ROTH FAMILY FOUNDATION

Music in America Imprint

Michael P. Roth
and Sukey Garcetti
have endowed this
imprint to honor the
memory of their parents,
Julia and Harry Roth,
whose deep love of music
they wish to share
with others.

The publisher gratefully acknowledges the generous support of the Music in America Endowment Fund of the University of California Press Foundation, which was established by a major gift from Sukey and Gil Garcetti, Michael P. Roth, and the Roth Family Foundation.

The publisher gratefully acknowledges the AMS 75 PAYS Endowment of the American Musicological Society, funded in part by the National Endowment for the Humanities and the Andrew W. Mellon Foundation.

FROM 1989, OR EUROPEAN MUSIC AND THE MODERNIST UNCONSCIOUS

FROM 1989, OR EUROPEAN MUSIC AND THE MODERNIST UNCONSCIOUS

Seth Brodsky

UNIVERSITY OF CALIFORNIA PRESS

University of California Press, one of the most distinguished university presses in the United States, enriches lives around the world by advancing scholarship in the humanities, social sciences, and natural sciences. Its activities are supported by the UC Press Foundation and by philanthropic contributions from individuals and institutions. For more information, visit www.ucpress.edu.

University of California Press
Oakland, California

Grateful acknowledgment is made to Purdue University Press for permission to reproduce an excerpt from Joel Brouwer's poem "Rostropovich at Checkpoint Charlie, November 11, 1989," from *Exactly What Happened* (West Lafayette, IN: Purdue University Press, 1999), 29–30. Courtesy of Purdue University Press.

Library of Congress Cataloging-in-Publication Data

Names: Brodsky, Seth, author.
Title: From 1989, or European music and the modernist unconscious / Seth Brodsky.
Description: Oakland, California : University of California Press, [2017] | Includes bibliographical references and index.
Identifiers: LCCN 2016040759| ISBN 9780520279360 (cloth : alk. paper) | ISBN 9780520966505 (ePub)
Subjects: LCSH: Music—Europe—20th century—History and criticism. | Music—Europe—20th century—Philosophy and aesthetics. | Modernism (Music)—Europe. | Nineteen eighty-nine, A.D.
Classification: LCC ML240.5 B76 2017 | DDC 780.9/04—dc23
LC record available at https://lccn.loc.gov/2016040759

Manufactured in the United States of America

26 25 24 23 22 21 20 19 18 17
10 9 8 7 6 5 4 3 2 1

To Jude and Lev
In memory of Daniel Albright

What we lack is a shared perception of the situation. Without this binding agent, gestures dissolve without a trace into nothingness, lives have the texture of dreams, and uprisings end up in schoolbooks.

THE INVISIBLE COMMITTEE, *TO OUR FRIENDS*

Leopards break into the temple and drink all the sacrificial vessels dry; this keeps happening; in the end, it can be calculated in advance and is incorporated into the ritual.

FRANZ KAFKA, *ZÜRAU APHORISMS*

CONTENTS

ILLUSTRATIONS

ACKNOWLEDGMENTS

This book's cover features a wall with a hole in it, which seems about right to me: books are forms of closure and fixity and creaturely confinement, but strange ones, in that they want only to be opened, loosed, caught back up in conversations much like the ones that started them. In this sense, the book is the least representative form of what it stands for. The people I thank here are those without whom this book couldn't have been written, but they are also those whose minds, words, grace, and attention are the book in its better form.

I must first thank those with whom I started these conversations, above all David B. Levy and Scott Klein; each of them turned my wheel a degree or two, and changed my trajectory forever. Jürgen Thym, Martin Scherzinger, and Robert Morris will see little here of what they first helped come into being, but their counsel initiated the process, the questions, and the standard of thought. Justin Caulley, Robert Fink, Jeremy Grimshaw, Rob Haskins, Michael Klinger, Matthew McGaughey, Sara Nicholson, and Robert Wood were also among the project's first stateside interlocutors. Its Berlin wing, often involving site-specific encounters, includes Angela Ida De Benedictis, Pietro Ernesto Cavallotti, Talaya Delaney, Justin Caulley (again!), Bianca Charamsa, Heiko Hoffmann, Heidi Enzian, Thomas Richter, and Ehren Fordyce. Friends and former colleagues Richard Cohn, James Hepokoski, Gundula Kreuzer, Pat McCreless, Ian Quinn, and Michael Veal were invaluable early partners in thought. A 2012 workshop with the JACK Quartet—at that time Kevin McFarland, Christopher Otto, John Pickford Richards, and Ari Streisfeld—redefined the scope of the project. Questions, lunches, dinners, and more questions from Matthew Arndt, Lee Blasius, Robert Cook, Brian Hyer, and Jennifer Iverson also took things in happy unanticipated directions, as did help and inspiration from Peter Schmelz. Kaitlyn

Tucker was extremely gracious in sharing some of her exciting new work on the history of the Ljubljana School of post-Lacanians. I owe a special debt to Ilya Kliger, not only for his intellectual fellowship, but for introducing me to the thought of Jacques Lacan, and also to the peerless work of Bruce Fink. An American Musicological Society panel on music and psychoanalysis provided me some essential collaborators, among them Amy Cimini, Clara Latham, Fred Maus, and Holly Watkins. Deep writing wisdom from Elisabeth Le Guin and Tamara Levitz—the kind that takes a few years to reach the surface, where it then stays—came at the right time. Conversations with Mathias Spahlinger in early 2015 proved invaluable; while his music is not discussed in the pages of this book—his *passage/paysage* from 1990 deserves its own book—his influence and example run throughout as a silent current.

In concrete terms, this book is a fruit of my time so far at the University of Chicago. I cannot—and, evidently, could not—conceive it coming into being anywhere else than this school's enlivening air and ethos, and the wonderful people who make it breathe. They have provided me an intellectual camaraderie the likes of which I'd never known. Gabriel and Jonathan Lear were key supporters early on; David Levin and Eric Santner have remained constant companions of the project, as have Jessica Stockholder and Patrick Chamberlain; and Maud Ellmann and the whole Modernisms Workshop crew were vital interlocutors over an entire year. My colleagues in music, among them Philip Bohlman, Anthony Cheung, Thomas Christensen, Travis Jackson, Robert Kendrick, Marta Ptaszynska, Augusta Read Thomas, and Lawrence Zbikowski, never ceased to buoy and inspire my best efforts. I extend special thanks to the intrepid graduate students in my seminars on postwar European music, music and psychoanalysis, and modernism and repetition. Among other institutions I must thank the Paul Sacher Stiftung and the Alexander von Humboldt Stiftung; I cannot imagine my work without their early and enormous generosity. At the Sacher, Evelyne Diendorf, Matthias Kassel, Felix Meyer, Ulrich Mosch, Michèle Noirjean-Linder, Robert Piencikowski, and Heidy Zimmermann made my repeated stays a welcoming pleasure, never hesitating with expertise and patient guidance. Hermann Danuser was my host during my year as a Humboldt German Chancellor Fellow; a model for my research, he was also an early and invaluable supporter. A grant from the Deutscher Akademischer Austauschdienst introduced me to Berlin; a Morse Junior Faculty Fellowship from Yale University supported my extended return.

I am forever in debt to my readers, not one of whom failed to leave a significant mark on the text: friends and colleagues Nicholas Betson, Jinn Bronwen Lee, Christopher Burns, James Currie, Ryan Dohoney, Tom Eyers, Martha Feldman, Michael Gallope, Sumanth Gopinath, Ted Hearne, Berthold Hoeckner, Anna Kornbluh, Michael Lewanski, Steven Rings, Anne W. Robertson, Haun Saussy, David Schutter, Stephen Decatur Smith, Olga Solovieva, Hans Thomalla, and Jeffrey Treviño; former and current students Ted Gordon, Lester Hu, Chaz Lee, Trent Leipert, Maria Perevedentseva, Marcelle Pierson, and Martha Sprigge, among others; and of course my two anonymous readers, whose simultaneous scrutiny of and commitment to the project was remarkable by any standard. Brian Kane and Seth Kim-Cohen, my Borscht Belt brothers, ought to be credited as co-thinkers; their patience in pondering (and laughing) with me was boundless.

The production of this book was, unsurprisingly, also a thoroughly collective affair. Mary Francis, my former editor, was its constant, patient steward from the beginning until her departure. Raina Polivka, with equal patience and acuity—and the meticulous help of editorial assistant Zuha Kahn—saw it through. Press editors Rachel Berchten and Lindsey Westbrook did beautiful and swift work to bring the manuscript to its final state. Andrew McManus's fantastic engraving work and the mad design skills of George Adams made the examples sing; Ted Gordon's early proofing of the manuscript was key; and David Giordano's cover art gave me the very picture of the book, an image as unforeseeable as it now is defining. At this point, Josh Rutner knows this book better than anyone alive, including me; he has edited every line of it with strigine sharpness and the passionate dedication of a bibliophile. His eye and care could not but make every book better. Their work was partially subsidized through generous subvention grants from the University of Chicago and the AMS 75 PAYS Endowment of the American Musicological Society, funded in part by the National Endowment for the Humanities and the Andrew W. Mellon Foundation. I am indebted to many more people for less "direct" but no less essential forms of production help, among them my 2015–16 course assistants Meredith Moretz and Lindsay Wright, and graduate student Owen Hubbard for his emergency Bodleian expedition to scan an example. Irmi Kocian and Peter Maunu provided the sunlit, wood-paneled, origami-chaired room where the book was finished, and Alican Çamcı the conversation and tea to bolster its last pages.

Every book needs a space in which to unfold; most books unfold in less-than-ideal spaces. As if by a miracle, my own book found the Writer's Workspace on Broadway Avenue in Edgewater, Chicago, and this turned out to be the best, most right space. I thank Amy Davis for her saint's work opening and maintaining it; she and it are godsends.

I must thank two people who sadly did not live to see this book in print. One is Dirk Deichfuss, my first German teacher and first on-the-ground guide to Berlin. An East German defector—he escaped by swimming—he had a musical and literary capture of the city's every corner, East and West. Because he gave me a new language, and gave so willingly and with such inspiration, he will always be for me the image of goodwill.

The other is Daniel Albright. It is hard to express how much his work and companionship meant to me, and how much they inspired and guided this book, which little resembles his own many volumes. I think of Gertrude Stein's motto "We are always the same age inside"; Daniel was always young, always beyond his years, always ageless. He was as early as his subjects were late, and was always going to leave too soon. He should have been able to read this; instead I offer it in his memory.

If books are forms of fixing and closing, however premature and transitory, it seems to me that they cannot emerge from anything but enduring loves, and go back to them. During this book's writing, I have seen my brother Chance become a medic, my sister Cordelia a yogi, my mother Barbara a grandmother, my father Bernard a novelist (once again). To see them transform so profoundly while enjoying the constancy of their love and support has been an indescribable joy. This book is dedicated to the greatest loves I will ever know, for my wife and constant companion Jude Susan Stewart, and for our son, Lev Henry. Neither is a love I even half know; neither love is fixed or closed; neither is anything but a balm for any creaturely confinement, and a dare to resist the merely possible. Their love, always everywhere, is my home, my better form.

INTRODUCTION

"But supposing He does not come"

Parapraxis:
Act whose explicit goal is not attained.

—JEAN LAPLANCHE AND JEAN-BERTRAND PONTALIS, *THE LANGUAGE OF PSYCHO-ANALYSIS*

I am sitting in a foyer. No, not quite a foyer. I am sitting in a large, manifold, torquing passageway, open seemingly on all sides, connecting the small and large halls of the Berliner Philharmonie. I am confused, and also stunned. Not unpleasantly: Hans Scharoun's organic, neoexpressionist architecture, rejecting all symmetries and rectangularities, has done a fine job of helping these feelings along.

It is September 2011, and I have two concert tickets in my hand. One is for a performance of Gustav Mahler's Eighth Symphony from 1907—the "Symphony of a Thousand"—with the Philharmoniker, eight soloists, and no fewer than four choirs, directed by Simon Rattle. The other is for Luigi Nono's *Prometeo* (1981–85), a "tragedy of listening," involving the Schola Heidelberg, the Experimental Studio of the Southwest German Radio (SWR), and the Konzerthausorchester, originally the main orchestra of East Berlin. The latter work, requiring two conductors, is led by Arturo Tamayo and Matilda Hofman; Nono's old friend and close collaborator André Richard directs the electronics.[1] Both tickets are for Saturday, September 17, at eight o'clock in the evening. Both concerts are taking place in the same building—the Mahler in the big hall, the Nono in the small one. The tickets were not cheap, nor easy to come by. How did this happen?

Perhaps I was simply too excited. Yes, this would have to be the explanation. Mahler is one of my favorite composers, and the Eighth is the most rarely performed of his symphonies. Theodor Adorno's buckling critique has made it harder for me to get entirely caught up in its world-breath—its caroling *Kinder* and balconied *Mater gloriosa*—but still I felt an almost bodily need to be there.[2] It is, after all, a bodily piece. There is hardly a way of escaping its exploding stage; the monstrousness of the forces agglutinates its audience. It is a symphony of and for the masses.[3] This is surely one of main things that offended Adorno: the piece cannot stop saying *We* when it still means *I*; it has committed one of Adorno's *ausgesuchtesten Kränkungen*, "choicest insults."[4] But so long as it comes from Mahler, I am helpless before this *We*. It promises an untold, but also *shared* plenitude, a binding agent for human—and, it would seem, divine—collectivity, and at least in the concert hall, it makes good on this promise. Its setting of the ending of Johann Wolfgang von Goethe's *Faust*, part 2, becomes a paradoxical acousmatic opera: perfectly visible, wildly theatrical, and yet ultimately imageless, all performers pointing to a consistency beyond themselves, in excess of all objects. The hall will become a vortex, everything will be drawn to the center—and then, in a final "chorus mysticus," through the power of *das Ewig-Weibliche*, Goethe's "eternal-feminine," upward.[5]

This, at least, is the fantasy. Adorno pops into mind again here, when he writes (of all things) about *Die Fledermaus*:

> Anyone wishing to find the *Fledermaus* beautiful must know that it is the *Fledermaus*: his mother must have told him that it is not about the winged animal but a fancy-dress costume; he must remember having been told: tomorrow you can go to see the *Fledermaus*. To be within tradition used to mean: to experience the work of art as something sanctioned, valid: to participate through it in all the reactions of those who had seen it previously. Once this falls away, the work is exposed in its nakedness and fallibility.[6]

This "Symphony of a Thousand" is here my *Fledermaus*, my chance to be told by tradition that I am *within* tradition, that (even) I can go see its imageless truths unfold. In my giddiness, I hastily chose the wrong date.

Am I excited for Nono's *Prometeo*? Absolutely. But in an indescribably different way. It has nothing to do with those head-versus-heart clichés, that phooey about "intellectual" music. My body is compelled, my "heart is in it." I want to be there when it happens. But it is less clear to me what will happen—what will have happened. If something like the pleasure principle compels me toward Mahler—*it* felt great last time, I can't wait to feel *it* again—then the prospect of the Nono pushes into a kind of beyond-the-pleasure principle. I am nervous to hear this "it" I can neither identify nor place so easily. I know it only from two recordings, heard many times, but never in their uninterrupted entirety. It is, obviously, a far rarer piece in all ways. I can imagine how it will work in Scharoun's *Kammersaal*. Like the *grosse Saal*, in the round, but tighter, more crenulated. Groups, from large to small, will be distributed throughout the space; voices will come from everywhere, both as bodies and as disembodied sounds, processed through elaborate, often improvised electronic means. Though larger ensembles will occupy the center stage, there will be no center to the sound, at least in any traditional sense; the aural gravity will tend toward the edges. Not centrifugal—which was a fantasy anyhow—but centripetal. The acousmatic will play a role here, too, but in a doubly opposite way. In Mahler, I will know exactly where the sounds are coming from, while being helplessly convinced there is another, greater source, beyond imagination. In Nono, I will often detect sounds I cannot place—either their cause *or* their source—while at the same time hearing their fragile materiality laid bare. I know the work will be long—more than two hours—and that it will test my capacities, my patience, my attention, my good will. I will be stuck in its stuck-ness, its annulment of elsewhere. I recall a conversation between Nono and his librettist, the philosopher Massimo Cacciari: the work should effect a transition from "believing" to "perceiving." A gentler way of affirming Max Weber's paraphrasing of Friedrich Schiller: modernity, the "disenchantment of the world."[7]

I also know *Prometeo* will end in what seems like an absolute inversion of Mahler's finale. Not a messianic swell, obliterating all silences and interstices, enveloping all the hall's bodies in its unstoppable tide. Instead, a severe reduction and retraction, a shrinking in space and force, an arresting of all motion, ceaselessly halting, always returning to its only real consistency: the rest. (A cryptic phrase often echoes throughout the work: "this weak/messianic force." What could express this better than the recurring grand pause?)[8] The singers—now no longer a "chorus mysticus" but "mitologia-coro"—will not tell of an eternal feminine to come, but of a genderless, lithic law, a "NOMOS" beyond all identification. "One person but with various names," it will seize all times and condense them into a quietly pitiless "IS": "IS: transgressing, reestablishing," "IS: bringing down, defending," "IS: that which takes away all consolation," "IS: that which is only revealed in the ring of fire." Cacciari's words here seem like willful misprisions of Goethe's closing lines, "All that passes away / Is only a likeness; / The unattainable / Here finds fulfillment." Imagining how *Prometeo* ends, I can see it "take back the Eighth." Quite literally: I can hear the symphony collapsing from arc into instant, sense its oceanic feeling drying up:

> IT FLASHES
> AND IN THE DESERT IS INVINCIBLE

So: excitement, of two quite irreconcilable kinds, and careless haste. It all seems obvious enough. But as I sit there, reviewing my hypothesis in Scharoun's foyer-that-is-no-foyer, I start to feel as if my mistake was not a mistake at all. It went according to script. Whose?

• • •

Probably the best way to introduce *From 1989, or European Music and the Modernist Unconscious* would be to parse its title. I see four claims in it: it is a book about a year; about European music; about psychoanalysis; and about modernism. I will take up that last term first and at greatest length, not only because it is the most fraught, but because I remain most uncertain about it. *From 1989* is not a resolution of this uncertainty so much as a documentation, an illumination and narration of it—a way of making it appear clearly, without making it appear clear.

Before launching into this discussion, I should stress, however, that this book is very much about *all* four of its titular terms. A more provocative way to put this is that *From 1989* is a deliberately under-disciplined book, situated at symptomatic points between a number of distinct disciplines. The Great Disciplinary Between is increasingly the humanities' most orthodox agora, but in practice this can irritate. Those anticipating—however unconsciously—a book centrally on New Music, or on the political meaning of 1989, or on the fate of late twentieth-century modernism or a collective "aesthetic unconscious," will sometimes find themselves in a very different discursive milieu, one they didn't necessarily sign up for.

I think the more challenging aspect of the book may be its interference at partition points *within* certain larger fields: that point where music history and music theory, or music theory and music philosophy, police their mutual alterity; or, in psychoanalysis, that still contentious division between theory and practice, between the humanistic space of textual interpretation and the clinical space of speaking and listening subjects. Nowadays, such divisions more often invite friendship—dialogue, collaboration, complementarity—than conflict. But this friendship still requires divisions in both the imaginary and the symbolic, the clearer the better: partitions that coordinate, quite literally, distinct self-images: "Me" and "You." Distinct *technê* too, and the differential designs they afford—here is how a historian would *see* it, here is what a theorist or clinician would *do* with it, and so on. *From 1989* enacts a strategic confusion of such partitions. I am aiming here for a certain *inconsistency*, the kind that comes from loosening and collapsing the partitions that grid over worlds, that legislate difference and allow us to *tell* the difference, to discern and narrate it at once.

If I do this, it's not out of any great pretension for a particular field or set of fields. I'm skeptical of a utopian synthesis between disciplines or even subdisciplines, in part because I'm not so sure such a synthesis—say, between music studies and psychoanalysis, or psychoanalysis and modernism studies—bears that much promise. (Both have had their day, for better and worse.) Moreover, friendships do benefit from consistency, not least of their coordinates, of friends knowing where they stand. If I am after something in this book, it is not so much about preparing the ground for a certain kind of future, and even less about trying to program that future. It is more about maintaining fidelity to a certain kind of past that is not so past at all. I want to argue that "modernism," at least as the attempt to designate a historical aesthetic phenomenon, is the signifier of precisely such inconsistency, such loosening and collapse. What aesthetic modernism is *is* inconsistency: a de-partitioning and un-gridding of worlds, a de-regulation of differential coordinates.

The bulk of modernism's history—its long tail of endless internal differentiation and ismatic dispute—would seem to say otherwise. Modernism is more often the signifier par excellence of partition, of breaking definitively with pasts and drawing lines in the sand of the present. It calls for futures, and then programs them; it *re*-grids the world according to new demands, demands for the New. Aren't these tasks essentially campaigns in consistency? What are form and flatness, or tone and technology, but master signifiers that any one of modernism's moments calls upon to give its projects continuity? What is modernism without this calling—without apostrophe, arguably its greatest trope? "Send us, bright one, light one, Horhorn, quickening, and wombfruit": Isn't this a call not just for inspiration, but for consistency? A prayer that the New, even after the shock of its birth, go on going on, live and grow as some kind of continuing-itself?[9]

Yes, absolutely. Aesthetic modernism is the history of ceaseless attempts to live out the self-supplied letter of the little law made big—to be, and act, auto-nomos-ly. But this book will argue that such a history is also one of *desire for such law.* Which is to say, the experience and enjoyment of its lack. This lack, this desire, is nothing natural. Modernism had to learn, again and again, how to desire, better yet what to wish for, what fantasies to entertain, and how to sustain them. Here modernism was anything but consistent. Did it desire order or disorder? Yes! Overwhelming presence or plunging void? Yes! Most visceral heat or coldest calculation? Yes, and again, yes! Affirmation is not, admittedly, the first thing that comes to mind when thinking of modernism. But the very invocation of modernism generally works affirmatively, gathering the sprawl of negativities—presence must be *overwhelming*, the void must *plunge*—under one covering sign. It serves a universal copular function, a way of rendering what might have been so many solipsisms into a potentially infinite series of pairs: Arnold Schoenberg *and* Igor Stravinsky, to cite just one. This vision is not some ex post facto historiographical invention, but modernism's own, there in its imaginary and symbolic orders, its compulsive picturing and languaging of difference.[10] It is the map and the manifesto, the showing-and-telling of so many partitioned utopias properly spaced. *Here* is my no-where, *there* is yours. It is a vision, if not of friends, then of frenemies, who at least know where things stand.

While no book on aesthetic modernism can remain uninvolved in such visions, I'm far more interested in the condition for the possibility of such endlessly coordinated agon, bolstered by new desire, new fantasy, new law. It is, initially, a matter of simple logic: If modernism was a new kind of desire—for a new consistency, a consistent New—it must at certain moments have forgotten how to desire. If it persistently produced radically new fantasies, it must have persistently experienced the liquidation of old ones. If it wished radically new law into being, it must have once known radical lawlessness. To put it another way, modernism might also be the signifier of a kind of syncope in the aesthetic regime—a fainting spell, a moment of blackout leading to new visions, not least of white squares.

A nay-saying modernism, which does not gather and include, partition and coordinate, so much as test, break, deny, and disperse, invariably summons Adorno to the scene. His *Philosophy of New Music* (1949) is, after all, not really a text on frenemies, but on how Schoenberg is *the* solipsistic soul of modernism, its monad-Moses, authentic bearer of inexpressible truth; on how Stravinsky is utterly unfit even to be his Aron; and—most essential, I think, because it enacts the primary repression that allows the book to work its magic—on how *die gemäßigte Moderne*, "the moderate modernists"—composers like Benjamin Britten and Dmitri Shostakovich—are a middle road not even worth countenancing, let alone discussing.[11] Following the cues from modernist studies in art and especially literature, studies of musical modernism in the last decade have been undoing this repression with special relish, and they are absolutely right to.[12] If Edward Elgar is a modernist, then Adorno is no longer our unconscious, and modernism is no longer an imaginary affair, something that necessarily *sounds like* atonality, or *looks like* abstraction.[13] Always cosmopolitan, modernism now becomes worldly. It might show up anywhere. It might look like—sound like—anything. Here is modernism's inconsistency in the flesh.

But there are many different kinds of "no," and another of *From 1989*'s provocations is to push Adornian negativity to the side—or rather to repress it temporarily, since it returns in force at the book's conclusion, its inevitable object of inquiry. For much of the book, however, I side with the art historian T. J. Clark's later dissatisfaction with his own earlier, Adornian formulation that "the fact of Art, in modernism, is the fact of negation."[14] Clark's reformulation, some two decades later, gets much closer to my own aims, and is worth citing in full:

> Once upon a time I called this exacerbation of means and push to the limits in modern art its "practices of negation." But I do not like that formula any longer. I think it wrong to opt for either "negative" or "positive," or "beautiful" or "ugly," as descriptions of modernism in characteristic mood. The point is that modernism was always on the lookout for the moment, or practice, to which both descriptions apply. Positive and negative, fullness and emptiness, totalization and fragmentation, sophistication and infantilism, euphoria and desperation, an assertion of infinite power and possibility alongside a mimicry of deep aimlessness and loss of bearings. For this, I think, is modernism's root proposal about its world: that the experience of modernity is precisely the experience of the *two* states, the two tonalities, at the same time. Modernism is the art that continually discovers coherence and intensity in tentativeness and schematism, or blankness lurking on the other side of sensuousness. And not on the other side, really—for blankness is the form that sensuousness and controlled vivacity now actually take.[15]

In the context of my own thinking, Clark's words issued a veritable "Borges-Wilkins moment," a precipitation of "shattering laughter," which began to cave the partitional logic of the modernism I thought I knew.[16] If *From 1989* moves beyond

Clark's basic point—so simple, so difficult—it is in the direction of formalism. An exacerbating formalism, less interested in totalizing than in testing.

This testing formalism begins with a small but important disagreement. Clark is rash in dismissing "practices of negation." Because, if I read him correctly, he is speaking of another kind, another register, of the negative. Not a grammatical negativity, not "no" as a codified part of speech, a pre-allocated way of declaring what one isn't or doesn't or couldn't—Samuel Beckett's "First I'll say what I'm not, that's how they taught me to proceed, then what I am."[17] This is precisely what Clark remains dissatisfied with: the story of a Manichaean modernism, whose aggressively intentional ugliness depends for its life on a memory of prior, placeable beauty, or whose brazenly schematic new beauty reads as a retort to the world's old repository of reliable uglinesses. Clark's claim is that modernism, at least at formative points, forced itself to lose the very languages of dialectic, the speech in which it could say or sound out "no" to anything, in which it could picture what "denial," or "ugly," or "absence" might look like. "This catastrophe we allowed to take place": Morton Feldman's reminiscence about the emergence of radically indeterminate music in the 1950s speaks to a scene witnessed again and again in the history of aesthetic modernism, in which the speaker or sounder or image maker points, with deictic desperation, to the place where the symbolic and imaginary falter, where they fail to tell differences any more.[18]

Such moments are anything but dialectical. They are not Hegelian negations of the negation. They are arrests of the progressive movement, the insertion of a gait into the dialectical next step. They are marked, or burdened, or—why not?—emancipated by an overwhelming uncertainty. Not least as to their own authenticity. Few write more eloquently about having "completely lost the ability to think or speak coherently about anything at all" than Hugo von Hofmannsthal's Lord Chandos, long taken as an icon of the Viennese fin-de-siècle *Sprachkrise*, but also of a larger, grander crisis of language.[19] Is it a put-on, or the thing itself? The difference is never so clear, nor is it clear that the modernist could discern this difference. Arguably modernism's fate—one of them, in any case—is this deep unsureness as to whether it is allowing actual catastrophes to take place, or staging theatrical fantasies of incapacity. The ancient Roman genre of the *recusatio*—the poem announcing the poet's failure to write the requested poem—haunts modernism at every turn. It is modernism's doppelgänger, marring the scene by reminding it that all its catastrophes can become—and might already be—generic.[20]

To my formalisms: there is indeed a negativity at work in Clark's proposition of a modernism that collapses or confuses "positive and negative, fullness and emptiness, totalization and fragmentation, sophistication and infantilism, euphoria and desperation." It is not the negativity of the symbolic: the differential coordination afforded by the network, grid, or list, a diacritical system that assigns supposedly arbitrary signs distinct positions. Nor is it the negativity of the imaginary: the register of like and unlike, mimesis and rivalry, fidelity and its lack. It is, rather, an ontological conception of negativity: a negativity that does not figure *within being as its opposite*, but is perpetually being reborn alongside it, its always missing twin. In political theory, this is what Ernesto Laclau and Chantal Mouffe call antagonism, the "limits of all objectivity," that point of deadlock that founds all discourse, and from which discourse provides the possibility of at least temporary escape.[21] Hegemonic struggle, the struggle between parties to master the common discourse, becomes a way of escaping antagonism by making it *appear*, with all the instability appearance implies. As antagonism emerges into the symbolic and imaginary, its instability also becomes a site of possibility; it becomes workable, fruitful, kinetic.

While Laclau and Mouffe come and go throughout this book, it is the Lacanian concept of the Real that provides my central means of coordinating modernism's "other" negativity.[22] Jacques Lacan's formulation of the Real, originally in the context of his psychoanalytic theories, is a complex and in some ways notorious one; certainly it is always threatening to turn into what it was expressly intended to avoid—the impression of an autonomous domain, a gnostic beyond or bad sublime lying in wait to traumatize the subject, or bring it bliss. McKenzie Wark's dismissal of the Lacanian Real—"always something terrible, formless, lawless . . . a modern version of the serpents that . . . Apollonian thought has to slay, again and again"—is perfectly right in all the wrong ways. But it's hardly inappropriate; the Real is easy to reify, and even easier to villainize.[23] The concept evolved over Lacan's career, sometimes with maddening fluidity; but the philosopher Tom Eyers has shown that the Real maintains a surprising consistency throughout Lacan's work.[24] It is a way—always inadequate—of marking on the one hand the persistent failure of the symbolic or imaginary to "capture it all," and, on the other hand, their constant production of a surplus, of more than they bargained for. In essence, the Real is an emergent property, an inconsistency produced alongside all symbolic and imaginary attempts at consistency. If the Real is, according to Lacan, "that which resists all symbolization absolutely," it is a resistance immanent to symbolization, its constant by-product.[25] *From 1989* adapts a number of Lacanian concepts—in particular desire and fantasy—in order to schematize this "Real" negativity in relation to modernism. I eventually suggest, for instance, that the modernity to which modernism proclaims its tormented fidelity, on which it heaps love and hatred at once, can be understood as its *objet petit a*—a "Real object." Modernity becomes modernism's turn-on, and also its objectification of what it experiences as impossible—another way of saying that modernism is turned on *by* impossibility.

The core of my argument rests, however, on my hypothesis that aesthetic modernism has two recurring "moments," often coincident in any historical situation, but nonetheless linked by the temporal logic of sequence. The second of these moments is the (still largely) hegemonic one: modernism as a desirous call for the New. Modernism as so many futuristic fantasies and the factional disputes they engender, their "frenemization" of discourse; as a dialectical negation of the past, taking up the break and the progression as its axioms; and as the fabrication of new consistencies—modernism's egos, as it were, its often exhausting "let me tell you all about myself" insistence.

But this second moment depends upon a first. And I think this first moment is modernism's more properly ontological intervention in the aesthetic regime—what, simply, makes it so different. In this first moment, modernism can be understood to designate a phenomenon in which a desire already consuming the surrounding culture is compromised or neutralized; in which culture's already robust fantasies—good and bad—about its future, past, and present are disenchanted, and the partitions separating these fantasies from life undermined; in which the very possibility of a dialectical next step, a negation of the negation, is temporarily undone; in which the self-identity of future, past, and present are shown, or staged, as inconsistency itself. This is indeed a strange thing to imagine: a modernism that was not progressive in any strict sense, but precisely that force that, at least in the aesthetic realm, threatened or humiliated its culture's most reliable dreams of progressiveness. Modernism only emerged, and seemingly could only emerge, within cultures that already knew their New, and already possessed extraordinarily sophisticated know-how *for* it, enjoying, desiring, and fantasizing it in multiple forms. I want to suggest that modernism emerged, initially but repeatedly, as the disruption, and often the sabotage, of precisely this know-how, this desire and enjoyment, these fantasies—a New with no know-how.

The longer-range argument of this book, developed in a roundabout and rotational way, is that the history of aesthetic modernism can be read as a constantly reenacted passage between these two moments, and that the logic of this passage can be likened to that of trauma and repression. Modernism's paradoxical "passion for the Real," as Alain Badiou puts it, opened up something remarkable in the aesthetic regime: the attempt to stage antagonism itself, to make constitutive negativity appear, to treat the groundlessness underlying its own inherited practices as if this groundlessness *were* its absolute, and to demand that this absolute show itself.[26] The trauma, I think, involves an encounter with impossibility: absolute negation is impossible, and nothing makes this clearer—makes a show of this impossibility more—than aesthetic activity, where what is shown always carries with it the surplus of what is not shown, and where one element's negation is supported by another's repetition. Not only is negation a subjective activity; nothing reveals an aesthetic actor's subjectivity more reliably than his or her choices—in the end, always arbitrary, contingent, groundless—about what to negate. The encounter with the Real, as Lacan rehearses again and again, is a missed encounter, a *rencontre manquée*.[27]

Modernism's more official histories needn't be contradicted in order to suggest that they are nonetheless histories of reaction. Or, more precisely, repression, of something modernism itself uncovered or initiated, its traumatic missed encounter with the Real—its founding parapraxis, one could say. Modernism has had a notoriously difficult time taking responsibility for its own initiating hand in these "first moments." It is, without a doubt, an extraordinary kind of invention, one that takes up so many Big Others of aesthetic practice—Tonality, Representation, Narrative, and so on—and *makes them go missing*, such that modernism can stage the emptiness of their place, from which it necessarily emerges. The creativity involved in this "obsoleting," this making-lost, is often taken for its opposite: necessity, the demands of history, the situation in which one finds oneself forced to act. Or to let happen: "this catastrophe we *allowed* to take place." But I think precisely this self-situating is modernism's greatest innovation, its formative act of creation. Certainly it is an act modernism pays for, time and again. "No" is its founding crime, "New" its alibi: modernism's guilt, but also its consolation and reward.

The narrative logic of *Totem and Taboo* (1913), often regarded as Sigmund Freud's greatest alibi of origin, may come to mind here. "The dead father became stronger than the living one had been," he writes.[28] Something like this seems to have happened with modernism: the dialectics of desire and the desire for dialectics, murdered, return with a vengeance, in forms bolder and wilder—more systematic *and* more intuitive, more mechanized *and* more natural—than anything previously imaginable. Tonality returns *as* dodecaphony, or integral serialism, or spectralism; representation *as* abstraction, or collage, or photorealism. The reincarnation glares at its deposed body. Clark puts the words in Pablo Picasso's mouth: "You think that modernity is a realm of appetite and immediacy! I'll show you appetite! I'll show you immediacy! I shall, as a modernist, make the dreams of modernity come true."[29] This play-Picasso, jittering madly between zeal and contempt, speaks to the premise that modernism found the antagonisms it unveiled as unbearable as did its parent cultures. They entered into a Kafkaesque pact: modernism can be the leopards, breaking into culture's temples to drink its sacrificial vessels dry, so long as culture can be allowed to calculate this invasion in advance, and incorporate it into the ritual.[30] Such is modernism's cultural life, the life of its "second moment": the ritualized invasion, the expected leopard.

Something I want to argue in this book is that musical modernism in Europe had, by 1989, gradually transformed into a third stage in Franz Kafka's parable, one he surely anticipated. All over Europe, in forms and signs perfectly inconsistent with one another, music was staging its own de-coordination, its partitional collapse, the breaking in of leopards, as if this scene were the *whole ritual itself*. As if it were happening for the first time, as if modernism, now perpetually caught in its "first moment," were not at all coming to an end, but incessantly trying to begin again.[31]

. . .

"This is not yet another book about modernity," Françoise Meltzer writes at the opening of her 2011 book *Seeing Double: Baudelaire's Modernity*.[32] It is, of course, and about many other things. *From 1989* is also not about modernity, but, in the end, really about modernity. How could it not be? Not only is it about modernism, it is about New Music, and about the psychoanalytic unconscious, one of modernity's stranger and more intractable concepts, officially minted in the early writings of Freud, but arguably already there with the coining of the Cartesian *cogito*.

But compared to Meltzer's nineteenth-century Paris, this book's temporal and geographical coordinates—which begin in 1989 Berlin—would seem a bit off base. Modernity here? Really? Jürgen Habermas's famous formulation of modernity as an "incomplete project" was already a self-consciously untimely plea in 1980, directed at the foaming tides of a discourse increasingly convinced of modernity's obsolescence, or stagnancy, or foreclosure—which is to say, modernity's past-ness, a premise only modernity could think up.[33] By 1984 Habermas was speaking of a "new obscurity," the "retraction of horizons," and by 1989, postmodernism was entering what Steven Connor, surely aware of the Sisyphean nature of periodizing the term, has called a "third phase": a moment of entrenchment, whose epicyclic looping of production and feedback would inevitably bring with it a dissipating of energies and a fading of prospective (post- and anti-modern) futures. What now lies ahead is only the intellectual bureaucracy of making sure stories about postmodernism more or less check out.[34] Fredric Jameson's *Postmodernism, or the Logic of Late Capitalism*, hardly a bureaucratic exercise, would be published less than two years later, becoming a source of dark methodical enchantment for a decade's theorists. By the time I enrolled in graduate school in the late 1990s, it was the kind of text to be handed to students like me as a Book of Wisdom, a way of understanding Our Time. First axiom: this is not the time of modernism.

And of course there is 1989 "itself": the joyful emancipations, the bungling and crumbling and coming clean, the brutal acts of retrenchment. Not a week in its events remains unchronicled, nor, as the years pass, does their meaning escape constant revision. Francis Fukuyama's neo-Kojèvian declaration of the "end of history" is certainly among the revised, so much so that its gradual fading throughout the 1990s, and veritable disgrace in the early aughts, have given way of late to—not even renewed defenses, but amnestic assumptions that it was right all along.[35] But if the thesis inspires a general incredulity today, nonetheless it still constitutes something like what Freud called a *proton pseudos*: a "first falsehood," an illusion that begins to constitute the concrete reality of the moment, and so becomes its history, demanding a proper recounting.[36] In some sense this is precisely what leftist historians—who could not possibly condone Fukuyama's hubristic thesis—did. The moment of the Fall of the Wall became, for Clark, one of almost Shakespearean conjoining-in-death, the double expiration of socialism and modernism. His focal question in *Farewell to an Idea* (1999) would be to ask whether this also meant that "in some sense they lived together, in century-long co-dependency."[37] For Eric Hobsbawm in 1994, the events of 1989 to 1991 at least put an end to the twentieth century, making it the psychotic younger sibling of the "long nineteenth."[38] After this "short century" of ceaseless catastrophes, anyone, historian or otherwise, would have to be a fool to forecast the future.

And yet: Hobsbawm chooses to end his tome by raging against the new obscuring of the possibility of the new: "We do not know where we are going. . . . However, one thing is plain. If humanity is to have a recognizable future, it cannot be by prolonging the past or the present. If we try to build a third millennium on that basis, we shall fail. And the price of failure, that is to say, the alternative to a changed society, is darkness."[39] The conviction, written at a moment when Western history seems caught between what Joshua Clover calls Fukuyama Pop and Jameson Pop, comes in the book not long after Hobsbawm has proclaimed that the "smell of impending death rose from these avant-gardes. The future was no longer theirs, though nobody knew whose it was."[40] But the demand—the future absolutely depends on a break with the present and past—has an uncanny modernist ring to it. It is the infinitely sadder, older apogee of Arthur Rimbaud's impatient "enough," his wide-eyed call to "Depart, into new noise and affection!"[41] Like Habermas's call for an "incompletion" of the present, however, Hobsbawm's warning is untimely. The two pleas sit on either side of a year that still stands as a freezing point for the temporality we call modern and modernist. Bruno Latour, writing about the year from 1991, gazes anthropologically upon those who "intend to remain resolutely modern," who still "believe in the promises of the sciences, or in those of emancipation, or both." Peering in "art galleries and concert halls, along the façades of apartment buildings and inside international organizations, you can feel the heart is gone. The will to be modern seems hesitant, sometimes even outmoded."[42] So much for "*by* 1989" and "*in* 1989." What about "*from* 1989"?

The phrase was chosen carefully. It is meant to let the signifiers hover between "repository" and "perch," 1989 as a locus of origin and 1989 as a place from which to assess, at a distance and skeptically, origins. The book takes plenty of its artifacts from that year; some involve music, others do not. They are a motley collection, traversing practical and clinical sites, the purview and métier of artists and performers, philosophers, historians, political theorists, and psychoanalysts. And they often push the bounds of the book far outside its titular territory. As such, it can be said to fall into a now-robust genre initiated by a number of microhistorical endeavors beginning in the late 1990s from such scholars as James Chandler, Michael North, and Hans Ulrich Gumbrecht.[43] Music studies has produced some remarkable endeavors in its own right since then—James Q. Davies's dissertation on music in 1829 London; Hugh Macdonald's musical "biography" of the year 1853; Joshua Clover's acid meditation on pop around 1989; and Tamara Levitz's extraordinary reweaving—I cannot help hearing in "history" *histos,* "loom"—of the three days of *Perséphone*'s premiere in 1934 Paris.[44] Each of these efforts has inspired the current book, the latter two serving at times as models.

But I take some measures to differentiate from the genre as well. The equivocal "from" in my title is also intended to push against the premise of the origin story, whether those origins take the form of break or rupture on the one hand, or genesis and emergence on the other. *From 1989* is an attempt at precisely the opposite: a story of non-origins, botched genesis, missed encounters. If anything, it is an initial attempt to speculate the musical prehistory of such missed encounters, which could be thought of as the larger missed encounter between modernism and revolution—modernism's "failure" to execute a temporal revolution it is always auguring, and its correspondent "success" as a repeated turning in place, a constant coming back to where it started. In this sense, Gumbrecht's goal in his book *In 1926: Living on the Edge of Time* (1997) is the opposite of mine. Gumbrecht writes of how his book "should produce the effect to which [its] title alludes: you should feel 'in 1926.' The more immediate and sensual this illusion becomes, the more your reading will fulfill the book's chief aim."[45] By contrast, *From 1989* is more interested in the "production of absence." It trains its gaze on what continues to fail to happen, to *not* make itself into sensual immediacy, to fall short of a present otherwise deliriously devoted to picturing itself "in the moment."

I do not, however, want to imply my own resolved stance on the matter, least of all to assess aesthetic modernism's *historical* failure, a failure inviting something like Clark's magisterial farewell, which strikes me (and others) as wishful in its melancholy.[46] Perhaps mourning in the right key can preemptively kill its object. But I think aesthetic modernism is here to stay, not so much as a recognizable and conscious artistic praxis—a "crisis of representation," say, or a commitment to the tendency of the material, to abstraction or fragmentation or autonomy, and so on—but rather as a misrecognized and unconscious *parapraxis*, a repetition of acts "whose explicit goal is not attained."[47] If 1989 is a special moment in this history, it is because it stages the proximity—and sometimes the stark juxtaposition—of two irreconcilable "negative turns." This is how Quintilian defined trope, a turning away, and it works here: world politics, witnessing a turning away from the very possibility of Revolution through one last soft revolution; and musical modernism, aloof from these remarkable events it simultaneously dreams about, turning in place, continuing to practice its most venerable trope: the supposedly good work of breaking ground, of losing, failing, waiting, readying, in preparation for a Revolution to come.

. . .

In terms of sheer number of artifacts, the book's pride of place is granted to "composerly production" across greater Europe. Hundreds of regional and world premieres were collected in the course of research, with as much of their discursive fabric intact as possible: notes, reviews, previews, and interviews, contemporaneous analyses and interpretations. This is in large degree how the book began—as a playful project in seeing how much New Music I could unearth from a single year, how much of the mycelial network I could recover or at least trace, and what it might tell me upon re-activation, or in this case re-audiation. The idea was initially suggested to me by Anne C. Shreffler's wonderful (and, in terms of repertoire, quite catholic) seminar at Harvard on "music of the last ten years." What about music of the last one years? And what about removing the curatorial filters, and beginning to let in the good, the bad, the ugly, the utterly forgotten?

Contemporary European composition here presents a kind of inversion of many other fields of creative musical labor that fall into the "modernariat," Paolo Virno's term for the "historiographical genre" that prioritizes and enjoys "the memory of the present."[48] Online forums and databases like discogs.com testify to passionate and encyclopedic communities of individuals invested in musics that enjoy a far richer afterlife than they ever did in their own (often-unnoticed) moment. Many of the texts and objects I uncovered were, by contrast, born under state-subsidized spotlights, shining equally on concert stages and discursive platforms. Pieces would arrive to a bit of journalistic fanfare, would greet first listeners with expansive philosophical essays, and would often receive published in-house analyses via resident musicologists or intendants involved with the institution or festival. Sometimes even a recording would follow, often through further subsidy from the state. And then—oblivion. No more performances, no libraries with recordings, no online forums, and, often enough, no hits on Google. An uncanny if dystopian realization of an old modernist wish: to fashion the pure object, monadic in its self-enclosure. The online composer databases that began to appear in the late 1990s and early aughts have alleviated this tendency while paradoxically intensifying it: the symbolic big Other will retrieve the information from the grid at a click, but it comes from the object; the subject is still quite hard to find.[49]

There are of course many factors involved in this process, and they lie mostly outside this book's intentions. But one of them becomes increasingly important as the book enters its third part: the old problem, still so aptly read by Robert Morgan back in the 1980s, of musical modernism's "secret languages."[50] If there are still no "private languages," anyone who has spent time in the Paul Sacher Foundation in Basel, Switzerland, can certainly say a thing or two about secret ones, specifically the often labyrinthine compositional and pre-compositional practices presented in so many European composers' sketch materials. Each presents anywhere from a radically new way of making works, to a series of variations on a post-serial *lingua franca*, which, in their idiosyncrasy, "change everything." This has led to what I consider a reasonable enough hegemony in scholarship on European New Music: a commitment to recuperating composers' aesthetic intentions through excavating the systems, methods, and means through which they consciously generated their works. The manifold historical breaks with musical modernism were in part breaks with the very premise that a work's meaning *is* its making; but still, that premise is hardly defunct. Pietro Cavallotti's 2006 study of Helmut Lachenmann, Brian Ferneyhough, and Gérard Grisey is a peerless feat of decryption and reconstruction, and still one of the best arguments that, within a certain "art world," construction *is* one of intention's irrefutable modalities.[51] If it was written, it was thought; perhaps more importantly, if it was written, it now "thinks itself," takes on a life of its own within what Lacan, in his famous 1964 seminar, called "the *automaton*, the return, the coming-back, the insistence of the signs."[52] The legacy of musical serialism is inextricable from such insistence, endlessly moving between its celebratory negation of all previous forms of guidance and the promise of guidance by a higher, "luckier" hand: a new or old nature, law, or the return of inspiration, now purified into a modernized, disenchanted genius. Such *automaton* is, in a dual sense, serialism's "fate."

Lacan introduced the notion of *automaton*—adapted, like so many of his working concepts, from someone else—as a companion of what he called *tyche*. Both are derived from the Aristotelian formulation of cause, and serve as causality's formal remainders. If *automaton* involves a "spontaneous" repetition of the signifier, something iterable, something that by definition *can* be repeated, *tyche* designates the "chance" repetition of what cannot be repeated: something that lies "beyond the *automaton*." *Tyche* repeats itself not as something positive, but as "impediment, failure, crack"; it is in this context that Lacan introduces the notion of the missed encounter, the *rencontre manquée*, likely inspired by André Breton.[53] Never short on hubristic claims, Lacan maintains of *tyche* that "it is quite obvious, throughout Freud's research, that it is this [missed encounter] that is the object of his concern."

This is the territory of Freud's "unconscious intention," but in a way that emphasizes the negativity involved. Lacan here takes to the letter all of Freud's terms for how unconscious intentions manifest themselves—specifically the first three letters, *ver-*, as in "*das Vergessen* (forgetting), *das Versprechen* (slip of the tongue), *das Verlesen* (misreading), *das Verschreiben* (slip of the pen), *das Vergreifen* (bungled action), and *das Verlieren* (mislaying)."[54] All these terms imply a conception of the unconscious as something perhaps still contrary to common perceptions. It is not a locus of repressed but nonetheless coherent knowledge, steering the psyche toward its own prohibitive designs; rather, it is a place of disjunction, confusion, the concordance of opposites—in a word, impossibility. In this reading, unconscious knowledge is not so much open to interpretation and understanding as it is to assumption, to being taken up and taken on as something that, as an act of ever failing "to attain its explicit goal," must be given a place within conscious life while still retaining its status as alien, extra, "extimate." Mladen Dolar considers this

> what constitutes the proper domain of psychoanalysis at its minimal: phenomena which are irreducible to intentionality, to *causa finalis*, to conscious intentions, and which are at the same time irreducible to the causality of nature, to natural processes beyond conscious control, to the somatic. Neither consciousness nor nature; neither

> the (conscious) mind nor the body. In a nutshell, what psychoanalysis is interested in is always something which happens "by coincidence," "by chance," yet it keeps recurring, it keeps repeating itself, but without constituting a positive causality apart, while irreducible to both natural and conscious causality.[55]

Here, with something that seems to happen "by coincidence" or "by chance," yet that "keeps recurring," "keeps repeating itself," is the focus of my book's engagement—with music, but also with modernism and, in a sense, with psychoanalysis. I might provide as only one example four composers who I think embody the range of European musical modernism in 1989, and who could be taken to stand in for the many others discussed throughout its pages: Luciano Berio, György Ligeti, Helmut Lachenmann, and Wolfgang Rihm—a motley crew, undeniably. Each composer has his own *automata*, his own collection of insisting signs that reaffirm themselves in work after work. Such signs migrate from category to category, depending on the designs of the reader and listener. Are they elements of style? poetics? technique? voice? method? Yes! But among such self-scripting reliables, one is hard pressed to find a surer hallmark of Berio's work than his gradually evolving harmonic fields, providing an ever-expanding ground over which can unfold, like a storm front, the most turbulent and unpredictable of semiospheres; or, in Ligeti, the tendency to stratify sound layers rhythmically and harmonically, aiming at an impossibly dynamic stasis, always precarious and "hovering"; or Lachenmann's "building" and "playing" of new meta-instruments, engendering an almost fugal polyphony of extended techniques and sound families; or Rihm's persistent, seemingly asystematic insertion of the most violent displacements into otherwise continuous fields of intensifying activity until they "break open" and "break through." These, one could say in Freudian-Lacanian terms, are *compositional drives*: while remarkably productive, they also seem to operate independent of formal dictates, "by themselves" (*auto-matos*). They do not yield an intentional form, do not and cannot lead naturally or inevitably to "the finished work," and in this sense they could be considered constitutionally aloof from or even detrimental to the "end"—if not the aim—of notated compositional activity, what the symbolic Other expects of the signifier "composer": to be one who makes works. Here, then, would be the domain in which sketch-study unfolds its riches: the domain of the written, the iterated, the recuperable intention of the insistent sign.

But there is another register that comes into play, one that tends to leave serious engagement silent. It concerns what, after a 1966 essay by Ligeti, one might call "the imagination of the form," the way in which so many works of "the New Music" take seemingly spontaneous turns, or suffer certain strangely consistent chance encounters—how "something keeps repeating itself" beyond the signifier.[56] And here is where the psychoanalytic conception of unconscious fantasy can be brought into play: a way of postulating how an antagonism—an ineliminable conflict, a repeatedly missed encounter with impossibility—can become veiled, namely, as a possibility that fails to pass, that remains desired and keeps desire alive.

This, as I argue at various points in the book, is a productive way of beginning to come to terms with what is often most elusive in much of this music: the way in which so many of Berio's works, after their astonishing multi-domain expansions, their building of worlds, shudder, shrink, and self-retract; the way Ligeti's hovering-quivering-glittering poly-harmonic-rhythmic meshes, aiming toward a utopian "abolishing of time" itself, are suddenly, brutally cut off—woodblock as clock, clock as guillotine; the way Lachenmann's airy, noisy, hyper-reverberant sound structures gradually freeze and self-evacuate, their final toneless noise crushing all resonance; the way Rihm's ceaseless trains of prolixity and breakthrough so often lead to a choked silence, alternately horrified and confused at its utter incapacity to produce. Such moments are, I think, the dark doubles of sketch-study. Whereas the latter tracks *automaton* in the thick forest of secret languages, the former offers a way of tracking *tyche*, precisely *not* as a secret language but as a *lingua franca*—understanding how European musical modernism may have as its most common locus not a positive object, but a negative one: an axiom of failure, a shared parapraxis.

It is a handy axiom for the modernist, as someone whose problem with the old is always twofold, always a matter of biggest and most particular others, of language in general and the unmistakable timbre of specific voices, the "infinity of the stars" and the "infinity of our father."[57] Jameson cites Walter Benjamin citing Paul Valéry on Charles Baudelaire: according to Valéry, Baudelaire's central difficulty was "how to be a great poet, but neither a Lamartine nor a Hugo nor a Musset."[58] The axiom of failure is everywhere in the musical mycelium of 1989 Europe: in works that miss encounters with actual personages, with Schubert, Bach, Mahler, Beethoven; with genres such as opera, the symphony, the string quartet; and even with the great tropes of Western modernity itself, with utopia, knowledge, revolution. There is, of course, no one way to fail, and so one finds in failure as an axiom a felicitous—and achieved—encounter. Those seemingly timeless tests of strength for any creative artist, *ingenium* and *iudicium*, invention and judgement, meet up "by chance" with the test of strength for any aesthetic modernist: originality. There is much originality in these works of 1989, and much invention and judgment—some good, some bad, some inscrutable. But there is also a common tone that calls to mind Jorge Luis Borges's "aesthetic fact"—already a modernist formulation in its own midcentury moment: "This imminence of a revelation as yet unproduced."[59] If there is a pathos that motivates *From 1989*, it involves this continued aesthetic insistence on un-production at a moment when, for at least a brief spell, utopia seems to have shown its flickering face. While I am critical of that face, I remain ambivalent about the notion of turning away. There is something sad and ghastly about the thought of having missed it. At the least, no one outside a revolutionary moment—certainly not the historian—has much jurisdiction to say what its actors ought to have done, or not done.

. . .

If the role of psychoanalysis in *From 1989* is a manifold one, it first appears in a quite restricted role: a heuristic, a lens, an apparatus. It is initially a matter of propinquity, of coming upon a "found object" from that year, published just before the Wall cracked open: Slavoj Žižek's strong political and cultural (mis)reading of Lacan in his 1989 *The Sublime Object of Ideology*. It was Žižek's first book in English, and the rest, as they say, is history. I was especially interested in Žižek's adoption of Laclau and Mouffe's concept of antagonism, itself reformulated from Karl Marx; essentially Žižek conflates this notion, which involves the "limits of all objectivity" in the field of political discourse, with Lacan's concept of the Real, as "that which resists symbolization absolutely." The conflation is not without its symptoms, but they are also extremely productive, especially as they extend into the domains of ideology (for Laclau and Mouffe) and unconscious fantasy (for Freud and Lacan).

This book's part 1 is an exposition and development—and, in some ways, a recapitulation—of these concepts as they relate to what I consider three of 1989's most spectacular musical scenes. They are, I argue, also three of its most fantastical and ideologically freighted: Leonard Bernstein's doctored performance of Beethoven's Ninth on Christmas Day (*Freude* replaced with *Freiheit*), Mstislav Rostropovich's impromptu recital of Johann Sebastian Bach at a newly opened Checkpoint Charlie in November, and David Hasselhoff's sublimely goofy lip-sync of his hit song "Looking for Freedom" from a crane at the Brandenburg Gate on New Year's Eve. All are rather Žižek-friendly events, open to the wide analytic lens (or maw) of a post-Lacanian ideological critique. But to my knowledge, none of these events have been brought together with the other two, and if they have something new to tell us, it is as a triad, its tones gleaming as irresistibly, and decaying as surely, as those depicting Wozzeck's coins in act 1 of Alban Berg's opera.[60]

What they have to tell us is twofold. First, they can be used to construct and analyze some of the historical moment's more robust cultural fantasies as they implicate music. In what might seem like mere occasional fluff—or, as one early reader of the book surmised, desperate stunts to revive flagging careers—I argue that we can nonetheless find three specific, highly visible and audible forms by which culture "already knew its New," and through which it was able to desire and enjoy it in reliable and effective ways. These *were* stunts, no question; but this is all the more reason to look behind their curtains. In their brash ad-hoc-ness, they used the fantasy machinery they had on hand, and that machinery's uses extend far beyond them.

The second thing these performance spectacles have to tell us concerns musical modernism directly. It will no doubt strike some readers as odd that a book ostensibly about contemporary European composition would spend the whole first of its three parts on an entirely different world, perfectly divorced from, say, the preoccupations of a Louis Andriessen, Adriana Hölszky, or Pascal Dusapin. Another of the book's provocations is to contend that, fantasmatically speaking, they are not divorced at all. Anything but: we cannot understand the one without the other, and I would wager that some of the most extensive and counterproductive misunderstandings of musical modernism stem from attempts to pull the two apart—whether to proclaim them mutually autonomous or hierarchically attached. I argue instead that fantasy is their—often elusive—common ground. It is in their designs that they differ: while the stunts of Bernstein, Rostropovich, and Hasselhoff needed such fantasies to *work*, using the master signifier "freedom" to veil and wall up a radical historical breach, the latter needed such fantasies to *fail*, to fall apart, to unveil a historical Real. If European New Music in 1989 didn't consciously know itself as such, it was nonetheless still an art of fantasmatic sabotage; its otherwise irreducible practices congregated around a common libidinal know-how, and met that know-how analytically, armed with myriad forms of not-knowing. To think in rather nineteenth-century terms: if we are to understand these forms of not-knowing, these arts of sabotage, we must understand the factory, and the unconscious knowledge it produces. This is the first part's basic aim.

The three odd-numbered chapters of part 1 constitute three rotations through the same material, hence their common title. They are forms of rehearsal: they read, watch, and hear Hasselhoff again, and then again, each time uncovering new aspects of the fantasmatic apparatus that supports his performance. In this sense, they treat their scenes as the Freudian clinic tried to treat dreams: material to work through, whose content may be alternately lurid or banal, but whose form only emerges through telling, and whose form *is* its most essential content. The two even-numbered chapters are significantly larger and more theoretical in nature, less case study or dream interpretation and more metapsychology. Chapter 2 slowly teases apart a psychoanalytic notion of fantasy from the more common parlance, to illustrate not simply the differences between "fantasy and *fantasy*," but also their antagonism. While common everyday fantasy is always on some level a site of freedom—or at least its image—psychoanalytic fantasy is a site of bondage and constraint, a way of being framed, often enough for a crime the fantasist can't recall committing. In a serendipitous turn, this tension also plays out in the Western historical genre of the musical fantasy, and it becomes the chapter's emergent aim to identify an uncanny repetition of sorts between the discursive logic of musical fantasy in middle- and late-period Beethoven and that of Bernstein et al. in 1989.

Chapter 4 deserves special attention, and perhaps even a caveat. It is the book's theoretical engine, its "systems folder," where the key concepts and logic that undergird the book's remainder are laid out in as consistent and detailed a fashion as I could muster. Given that they come centrally from Freud, Laclau and Mouffe, Žižek, and, above all, Lacan, this doesn't make for the easiest reading. At the same time, I felt strongly that it would have been irresponsible to leave its material out—to outsource it to other already-existing primers and "Introductions-to . . . ," for instance. With much of this material, and especially with so cumbersome an apparatus as Lacan's, there is no such thing as excursus; retelling is always telling anew. Lacan's teachings were initially an oral practice, and his most important concepts often couple a form that is iterable but empty—his (in)famous mathemes, for instance—with a radically open and proliferating content. Rehearsal, like dream interpretation, *is* the work. While my own extra-excursus doesn't pretend to be a revolutionary reading of Lacan, it does take up the challenge of retelling itself, and provides what I hope will be one of a growing number of important resources for music students interested in the Freudian-Lacanian lineage.

Part 2, unfolding under the signifier "New," constructs a kind of "counter-site" to part 1, not least by taking the notion of counter-site as its subject. It conceives of European New Music as what Michel Foucault called a heterotopia, an "other space," quasi-utopian and also actually existing, in which "other real sites that can be found within the culture are simultaneously represented, contested, and inverted."[61] Chapters 6, 9, and 10 take this premise quite literally. In chapters 6 and 9, I engage three works that in a number of ways can be seen as "counter-events" to Hasselhoff, Rostropovich, and Bernstein: Heiner Goebbels's *Befreiung* for speaker and ensemble, Paweł Szymański's solo cello piece *A Kaleidoscope for M. C. E.*, and Luciano Berio's *Rendering*, his "restoration" of the sketches to Franz Schubert's Tenth Symphony. In no way can these events compare—in terms of audience, mediation, or historical power—to the mega-events of part 1. But this is in part the point: their restaging of similar materials and scenarios in "contested" and "inverted" form is done in a kind of cultural nighttime, reconfigured as dreams configure the day's waking reality, its "recent and indifferent material," as Freud puts it. My wager is that the power these new compositions lose as representatives of the year, they make up for as representatives of a certain truth, the truth of a collective unconscious desire—again, as dreams can tell the subject something about the truth concealed by its days. Chapter 10 expands the aperture—or, better, auditorium—considerably, zooming out to a number of "counter-networks" in which New Music reconfigures older music via certain master signifiers—"revolution," for instance, or "Schubert," or "Bach."

Chapters 7 and 8 go into considerable depth about what I think this reconfiguration consists of. Here the material first engaged in chapter 4 is revisited and "applied" to New Music; chapter 7 in particular attempts to expound a Lacanian discursive theory of New Music, and of aesthetic modernism more generally—a theory not just of how actors and subjects "talk" New Music, but how they more broadly "language" it, forging social links and desiring structures through the excessive materiality of music as much as the denotative operations of the signifier. What kind of subject—what "little God of the world," as Goethe put it in *Faust*, part 1—is the modernist? What sort of desire founds its subjectivity on the new, literally throws itself under this mastering signifier of the not-yet?

The book's third part initially makes explicit what the second part had implied: that the enclosure of the psychoanalytic clinic—an ambivalent one, endlessly provocative of intense debate—can be read as *isomorphic* with the heterotopian "other space" of New Music, a space that was in 1989 (for better or worse) as autonomous a musical scene as any the world had ever produced. In this counter-site, the dominant fantasies of New Music's own cultural milieu are invited in and taken up as subjects bearing their own particular pasts; they are brought to moments of traversal and subjective destitution, made to witness their own "imaginary decline of the world," as Lacan puts it.[62] The space is not only a matter of the noumenal site of the work, or the actual physical location of the concert hall; it is also a discursive space, linking subject with other through the use of languages. But if part 2 constructs an isomorphism, an equality of forms that nonetheless do not generate or equal each other, in part 3 I try to take things a bit further. Here, under the larger rubric of "repetition," I begin to expand the temporal frames and historical claims of the book. This entails beginning to think of my found heuristic, the Freudian and Lacanian psychoanalytic clinic, as an *example* of a modernism, quite like the one I had been constructing in part 2. I argue for the possibility that my "apparatus" is not so much a distancing lens on an objective material, a way of getting some perspective on things, as it is *another repetition*—of a scene, a performance, a logic—that characterizes the dynamics of a much longer "moment" of European modernism. (As I suggest in chapter 13, perhaps the Lacanian field is not what psychoanalysis looks like when it finally receives or is overtaken by postmodernism; it is what modernism, losing its hegemonic grip on the arts, begins to look like when it migrates back into psychoanalysis, when the linguistic turn invites the human psyche to become as pushable, as testable, as absolutely decomposable as modernism's other tormented mediums.) In chapters 12 and 13, I return to Lacan's discourse theory, and offer a formalization of two moments of modernism, each of which can be understood through one of Lacan's discourse schemata: a "master's discourse," and an "analyst's discourse." I argue that the history of aesthetic modernism can be understood in part as a constant, tense passage between these two discourses, ever implicated in one another, each ever incipient as the dominant mode.

Chapter 14 jumps back eighty years to the Viennese *Sprachkrise*, and to Schoenberg's *Erwartung* (1909) as a striking example of, and precedent for, such an analyst's discourse. Indeed, emerging as it does at the moment of Schoenberg's own "end of analysis," *Erwartung* can be shown to have much in common with many of the inspired failures and missed encounters that structure the landscape of New Music in the Europe of 1989: its monstrous stylistic impurity; its strange hybrid of "blind technique" and asystematicity; its undoing of conventions without offering substitutes; its exposure of antagonisms that threaten the symbolic order out of which it emerges—in short, its loss, not just of the rules, but of the rules governing the rules. What lies between these two moments of "analytic modernism" is, among other things, the much longer historical transformation of Schoenbergian modernism into a master's discourse. It is not a history of "programming the absolute," as Berthold Hoeckner memorably put it about music in the "long" nineteenth century, so much as programming the antagonism: staging a radical inconsistency as consistent, erecting new armatures of fantasy in support of newly named desires, restarting the dialectic.[63]

Thus can the history of aesthetic modernism be seen, at least in part, as a consummate Freudian dynamic: founding trauma and repression, a murder of fathers, an exposure of antagonisms, and the laying down of a long veil, one onto which new fantasies of a master can be projected. "After great pain a formal feeling comes," goes the line from Emily Dickinson. She is not the first person I think of when discussing European musical modernism, but her words are apt. Keeping in mind Freud's maxim that anxiety is the only honest affect, perhaps the great pain of modernism's analytic moments is also a source of prohibitive pleasure; perhaps the longer, soberer melancholies of its master moments are but a redistribution of same. To put it more concretely: maybe Moses, as he "sinks to the ground in despair" at the end of act 2 of Schoenberg's *Moses und Aron*, is not so despairing after all. Maybe his famous exclamation of not-having—"O Wort, du Wort, das mir fehlt!" (O word, thou word, that I lack!)—is the very thing keeping his desire alive.[64] The Frau's last words in *Erwartung*—"Ich suchte" (I was searching)—are in this sense not so different. A theater of incapacity keeps alive the libidinal flame of the creative act; what ended *Erwartung* as a now-iconic gesture of un-closure is formalized into a constitutive act of de-completion.

Chapter 15 returns to the book's own present, but drags fin-de-siècle Vienna with it, exploring a network of "Mahler pieces" from 1989. The network emerges partly out of unrelated, stylistically disparate works, some of which explicitly cite or allude to the composer, others of which stage Mahlerian scenes or tropes. But the bulk of the network is the result of deliberate effort—European cultural institutions commissioning composers to fantasize on their behalf, to produce collective scenes in which "Mahler" serves as a musical representative of "Europe." Unsurprisingly, the composers respond in the negative—not with scenes, but with their dismantling; not with representations, but their travesty, ruin, or residue. The remainder of the chapter stumbles into what I think is fair to call the book's central repression: the presence of Theodor Adorno, whose 1960 monograph on Mahler I take as an uncanny guide to these later works. The book ends with an extended consideration of Adorno's place in a Lacanian account of European musical modernism.

. . .

A few words on how this book is laid out. It is, without my wanting to come off too pretentiously, an achieved ambivalence, in the way Harold Bloom once described poems as achieved anxieties.[65] Which is to say: it begins ambivalently, and ends ambivalently, but along the way hopes to have done something with this ambivalence, such that it ends up in a quite different place—an appearing-clearly, if not appearing clear. In this sense it operates through at least a minimal identification with its main object of inquiry. Ambivalence is, I think, one of the most constitutional properties of aesthetic modernism. Where modernism is, there ambivalence will be, and also uncertainty. Its historical actors often put on a great show of appearing otherwise. "So cold and optimistic, modernism," writes Clark in *Farewell to an Idea*. "So sure it will get there eventually."[66] But I think Clark is being a bit glib here, and wouldn't be surprised if he admitted as much; modernism's surenesses can fade in seconds, cracked open by another, opposite possibility. If this book performs something of a working-out, it will in the process invariably appear at moments to fall to one side or the other, to have made up its mind. But don't shoot too soon, as Žižek puts it in one of his favorite jokes.[67] I state here for the record: the ambivalence will have remained unreconciled by the end.

The structure of the book is probably the most concrete manifestation of the influence of psychoanalysis, particularly the Lacanian orientation: its chapters could be read as variable-length analytic sessions. They are mildly but consistently paratactic, shot through with interstitial breaks, which one might read as pauses, silences, even prompts. The chapters, even the longer ones, "scand," or break off, always ending a bit too soon. All this happened rather spontaneously, though, by default, nothing in a book on psychoanalysis is spontaneous.

The book is not, however, a series of fragments. Ideally it would be read in order. Here too, the analytic analogy is helpful: the progression is not a dialectical one, in which each step declares itself forward through a negation, and then a negation of the negation. The book's ideas very much build on each other, but as an accumulation, effected by a persistent returning to the same material, its rereading, thinking again, repetition. Rotation as a means of getting somewhere. Again: less Hegel, more Kierkegaard.

. . .

The 1988 performance of Prometeo *in the Berlin Philharmonic's chamber music hall in presence of the Venetian is unforgotten. The finale of the* musikfest berlin *2011 brings the* Tragedia dell'ascolto, *alternating and simultaneously with*

> *Mahler's Symphony of a Thousand in the large hall, back to this place. Two large designs of a world, transcending traditional forms, supported and fascinated by the human voice. Two monumental conceptions: One of them stands at the beginning of the 20th century, Faustian, before the outbreak of the First World War, the other one at its end, Promethean, before the beginning erosion of the soviet empire. Faust and Prometheus then also constitute the two mythical threads that partly openly, partly subcutaneously pervade the programme of the* musikfest berlin *2011. (Musikfest Berlin 2011, introductory essay to the program book)*

Professor Doctor Joachim Sartorius and Doctor Winrich Hopp, respectively the intendant and artistic director of Musikfest Berlin 2011, are smart fellows. A bit diabolical, but smart. That is what, while I hold my tickets, one in each hand, I am thinking. I was indeed reading the script, unconsciously following the insistence of the signs, and it briefly made me myself into an *automaton*. But again: Whose script? Whose signs? Sartorius's? Hopp's?

To say it was no one's but my own would, arguably, be the proper psychoanalytic answer: the answer of someone who has learned what Lacan called the "big secret of psychoanalysis: there is no Other of the Other."[68] There is some truth to this; here I am, having written a book about European musical modernism's constitutive antagonisms, about how it puts itself in binds again and again of its own accord. The vision is perhaps not so distinct from my "symptom." To say it was Europe's fault is, I think, the historian's answer, and one I feel some pressure to levy. Sartorius and Hopp are here not the origin of this script, they are themselves readers. With this festival they are presenting a scenario that has been repeated again and again on Europe's concert stages for decades, and will only grow more reliably into what it is in the years to come: a Freudian *fort-da* game, being played on an infinitely grander scale than the one Freud first beheld, the vision of his grandson Ernst tossing a bobbin on a string over his pram, shouting *fort!* (gone!), and reeling it back in with a gleeful *da!* (there!).[69] Modernism—in this case, *Prometeo*—provides the *fort!*, and to absolutely stunning effect: an arresting of dialectical motion, a tychic repetition of the gap, a centripetal disintegration of the center that couldn't hold. And a traversal of one of Europe's oldest and most irresistible fantasies, modern before modernity: Prometheus, the promise of power and progress—the very birth of dialectics?—through emancipatory instrumental reason. Such fantasies are left in destitution by the end of Nono and Cacciari's work, literally desert-ed. The revenge of the centripetal Real on the (Mahlerian) fantasy of centrifugal force.

But then, a resurrection. Mahler: *da!* The eternal feminine saves the day, converts a pagan Prometheus into a Christian Faust—belief wins out over perception—and the pleasure principles of countless Philharmoniker subscribers are reactivated. In his critique of the Eighth, Adorno couldn't resist quoting a *bon mot* from the composer Hans Pfitzner, who allegedly responded to the symphony's opening "Veni Creator Spiritus" with a crabby plea for the missed encounter: "But supposing He does not come."[70] Here the Musikfest provides the ultimate retort, the most resounding *DA!* Mahler himself—already insinuated in the ears of the Eighth's early unbelievers—is the Creator the work was always calling.[71]

It is a gripping finale. But the Musikfest directors, ingenious in the breadth and detail of their conception, are not terribly original here: the same scenario is being played out in so many festivals and concerts throughout Europe in 1989. There, for instance, a spectral Franz Schubert will come and go and come and go on the first half, in a work of Adriana Hölszky or Stefano Gervasoni or Rolf Riehm; and, on the second half, he will be brought stunningly back to life as Schubert in the flesh, his full color and body impossibly restored. This might be thought of as Europe's learning-to-live with modernism as its symptom: its embrace of the constitutional hole in itself, even its coming to identify with it, in the knowledge that it is not going away. Or it might be thought of as a cunning and cynical neutralization of whatever is, or was, progressive in aesthetic modernism. Either premise is an uncomfortable one. This book was finished in the spring and summer months of 2015, months in which—from the Greek "Grexit" fiasco to the catastrophe (often falling into true horror) of its refugee crisis—Europe exposed an unbelievably ugly face to the world. In such a situation, musical modernism comes to look far more like an ego discourse—a means of showing the world an ideal image of oneself—than like a traversal of fantasy, or the catastrophic energy of dis-identification. Or even a gaffe: if one wants to see Europe's parapraxes in 2015—what it "really thinks"—it arguably takes the form not of any "official work of art," but of a Hungarian camerawoman tripping a Syrian refugee.[72]

I went to the Nono. But I also paid for another ticket to the Mahler. (The directors couldn't have been *that* cynical.) In the end, however, I think my gaffe was caught perfectly between the psychoanalytic and historical accounts. It *was* my fault, and mine alone, because the directors in no way intended, even unconsciously, to create an impasse. They were reading a script that told them how to *resolve* such impasses: *first* Nono, *then* Mahler. One must, after all, end with Mahler. (The last Nono performance was on September 17, the last Mahler on September 18.) The extraordinary Berlin premiere of *Prometeo* in late 1988 was, as the presenters say, "unforgotten," but it was also unrepeatable. A cultural praxis had grown around it now, and had produced, in its explicit narratives but also in the "material sincerity" of its very armature, a means of fabricating an account of what this music means—to a listener, to a public, to Europe, to tradition. *Prometeo*, as a locus of antagonism, a traversal of fantasies, had been transformed back into a fantasy, a way of resolving antagonism narratively, not least by being able to say, "I know what the Other wants, and I can provide it."[73] What does this Prometheus want? What is he waiting for, invincible in the desert? He is waiting to be converted—to be washed in the Mahlerian flood, to be hoisted to heaven by Goethe's eternal feminine.

This puts my own slip in a new light. My explicit goal, unattained, turned out to have produced something more properly psychoanalytic than I initially realized: a moment of nonsense that was also a moment of truth. I *was* giving audience, not to Mahler's comedy (it is, in the end, a comedy), and also not to Nono's tragedy (where the ear is chained to the mountain, and suffers its own unrelenting sequence of tormenting pleasures). Sitting in this no-place, caught in a neither-here-nor-there, I was giving audience to an antagonism that wants only to hide, and which, like most antagonisms, it is culture's very life to conceal.

PART ONE

FREE

1

DREI PHANTASIESTÜCKE (1)

Sehr innig zu spielen

—ROBERT SCHUMANN, *PHANTASIESTÜCKE*, OP. 12/I. "DES ABENDS"[1]

1. Phantasiestück. David Hasselhoff has ants in his pants. It's late evening on December 31, 1989, in Berlin, and the interviewer can't quite get his attention.[2] He's too busy whooping and hollering *Hallo!* at the massive crowds to his left, then his right, then behind him. He squirms, grins, giggles like a teenager who has seriously underestimated the scope of a prank he's just pulled off. He catches the camera's gaze, purses his lips, and silently mouths "Unbelievable!"; he bugs out his eyes and flares his nostrils. Still mugging for the camera, he points to the throngs behind him and drops his jaw in self-conscious awe. The interviewer finally locks him down: "David, why did you want to come exactly *here* to the Brandenburg Gate?" Hasselhoff suddenly modulates into wistful-rugged voice-over mode: "One year ago we did 'Looking for Freedom,' and it was a *dream*." He is referring to his hit single, which squatted in the number one spot of Germany's pop charts for eight weeks in late spring of that year.[3]

And now David Hasselhoff is here to sing it "live."[4] The music is switched on, and begins to pipe through the frigid speakers. He tightens his piano-patterned silk scarf, reaches into his leather jacket, and pulls on something. The jacket begins to sparkle in randomly distributed clumps of triangle-shaped lights. Hasselhoff starts belting out the famously diminutive first verse, voguing iconic Elvisian poses for each half clause: "One morning in June some twenty years ago, / I was born a rich man's son. / I had everything that money could buy, / but freedom, I had none." As the crane-platform he is standing in commences its ascent, lifting him some hundred feet in the air, Hasselhoff sings the chorus. An anodyne American-export alloy of mid-1980s country and demo-button synth is fleshed out with a generic backup gospel chorus. Even on the heavily compressed web clips of the

FIGURE 1. David Hasselhoff at the Berlin Wall, December 31, 1989.

event, one can hear the many thousands of voices below—on the freezing ground, on either side of the crumbling Wall, swaying on the Wall itself—automatically erupt in unison. Hasselhoff, despite his antics, seems to find himself surprisingly moved, his quivering "live" voice breaking up behind the prerecorded vocal track. "Everyone was singing my song," he remembers, "and I was singing, crying and freezing all at once. As the great chorus rose up in the night sky above the Brandenburg Gate, you didn't have to be German to find it emotional."[5] He leans over the platform's edge and pumps his fist high in the air, and a large firecracker soars inches over his downturned head; moments later, another breaks apart against his stomach. As a composition, the song is pap, oxymoronic pure kitsch. But as an event, it is undeniably uncanny: a collective celebration, but also a kind of strange Brechtian "teaching piece" whose words demand not simply to be heard, but to be repeated, installed directly into the crowd's mouths, its souls following suit:

> I've been looking for freedom, I've been looking so long.
> I've been looking for freedom, still the search goes on.
> I've been looking for freedom, since I left my hometown.
> I've been looking for freedom, still it can't be found.

Amid all this spectacle, Hasselhoff comes off not only as a master of ceremonies, a hybrid DJ and descending angel, but also, strangely enough, as a humble partici-

FIGURE 2. Mstislav Rostropovich at Checkpoint Charlie, November 11, 1989 (as seen live on French TV).

pant. He is spectacularly elevated, but equally subjected, thrown down below, rendered a slack-jawed man-on-the-street tourist. "All I could think," he reminisces in his autobiography, was:

> What an honor to be part of history. When I was lowered to the ground I grabbed a bottle of schnapps and took several swigs. Then I started chopping chunks out of the wall with a hammer and putting the pieces in my pockets. I took them home and gave them to the *Baywatch* crew on a little plaque saying "A little piece of freedom." When I got back to the hotel, the tape was still running in the VCR. I pressed "rewind" and "play" and there it was—I had that whole unforgettable night on tape.[6]

• • •

2. *Phantasiestück*. November 11, 1989. Philippe Rochot, Antenne 2's special envoy to Berlin, is standing on a walkway above Checkpoint Charlie, conversing with the anchor back in Paris.[7] A slice of Wall behind him is smothered in graffiti, some of it very recently revised: a large Mickey Mouse clothed in the colors of the German flag stands like a tour guide next to the words "Wilkommen in ~~Ost~~-Berlin." Rochot seems flustered; his tone is electrified, he is improvising. An unexpected scene is unfolding behind and below him: the legendary Russian cellist and exile Mstislav Rostropovich appears to be setting up for a performance of some kind. Someone is helping him with a chair while he, his back to the camera, unlatches his

instrument case. He has just arrived in Berlin from Paris, on a plane owned by his close friend, the French captain of industry and food tycoon, Antoine Riboud.[8] "It was a simple need," Rostropovich told a 1999 interviewer in *Fidelio*, the organ of Lyndon LaRouche's Schiller Institute. "I had to do it. And by myself, for sure. Because, this Wall was a symbol of my life, or my 'two' lives."[9]

The amplitude and affect of this mise-en-scène is an inversion of Hasselhoff's performance: a small semicircular crowd has swaddled Rostropovich into an intimate ad hoc amphitheater less than fifteen feet wide. "Rostropovich's 'theater,'" as two commentators put it shortly after the performance, can be seen as "situational—above all, personal. He deliver[s] no shrill monologue, his music accompanie[s] no raucous stage show calling for more political upheaval."[10] But it is a liberation scene nonetheless: an un-crossable border is crossed, a no-man's-land becomes a stage on which to monologue the individual's inalienable right to free speech, free song. Even for the fool: this spectacle is, among other things, a "mad scene," *la finta pazza*. Slava is Quixote vindicated. As the man begins to play—an act captured on hundreds of television channels, re-narrated in countless histories of the events of 1989, and in countless obituaries for the musician himself—an incandescent silence settles on the scene. One hears only the clicking camera shutters competing with the reedy-raspy tones of the unamplified, slightly out of tune, remarkably vulnerable cello.

Rostropovich plays Johann Sebastian Bach: in this French news clip, it is the saraband from the third cello Suite, BWV 1009; in another clip he is playing the iconic prelude to the first Suite. In Joel Brouwer's poem "Rostropovich at Checkpoint Charlie, November 11, 1989," it is the tumultuous, breathless prelude to the fifth Suite:

> The maestro sits
> in the shadow of the Wall, lifts his cello from its case, then
> lunges, stabs the bow across the strings,
>
> and instantly the street is possessed: Bach's Suite #5.
> The chords circle low, wary as a flock of crows, then vault
> into melody, retreat, begin again: threnody, aubade,
>
> threnody, aubade, like a man who wakes up
> on the morning he's longed for and finds he can think of nothing
> but the night just ended and the night to come.[11]

One may not agree with Richard Taruskin's appraisal of the performance—"the only time I ever hated the Bach Suites"—but it's hard to deny that the tone is "frightfully turgid, tempo glacial," and the entire affair feels a bit ponderous ("[Rostropovich's] jaw was jutting, his mouth was working furiously, his forehead was beaded").[12] He plays the suites more or less as he has played them in recitals, which is to say, as if no historical performance movement ever happened. The thick round tone wobbling with vibrato, the frequent portamenti suppressing any virtual polyphony—the general cadence reveals little trace of dance, each weighted tone instead betraying an emphatic *you. are. here.* But then, the scene itself has little truck with History, still less with historicism. If its moment is historic, its frame, for Rostropovich, is unmediated and eternal. When the interviewer in *Fidelio* asked Rostropovich why he chose to play Bach, the cellist responded with the language of sacerdotal servitude:

> We interpreters are the servants of the composers; we must be very modest and ought never to present ourselves—our ego—in the front lines; rather, the idea of the composer, which, on the contrary, is divinely inspired, should be presented. . . . In order to render [Bach's] music, I had to give up my "Russian personality"; because a composer as great as Bach actually needs hardly any "rendering" to come into being. It "suffices" to perform it as he wrote it. And that is true for all great composers.
>
> I have immense respect for Bach; he is one of the best examples, that art comes from God. As with a priest, it is not necessary that the Word of God be interpreted; rather, that God speak directly to man through the priest.[13]

. . .

3. *Phantasiestück.* The fourth movement of Beethoven's Ninth, just after the return of the *Schreckensfanfare.* Now it is Christmas Day, 1989, and Leonard Bernstein is conducting the work in Berlin's Königliches Schauspielhaus, the former home of the Berliner Sinfonie-Orchester, the Philharmoniker's East German rival.[14] Bernstein and the German musician-impresario Justus Frantz have spared no expense to globalize—still with a frisson of trespasserly transgression—the spectacle. The orchestra alone includes players from Munich, Dresden, Leningrad, Paris, London, and New York. The choruses come from West and East Berlin, including the Dresden Philharmonie's Children's Choir. All these voices now rush into the no-man's-land like air into vacuum, harmonizing on the famous lines "All men will become brothers" and "Be embraced, millions / This kiss to the entire world!" As the bass-baritone Jan-Hendrik Rootering begins to sing his plea for new tones, the young girls in the chorus behind him stare straight ahead, steeling themselves in the knowledge that they are being broadcast to the hundreds standing in the Breitscheidplatz (in the West) and the Platz der Akademie (in the East), and to a televised audience of thousands in thirty-six other nations.[15]

Bernstein brings down his left fist on the word *freudenvollere* (more joyful), and the orchestra hammers out an A-major chord. With noticeable boost in boom, Rootering proclaims—not *Freude*, but *Freiheit. Freiheit*, ricochets the men's choir behind him, and off Rootering goes, singing a version of Friedrich Schiller's poem that appears never to have existed:

> Freedom, beautiful spark of the gods, daughter of Elysium,
> Intoxicated with your fire, heavenly one, we enter your shrine.
> Your magic power reunites what strict custom has divided;
> All men become brothers where your gentle wing rests.

FIGURE 3. Leonard Bernstein conducting the finale of Beethoven's Ninth at the Königliches Schauspielhaus in East Berlin, December 25, 1989.

Perhaps not never: though Bernstein feels plenty "authorized by the power of the moment" in replacing all instances of *Freude* in Schiller's text with *Freiheit*, he does reference the old theory, dating back to an 1849 article by Friedrich Ludwig Jahn, in which "a planned paean to freedom by Schiller fell prey to the censor and had to be turned into 'An die Freude' to avoid recriminations."[16] But Bernstein concedes that the theory is probably false, and, in a Falstaffian spirit of *se non è vero, è ben trovato*, he barrels ahead:

> But legend or not, I feel this is a heaven-sent moment to sing "Freiheit" wherever the score indicates the word "Freude." If ever there was a historic time to take an academic risk in the name of human joy, this is it, and I am sure we have Beethoven's blessing.[17]

This "academic risk" takes some chutzpah; the famous Schiller statue by Reinhold Begas stands in Gendarmenmarkt Square directly outside the hall, even as the poet's verses are being rewritten within. But with the exception of a single newspaper review, the move is not received as cynical.[18] It is instead understood as the culmination in a series of gifted Beethovens, following Daniel Barenboim's November 12 Berliner Philharmoniker performance of Beethoven's First Piano

Concerto and Seventh Symphony (a "gift" specifically to the East Germans), and, nary a week later, Yehudi Menuhin's all-Beethoven concert (a benefit for the "reconstruction of the historical city center of Berlin"). Here, in classical music's arguably most mythic self-staging of the late twentieth century, the polis is given the gift of once again dancing around "the freedom tree of the Revolution."[19] Or, rather, they are given the semblance, the spectacle, which is enough. And it is the spectacle itself which designates the stage, which calls the shots, which allocates parts for everyone—the conductor, the singers, the instrumentalists, the critics, the media, the spectators and listeners. Everyone plays their part.

2

FANTASY & FANTASY (1)

In common parlance, fantasy is what you get up to when the surveying mind and surveying society are both looking the other way. Fantasy is supremely asocial. Doubly licentious, it creates a world of pleasure without obligation to what is either permissible or possible, outside the realm of fantasy, to do.

—JACQUELINE ROSE, *STATES OF FANTASY*[1]

Phantasiestück: the term wasn't Robert Schumann's to begin with but E. T. A. Hoffmann's, and in all likelihood it didn't originally connote "pieces" in the musical sense but something more like "scenes," something to be staged, to behold and get caught up in. In Hoffmann's case, they were already transmedial scenes. Perhaps they start as images—say, Jacques Callot's engravings—but soon they end up airborne, ballooning into associative networks, word into scenario into literary form. The three spectacles of chapter 1 close the loop, creating a circuit of transfixity. Scenes of image becoming word becoming music, they are also initiated *by* music. Music, or perhaps just the idea of music, provides a kind of proscenium or screen, some consistent-resistant surface. Chargeable with limitless affective intensity, it props up a multimedia spectacle, eventually yielding an exhaustively documented and commented-upon event exploiting all that late twentieth-century technology has to offer. What kinds of "fantasy scenes" are these? Not, at first glance, ones *sehr innig zu spielen* (to be played very inwardly), as Schumann directs the pianist in the first of his Op. 12 *Phantasiestücke*. They are vulgar megaphonic parades next to the crepuscular privacies of "Des Abends," with its encrypted "Clara theme," its chafing inner voices and crossed, caressing thumbs, its 2/8 meter disguised as 3/8, et cetera. Here, in rejection of everything these Berlin scenes stand for, is a music of sublime nuance, a music that categorically rejects the world, "becomes lost to it," absorbed only in its own song.[2]

Schumann's *Phantasiestücke* are relatively late, perfectly idiosyncratic additions to one of Western music's wobbliest but longest-standing genres, and in some ways there is little sense in speaking of a sixteenth- or seventeenth-century fantasy by Luis de Milán or William Lawes in the same breath as a nineteenth-century one

EXAMPLE 1. Robert Schumann, *Phantasiestücke*, Op. 12, No. 1, "Des Abends" (In the Evening).

by Schumann, or an eighteenth-century one by Carl Philipp Emanuel Bach, or twentieth-century fantasies by Ferruccio Busoni or Ralph Vaughan Williams. But if all these musics are so unlike one another in tone, technique, or "language," they are nonetheless shadowed at every historical turn by a common discursive logic that suggests family resemblances. There is, it's easy to see, a consistency between Milán's 1536 designation of the fantasy as springing "solely from the fantasy and skill of the author who created it" and Christopher Simpson's statement, in 1667, that a fantasizing composer "is tide to nothing but that he may adde, deminish, and alter at his pleasure . . . wresteth and turneth as he list, making either much or little of it as shall seeme best in his own conceit."[3] But this logic continues to rehearse itself in very different musics in the eighteenth and nineteenth centuries, when a musical fantasist "follows his whims completely without attempting to work out a specific plan"; or "depends too much on the caprice of his mood, on the peculiarity of his immediate frame of mind, to be able to aim at a particular end"; or "loses himself in a sea of modulations"; or "doesn't pay attention to what one plays [but rather] yield[s] oneself freely to exactly what one feels."[4] As one might expect, these later descriptions differ from the earlier ones in their emphasis on feeling. But discursively speaking, feeling occupies the same structural role as, say, "pleasure" for Simpson, and even that unarticulated force driving Milán's fantasist to work "solely": it is what comes from the author alone. The logic rehearses itself yet again in Hoffmann's own account of his *Fantasiestücke in Callot's Manier*, in which Callot's work "really *goes beyond the rules* of painting; or rather his drawings are but reflexes of all the *fantastic apparitions called up by the magic of his exuberant fantasy*. . . . Even the commonest subjects from everyday life . . . appear in the glow of a certain romantic originality, so that *one's thoughts are surrendered to fantasy*, and engaged in the most amazing way."[5]

The consistency in these generic formulations stands in striking tension with the inconsistency they seem designed to stage: "fantasy," as a title and generic name, becomes a way of encapsulating this tension. Within the symbolic matrix of musical-formal codes and conventions, "fantasy" comes to designate a collection of practices that eludes them—a code of no code, an executive order suspending order, a masterful un-mastery. On the one hand, a musical fantasy consistently stages an emancipation from various forms of consistency, whether classical rhetorical categories (*ingenium* and *iudicium*, for instance); structural-generic ones (suite, sonata, eventually symphony); or more generally whatever any musical-historical moment considers its primary, necessary constraints on imagination, its taming *technê*. A fantasy can at any time liberate the instrument, the will, the technique; it is what happens when an étude plays hooky.

On the other hand, this liberation is granted by a master, the master of genre. Only with its license—minimally, a contractual announcement to a listening community that "here and now will be some freedom"—can one pursue one's wildest, most formally transgressive wishes. The logic is hence complex, and a bit contradictory: a wish to break free, and a wish to submit; to let go of oneself, and to get swept up in something bigger, stranger, other. Most striking for my own designs in this book, musical fantasies—again, as a certain discursive consistency obtaining over multiple historical breaks—repeatedly enact a wish to show, and to hide. Rhetorically they purport to expose what goes on in the fantasist's head (and hands) before processes of censorship and revision can take hold, and before the demands of formal propriety (allegedly) set in. At the same time, they also stage—equally baldly—a paradoxical scene of opacity, casting an aural spotlight on the permanently occluded "real source" of invention. The turning of mentation into an aural theater is precisely what reveals its stubborn hiddenness: yes, yes, we just heard the act of inspiration itself, but—where did it really come from? Why did it inspire so? What, dear fantasist, were you really thinking? Or rather: What, in you, was really thinking for you? If autonomy is something of a master signifier for the genre—already there in Milán's throwaway modifier "solely"—it is nonetheless a pearlescent one, always about to invert its meaning. It is not just some special autonomy—say, the technical facility or inventive prowess of the artist—that allows the musical fantasy to materialize. The fantasy also allows autonomy to materialize; sanctioned by the genre itself, fantasy is what turns technical facility and inventive prowess themselves into a kind of performance. They, and not simply the resultant text, become the object of desire.

So from one perspective a maker of musical fantasies is radically alone, released from the other's demands that she make sense, hold things together, be a self-identical subject. In this context of breaking free, "pleasure," "whim," "conceit," and "feeling" all signify a wresting (back?) of the other's dominating power. And transgression, Hoffmann's "really going beyond the rules," naturally precedes this being alone. But simultaneously the fantasist also becomes a surrenderer, one who yields, gives up and over, becomes possessed—which is to say dispossessed, disenfranchised of a certain mastery, "surrendered to fantasy." Now sprung from self and self-rule, a fugitive of ego, the musical fantasist becomes a kind of eavesdropper on his or her own creation, which seems to come from elsewhere. It is possible here to put forth—if not a formula of musical fantasy, then at least a heuristic: *in fantasy, a (musical) self emerges from (musical) self-occlusion*. This self-occlusion, already there "at the beginning," creates a kind of constitutive gap, something that is, paradoxically, missing from the start.

But this constitutive gap is put to work. It generates a kind of momentum, a minimal productive instability. And along with it, an attendant logic of transposition and interpellation that becomes indispensable to the strange intersubjective sleight of hand musical fantasies often effect. The composer-performer, staging her own absorption, eventually cedes her agency and is surprised at what she finds herself delivered to. Now occupying the position of listener, she joins the audience, which comes to identify with her. Both then audiate with (supposed) surprise upon a third, apparently independent agency—a music for which no one is entirely responsible, and whose origins remain opaque, occluded. Not a love triangle exactly, but a desire triangle, almost farcical in its complexity. An operatic imbroglio, even: the position of master or cause now veiled, a little game of un-mastery, of aural hide-and-seek, ensues. The performing fantasist, lost to the world, becomes lost to herself, a proxy onlooker and eavesdropper. The actual onlooker-eavesdropper, lost in the performance, identifying with the performer, becomes a proxy fantasist.

• • •

Here is Annette Richards writing about Ludwig van Beethoven's *Chorphantasie* (Choral Fantasy), Op. 80, from 1808:

> The fantasy, then, enacts a quest from obscurity to light, a journey into knowledge; the composer/performer, the protagonist of the fantasy, is as the initiate/apprentice coming out of ignorance into self-awareness, discovering at the climax of the journey not the world outside, nature, but rather a mirror that throws back a now-clear reflection of the artist himself. But in the strange doubleness of fantasia as public performance, this private invention of the self is overseen, or overheard, in a voyeuristic moment: the fantasia, the artist's monologue and autobiography, offers what amounts to a titillating glimpse under the veil of secrecy into the intimate laboratory of the genius' imagination.[6]

Richards could not have described musical fantasy's logic of transposition and interpellation better. But she also articulates perfectly how such a logic constitutes the bridge from individual to collective fantasy. The complex circuit of desire it engenders reveals that the "sprung-ness" of fantasy depends constitutionally on the Other, on a continued being-together; fantasies, especially of aloneness, are never themselves alone. Richards's is still one of the most original and searching books on the Western genre of musical fantasy, and although its explicit topic is the relationship between the "free fantasia" and the picturesque mode from the mid-eighteenth century through the end of Beethoven's "heroic" period, it also charts the process by which musical fantasy "goes public," as it were.

The transition is hardly a simple one, of course, and it would be a mistake to succumb to teleological temptation and suggest that the hushed, quivering solitude celebrated by those "clavichord cults" around C. P. E. Bach gradually realized its destiny in the sublime collective thunder of Beethoven's *Hammerklavier*. All the same, it is clear that a sea change in the genre's meaning and influence occurs in the early nineteenth century, and that Beethoven's music has much to do with it. It is easily detectable in critical responses to Beethoven: it's through his influence that the fantasy genre is perceived as staging a coup, a literal takeover of (all the) other genres. In 1805, the *Allgemeine musikalische Zeitung* famously celebrates Beethoven's Third Symphony as "really a very extended, daring and wild fantasia"; a decade later, the same journal is publishing passionate editorials about the need for a containment policy: "Musical fantasies are usually forgiven the sins against form and rule, when a great spirit governs them. . . . But to transfer this characteristic of the fantasy to other pieces of music, and so to *make the musical fantasy rule in the region of the musical world*, can only lead to gross errors."[7] Richards cites an 1817 letter from one Ernst Ludwig Gerber extending the political metaphor further:

> It appears to me as if the fantasy, like a despot, has seized absolute power over music. . . . One can no longer perceive either any definite musical forms or any limits to the influence of the fantasy. Everything goes in all directions but to no fixed destination; the madder the better! The wilder and stranger, all the more novel and effective. In such a way we hear and play nothing but Fantasies. Our sonatas are Fantasies, our overtures are Fantasies and even our symphonies, at least those of Beethoven and his like, are Fantasies.[8]

Such passages can of course be read as evidence of a more general anxiety about the heterogeneous and disorientating effects of "modern music" and modernity tout court. "Fantasy" comes to signify, and indeed to contain in musical objects, otherwise ubiquitous worries about the simultaneous loss of bearings and moorings, the disintegration of rule and progress. In this sense, fantasy becomes a cipher for political anxieties, even as it continues to signify a refuge from them.

But at the same time, this more general account doesn't address what could be seen—above all in Beethoven's "middle period"—as a kind of recalibration of fantasy's generic code. By the time of the *Chorphantasie*, it has become the genre par excellence of theatricalized coordination, establishing in dramatic terms a scene of radical beginning, new bearings and new moorings. This trope is not in itself new; the toccata and prelude are venerable sites of musicalized beginning, of the warming of hands and machines. Richards rehearses how the German verb *fantasieren* designated already in the late eighteenth century not simply the "precompositional search for ideas" but a kind of preliminary music, a music not just of but before beginning.[9] For Franz Joseph Haydn, for instance, the improvisatory aspects of fantasy are marked by incipience; submission to mood initiates a process: "I sat down [at the keyboard] and began to fantasize," Haydn recounts, "according to whether my mood was sad or happy, serious or playful. Once I had seized an idea, my entire effort went toward elaborating and sustaining it according to the rules of art."[10] But whatever off-site or obscene implications remain in Haydn's gloss, they are eliminated under the newer Beethovenian paradigm. Fantasy becomes the generic signifier for staging the act of beginning as a music, and more precisely a musical work. The experience of inspiration and the labor of invention become the auditory scene itself; fantasy renders a musical theater of origins.[11] The heuristic I formulated above undergoes a revision. Musical self could still be said to emerge from musical self-occlusion; this self-occlusion is still put to work, mobilized as a kind of desire. But the scene is turned on its axis, "spun" even: it becomes an ontogenesis, a scene of birth, maturation, completion. This constitutive gap between sovereignty and submission, autonomy and dependence, is resolved—or, more exactly, masked—by being temporalized.

Essential to the increasingly hegemonic power of this musical origin-theater is what Daniel K. L. Chua has called "blank signs." Such signs are constitutive of absolute music, central to its power; they do not "annul the music's semiotic properties to gesture to various topics (horn calls, dance types, national styles, etc.) but [subsume] such meanings under larger philosophical and formal claims; under the banner of absolute music, the essence of music is more than the sum of its topics. Blankness, in this sense, requires an emptying of its content by mixing topics, like the colors of the rainbow, to produce a whiteness that is as full as it is empty."[12]

The blank sign is therefore beyond (or perhaps before) "positive" and "negative," which is to say that even though Chua calls it a sign, it does not participate in a semiotic game as one among opposing terms. Rather it becomes a placeholder for those moments where oppositions collapse. Chua considers "music's vacant sign of freedom" the quintessential blank for Beethoven; if fantasy is "the antiformal genre that parades the creative imagination of the composer as incipient content," then it is a work like Beethoven's *Chorphantasie* that provides the stage on which that incipient content becomes something like freedom "itself."[13] In Chua's reading, the work's opening two bars for solo piano are "a generic statement of creation *ex nihilo*," as blank in content (stolid C-minor arpeggios) as was the score's first page during its premiere (Beethoven evidently didn't have time to write the beginning down). In a dramaturgy that famously foreshadows the finale of the Ninth Symphony, this "blank state of freedom" engenders a series of variations for piano and orchestra before eventually enlisting the participation of a chorus that "sings of the harmonious power of art to fashion a new society. By the end," as Chua reads the process, "content and form unite. The escalation from the particular to the universal is an allegory of freedom and progress, a movement from the creative process to the created order, and from the individual subject to the universal law."[14] But, much like the individual subject's incipience, the universal law's appearance too must take the form of a blank sign: the word *Kraft* (power), repeated again and again in C major, twice leading to a Neapolitan E-flat major *tutti* chord. "Loud, shrill, and seemingly immovable, this harmonic shift ushers in the high-point and still-point of the entire [*Chorphantasie*]. . . . [It] represents the power of an art religion that tears us away from the phenomenal world toward the glorious reign of liberty."[15]

Chua is adamant that this "'Kraft' chord" not be taken as a static representation of freedom, "as if it were some eighteenth-century topic"—again, it doesn't operate from within a defined semiotic field as one among its differentiated terms. Rather, it marks a place or moment where that field breaks down. As such, this "freedom" is weirdly static, resistant to development and variation. If the fantasy's dramaturgy is itself "not a picture but a process," still it is pinned in place by a start and culmination that are picture-like, anti-processual.[16] An initial signifying vacancy—the beginning blank, blankness as beginning—finds its eventual realization in a second vacancy that is at once the completion and the repetition of the first. What manifests as a teleological process is actually a return to an impasse. And not a return to something "positive or negative," a "seed" or "crisis." Rather, the process itself is what masks a constitutional gap as an empirical one, what renders something "missing from the start" into something to be lost and found.[17] An obscurity or occlusion is repeated as its opposite, as something transparent and clarifying—Richards's "mirror that throws back a now-clear reflection of the artist himself."

Admittedly, this all seems as distant from Schumann's "Des Abends" as it does from the *Empfindsamkeit* and irony in the fantasies of C. P. E. Bach, with their distinct airs of intimate aloneness. But Ryan Minor offers a compelling argument for the *Chorphantasie* being less invested than it appears—than it wants to appear—in a vision of emancipatory communal will. It too is alone. Its "chorus of spirits" shows its seams to anyone willing to look; it is "entirely inorganic" and "simply echoes the valedictory melody announcing the pianist-hero's full emergence. These creatures did not learn to emulate their Prometheus, but to praise him."[18] Even as it embodies a new generic paradigm soon to threaten the symphonic genre itself, the *Chorphantasie* remains riven by the fantasy genre's older antagonism between mastery and un-mastery, autonomy as sovereign authority and as individual transgression.

But Chua's and Richards's readings, when taken in tandem, also testify to how a musical genre—especially one as discursively malleable as the fantasy—might metamorphose when gripped by a historical shift in discourse. The "inscriptionist" tendency of musical fantasies, their so often being fantasies on some preexisting text, is one of the genre's more transhistorical if banal features, but it illuminates nicely something in this discursive transformation. When the fantasy's ambivalent autonomy enters a field newly mastered by discourses of collective emancipation and self-determination, "freedom" becomes its urtext, a mortified signifier it is now tasked with revivifying and filling out. From within this new discursive horizon, all fantasies implicitly become *fantasie sopra "La Libertà."* Under the new Beethovenian paradigm, this freedom begins as a musical blank, the inscrutable opacity of a radical beginning; and it ends as the theatrical production, out of this opacity, of the urtext itself, now all too decipherable, as if it had really been there all along: *Kraft. Freude. Freiheit.*

. . .

If there is any historical path from the curtained murmuring of "Des Abends" to the whooping of Hasselhoff and his firecrackering throngs, it would have to be—as Richards might put it—a picturesque one, full of disorienting swerves, convolutions, overgrowth. But perhaps the better metaphor is not the path but the repetition—so long as it is understood to be a repetition with differences, a repetition in unrepeatably new contexts. Certainly these three Berliner *Phantasiestücke* repeat a much older discursive antagonism, along with quite a few other features of early nineteenth-century musical fantasies. Each is, for instance, a reflexive setting-up of freedom as a cause for music and music as a cause of freedom. Each also stages a performer wresting from a big Other some right, some wish-granting power. And there is in each scene also a "voyeuristic moment" of staged aloneness: sublime withdrawal made visible, supreme asociality socialized, in which Bernstein, Hasselhoff, and Rostropovich each appear to disengage from the parade and enjoy, as Jacqueline Rose puts it, a "world of pleasure without obligation to what is either permissible or possible, outside the realm of fantasy, to do." Hasselhoff thrusts his fist in the air, Rostropovich gracefully releases his bow, Bernstein drops his baton exhaustedly, and each, swaddled in eyes and ears and echoes, casts a long gaze deep into the interior elsewhere. The viewer may at this point feel she has witnessed something obscene, literally not intended for the stage—or, rather, that she and the public retroactively constitute not so much the recipients of this liberation scene as the fetish object on which the three alleged liberators got off: Lenny once again playing the empathic, lily-gilding exhibitionist, Slava again the Russian Orthodox music-soldier, "The Hoff" again as everyone's toothy dream-boy industry-tool. In this sense the vulgarity may be inseparable from what privacy the spectator is also privy to: offered up to the public is an otherwise invisible and inaudible zone of freedom, a place where, as "surveying mind and surveying society" (Rose) look the other way, an individual lets himself go.

FIGURES 4, 5, and 6 *(opposite)*. Leonard Bernstein, Mstislav Rostropovich, David Hasselhoff, and the elsewhere gaze.

This letting go follows musical fantasy's twist in discursive logic as well: the emancipation from a master is granted by a master, the letting go entails a getting-swept-up. In each case the master is opaque, self-occluding, absolute. Bernstein's freedom must be "authorized by the power of the moment"; Rostropovich must forfeit not only his "Russian personality" but his very self; Hasselhoff must imagine that the boundaries between his own voice and body and those of the crowd disappear into a "great chorus [rising] up in the night sky." "The intrusion of fantasy," the psychoanalyst Maria Torok writes, "causes the ego to give up its own self-government for a moment. . . . While remaining the seat of its actions, the ego momentarily refuses to be its author."[19] In all their Schillerian pomp, these three fantasy scenes may outshout Schumann's "Des Abends," but they are, from a certain perspective, still all musical daydreams—reveries, hallucinations, each shrouded in the half-light of their own specific unreality, each veiling a more intimate combination of transgression and servitude. Desiring to be "tide to nothing," they break free of the other; free, they desire to yield, to an (other) other.

But all these repetitions, striking though they are, are quilted in place by another, no less important for being so obvious. These spectacles are each attempts—rather Beethovenian ones—to stage freedom as an act of beginning, and to stage that beginning *as* music. Here they do not stop with music, of course. Rather, they seem to bring about a garish sublation of the logic of musical fantasy as a genre. They try to convert the constitutionally implicit nature of musical fantasy, its "paradoxical scene of opacity," into something absolutely explicit and transparent. To fantasy's veiled aural theater, staging the absolute as blank, as wordless possibility, the word itself is now added. With its saying, nothing is left unsaid. These *fantasie sopra "La Libertà"* take freedom as their subject, but it is "freedom"—as a signifier, a mortification—to which they become subject.

. . .

So far, I have been trying to fray the fabric that holds the word "fantasy" together, using two distant historical moments to tease out two seemingly irreconcilable threads: one based on emancipation and autonomy, the break and the opening, the other on bondage and opacity, the suture or veil. For the remainder of this book, I certainly don't intend to separate these two threads. Instead I want to appeal to what I consider one of the more robust discursive traditions devoted to keeping those threads entangled: that of the unconscious.

Histories of the unconscious are many. If still none are more exhaustive than Henri F. Ellenberger's 1970 tome *The Discovery of the Unconscious*, most nonetheless take Freud as their measure, and chart a genealogical or archaeological path back into all the sources and inspirations he so famously repressed.[20] In this context, Matt ffytche's recent work constitutes an intervention, an attempt to think Freud and psychoanalysis as themselves tropes in an ongoing history of a "broader unconscious" at once conceptually specific—a "formal problem"—and also a historical phenomenon precipitated by the pressures of its various times.[21] This unconscious is treated as essentially a discursive formation, a kind of solution, via language and its organs, to a problem that plagues its users ceaselessly. Its myriad "foundations" in a post-Enlightenment moment are "not detachable from nineteenth-century attempts to give an account of autonomy, originality and independence in the individual, or the wider desire to find new languages and new conceptions of human and social order."[22] Within this greater field of interests and needs, the unconscious becomes a conceptual inevitability, something whose actual ontological status pales next to its need to be fictioned, told and told again, employed as a "mediator." Maud Ellmann puts it nicely: this broader unconscious had no choice but "to be invented—and successively reinvented—whether it exists or not."[23]

As ffytche understands it,

> The increasing [early nineteenth-century] interest in an unconscious psyche reflects not simply the attempt to produce an adequate account of the phenomena of interior life, but also a concern with establishing the possibility of a self-caused self, or a self

> the logic of *whose development is irreducibly detached from more systematic forms of explanation*, or from the idea of its manipulation by external authorities or other determining causes. Such ideas would have an immense (if contested) appeal, particularly within liberal theories of individuality . . . [as] attempts to describe a stable "basis" to the self in the nineteenth century and beyond, into the domain of psychoanalysis itself.[24]

"Whose development is irreducibly detached from more systematic forms of explanation": herein lies the strangeness of the unconscious as concept. It is not, as ffytche is careful to maintain, simply a conceptual history of the demands of "the ideologues of liberal freedom" for more and greater freedom (in, say, political franchises, economic markets, the press, or individual determination). Rather, it is the more peculiar and problematic history of attempts to ground that freedom in a structural moment of opacity, obscurity, unrecoverability. This is what leads to ffytche's arguably most significant move, his focus on the early nineteenth-century work of the German philosopher Friedrich Wilhelm Joseph von Schelling: it is in Schelling's conceptualization of the unconscious that ffytche locates a kind of founding discourse.[25] Ironically it involves the assertion that, as ffytche puts it, "the beginning *must not be thought*." Moreover, it is precisely such an un-thought beginning that grounds human freedom, self-determination, and even historicity itself.[26] As Schelling puts it in his *Philosophical Inquiries into the Essence of Human Freedom* of 1809, "Understanding is born in the genuine sense from that which is without understanding. Without this preceding darkness creatures have no reality; darkness is their necessary inheritance."[27] For Schelling, this beginning "precedes all individual actions," constituting the "primordial deed which makes a man genuinely himself"; "immediately after it is put into exuberant freedom, this deed sinks into the night of unconsciousness."[28] Such a deed constitutes a kind of prehistoric choice on the part of the individual—an *Ent-Scheidung* or "de-scission" that cuts the individual off from origins to which he or she is nonetheless now bound. For Schelling, the deed is not reversible:

> For man to know of this deed, consciousness itself would have to return into nothing, into boundless freedom, and would cease to be consciousness. This deed occurs once and then immediately sinks back into the unfathomable depths. . . . Only in this way is a beginning possible, a beginning that does not stop being a beginning, a truly eternal beginning. For here as well, it is true that the beginning cannot know itself. That deed once done, it is done for all eternity. The decision that in some manner is truly to begin must not be brought back, because this would amount to being taken back. If, in making a decision, somebody retains the right to reexamine his choice, he will never make a beginning at all.[29]

This passage comes from Schelling's *Weltalter* (Ages of the World), a manuscript he first drafted in 1810, came close to publishing the following year, and eventually abandoned after two more substantial revisions.[30] Alistair Welchman and Judith

Norman call the text "a primer in the 'logic' of the beginning as such," and despite the manuscript's tormented and hermetic history, ffytche identifies it as a place of applied beginning, the start of an ongoing conceptual consistency.[31] It is for him where "the study of the unconscious properly begins," insofar as it is the study of a problem with "two sides": on the one hand, the problem of a need for absolute foundations, an absolute and irrefutable ground or beginning; and on the other, the problem of an absolute freedom that emerges from this ground's opacity or inaccessibility.

This is—as readers will likely have noted already—an ontogenetic scene. And indeed, some consider Schelling's most important philosophical intervention his attempt to provide an ontogenetic account of the "transcendental subject of thoughts" of late modern German philosophy.[32] For Adrian Johnston,

> Perhaps Schelling's key post-Kantian theoretical contribution is the asking and answering of the question regarding what, exactly, underlies the structural scaffolding of fully formed transcendental subjectivity as portrayed in Kant's critical apparatus. Whereas the Kantian transcendental system implicitly treats the subject, ensconced in experiential reality and its world of constituted objects, as always-already existent and operative, Schelling seeks to account for the very emergence of such subjectivity, for the origins of this agent-function. That is to say: Schelling, especially in his texts from 1809 and after, attempts to sketch the (transcendental) subject's (ontogenetic) pre/proto-history.[33]

Is this a fantasy? Is Schelling, in the years between the *Chorphantasie*'s composition and premiere, penning his own Beethovenian *fantasia sopra "La Libertà"*?[34] There is something vertiginous about the very question, since what is at stake for Schelling is the capacity of philosophy to give an account of how the faculty of fantasy can exist at all: it is the "eternally dark ground of selfhood" that provides the condition for the possibility of fantasy.[35] Slavoj Žižek, one of Schelling's most dogged interlocutors, puts it thus: if the Kantian "transcendental turn . . . desubstantializes the subject," then "*it is this very desubstantialization which opens up the empty space (the 'blank surface') onto which fantasies are projected, where monsters emerge*."[36] The strong implication—one that Lacanians like Žižek and Johnston make explicit—is that the transcendental, disembodied subject is not only capable of fantasy, but is a fantasy. Not a "mere" fantasy, not a delusion standing in the way of truer alternatives; rather, the transcendental subject emerges out of an obscure, unstable material situation as its inevitable by-product—a "symptom," a "violent reaction-formation precipitated by and setting itself up against the corporeal condition."[37] The premise is dizzyingly reflective. Fantasy becomes commensurate with fantasizing faculty. The subject, as a fantasy the body has about itself, turns to philosophy to give an ontogenetic account—a fantasy?—of its origins, now unrecoverable. At the same historical moment, it turns to music—to fantasies—to stage an ontogenetic theater of origins. What Schelling's philosophy denies itself as conceptual act—"For man to know of this deed, consciousness itself would have to return into nothing, into boundless freedom"—Beethoven's music puts forward as aesthetic experience.

. . .

Schelling originally wanted to begin the *Weltalter* with a famous proclamation of unrecoverable beginnings—the inscription borne by a statue of the nature goddess Isis at the Egyptian Temple of Sais: "I am that which was, which is, and which will be and no mortal has lifted my veil."[38] If the finer points of Schelling's newest manuscripts were not in wide currency at the time, the line itself was ubiquitous in turn-of-the-nineteenth-century German culture. As Pierre Hadot among others has shown, the "veil of Isis" was a wonderfully ambivalent figure, at once the absolute bar to self-knowledge and the self's most necessary passage to the absolute.[39] The antagonism between these positions was seemingly resolved along generational lines: for Goethe, it was vital to "seek no secret initiation / beneath the veil; leave alone what is fixed"; for the younger Friedrich Schlegel, it was "time to tear away the veil of Isis and reveal the mystery." For Friedrich Schiller, lifting the veil was a sin punishable by death, and a true disciple of the priests of Sais would resist; for the younger Novalis, "He who does not wish to lift the veil is no worthy disciple of Sais."[40] Beethoven too knew the inscription from the Temple of Sais, and evidently thought about it often: he copied it down himself and chose to frame his transcription, keeping it "in full view upon his desk in his later years," as Maynard Solomon points out.[41] For Beethoven the line seemed to suggest, appropriately enough, the power of beginning anew. "May God grant you the strength to enable you to reach your *Temple of Isis*," he wrote in a letter to Countess Marie Erdödy, "where the purified fire may swallow up all your troubles and you may awake like a new phoenix."[42] But it's tempting to read such a blessing as Beethoven's own way of resolving the generational antagonism between a Goethe and a Schlegel, a Schiller and a Novalis: the promise of a radical beginning *through* total liquidation, death *and* rebirth. For Richards, whose entire last chapter concentrates on the veil of Isis as a figure in early nineteenth-century musical fantasies, Beethoven's *Chorphantasie* completed the transposition of a musical picturesque, rooted in the actual landscape of the garden, onto the "difficult topography of the self."[43]

In ffytche's Schellingian history of the unconscious, "music" is curiously absent, not just as a topic but as a word; perhaps it's appropriate then that the word "unconscious" is similarly missing from Richards's history of the free fantasia. These twin gaps suggest room for a number of possible histories, which this book could hardly trace out in any great detail, but at the same time it is worth pausing here to speculate on at least two. The first is, in some sense, the obvious one, the low-hanging fruit of *Geistesgeschichte*: as Schelling and others begin to formulate the unconscious as the "dark ground" of human freedom, the musical fantasy genre begins to function increasingly as its sonic corollary, a "musical unconscious," as it were—both the unconscious of music and also a musical performance of the unconscious. Musical fantasy's long-standing status as the sanctioned site of disruption, disorientation, parataxis; its increasing figuration as the un-, pre-, or anti-formal other of the sonata, sonata's dark doppelgänger; its unfolding of un-predetermined futures out of "absolute" beginnings; its encoding as the private and collective fate of the individual.[44] Such lines of thinking weave easily into Wagnerian myth—absolute music's death and rebirth as music drama—but so too do they into later developments. The expressionism of the Second Viennese School, for instance, becomes the catastrophically complete ascendancy of musical fantasy, the apotheosis of disruption and opaque necessity; it seems no coincidence that it would also be taken as the musical enactment of a properly psychoanalytic unconscious, displacing Schelling's Romantic vision of a chthonic chaos of "rotary drives" with the labyrinth of the late Victorian libido. One might even posit an afterlife of this process in Adorno's speculation, in 1961, on a *musique informelle*. There Adorno envisions

> a type of music which has discarded all forms which are external or abstract or which confront it in an inflexible way. At the same time, although such music should be completely free of anything irreducibly alien to itself or superimposed on it, it should nevertheless constitute itself in an objectively compelling way, in the musical substance itself, and not in terms of external laws. Moreover, wherever this can be achieved without running the risk of a new form of oppression, such an emancipation should also strive to do away with the system of musical coordinates which have crystallized out in the innermost recesses of the musical substance itself.[45]

Here, in the paradoxical position of a de-individualized "late style" so late the present can only produce it as a utopian image, is something like the apogee of the fantasy genre circa "Beethoven 1808": a music in a state of perpetual *Ent-scheidung*, always re-beginning, and whose subjection to freedom is so absolute no form or law can constrain it. In a gesture that loops back to the philosophical moment before Schelling's intervention, Adorno admits that *musique informelle* "is a little like Kant's eternal peace. Kant himself thought of this as an actual, concrete possibility which is capable of realization and yet is nevertheless just an idea."[46] I am tempted to suggest that Adorno is here fantasizing an "ontogenetic pre/proto-history" of Beethoven's music: the musical "dark ground" out of which might emerge Beethoven's heroic style, a fantasmatic resolution of what it can no longer access.

Such a history shouldn't look all that strange: it parallels at a trot a now-outdated, unabashedly Germanocentric history of Western music of the last two centuries, one already anchored in place by master signifiers such as *form*, *freedom*, *expression*; only two "new" signifiers have been added, or at least stressed: *fantasy* and *unconscious*. If I resist this history, I still think it's important to rehearse it here, since the alternative history is in many ways its intimate opposite: not a history of how music developed concordantly with discourses of the unconscious, but a history of music as its antidote—a veiling or patching up of what discourses of the unconscious were concurrently introducing into their discoursing cultures. In this alternate history, music becomes one among myriad cultural forms and practices in which a prohibition is both acknowledged and defied. An opaque origin is sonically spotlighted. A beginning that "must not be thought" is nonetheless thought, or imagined, or—above all in the case of music—paradoxically presented as knowable in all its unthinkability, as blank or empty sign, as sensory and sensual revelation of what lies behind Isis's veil without its even being lifted. This scenario is infused with the dizzying reflexivity I articulated above: fantasy becomes co-constituted along with the impossibility it hides. The positing of an unrecoverable beginning is what gives rise to its imagined recovery; the notion of a constitutionally dark ground that "cannot know itself" is what produces aesthetic acts of ceaseless revelation. An "obscure conceptual vacancy" finds its consolation in "music's vacant sign," but also its refutation. Music brightens the obscurity, its own vacancy "fills in" what the concept has emptied out.

It's possible from this perspective to take a hypothetical long view of musical fantasy. Among its other cultural functions, it becomes a kind "reaction formation," a "symptom" of the Cartesian *cogito*. It provides a sensual "patch" for a disembodied subject," a semblance of *res extensa* produced by *res cogitans* itself. For "forms of subjectivity set against and resisting assimilation to material bodies," musical fantasy provides a way of at least seeming to give body back to subjectivity while actually sustaining its absence—"wresting and turning" while being "tide to nothing."[47] Schelling's revision of the Kantian transcendental subject is, more fundamentally, a revision of the *cogito*; it suggests that "there is no *cogito* as a transcendent, but an immanent *cogito*, completely implicated in the body that it was produced in order to exclude."[48] In such a moment, music appears to be staging its own reaction formation to this premise. In a work like the *Chorphantasie*—and all the more so the Ninth Symphony—the scene of "immanent *cogito*" is made to appear, and constantly revisited. The transcendental subject finds its body again, and through sheer force of thought "wrests and turns it" into something else. An antagonism between body and subject is resolved in narrative form. The work, the fruit of a "boundless freedom" it stages in its opening bars, fantasizes what Schelling in the same period proclaimed impossible: the scene of its return, transformation, and apotheosis. But it seems wrong, and certainly preemptively reductive, to think of Beethoven here as Schelling's "false consciousness." Fantasy is, in this model, not avoidable without forfeiting the subject altogether; borne out by an inaccessible, irreversible *Ent-scheidung*, it becomes the consummate free activity, what a subject does with its freedom. Self-cause and self-determination come to take the form of fantasizing, of making available to imagination precisely—perhaps only—what cannot in actuality be had. Freedom becomes the freedom to fantasize its own unimaginable grounds.

If this all sounds hopelessly abstract, it finds resonance in some of the most powerfully concrete and critical recent work on Beethoven. "There is evidently something about Beethoven's late public works," writes Nicholas Mathew, "that turns us into political Romantics."[49] He borrows both the term and its negative valence from Carl Schmitt to designate a "cast of mind" that replaces concrete political commitment and action with its fantasmatic alternatives, a "sublimation of action into hermeneutics," as Mathew puts it.[50] Instead of actual or actualized political music—say, "the vast number of political songs, piano pieces, and chamber works that circulated in the early nineteenth century—the proclamations of solidarity, resistance, and orthodoxy that ultimately sat on music desks in thousands of Viennese homes"—Mathew finds in the late public works an "explosive rhetoric and chaotic invitations to be read," and these are nothing less than "symptoms of a crisis of their own relevance."[51] In a scenario Schelling might have recognized, such works are not empirically but constitutively cut off from their moment, "created out of inaugural loss" of "the historical occasion out of which [they were] born." This loss becomes "the meaning of [great works]": they become "occasional works perpetually in search of an occasion," compelled by a "purely directional Freudian desire" beyond satisfaction.[52] The music of works like the Ninth is therefore, "in a profound sense, post-war. . . . The action has always just happened, the great deeds belong to history now, and the best we can do is recall or commemorate the past in reading and contemplation."[53]

It's clear that Chua and Mathew have their differences. Mathew strongly implies that Chua is in fact one of those present-day critics for whom political Romanticism is a deserving label. But in fact neither is so sanguine about the revolutionary content of Beethoven's music, and both authors make room, in distinct ways, for the possibility that the emancipatory theaters of Beethoven's middle- and (some of his) late-period music operated less as incitements, exhortations, calls to *Freiheit*, than as fantasies. Which is to say: they fantasized precisely what they did not have, or see, or think any longer entirely possible. Beethoven's heroism was the mask of failure, the sound of historically concrete failure fantasized as a triumph of the absolute. "Throughout its history," Chua asserts grandly, "absolute music has functioned as a blank flag hoisted above the parapets of some political crisis in the hope that the erasure of meaning would compensate for the reality of failure. The abstract reigns as a refuge when the politically concrete breaks down."[54]

Both Chua and Mathew eventually come around to Bernstein's 1989 Berlin performance of the Ninth, and, predictably, neither reads it at face value. For Chua, the work becomes "merely an arbitrary vessel" for an occasion that demotes its object even while hoisting it on high. For Mathew, it becomes a "symptom of anxiety that the great works of classical music might not mean as much as people have wanted them to."[55] This anxiety is old; it "goes back at least as far as Beethoven's late music—to the contemporary critics who sought to populate its potentially desolate entanglements, and perhaps even to the music's own allusive but obscure solicitations."[56] I hypothesized above that, from the perspective of Western music history, 1989 might be seen and heard as a repetition of 1808 (the year of the *Chorphantasie*'s premiere), or 1825 (the premiere of the Ninth), or even—absurd as it sounds—1837 (the publication of Schumann's *Phantasiestücke*). Mathew's point suggests a strengthening of that hypothesis: what Bernstein, Rostropovich, and even Hasselhoff were repeating was the musical use of fantasy to patch up a break they themselves were celebrating. This too was Beethoven's move, this too is his repetition: to render musically, in the same common sweep of phenomenal time, the emancipatory break and the suture that closes it back up. These 1989 performances suggest how, in the most semiotically overdetermined of situations, music might nonetheless "stay 'absolute' even after the words are put back in."[57]

. . .

In most of the chapters that follow, I leave Schelling aside, as well as the early nineteenth century, which I have been scurrying around with a certain admitted recklessness. In the intervening span I instead turn most often to Freud, and to arguably Freud's strongest—most original, most damaging, most fruitful—psychoanalytic reader, Jacques Lacan. While this counteracts the efforts of ffytche to tell a less psychoanalytic story of the unconscious, it also updates the present book to a range and milieu more in keeping with its title: the late nineteenth and twentieth centuries, and the history of musical modernism that courses discordantly through them.

If I belabor these points about the discursive "foundation of *the* unconscious" and the contemporaneous vicissitudes of musical fantasy, it is because no discussion of *an* unconscious—least of all modernism's—is worth much without its prehistory. Whether one thinks with Schelling, or Freud or Lacan, the unconscious is not something to be left behind; one might call it a "constituted eternal," some register of permanent past-ness that props up the present's present-ness, even as it constantly intrudes upon it. When thinking through modernism as a series of cultural phenomena gathered around the ethics of the break, such a register becomes more, not less, intense. It seems to me that some of modernism's pathos comes from the fact that, to paraphrase Maud Ellmann's line above, it also had to invent its own unconscious, which inspired and tormented it in equal measure—a chasmic reservoir of distant imaginary pasts with which to estrange the present, and a constant reminder of its failure to break with actual pasts more recent.

Over the course of this book, I will be relying on a conception of the unconscious perhaps less lurid than Schelling's, but no less negative. Freudian psychoanalysis as a practice might seem antithetical to any assertion that "the beginning cannot know itself"—what is all that couch-bound yammering for, if not uncovering knowledge of one's past? But one of the most dogged strains in Lacan's "return to Freud" is his emphasis on the negativity of the unconscious already there in Freud's conceptualization. It is not merely another register of mentation, resistant to access but, with the right pressure and technique, accessible all the same; it is no veiled Isis. The Freudian unconscious is rather something radically other. It is a topography, a *site*, "at all points homologous with what occurs at the level of the subject": the locus of drives (at the border of psyche and soma), and also of "contents" (particular desires, wishes, fixations, formations, symptoms), all of which cannot but appear in distorted form.[58] It is also a dynamic, a *logic*. As Freud famously charts it, the unconscious is exempt from laws of non-contradiction, from the passage of time, from negation, doubt, or degrees of certainty. It is not subject to "secondary processes" such as reflection, evaluation, and reasoned reorganization, but rather obeys the "primary processes": condensation and displacement, metaphor and metonymy. It is allegiant to its own psychic reality over any "external" reality or reality principle. This is what justifies its status as a kind of unknown knowledge—not simply its being elusive, difficult to recognize or admit, but rather its possessing a certainty anathema to the very idea of knowledge, which is its discursivity, its openness to debate and changeability, to design and manipulation.[59]

Most important for my purposes in the coming chapters, the Freudian and Lacanian unconscious is an *effect*: an insistence, a repetition. But a curious repetition, not of a positive content, of knowledge or memory in their common sense, but of an impasse. Hence Freud's terms, mentioned in the introduction, for how unconscious intentions manifest themselves, all negatively formulated: "*das Vergessen* (forgetting), *das Versprechen* (slip of the tongue), *das Verlesen* (misreading), *das Verschreiben* (slip of the pen), *das Vergreifen* (bungled action), and *das Verlieren* (mislaying)"—or, as Lacan more tersely puts it, "impediment, failure, crack."[60] Strictly speaking, the eventual first commandment of the psychoanalytic clinic—speak whatever comes to mind—was not meant to "produce" the unconscious, but to lay bare its insistent incapacity to be produced, and the specific, idiosyncratic logic of this insistence. The psychoanalytic clinic was from its origins a place where this repeated incapacity was transformed, from nullity to proper name, from the essentially forgettable—as accident, glitch, or non-meaning—into that which refuses to be forgotten. At its limit, this model of the unconscious presents it as a *radically significant non-meaning*, some gap or lack, some "impossible." A kind of unmoved mover in negative form, it provides something like the cause of the speaking subject. Not a sublime birth, but a banal cause: a hiccup, a hocket, an at-bottom-arbitrary lurch, which cracks something open and gets it moving.[61] One of Lacan's foundational concepts comes out of this: "$" the split or barred subject. To call a subject split is to say nothing more than that it has an unconscious dimension: that it will never be fully present to itself, and that this experience of always-partial absence is the subject. The correspondences to Schelling's thinking in the *Weltalter* are, as Freud himself might have noted, uncanny. But of course there were, and are, differences. Among the most important: psychoanalysis is not philosophy. It is not a way of putting things together, but of taking them apart.

• • •

> *. . . mit seinen Nachtmützen und Schlafrockfetzen*
> *Stopft er die Lücken des Weltenbaus.*
> *(. . . with his nightcaps and tatters from his dressing-gown*
> *he patches up the gaps in the structure of the universe.)*
> —HEINRICH HEINE, "DIE HEIMKEHR," LVIII

Whatever promise of reconciliation psychoanalysis might seem to offer as a therapeutic practice, Freud himself was no great fan of patching things up. He often cited with relish Heine's derisive line about "philosophers" (though Heine himself was addressing "the German professor").[62] Freud took the word "analysis" quite seriously, and would sometimes stress the word's chemical aura. Analysis ought "break up" and "separate out" psychic formations of an otherwise "highly composite kind"; it ought isolate "the fundamental substance, the chemical 'element,' out of the salt in which it had been combined with other elements and in which it was unrecognizable." If this smacks of essentialism, Freud was quick to counter by emphasizing the ceaseless contingency of the endeavor: "In mental life we have to deal with trends that are under a compulsion towards unification and combination. Whenever we succeed in analyzing a symptom into its elements, in freeing an instinctual impulse from one nexus, it does not remain in isolation, but immediately enters into a new one."[63] Lacan, characteristically, was more merciless and histrionic. But his rereading of Freud emphasized the same chemical process. The "end of analysis" should bring the analysand to a point of breaking down: a moment of "subjective destitution," a dissolution of the coordinates of selfhood. The subject's identifications should undergo "a twilight," an "imaginary decline of the world, and even an experience at the limit of depersonalization."[64] The analysand would in the process come to "know the domain and the level of the experience of absolute disarray."[65]

The analytic metaphor arguably finds its clearest "medium" in the concept of fantasy. It is fantasies that are analyzed, teased apart, broken up and broken down. Fantasy is the consistency, the fabric or mesh, upon which psychoanalysis sets itself as a negative agent. Lacan is, again, the more merciless: an analysis, in order to reach its end, must "traverse the radical fantasy."[66] What this entails is not a reaching back, or down, to the analysand's oldest or deepest truth, but rather reaching past it. In Schellingian terms, one might say, the aim is not to "bring the beginning back," to "return into nothing, into boundless freedom," but rather to realize that precisely this—this hope of closing the loop, of radical self-consistency or self-fabrication—*is* the fantasy. In this sense the psychoanalytic subject really is "tide to nothing," but it is a nothing that continues to intrude upon the subject, and prevents it from closing itself up.

If there's something deeply concordant between what Rose calls "common parlance" fantasy and the logic of musical fantasy, it would seem to have something to do with disavowing this nothing. But it is a paradoxical disavowal. The "gaps in the structure of the universe" are covered over by smooth, consistent images, yes, but they are often images of break and liberation, scenarios staging an individual and collective escape from law and lifeworld into the erratic flows of desire. The Freudian-Lacanian unconscious would appear in many ways to represent the opposite of this: un-freedom at its most structural, a site of hedged possibilities and unknown knowledge; the constitutional inability to change over time or adapt to new circumstances, to "learn from reality"; the constant falling short of true indeterminacy; the repeated missing of an encounter with the truly unimaginable. This suggests an inverted thesis: that musical fantasy and fantasy in general, as ways of staging the experience of freedom, constitute the means through which the experience of the unconscious—as an impasse, an impossibility, an intrusive nothing—is repressed. Fantasy, and its extension as a genre of musical performance, become an especially inspired form of disavowal, a magic trick: making nothing disappear.

When Rose articulates fantasy's common parlance, she means to distinguish it from the seemingly paradoxical premise of unconscious fantasy. "Radical fantasy," "primary fantasy," "fundamental fantasy," "core fantasy": each of these terms had over the course of Freud's and Lacan's work attempted to designate something in essential distinction to conscious fantasy, as daydream, reverie, flight from reality. Each of these Freud increasingly gathered under the term "imaginativeness," as an "autonomous psychic activity characterized by the fact that its intentional objects do not 'really' exist," and by its imagining subject consciously knowing this to be the case.[67]

To designate a fantasy as unconscious is to designate almost the opposite: not a space of make-believe into which the subject takes flight, but the reality itself from which the subject takes flight. This was essentially the lesson of Freud's abandonment of "seduction theory." When he confessed to Wilhelm Fliess that he no longer believed in his *neurotica*—his assumption that his patients' traumas were always based on actual experiences—Freud opened the way for what he would call "psychic reality," and eventually "construction," the premise that an unconscious formation, composed of all manner of material at hand in the patient's experience, could form a fictive basis for their reality, including both future memories and fantasies.[68] The Oedipus complex became the best known of these constructions. An elaborate fiction formed around a "kernel of truth," it would come to provide

Freud and some of his followers with an ersatz psychic unity of the subject, the source and matrix for all the seemingly spontaneous emancipations of desire "commonly" called fantasies.[69] It would, one could say, help this "German professor" patch up the gaps in his structure of the universe. Lacan, among others, would eventually play Freud's Heine, trying to restore—sometimes with gleeful derision—the gaps Freud had tried to close.

If quotidian fantasies often stage a structural breach, an escape from the other (as law, language, or listener) into an individual, subjective desire, then unconscious fantasies could be said to constitute precisely those laws and languages—some other other—that make desire possible in the first place, that turn it on, sustain its flow, direct its course. To put it another way, there are the scenes to be witnessed—the flights of fantasy, the performances of "freedom"—and then there are the psychic stages on which they unfold: the scenic armature and apparatus, the choreography, the lighting and camerawork and costuming, the constitution and positioning of an audience, and so on. Psychoanalytically speaking, these are hardly sites of the loss of coordination, but rather sites where a pseudo-loss, a semblance of freedom, is coordinated. C. P. E. Bach may, according to Johann Friedrich Reichardt's description, lose himself in a "sea of modulations," but from a psychoanalytic perspective, this is a spurious loss. Or rather, this loss is meticulously positioned, clearing a perch from which to behold a scene being staged—in this case, the scene of Bach's "himself" disappearing so that another "himself" can materialize in its place. The brilliant positioning of hands and fingers is secondary here. The primary challenge, always met by unconscious fantasy, is to position the coordinates of one's own un-becoming, such that an other—more or less of one's choosing—can become.

. . .

"An Phantasie fehlts, Gottlob, weniger als je zuvor" (Of fantasy, thank God, there's less lack than ever before). This was Beethoven's alleged response when his personal assistant Karl Holz asked him which of his late quartets was his greatest. "Each in their own way" was Beethoven's testy initial response, but the conversation soon turned to Op. 131 in C-sharp minor, with its "new manner of voice treatment." Holz claims Beethoven eventually settled on it as the best of them.[70] As the early reception of Beethoven's last works famously testifies, critics did not agree. The profusion of *Phantasie* was, in fact, the problem. "The ideas sat perfectly clear on paper and pleased the eye," confessed an anonymous reviewer in 1829, "but in performance often became a wild tangle [ein wüstes Gewirr]."[71] The French critic Alexandre Oulibicheff put it more bluntly: these last works were "the negation of music itself."[72]

By the time of Joseph Kerman's watershed 1966 book on the quartets, accounts had been squared: Op. 131 was the greatest. Kerman could now praise Beethoven's line about *Phantasie* as "an understatement to leave us all speechless."[73] The line returns at the end of his virtuoso reading of Op. 131, a reading also meant, I think, to leave us all speechless. Gathered under the rubric of "integration," Kerman's interpretation leaves no stone unturned in its attempt to demonstrate that, despite appearances to the contrary, the quartet is "the most closely integrated of all [Beethoven's] large compositions," and could be viewed "as the culmination of his significant effort as a composer ever since going to Vienna."[74]

The work of Stephen Rumph and the late K. M. Knittel has performed a remarkable excavation of "Beethoven's late style"—how it was retroactively constructed, revised, inverted, how it has its own vicissitudinous history.[75] Vicissitudinous, but not picturesque. It does not meander. It zags, between two "conditions" to be "diagnosed," and for which Kerman's own chapter title "Disassociation and Integration" (comparing Op. 130 and Op. 131) is a decent enough rubric. There is the long history of pathologizing the late works, thinking them the fruit of madness, deafness, depression, a destitution of the soul. And there is the counter-history—overlapping largely with what Rumph calls Beethoven's "modernist" reception—of marveling at how healthy the works are. Healthier in fact than any human body, falling as it does inevitably short of the sublime cohesion of the last quartets and sonatas. If the latter history concords with universally positive valuation, the former is itself an agonized scene: for Oulibicheff, the works are sick, and that is why they are bad; for Richard Wagner, the works are not sick, but suffering, and this is their sign of health;[76] for Adorno, the works are suffering because they are sick, and this is itself a sign of truth, a truth no other music of the time was willing to tell. Culture made them sick, and they refused to hide it.[77]

"Of fantasy, thank God, there's less lack than ever before." It is such an odd phrase. But in it, fantasy's irreducibly double meaning reveals itself nicely. Clearly Beethoven meant by "fantasy" an eruption of invention, a fructified imagination; fantasy here still relates to Haydn's *fantasieren*, to a preliminary music full of disruptions and parataxes, searching, finding, and seizing. What he probably didn't mean—at least by the phrase itself—was that such works were "the most closely integrated of all his large compositions." This, one could argue, is the fantasy in the psychoanalytic sense, the radical or fundamental *unconscious fantasy*, which framed and fueled the cultural reception of Beethoven's late works throughout the twentieth century. It is the fantasy that these strange scores, so overtly and enigmatically disruptive of the tradition from which they emerged, are actually entirely of a piece—not only cohesive, but more cohesive than the "middle period" works, which had created a new standard for cohesion. There is something almost specious about the premise: the more disordered the appearance, the more it serves to evidence a deeper order. With swift elegance Rumph lays out the visions of Walter Riezler and Heinrich Schenker, of Joseph Kerman and Charles Rosen and Maynard Solomon. Each modulates in his own way the same fantasy of Beethoven's late works: that they are "fresh proof of the perfect consistency and homogeneity of his development," and he bends their contrasts to his will "to safeguard the unity of [the] work" (Riezler); that they are "bound by universal law," and consummated "through the artwork" (Schenker); that they "derive from a central and unifying idea" (Rosen); and that they "map the infinite without losing hold of the center" (Solomon).[78] If this is what modernist criticism looks like, then one might fairly call modernism a kind of unconscious fantasy. A Schellingian one, in fact, since it is precisely these works' performative existence as a "wild tangle," *ein wüstes Gewirr*, that grounds their critics' own subcutaneous "search for order," as Solomon puts it. By that phrase, of course, Solomon wanted to say that Beethoven himself was embroiled in such a fantasy: the Ninth is for Beethoven what Op. 131 was for Kerman (and for Beethoven). Lacan's old saw about desire—that "desire is the desire of (or for) the other"—is rather schematically presented here. But in this integrationist history of the late works, both Beethoven and his exegetes stage an uncannily similar ontogenetic scene. An "obscure, unstable material situation" yields, as its inevitable by-product, its "reaction formation," the very faculty of fantasy. An activity of "patching up the gaps" ensues, opened up by the material itself. Freedom remains bound to contemplation of its unrecoverable grounds.

What then to make of Adorno? He too was no fan of patching. Rumph includes him as the last of his modernist critics, which makes enough sense; what is Adorno if not a modernist? But Rumph clearly needs Adorno to serve as a corrective to the preceding five voices: a voice who refuses to ring an increasingly hollow bell of order and classicism for these works, and who focuses with pitiless intensity on their status as "catastrophes."[79] According to Rumph, in Adorno's reading, "The sense that the individual work is somehow discovering universal laws, falls away. Instead, the music accumulates strangely opaque features, wholly foreign to the middle period—archaic modality, unpenetrated lyricism, conventional ornaments and formulae."[80] This combination of opacity and sense is what gives rise—this is Adorno speaking now—to "the nonsensical circumstance that Beethoven's final works are deemed both subjective and objective at once. Objective is the brittle landscape, and subjective the light that alone can set it aglow. He does not bring about their harmonic synthesis. Acting as a force of dissociation, he tears them apart in time in order that they might, perhaps, be preserved for the realm of the eternal."[81]

How, according to Rumph's metric at least, is this modernist? What does it have in common with the fantasies of a Riezler or a Kerman? It would seem here that Adorno is not on the side of fantasy at all, but of analysis and traversal, an unmeshing or breaking down, taken to its very end. And, as Adorno's now-classic account goes, it is nothing other than Beethoven's own "heroic style" that is being unmeshed; this is music about music.[82] The heroic style is a fantasy Beethoven himself "tears apart in time." "In late Beethoven," Adorno writes in the fragments for his unfinished

Beethoven book, "there is no longer any 'fabric.' . . . At the very place once occupied by dynamic totality, there is now fragmentation."[83] From an Adornian perspective, a Kerman or a Riezler disavows the late style altogether; both are desperate to demonstrate "fresh proof of the perfect consistency and homogeneity of [Beethoven's] development." The proof of their desperation is that they describe Op. 131 as essentially a more sophisticated version of the "Eroica." Or, better, the *Chorphantasie* as a shameless theater of total self-fabrication, of origins recovered and transformed, "a mirror that throws back a now-clear reflection of the artist himself." Not only does Adorno oppose this image, but he opposes the very capacity for image, for the fantasizing faculty. In the last works, Beethoven "no longer gathers up the landscape, now deserted and estranged, to form a picture."[84]

Here then is the other—Adornian—way of reading "Of fantasy, thank God, there's less lack than ever before": a profusion of disruptions, parataxes, obscurities, "strangely opaque features" that, overwhelming consciousness with their "wild tangle," compromise the capacity of unconscious fantasy to keep things patched up. There is indeed something pathological about this premise, and in a very specific way. It resembles an autoimmune disease, in which a body's defense system—in this case the fantasizing faculty—attacks itself. I can imagine Mathew being happy enough labeling this phenomenon "modernist alienation" and including it as just one among a list of "late style" equivalencies—"all the trumpets and drums, hymns, and heroic outbursts, and all the attendant talk of foreign invasion, popular sentiment, historic deeds, resistance, Modernist alienation, and conservative counter-revolution."[85] Rumph seems to perform a similar gesture in including Adorno as his sixth and last modernist critic. Ultimately I think they are both more or less right. The trumpets and the alienation belong together.

But the remainder of this book wagers that, nestled in these two necessarily ad-hoc lists, is a key to understanding musical modernism slightly differently. Slightly, but crucially. Though Adorno is nowhere to be found in the index to Kerman's book, in the larger scheme of things there can be no Kerman without Adorno, at least as far as late Beethoven is concerned. The integrationist fantasy is a reaction formation, a symptom of the conditions critics like Adorno claimed to hear and see in the late style. Adorno was not the first. They saw and heard it already in 1829: it was in fact the first reaction. Adorno's short foundational essay from 1937 was only a return to the wild tangle experienced by that anonymous reviewer, and better still to Oulibicheff's charge that this was "the negation of music itself"; it was a return and a positive revaluation. Is Adorno's appraisal "beyond fantasy"? Of course not! As an integrationist tale, his account of the late works bests Kerman's by miles. The coherent image it fabricates is unmatched in teleological sweep and intensity. It is an image of hell, one that Adorno's own exegetes, none more passionately than Chua, try to realize in analyses of the kind Adorno himself never provided. The "Galitzin" quartets foreshadow the Enlightenment dialectic's historical transformation of reason into barbarism. The *Grosse Fuge* "prefigures this history as the techniques of reason become those of tyranny"; it ultimately becomes a "prophecy of Auschwitz."[86] This is grand vision. Unutterably awful, but grand. Surely enough to patch up the gaps in the structure of the universe.

• • •

I am coming close here to suggesting that musical modernism begins in the West with Beethoven's late quartets. If I had to, I suppose it would be a good enough moment; certainly I am not the first to make the suggestion, or to feel the pressure to do so. "Books about modernism tend to go in for inaugural dates," T. J. Clark writes in the opening chapter of *Farewell to an Idea* (1999), his provocatively gap-filled "episodes from a history of modernism." "It all began in the 1820s, they say, or with Courbet setting up his booth outside the Exposition Universelle in 1855, or the year *Madame Bovary* and *Les Fleurs du Mal* were put on trial, or in room M of the Salon des Refusés."[87] Clark is cagey, for a while, but at the end of this chapter on Jacques-Louis David's 1793 painting *The Death of Marat*, he asserts that "ultimately I do believe it began with the French Revolution."[88] Clark even calls Beethoven "David's brother," and hears modernism's "decisive new structuring of time" in finales of the Fifth and Seventh Symphonies.[89]

I am less sanguine that Western musical modernism began in 1820s Vienna, and even less so that it began with the late quartets, or sonatas, or the magical passage into "late style." I want to suggest something more oblique, less work-based, and more psychoanalytic: that something like modernism can be seen to begin with *the reception* of Beethoven's late works, which is to say, with their "delayed activation" or "deferred action." These phrases are attempts to translate Freud's tricky German term *Nachträglichkeit*, literally "afterward-ness" or "reaching-backward-ness." The concept is one of the more complex and foundational in the Freudian tradition, already there in his early "Project for a Scientific Psychology" from 1895, and, as the term *après coup*, it comes to support Lacan's whole conception of psychic temporality.[90] I resort to it here as a way of theorizing how an event—often what is later understood as a trauma—can intrude upon psychic life without yet *meaning* anything, and therefore without being ascribed a place, positive or negative, in that psyche's lifeworld. A kind of shocking enigma, an excess that short-circuits the capacity to understand, it comes to be psychically coordinated only retroactively; meaning locks in place some kind of radically resistant non-meaning. It is not a matter of the child who, after almost falling off a bridge, develops a perfectly reasonable fear of heights. It is more about how that child, having enjoyed a bout of reckless, "thoughtless" play on that same bridge, later hears a macabre tale of a boy falling to his death. A certain thoughtlessness is suddenly given a place; the child views it now through a new aperture, fastened together by the signifiers "height," "play," "death."

In Freudian terms, we are being potentially traumatized all the time and, thankfully, will never know it, because such moments are never "activated." And I'm tempted to think here of all those moments in Western music pre-Beethoven when the supposedly grand tread of history came upon a wild tangle, a moment when a mode of musical-creative activity seemed to develop an autoimmune condition, when a "language" or technology attacked its fantasizing faculty, its own fluency and know-how: the *ars subtilior*, or the "mannerist madrigal," to cite just two instances.[91] If they prompt a historiographic eye roll, so much the better for my larger point: they are moments made famous by "modernist critics," moments when a modernism already in place sought to know, or to fantasize, its "unrecoverable beginnings." If I don't consider such moments beginnings, it's not a matter of constitution. Who am I to scoff at the rhythmic mind-benders in the Chantilly Codex, or the goth pallor of Michelangelo Rossi's madrigals? One can hear in them not only transgression and experimentation, but a coming apart or breaking down of the very "linguistic" consistency of their inherited practices. They were wild tangles if ever there were. No, it is not a matter of inherence, but of reception, of the delayed activation brought about by fantasy: these moments had no fantasmatic future. Their parent cultures weren't turned on by them, or weren't turned on for long.[92]

The same could of course be said for late Beethoven, at first. A shocking enigma over which nothing much was made. And ironically, that anonymous reviewer's assessment may have been more Adornian than Adorno's own: it was a reasonable if unimaginative response to witnessing an artwork attacking its foundations, an autoimmune attack by fantasy upon itself. Which is to say, the reviewer, honoring Adorno's prohibition on fantasy before the fact, took the works' cues, and did not then try to fantasize about them. He simply left them tangled. But this is not the history of modernism. The history of modernism is a repeated endeavor to engage such moments, to not leave well enough alone. To attack, break down, and traverse the fantasizing faculty with what inevitably become fantasies of traversal, breakdown, attack. The paradoxical by-product of such a history—its symptom, one could say—is to ensure, "thank God," that there is less lack of fantasy than ever before.

3

DREI PHANTASIESTÜCKE (2)

What happens if we read the three liberation scenes at the Wall anamorphically? If we angle their transgressive foreground to reveal the constructed-ness of the "scenic armature" against which they unfolded?

The battered, palimpsest-ed patch of the Wall behind Rostropovich, for instance, can be read not only as the panorama for his performance, but as a necessary antagonist. It is precisely the Wall, in all its candy-colored gimcrack vulgarity, that props up Bach the eternal. The relationship is perfectly reflexive: Bach and Wall are re-encoded *as* antagonists in the very execution of the scene itself. Scraped out into cold, damp November air on an old wooden box by an old man on an old chair, Bach is nonetheless offered up as the undying patriarch, his immortal presence affirmed by the Wall, which, in all its dreadful design, cannot but tumble into dust. It becomes the signifier of a wretched historical caesura, a political *Unzeit*, "un-time," shamed into disintegration by the "timelessness" of a music that, unlike mere political regimes, remains "unstained by blood."[1] In this sense, the scene is also revolutionary, but in a patently pre-1789 sense: *de revolutionibus orbium caelestium*, a revolution of celestial bodies, it participates in a kind of bracketed time where "the stars run their circular course independent of earthly men, while at the same time influencing or even determining their lives."[2] Such revolutions are not at all cataclysmic. They happen slowly, cyclically; they lead inexorably toward restoration. And in this case, it is a restoration of the father, Papa Bach, whose return forces even the great Slava to disintegrate, to become "the servant of the composer," "give up [his] 'Russian personality,'" coordinate his own self-loss, as "God speak[s] directly to man through the priest." From this perspective, even the crowd itself is magnetized into a necessary prop: the brittleness of the cello virtually obliges the formation of a small, swaddling, quasi-monastic audience. To get bogged down in debates about whether composers are divine or not, or whether Bach's music is appropriate here, or how to play it "authentically," is to miss the point. In his *Fidelio* interview a decade after the event, Rostropovich lays out in bald terms the armature of his fantasy scene, perhaps even his fundamental musical fantasy. On the one hand, it follows the structural logic of kenosis, according to which Christ "emptied himself, taking the form of a slave, being born in human likeness." ("Emptied himself" has been alternately translated as "made Himself nothing," or, in the King James Bible, "made himself of no reputation"; the the Greek verb is ἐκένωσε [ekénōse].)[3] The term *kenosis* is still a highly fraught, frequently debated concept in Christian theology, but humanistic discourse probably knows it better as one of Harold Bloom's six revisionary ratios, and it certainly functions in a Bloomian way here.[4] But one needn't subscribe to Bloomian theory in order to see that Rostropovich's kenosis is profoundly double-sided. A fantasy of submission to the divine authority of the power of moment, it is also one of 1989's more spectacular acts of self-aggrandizement, masquerading as the inversion of the Freudian formulation of the ego: "Wo es war, soll ich werden" (Where it was, I shall become). For Rostropovich: "Where *I* was, *it* shall become."

. . .

If nothing else, Rostropovich and Hasselhoff have this coordinated self-loss in common. In the latter's place, it is not Bach but Hasselhoff's German agent Jack White (née Horst Nußbaum) who masterminds the elaborate, cynical publicity stunt at the Brandenburg Gate—the elevating crane, the TV spots, maybe even the ridiculous jacket and piano scarf. More importantly, it was in fact White who originally composed and produced the music to "Looking for Freedom," in 1978.[5] Initially sung by the largely unknown Marc Seaberg with English lyrics by Gary Cowten, it was soon covered with new German lyrics ("Auf der Strasse nach Süden"—something like, "On the Road Down South") by the West German Schlager singer Tony Marshall, and only then did it top the charts.[6] The following year, the East German star Uwe Jensen released a cover of *that* version and it went on to become a hit on the other side of the Wall. So when White insists Hasselhoff resurrect the song in 1988, he is surely (and quite literally) banking on the musical memory of both West and East Germans as much as he is the celebrity status of the guy from *Knight Rider*. The audience, split geographically, is nonetheless brought together in an almost automaton-like fashion by the driving refrain. Hardly asking their permission before repeating itself incessantly, it at once presents a signifier of division—the East Germans listening in the late 1970s could hardly just set off for Bavaria—and a signifier of a pre- and post-Wall unity: West or East, "free" or "unfree," who *doesn't* feel a sudden gust of *Sehnsucht* for the south?

But the brash pop-will-bring-us-together-ness of the show belies another register in which Hasselhoff is not merely a cipher, a prop of the spectacle, but also a kind of radical voyeur. The entire scene could be said to prop up Hasselhoff's own fantasy of looking and being looked at, both actions caught up in an autoerotic loop that perfectly circumvents the apparently communal spirit of the event. At the start, we have the mugging and nostril flaring for the camera; at the end, we have Hasselhoff himself in his hotel room pressing "rewind" and "play," "that whole unforgettable night" captured on a VCR tape. In between these two poles unfolds an uncanny rehearsal of the panoptic nightmare of East German surveillance: "the Hoff" being lifted above the crowd, transformed from tumescent phallus into border tower, voyeur into armed guard. He may be thrusting only a microphone into the air, but on some level his audience intuits that it may as well be a rifle, and that it is now their prerogative (and pleasure) to fire back—hence the barrage of firecrackers that assault the voguing ascendant. The carnivalesque inversion extends to Hasselhoff. On the one hand, he is the nothing through which the prerecorded song is piped, an extreme case of "the servant of the composer." On the other hand, he is a central void filtered through a web of transpositions. As Žižek puts it, such an event "creates a multitude of 'subject positions' among which the (observing, fantasizing) subject is free to float, to shift his identification from one to another": exhibitionist/voyeur; in front of the camera / in front of the TV; in the sky / on the ground; "part of history" / parasitic publicity stunt.[7] The subject here is the slash, the very division linking incompatibles.

• • •

Where is Bernstein? Also in multiple, contradictory locations. Certainly he is his own characteristically libidinous "imp of perversity," a man who cannot help but enjoy "too much." In this case he becomes a kind of ersatz Don Giovanni, in his palace having his way with Beethoven while Schiller's "stone guest" lurks outside.[8] But he is also the bearer of the imperial message, an infringer nonetheless "sure we have Beethoven's blessing." When the choristers sing the lines "Brothers, surely a loving father / dwells above the canopy of stars. Do you sink before him, Millions?" they could be singing *about* Beethoven, rather than *as* him. And to some extent they could just as well be singing of Bernstein, whose editorial transgression transforms into the *support* of his authority. A Beethoven *in loco parentis*, he positions himself as the shepherd of Schiller's "truer" message, faithful to its spirit over its letter (and, no less, history's own letter debunking the Jahn myth). On another level, the transgression is arguably not such a transgression at all: an enormous affirmation of the identity and authority of multiple states, the event is not so much a celebration of an internationalist or cosmopolitan "rights of man," but becomes (certainly retrospectively) the inevitable apotheosis of state-supported celebration, something explicitly anticipated and endorsed by politicians, and

FIGURES 7 and 8. Friedrich Schiller (versus) Leonard Bernstein.

covered by state-supported media. Bernstein's move coincidentally (re)produces the cultural moment's ubiquitous signifier, from which there is now finally no escape—other than for "he who cannot rejoice" to "steal away weeping."[9]

The *Augenblick* is thus fashioned in the form of a supplicant, calling for, waiting for Beethoven, for the Ninth, for someone to come, wake it from its supposed slumber, and provoke, courageously, its reply—make it sing directly back to the citizens "not only in the German Democratic Republic and the Federal Republic, but also in all of Europe and the whole world."[10] When Bernstein arrives, the still-unpatched body politic is all too ready to grant him his infraction. Again, the fantasmatic logic writes itself quite smoothly into the prose of its early documentarians, such that Klaus Geitel, doyen of German music critics, could portray Bernstein as nothing less than the Western world's music pope:

> All were to combine to achieve the common goal of ringing the bell of emotion, of joy at this great, historical moment which Leonard Bernstein had conceived. He was

> truly more than a conductor; he shook people awake from the rostrum, surrendering to Beethoven's music and yet rendering it with all his heart and soul at the same time.... Combined under Bernstein, [the performers] gave more than a concert: they lit a torch for the love of freedom and the longing for freedom that extended far beyond the occasion.... Bernstein, Beethoven's sceptre in his hand, joining in the call for freedom.[11]

"All the ends of the earth," goes the famous Christmas gradual, "have seen the salvation of our God.... The Lord has revealed His righteousness in the sight of the nations." The decision to perform on Christmas Day is perhaps the most important "prop" for this thoroughly catholic Beethoven. In both senses: its fantasy frame is scarcely less liturgical than a piece of Notre Dame organum.

• • •

It would be all too easy to cordon off these fantasies of beginning within the individual psyches of Bernstein, Rostropovich, and Hasselhoff. Certainly they seem consistent enough with what we know from biographies and autobiographies: we know of Bernstein's epic egotism, of Rostropovich's increasing religiosity late in life, of Hasselhoff's "tool being." But this would be a mistake. There is nothing "merely psychological" here. It is precisely in the nature of these fantasies as unconscious formations that they are intersubjective—both inside and outside, intrapsychic and "out there." They implicate, inculcate, interpellate their audiences, and their audiences do the same. Each party says not only "This is what I want!" but also, arguably more emphatically, "This is what *you* want!" The historicity of the texts involved provides a crucial common material. Music, when it is "known by heart," is, after all, an ideal unconscious knowledge—if not exactly repressed or "unknown," nonetheless a kind of pre-subjectivized knowledge, something that automates a subject, speaks itself before the ego can say "I mean this," or even "I am this." But fantasy provides the actual binding agent: an assemblage, an unconscious *formation*. Jacqueline Rose stresses that Freud, as early as his letters to Fliess in 1897, linked unconscious fantasy "to what makes group identifications possible and impossible at one and the same time.... Fantasy is not... antagonistic to social reality; it is its precondition or psychic glue. But fantasy surely ceases to be a private matter if it fuels, or at least plays its part, in the forming of the collective will." Rose maintains that unconscious fantasy, as the formation of a psychic reality that can actually constitute the world, is also at bottom a matter of "how subjects tie themselves ethically to each other and enter a socially viable world"—for Freud, nothing less than a way of conceptualizing, after Friedrich Nietzsche, "the source of morality."[12] If these three scenes are *Phantasiestücke*, they are—no less than Schumann's "Des Abends," if less modestly—also a form of collective world making, a collaborative, highly distributed subjectivity trying make something *appear*, to show something back to itself. Though they may at moments be dreamlike, these scenes are not dreams. They do not "travel back from perception to unconscious, disintegrating and reordering themselves as they go." As fantasies, they are instead "progressive. Never completely losing their grip . . . [they are] always heading for the world [they] only appear to have left behind."[13] *Et vitam venturi saeculi. Amen.*

4

FANTASY & FANTASY (2)

"$\$ \lozenge a$": Jacques Lacan's formula, or "matheme," for fantasy. If it inspires wariness in those unfamiliar with the Lacanian rhetorical forest, it can provoke outright irritation among those who do know a thing or two about it. They might know it's generally read as "split subject (or barred subject) in relation to *objet a*," where the latter stands for *objet petit autre*, the "object little-other," in distinction to "A," for big Other. If this is already a tad finicky, wait: they (you) might also know that the *objet a*, often hastily rendered as "object of desire," is in fact not in any common sense an object of desire, but precisely the opposite—the object-*cause* of desire. Not so much what the (split) subject craves, fantasizes, or pursues, so much as what gets it going in the first place—desire being pushed, not pulled. It is in this sense a bit of happenstance, a *je ne sais quoi* the subject nonetheless "knows when it sees"—but this *a* doesn't technically exist. Here the irritation might set in: technically, "relation" is not the right word for that "punch" or *poinçon* between the two figures, which is in any case "merely a mark rather than a function," as Jacques-Alain Miller put it.[1] There *is* no relation between $\$$ and *a*, which is exactly what the formula attempts to elucidate. But, as a more Talmudic reader may point out, Lacan took pains to articulate that the *poinçon* can in fact "be understood as referring to the operations of union and intersection in set theory and the psychoanalytic operations of alienation and separation." And, moreover, that it "stands for the fact that each subject is characterized by the whole of the L Schema [another, more complex matheme], by all four vertices of it involving imaginary and symbolic axes (but not *a* as real)."[2]

Such sprouting vines of arcana often put people off Lacan. They can be exasperating; they corner the logic into paradox, where it squirrels and echoes, turning oracular. When they combine with anecdotes about the man himself—a charismatic but not endearing figure—they can create a force field of dissuasion. This didn't especially trouble Lacan. Though his *séminaire* grew considerably in attendance in later years, he continued to maintain that his was primarily a teaching practice, meant to educate, and trouble, those already versed: the community of practicing psychoanalysts. Given his largest audience ever—during an hour on prime-time Saturday night French television in 1973—he offered a perverse admonition: "Now don't get the idea that I'm addressing everyone at large [*la cantonade*, a pun on Lacan's name]. . . . I am speaking to those who are in the know, to the non-idiots, to the analysts I take to be in my support."[3]

So when Slavoj Žižek's first English-language book, *The Sublime Object of Ideology*, hit the shelves in December 1989, it might have been easy enough to misconstrue it as a cultic token to the master teacher. The wild, disruptive performativity and magpie erudition; the constant proximity of paradox; a high-density but meandering argument; an undisguised disdain for "university discourse," for speaking as an expert representative: they are all there in droves. They render the volume neither "a book in the classical sense, [nor] a collection of essays," as Ernesto Laclau put it in his preface, but "a series of theoretical interventions which shed mutual light on each other, not in terms of the progression of an argument, but in terms of what we could call the *reiteration* of the latter in different discursive contexts."[4] Perhaps Laclau was nodding at Lacan's infamous verdict on his own *Écrits*—"they were not meant to be read"[5]—but regardless, the assessment suggested not only a book about Lacan, but a Lacanian book, a not-meant-to-be-book.

In fact the volume was not very Lacanian at all, at least in approach. Years later, when the anti-program introduced by *The Sublime Object of Ideology* had helped turn Žižek into "one of the most influential and indeed popular public intellectuals in the world,"[6] he would confess—in a documentary titled *Žižek!*, no less—that he found Lacan's actual approach "ridiculous. . . . What interests me are his propositions, the underlying logic, not his style. His style is a total fake, I think. I try to forget it, I try to repress it." Nonetheless, Žižek was still "for Lacan," and would maintain that "the whole point of my work is that you can translate Lacan into clear terms."[7] This was in essence a recapitulation of one of the goals of *The Sublime Object of Ideology*, namely, to be as clear and indeed reasonable as possible, thereby intervening in an already well-established tradition of preserving and extending the Lacanian oracularity. "Against the distorted picture of Lacan as belonging to the field of 'post-structuralism,'" Žižek wrote pointedly in the introduction, "the book articulates his radical break with 'post-structuralism'; against the distorted picture of Lacan's obscurantism, it locates him in the lineage of rationalism. Lacanian theory is perhaps the most radical contemporary version of the Enlightenment."[8] This was only the first of the book's three explicit interventions. It also aimed to "accomplish a kind of 'return to Hegel'—to reactualize Hegelian dialectics by giving it a new [Lacanian] reading," and, no less, to reboot ideology critique from its post-Althusserian freeze.

If these aims helped contribute to an often electrifying piece of critical philosophy (book or not), they also made *The Sublime Object of Ideology* a rather untimely endeavor, something that could just as easily have had no future. A return of Hegelian dialectics, at the end of 1989? Only months earlier, Francis Fukuyama had famously leaned on Georg Wilhelm Friedrich Hegel and his twentieth-century reader Alexandre Kojève to declare dialectics finally at an end. But here was Žižek, arguing that not only had the End of History not yet arrived, but that it never would; Hegelian "absolute knowledge" was "nothing but a name for the acknowledgement of a certain radical loss," the late awareness that the negativity of dialectical movement is constitutive, not empirical—a loss dialectics never recoups but only repeats.[9] Likewise, the notion of reimagining ideology critique was more than a bit quixotic. It was less a matter of overturning Daniel Bell's (ideologically committed and proto-Fukuyaman) pronouncement in 1960 of the "end of ideology," and more a matter of challenging a profound skepticism, by 1989, about what else there might be amid the hypostatization of concrete ideological positions.[10] Recasting Lacan, too, was a contrary proposition. As Anna Kornbluh stresses, by 1989 Lacan already enjoyed entrenched coordinates beyond the clinic; within academic and critical-theoretical circles, he was an indispensable member of the "poststructuralist 'trinity,'" a "prophet of lack copacetic with Derridean *différance*," and an underwriter of countless Foucauldian "encounters with the Other."[11] Žižek's "Enlightenment Lacan" performed quite an inversion: a brash reassertion, in the midst of establishment postmodernity, of the *cogito* and the always already structured-ness of Cartesian subjectivity.[12] Contrary to Bruno Latour's assessment of 1989 Europe cited in the introduction—"The will to be modern seems hesitant, sometimes even outmoded"—Žižek was shamelessly insistent: we have always been modern, and this is our most general symptom, the cause of our fantasies (among them, that we have never been modern).[13] While there's nothing especially remarkable about a book swimming against multiple tides, it is worth noting how, in the case of *The Sublime Object of Ideology*, each of its tides became (even more) hegemonic in the decade following the book's publication. It wasn't technically a harbinger of the 1990s at all, but its Minervan owl, taking delayed flight only with the new millennium's Grand Guignol renewal of historical and ideological conflict.

And yet, I find it irresistible to imagine—yes, to fantasize—Žižek's book on the shelves of Berlin's English-language bookstores as Bernstein, Hasselhoff, and Rostropovich assembled their audiences. It is, to say the least, a telling non-encounter. While the people celebrate a release from the iron grip of ideology, there Žižek's book mutely sits, sour if not bitter, wagging its finger, upbraiding readers with the Althusserian adage that "the idea of the possible end of ideology is an ideological idea par excellence."[14] As "freedom" becomes the moment's master signifier, emitting from thousands of mouths, ringing in thousands of ears, Žižek insists on the word's "logic of exception," on how "every ideological Universal—for example freedom . . . is 'false' in so far as it necessarily includes a specific case which breaks its unity, lays open its falsity."[15] As the crowds appear finally to awake from the nightmare of history, Žižek rehearses "the Lacanian thesis that it is only in the dream that we come close to the real awakening."[16] Ideology is indeed a kind of unconscious or fundamental fantasy, but fantasy is itself on the side of reality, not dream. The fantasmatic nature of ideology "is not a dreamlike illusion that we build to escape insupportable reality; in its basic dimension it is a fantasy-construction which serves as a support for our 'reality' itself: an 'illusion' which structures our effective, real social relations and thereby masks some insupportable, real, impossible kernel. . . . The function of ideology is not to offer us a point of escape from our reality but to offer us the social reality itself as an escape from some traumatic, real kernel."[17]

In pitting Žižek against Hasselhoff, Bernstein, and Rostropovich, I of course risk turning them into the moment's mere antagonists, their disagreement no less real for being unintentional: a Jeremiah howling vainly at Joyful Noise, or a rueful post-Marxist bemoaning the foreclosure of the socialist horizon as the "other side" gloats. A matter of contest and contention, irreconcilable interests, standpoints—a tempting picture, but, I think, the wrong one. In reducing it to rivalry, it coerces the scene into what Lacan might have called an imaginary disagreement, a fantasmatic factioning of an otherwise more complex relationship. And a stranger one: Žižek's book is not so much taking sides as, without meaning to, articulating precisely the grounds by which the world around it is busy creating the reality it simultaneously celebrates and enjoys. *The Sublime Object of Ideology* offers an expansive, digressive, spiraling account of how—as I put it in chapter 2—one might render in the same common sweep of time the emancipatory break and the suture that closes it back up. Amid so many choral fantasies, it is a curmudgeonly "wild tangle."

Key to this account is Žižek's development of the Lacanian concept of the Real, at which he hints above in the notion of "some traumatic, real kernel." The Real is more an anti- or un-concept, Lacan's term for "that which resists symbolization absolutely," or "this something faced with which all words cease and all categories fail, the object of anxiety par excellence."[18] Such designations suggest the Real as a kind of autonomous, radically resistant material, the elusive stoniness of stone, the monolith, the spirit-as-bone. Lacan seems to countenance such interpretations when he speaks of the Real as a smooth, paralyzing plenitude "absolutely without fissure"—"there is no absence in the [R]eal."[19] And yet, it gives to the Real too much substantiality, too much consistency, to think of it this way. It does not inhere, even less does it reside; it is not substance, not a state of things. Because the Real is "always and in every case in its place," it does not as such *appear*, since this would necessarily engender aspects, modalities, ways of seeing. The Real is hence its own self-occluding ground; because it "carries its place stuck to the sole of its shoe," paradoxically it cannot be located, let alone considered from this or that angle.[20] This in turn suggests the Real as the opposite of material—as a gap or void, a ceaselessly missing thing. It ought be no surprise that elsewhere Lacan supports this notion as well, speaking of the Real as a persistent radical negativity, a constant failing, something that "doesn't stop not writing itself" (ne cesse pas de ne pas s'écrire); at its simplest, it is "the impossible."[21] These notions bring the Real close to Lacan's tersest definition of the unconscious, cited earlier: "impediment, failure, crack," unconscious as (negative) effect.

Such talk may rightly return us to the irritation I mentioned at the beginning of the chapter. Is the Real full or empty? A stifling too-muchness or an abyssal lack? Yes, and yes, Lacan seems to say. And there's something perfectly shifty about the decision to give such radical inconsistency a single term. At one moment it seems to come out of the roaring maw of the Gatekeeper in Franz Kafka's parable of the law, at another, from the mouth of one of Samuel Beckett's tramps, prattling on about the futility of prattling on. But one of the central achievements of *The Sublime Object of Ideology* was to transpose the Real from a peripherally persistent figure in Lacan's own work to a center of sustained critical theorization. Indeed, at moments the book's "whole point" seems to be to "translate [the Real] into clear terms," as both concept and effect. On the one hand, this entails what Kornbluh calls a "vertiginous" definition of the Real, its compression into a self-nullifying antagonism: "a point of the immediate coincidence of . . . opposite poles: each pole passes immediately into its opposite; each is already in itself its own opposite."[22] But on the other hand, Žižek proposes a strategy of, if not resolving, at least "gaming" the Real, entraining his breathless analysis to its continuing arrhythmias. It may be that the Real is, "in a first approach, that which cannot be inscribed, which 'doesn't cease not to inscribe itself'—the rock upon which every formalization stumbles. But it is precisely through this failure that we can in a way encircle, locate the empty place of the Real. In other words, *the Real cannot be inscribed, but we can inscribe this impossibility itself, we can locate its place: a traumatic place which causes a series of failures.*"[23] I think again of my Berlin bookstore. Regardless what side of the newly opened Wall it sits on, it is, in my mind's eye, as untheatrical a space as could be imagined. The perfect antipode to what music is doing to the rest of Berlin at that very moment: rendering the city a proscenium on which "music's vacant sign of freedom" can be fantasmatically projected, transformed from a "blank" into the shimmering semblance of something concrete, enduring, re-findable. Silently, on the shelf, hiding, a plea for another kind of stage, where the player encircles, again and again, "a series of failures." A theater of truancy. Kafka and Beckett after all.[24]

• • •

"$\$ \lozenge a$": the formula is, unsurprisingly, a bit of a paradox in itself. It proposes a way of inscribing—if not the Real, then at least the subject's own attempt to "encircle" what remains Real to it, what the subject continually returns to as its impossible-to-write, its inscriptive failure. Also unsurprisingly, Žižek makes much of Lacan's formula. It turns out to provide great material for a para-process of incessant encircling, for all those "reiterations . . . in different discursive contexts" of which Laclau wrote in his preface. As such, it offers one among multiple reflexive "cores" to Žižek's practice. If fantasy is, as Lacan put it, a "window on the real," then Žižek's exegetical reiterations of the formula constitute a kind of fantasizing on their own, a way of putting the formula's own radical negativity to work—setting it off, making it go, aspecting and displacing something "always and in every case in its place."[25] But I shouldn't overstate the case: "$\$ \lozenge a$" can indeed be translated "into clear terms," so long as one allows that both the terms and their non-relation inscribe a series of contradictions, a way of *dealing* with radical negativity, if not dispensing with it. Since the formula provides a conceptual anchor for the ensuing chapters, I will risk getting a bit schematic here in unpacking what is most pertinent to my purposes. I begin with the first figure, which I introduced in chapter 2: $\$$, Lacan's barred or split subject.

$\$$ is, as I wrote above, Lacan's way of writing what he took to be Freud's most revolutionary intervention in the Cartesian subject: the claim that the subject has an unconscious dimension and as such will never be fully present to itself. And moreover, that this constant lack of self-presence is the subject; if stones are not subjects, it's not just because they don't possess consciousness, don't "know themselves," but also because they *are* fully present, and lack for nothing. The split subject, by contrast, is constitutionally lacking, born already missing something. For Lacan, this birth is not coincident with the subject's physical emergence, but with its introduction into language, a symbolic order, a "universe of symbols" whose infinite mesh of internal differentiations and combinatorial protocols "carves up [the individual's] body" according to a structure "which has nothing to do with anatomy."[26] This "shearing" is double-sided. On the one hand it inscribes in the individual a register of dead letters, inert and objective forms that fragment and dis-integrate that individual; on the other hand, it is these letters' very deadness and dis-integrating power that produces the spaces in which subjective desire and libido can emerge, in which the prohibitive enjoyment Lacan calls *jouissance* can collect and coil. The subject inevitably attempts to assign these desires and enjoyments names and meanings, and often enlists the very signifiers that engendered them in the first place. So the symbolic order takes away and gives back at once: its permeating absences provide the very anti-stuff of desire, but also the signifiers, syntaxes, grammars, and codes in which this desire can be formulated. It is, in this sense, a classic *pharmakon*, a poison and cure at once.

It's important to stress the strange temporality of this process by which the subject is "installed" in a symbolic order: there is no subject lying in wait before its shearing, but only a subject already split, literally thrown under (*sub-iacta*) the dead letter. $\$$ is not an essence but a deduction, "simply an underneath, a subject, a *hypokeimenon*."[27] As such, the subject is for Lacan marked by a shimmering intermittency—a sonar subject, the blip and ping of signification hitting on a special kind of nothing. Essential to this sonar process are two other Lacanian figures, S_1 and S_2, designating respectively the "master signifier" and "all other signifiers," or what Lacan later simply calls "knowledge." S_2 as a concept harmonizes relatively easily with common conceptions of language: the domain of the writable, the iterable, the substitutable, a fundamentally synonymic space; it is hence also a kind of anti-Real, where nothing remains "always and in every case in its place," but is often all too movable, slipping from one signifier to the next via potentially infinite semiotic and material links.

S_1 is, on the whole, a much more complex concept. It is still a signifier, but, in terms of the subject's psychic structure, it remains largely unconscious. Though it licenses the subject's installation in language, the master signifier is itself repressed, opaque, resistant to meaning. Even as it performs the first shearing, its structural role prevents it from being pulled into the combinatorial games enacted by S_2; it remains aloof, thing-like. Instead it functions as what Lacan calls a *point de capiton*, a "quilting point," a signifier out of which "everything radiates . . . and is organized around, similar to this little line of force that an upholstery button forms on the surface of material. It's the point of convergence that enables everything that happens in [a] discourse to be situated retroactively and prospectively."[28] Lacan is adamant: master signifiers are not meaningful "in themselves," they are not numinous symbols glowing with deep significance. Discourse may come retroactively to invest them with such, but Lacan remains dedicated to the premise of analysis as a process of unearthing master signifiers in all their contingency and arbitrariness, as purely formal punctuations in an otherwise unfissured, Real fabric.

Hence the metaphor of an upholstered surface rather than an architected space. S_1 is not an anchor, not a means of grounding the subject, but the autarchy of randomness, pure chance as absolute master. Once in place, it organizes the subject's discursive field: not just its identifications but its disidentifications, loves and hatreds, fears and hopes. Though it is not quite the same thing as Freud's *Ich*, it is what ego builds itself around. In this sense, ego is the product of the linkages *between* S_1 and S_2: if S_2 is the vertiginous field of infinite metonymy, S_1 is what magnetizes that metonymy, polarizing its movements. "I" is an emergent, highly contingent property of these semiotic adventures. It is an avatar, the subject's attempt within the symbolic order to know itself fully, to achieve absolute self-presence, to overturn once and for all the shearing, dis-integrating power of signifiers. In this sense, it is a modern reincarnation of a correspondence theory of truth, what Thomas Aquinas called "adaequatio rei et intellectus" (the adequation of thing and intellect), where S_1 is the "thing" and S_2 the domain of intellection. The "I" emerges from an attempted holophrasis, the compression of a complex, infinitely mutable constellation of ideas into a single adamant word.[29] This process is doomed to fail, of course; signifiers are being used to overcome the shearing power of signification. But the subject emerges out of this failure as its belated cause, what Lacan would call a *béance causale* or causal gap.[30] Where these semiotic adventures in the symbolic, these games of egoistic adequation break down, precisely there is where the subject emerges—paradoxically, as a gap.

This is a strong, unabashedly ontogenetic account of the subject. And one shouldn't let Lacan's terminology—coined after the linguistic turn and the inheritance of structuralism—conceal its debt to Freud. If it diverts, it is less through revision than through the distorting power of its formalism; or rather, formalism is its "revisionary ratio." But that ratio is not Žižek's. Although this ontogenetic account underwrites Žižek's treatment of the subject in *The Sublime Object of Ideology*, his book swerves in another way, trading formalism for expansion, hyperbole, brazen synthesis. Among the most compelling is a synthesis that makes the volume sit even more restively in its Berlin bookstore—a link to the 1985 book *Hegemony and Socialist Strategy* by the post-Marxist political theorists Ernesto Laclau and Chantal Mouffe. There the authors argue for a radically discursive conception of society, one in which society exists only as a word, the signifier "society"—hence marking, like all signifiers, the place where something is missing.[31] Laclau and Mouffe certainly don't doubt the reality of masses, groups, or individuals, but precisely such actors are engaged in "hegemonic struggles" to define society, to make something "bigger" appear within the domain of the symbolic—something that can adequately represent the truth of those groups. Here the authors introduce their twin notions of *empty signifiers* and *articulations*. Political struggles are always dual struggles: first, to fix in place empty signifiers that might organize the discourse, and second, to articulate links between such empty signifiers and concrete, specific, worldly terms.[32] In a later interview, Laclau gives the example of "justice for all"—a signifier at once boomingly righteous and utterly void of meaning—and articulations that might begin to "fill it up": the environment, gender, class, education, et cetera.[33] The hegemonic struggle is, structurally speaking, impossible to complete: no quantity or intensity of articulations can fill the emptiness of the empty signifier, and moreover, every articulation is contingent, relative, precarious. At the same time, the struggle is only possible in the first place because its absolute realization is not: "The social is articulation insofar as 'society' is impossible."[34] Hence the reality of social struggle is grounded negatively, emerging out of what Laclau and Mouffe call *antagonisms*—"not objective relations"—that is, not relations between opposing political bodies or articulated positions, but rather the "limits of all objectivity."[35]

Although—or perhaps because—he is a clear influence on the authors, Lacan appears only once in the body of *Hegemony and Socialist Strategy*, and again in a (rather epic) footnote. But among its other immodest interventions, Žižek's book

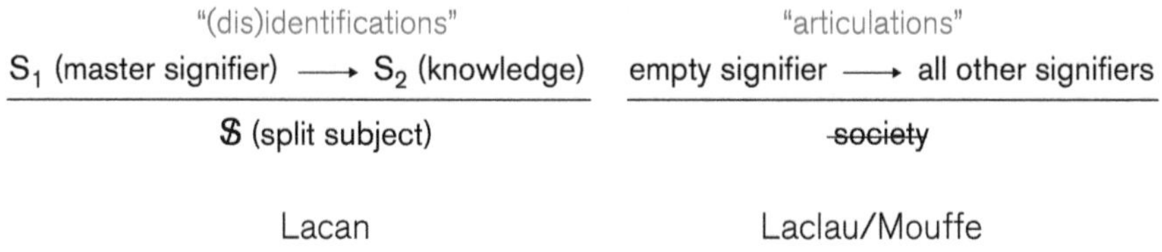

FIGURE 9. Two schemata of radical subjective negativity.

draws out this repressed relation, and essentially maps Laclau and Mouffe's account of hegemonic struggle onto Lacan's ontogenetic account of the subject. The barred subject is just as easily a barred society as it is an individual neurotic; both are figurations of a consciousness sheared by the signifier, thrown under the letter, simultaneously barred from absolute self-presence and engendered *by* that barring. Society, like the subject, is unconscious—a negative, opaque ground for fundamentally contingent discursive adventures. Those adventures represent the subject, in both the individual and the political sense. But—to employ Lacan's tricky definition of the signifier—these endeavors in the symbolic never present the subject to other subjects, but *to other signifiers*.[36] That is, the price for "getting in the game" involves leaving oneself behind. Or "below," on the level of the unconscious. One can model Laclau and Mouffe's struggle to hegemonize the empty signifier with concrete articulations quite easily after Lacan's schema for the subject's installation into language: above, a semiotic adventure defined by trope and substitution, constitutively incomplete and infinitely open to contestation; below, an ineliminable Real antagonism, serving as the unrecoverable ground. Political discourse emerges as an attempt to produce and stabilize a societal ego, to give society the promise of a fully self-identical "I" it will never quite be.

In terms of the history of psychoanalysis, Žižek's synthesis emerges as only the latest in a century's worth of endeavors to move from couch to commons, from the morbidly private world of individual micro-history to the fate of civilizations. In this he follows a long line of leftist writers such as Otto Gross, Wilhelm Reich, Erich Fromm, Herbert Marcuse, and to some extent Adorno, too.[37] But in Žižek's case, it all rests on the power of the letter. On the shelf, the closed book quivers with import. As Bernstein, Hasselhoff, and Rostropovich each fight their hegemonic struggle to fill the empty signifier "freedom," the book explains why this is impossible—why their music, perhaps any music, is a sleight of hand, a ruse meant to cover over an almost prosaic discursive operation, an endeavor in reprogramming the code.

But to say that language is what grounds both schemata isn't quite right. It is exactly there, where the line cuts the letter, that language precipitates what it simultaneously fails to capture. And here Žižek is dogged. It is a matter upon which Laclau and Mouffe's account seems to fumble, the matter of that titular "sublime object," or what Lacan calls *a*.

. . .

Lacan coined the formula "$\$ \Diamond a$" in his fifth seminar (1957–58), at a point where *a* had yet to become a figure that would launch a thousand ships in the theoretical humanities, and that even Lacan himself would consider his "most significant contribution to psychoanalysis."[38] At the time of the seminar, it simply stood for "little other," a piece or remnant of the big Other—law, language, the symbolic—that remained resistant to symbolization. Essential to this late-1950s conception of *a* was Lacan's notion of the imaginary, a third "order," reducible to neither the symbolic nor the Real. If the Real is the order of "one"—immobile, unparseable, impossible—and the symbolic the order of "three"—the endless triangulation of split subjects via mediating signifiers, S_1 and S_2—the imaginary is the order of "two": the dyad, the inherently volatile domain of sameness and difference, the mirror, the semblance, the lure.[39] The imaginary in some sense precedes the symbolic. If the stuff of the symbolic is suddenly one day there—Lacan's "universe of symbols," taken over from Claude Lévi-Strauss—still it is not quite an order at first, but exists piecemeal, congealing into images, smooth and resistant signi-things.[40] At this stage of Lacan's teachings, fantasy is the consummate "imaginary activity," a leftover of the transition from an imaginary or "mirror stage" to a fuller installation in the symbolic. In the fifth seminar he defines fantasy "as the imaginary caught up in a certain signifying use [*usage de signifiant*]," and a few years later, he refines the operation, confidently proclaiming that "the notion of unconscious fantasy no longer presents any difficulty once it is defined as an image set to work within a signifying structure."[41] Fantasy is a record of the subject's incomplete existence in language as a symbolic order. "Carved up" by a proliferating network of signifiers, something in the subject nonetheless resists the shearing. An image—flat, plenitudinous, literally indecipherable—clogs the network. Already here, there is the strong implication that such fantasmatic images are not themselves prior to the symbolic, but its precipitates. It is as if the subject, split by the letter, caught up in the endless combinatorics of language, produces a bit of un-symbolizable excess in the process. As Lacan continues to formulate *objet a* throughout the 1960s, this premise only intensifies.

Defining the *objet a*, or as I called it at the beginning of this chapter, the "object-cause of desire," is now something of a cottage industry in certain academic and theoretical circles. The task is an object-cause in itself, in part because of its paradoxical richness and oracularity, in part because, as Bruce Fink puts it, "few concepts have so many avatars in Lacan's work."[42] So while I hope to clarify some of the concept's logic and function here, I will err on the side of pragmatism and selectivity, highlighting those aspects most essential to my arguments in the ensuing chapters.

Here it's worth revisiting and expanding on Lacan's idiosyncratic notion of desire, hinted at in this chapter's opening paragraph. It is an almost perfect inversion of the common-sense conception: desire is pushed, not pulled. It is not a want, a desire for some concrete object—a man or a woman, a Snickers or a Coke, or even a looming abstraction like happiness or honor. Desire has no object, including the direct object of the sentence in which it appears here—desire is never a "desire for." Instead, desire is a condition, a way of activating and mobilizing an otherwise inert lack. It is prompted, sparked, jolted into being by objects. Whatever concrete objects its subject then pursues is another matter—and, for Lacan, almost invariably a matter of error. (The Snickers never satisfies, the Coke makes you thirstier, happiness remains elusive, et cetera.)

Framing desire this way suggests that, if an object is to be involved at all, it must be quite a peculiar one. And the canonic Lacanian example of peculiar perfection is the gaze. The premise is easy to misinterpret. It cannot be an entirely intelligible gaze, a gaze whose own object is clear to the subject: "he wants my wallet," "she wants my attention," even "they want me." Rather, the gaze as object-cause of desire must be enigmatic, and constitutionally so. Amid the profusion of examples in post-Lacanian literature, the philosopher Levi Bryant provides a remarkably clear case. It involves the sadomasochistic romance between a secretary and her boss in the 2002 film *Secretary*, and specifically "the way the heroine . . . experiences herself perpetually under the gaze of her boss":

> It is this gaze, a gaze of which she is never certain, a gaze which she is forever unable to determine as to whether it is truly taking place, that ultimately wins her love. She does not feel gazed upon because she loves her boss, but rather she loves her boss because she wonders whether she is gazed upon. The gaze is the object-cause of her desire. Her desire for her boss is the effect of this cause. This, then, is the crucial, not to be missed, point: [t]he fantasy does not conjoin the woman with her boss, but rather conjoins the woman with the gaze. . . . She is conjoined with that remainder, that point of excess that always escapes within her signifying economy.[43]

This example foregrounds the paradox of *objet a*, one that will assume considerable import in the chapters to follow: *objet a* does not exist. But its nonexistence is of a different sort than, say, the void in the split subject, or Laclau and Mouffe's "impossible" society. Subject and society are "born split": the subject only emerges as already missing something, society only appears as a struggle to define "society." In both cases, loss is constitutive, not empirical; there is, in a strict sense, nothing to be done with this loss. It is a Real loss, unparseable and irreplaceable. But it's here that unconscious fantasy emerges as, in a sense, a refusal to take "no" for an answer. Instead of doing nothing, it does the impossible. Quite literally: fantasy renders this Real loss into an image, something radically resistant to symbolization, and then sets this image-of-nothing to work "within a signifying structure," that is, within the very symbolic order that precipitated the loss in the first place.

In the eleventh seminar from 1964, Lacan stresses that "fantasy is the support of desire; it is not the object that is the support of desire."[44] I take this to mean that *objet a* comes second, so to speak; it is the fantasy that comes first, as an encircling that constitutes its circled object as enigmatic.[45] In this sense, the theater metaphor is not a casual one. Fantasy sets the stage, calls the shots, and so on. But what I find most striking is the strong implication that, in staging the object-cause of desire, fantasy stages a kind of non-appearance, or the appearance of something failing to take place. This is in essence what the secretary and her boss both experience: in directing their smoldering gazes at each other (the attraction is mutual), they also train their mutual lack on one another; each perceives not what the other is missing, but that the other is missing *something*. And precisely this is what turns them on, fills them with desire, letting them "enjoy what they don't have," to paraphrase Todd McGowan.[46] In activating a constitutive loss in the other, and transforming it into something enigmatic, the gaze creates its own Beckettian theater of truancy. It becomes a way of encircling the place where something "doesn't stop not writing itself." And, at the same time, a way of rendering that non-appearance as if it were something—something obscure, opaque, not-quite-there or not-quite-yet.

In this sense, *objet a* becomes an unconscious structural hack, and a cunning one. Framed by the window of fantasy, the object-cause suggests that the subject's own constitutive lack is actually empirical, that the hole—the Real—around which it has formed might be eliminable, that the lost object might be re-found and restored to its proper place. To the subject's own intermittency, its shimmering between signifiers, *objet a* presents itself as a shimmering vision of stability. The object's insubstantiality and inconsistency, mirroring the subject's own, are nonetheless mistaken for exactly the opposite: an impossible promise of substance, consistency, completion. Fantasy is what renders this promise so compelling, so irresistible. And it does so brilliantly, by tying the subject to its own "nothing," by "wresting and turning" it, and calling this a relationship.[47]

. . .

"$\$ \lozenge a$": Žižek, as I'd said above, has grand designs on the formula. It is, among other things, a means of understanding ideology anew, and of resurrecting ideological critique at a moment when it seems increasingly obsolete. If unconscious fantasy veils the subject's constitutive lack with the impossible promise of a "Real object," how might ideology be understood as unconscious fantasy en masse? Instead of conceiving ideological commitments as conscious investments in one or another concrete position, how might one understand ideologies as ways of unconsciously masking a deeper contingency, of disavowing an ineliminable Real in the social and political fabric of reality? Here Laclau nicely distills the inversion at work for both him and Žižek: under this new paradigm, "the ideological would not consist of the misrecognition of a positive essence, but exactly the opposite: it would consist of the non-recognition of the precarious character of any positivity, of the impossibility of any ultimate suture."[48] Conversely, ideological critique would involve overturning this non-recognition, exposing the precarious character of reality and affirming the Real antagonism grounding all attempts to hegemonize, to complete the sociopolitical ego.[49] Here psychoanalysis assumes a particularly radical form of critique, in that its goal is—as I wrote in chapter 2—to "traverse the radical fantasy," to help society reach not back to its "oldest or deepest truths," but past them. If ideology is unconscious fantasy en masse, then the psychoanalytic critique of ideology is indeed a form of ana-lysis, an unmeshing of the sociopolitical fabric. It stops not at a positive insight, nor at a negative refusal, but at a Real encounter, at what Lacan called "the big secret of psychoanalysis: there is no Other of the Other."[50] That is, there is no "language outside language," no metalanguage, that can vouchsafe its meaning, that can pin down the signifier as more than a signifier, more than a contingent point in an ongoing process. The subject, as the subject of language, or the discoursing society, "subjectivizes itself indefinitely . . . with no reason for stopping."[51]

Naja, jut, I hear the bemused Berliner mutter to himself as he pages through *The Sublime Object of Ideology* in the musty bookstore. "Yeah, OK." Despite Lacan's big secret, he has no trouble stopping his subjectivization at the hands of Žižek. He puts the book down and continues on his way to Breitscheidplatz to see the Ninth on a screen, or to the Brandenburg Gate, to sit on the Wall and listen to the Hoff, whom he finds ridiculous, but at this historic moment, who can resist? It is impossible not to enjoy. And yet, had my imaginary patron kept reading, he would have found in Žižek's book at least an attempt to explain why this is so—why the grip of fantasy makes it impossible not to enjoy. And he would find that it resides—not in \$, or S_1 or S_2—but in *a*. The schema is not triadic but quadratic. Only insofar as the split subject is embroiled in unconscious fantasy can the phenomenal world—as both semiotic adventure and "mere reality"—exist. Traverse the radical fantasy, untie the split subject from its Real object, and reality itself comes apart. Upper and lower registers of same psychic model, they are perhaps better described as two sides of the same fabric: to unmesh one is to unmesh the other.

The last Lacanian concept central to this book requires a brief swerve, away from Žižek's Falstaffian appetite for synthesis and back to Lacan's formalisms. It involves the introduction, in his well-known seminar of 1969–70, "L'envers de la psychanalyse" (The Other Side of Psychoanalysis), of a full suite of quadratic schemata, each intended to "mathematize" one of four discourses, four forms of "social link": the master's discourse, the university's discourse, the hysteric's discourse, and the analyst's discourse. Each is derived, respectively, by a clockwise quarter

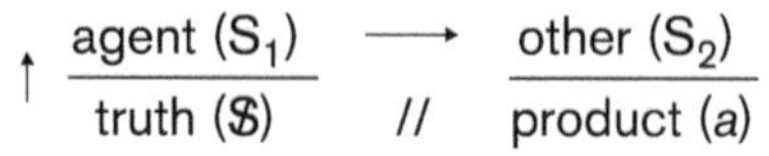

FIGURE 10. Jacques Lacan's schema of the master's discourse.

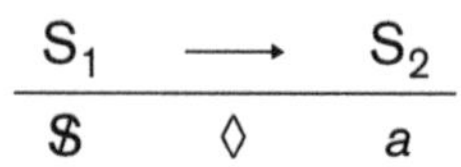

FIGURE 11. The master's discourse anchored by unconscious fantasy.

turn of the previous one, and all are ways of trying to write, or at least encircle, the Real as it exists in social relations.[52] Each discourse puts the Real to work, setting its impossibility of inscription in motion. As such, each discourse formalizes a different type of impasse, but also the way that impasse still engenders roles and effects—agency, otherness, production, truth.[53] But Lacan stresses that these discourses are not all equals. The master's discourse, appropriately enough, holds the other three in its frame, and their attempts to break away from it are only ever partial. It is the "other side of psychoanalysis."[54] In being schematized, the discourse of the master "can be uncovered in a sort of purity—and this, through something that we experience directly, and at the level of politics. What I mean by this is that it embraces everything, even what thinks of itself as revolutionary, or more exactly as what is romantically called Revolution with a capital R. The master's discourse accomplishes its own revolution in the other sense of doing a complete circle."[55] It would make sense that the master's discourse holds sway here, and also that it constitutes the other side of psychoanalysis. Though Lacan intends it to address multiple subjects in real-world interactions, it also presents in formal (Lacanian) terms the psychic structure of the classical Oedipal neurotic—which is to say, the "I" who "is not master in its own house," as Freud famously put it.[56] The master's discourse hence demonstrates how the subject is itself mastered by discourse, and how it tries to turn this subjected-ness to its advantage. "What I am trying to spell out," Lacan says in a remarkable protest-intervention during the seminar, "is what dominates [society], namely, the practice of language."[57]

The "truth" of the discourse, then, is not the master signifier, but $\$$; while S_1 engages S_2 as a master does a slave—Hegel, not Aquinas, is Lacan's model for the discourses—S_1 is revealed as an avatar, a "semblant."[58] The truth of the master is that it is a signifier held up by a split subject: the real master, like any subject of language, lacks. Meanwhile, the hegemonic struggle up above becomes a struggle for recognition, Hegelian dialectical tensions in tow. The "agent," as semblant of the master, demands that the other, as repository of all knowledge, "slave away" on its behalf, and serve it up a proper knowledge of itself, what it "really" is. But this is impossible. The demand is made by one signifier to another, each functioning as not-each-other within a differential system.[59]

If $\$$ is the co-constitutive "cause" of the adventures between S_1 and S_2, then *a* is the result of their failure, the precipitate of their breakdown. In the master's discourse schema, it occupies the position of product or by-product, a kind of surplus value or enjoyment: the spoils of slave labor.[60] But it is not an accessible enjoyment, and certainly not a pleasure. The subject has a notoriously hard time "enjoying" this enjoyment. Lacan calls this *jouissance*, a word for which there is (appropriately) no satisfying English translation.[61] In common French it signifies orgasmic bliss, but also the exercising of a legal right, to property for instance; in a late seminar Lacan compares it to usufruct, to "what serves no purpose."[62] In general it signifies in the Lacanian field what *Schmerzlust* and *Unlust* did for Freud: the collapse of pleasure into pain, a beyond of the pleasure principle, whose commandment is "enjoy as little as possible."[63] *Jouissance*, by contrast, is a prohibited and prohibitive enjoyment, an enjoyment before and outside the signifier. In Freudian terms, it is also "the kind of satisfaction which the symptom brings . . . unrecognizable to the subject, who, on the contrary, feels the alleged satisfaction as suffering and complains of it."[64] Hence it is an enjoyment we can't have—being forbidden by the signifier—and an enjoyment of what we do not have—of the lack that founds subjectivity, and that returns to it in the not-quite-form of *objet a*.[65]

The upper register of Lacan's schema models language, the "locus of the Other," as a hegemonic struggle between signifiers—the duking out of public discourse or "ego-talk," the vicissitudes of the debating collective or the neurotic's self-tussling. In both cases, consensus—holophrasis, identity—is their asymptotic point, a necessary illusion veiling an ineliminable antagonism. But it is Lacan's lower register—the register of $\$$ and *a*, as "truth" and "product"—that renders the model properly psychoanalytic, going beyond Laclau and Mouffe's model. The double bar between $\$$ and *a* also represents an impasse, a breakdown of signal into noise, but of a different order than the one above.[66] If the relation between S_1 and S_2 is marked by incompletion and contingency, the relation between $\$$ and *a* is marked by impossibility: it does not technically exist, because *a* itself does not exist. While the union between agent and other can't be completed, the connection between truth and product can't begin. It is an impossible relationship, or, more precisely, a relationship out of impossibility, a way of making impossibility into a sustainable—and enjoyable—resource.

A last point, about *a*. It still matters that it stands for *autre* (other). If Lacan's "big secret of psychoanalysis" is that there is no "Other of the Other," it is fantasy that keeps this secret secret. Moreover, it conceals this greater Otherless-ness through its own "hidden work"; it hides its act of hiding. In a later seminar, Lacan compares the "fundamental fantasy" to an axiom in geometry or set theory. It is "not something to be proven or demonstrated per se, but something which generates all of the allowable statements within a certain field."[67] The fantasy is hence a kind of given or uncaused cause, a paradoxical absolute whose function is to conceal the fact that absolutes—grand, guaranteeing Others—don't exist. If, like any axiom, it provides a frame, a stage, an open space, it is less so that concrete objects can fill it up, and more so that the subject can enjoy that emptiness, that not-having. To return to Hans Pfitzner's snide comment in my introduction about the "Veni Creator Spiritus" movement in Mahler's Eighth, the subject in the grips of its fundamental fantasy isn't worried that the Creator might never come. The fantasy prevents Him from showing up. It allows the subject to enjoy His truancy, and to coordinate with it a dual absence: the absence of the big Other always about to arrive, and the mirroring absence of the split subject's constitutive lack. So long as He continues not to show, the subject knows where it stands. The fantasy entrains the subject to His absence, and "teaches" it how to desire.[68] Veiling the Other's inconsistency and insubstantiality, its organization around a stubborn nub of non-sense, fantasy fabricates an always preemptive answer: "I know what the Other wants, and I can provide it."[69]

. . .

Žižek glares at the camera, his arms slicing the air like a marionette conductor. He wears a black T-shirt bearing Bartleby's slogan: "I WOULD PREFER NOT TO." "Are we aware," he asks, "to what extent, when we freely choose, our choices are predetermined?" The moment comes early in "Slavoj Žižek: What Is Freedom Today?," an "Opinion weekly video" in the *Guardian*'s online philosophy section.[70] It is December 2014, exactly a quarter century after the Wall's fall, but Žižek's take on freedom is perfectly consistent with the anti-program of the not-quite-book from 1989: don't get duped. "Freedom" is a great signifier, sure, but invariably it comes off the lips of speaking beings, whose subjectivity is always grounded in an unconscious—which is to say, a deeper, structural un-freedom. Looking back at Matt ffytche's description of the "broader unconscious" of the European nineteenth century in chapter 2, it's hard not to see Žižek here as a contemporary vindicator of Schelling's stifled *Weltalter* project, tirelessly disseminating his own ontogenetic account of, as ffytche puts it, "a self-caused self, or a self the logic of whose development is irreducibly detached from more systematic forms of explanation."[71] The video's 23,000 shares and 205 comments suggest that "such ideas [still] have an immense (if contested) appeal, particularly within liberal theories of individuality."[72]

The comparison is not a casual one. If *The Sublime Object of Ideology* helped introduce a new "Lacan of the Real" to audiences in 1989, it seems never to have been Žižek's most urgent aim, or deepest desire. He confessed almost cathartically in a long 2003 interview:

> I'm trying to do what Deleuze forgot to do—to bugger Hegel, with Lacan [chuckles] so that you get monstrous Hegel, which is, for me, precisely the underlying radical dimension of subjectivity. . . . But again, the basic idea being this mutual reading, this mutual buggering of this focal point, radical negativity and so on, of German Idealism with the very fundamental . . . insight of psychoanalysis. It's a very technical, modest project, but I believe in it. . . . Do [I] ultimately use Hegel to reactualize Lacan, or the other way around? I would say the other way around. What really interests me is philosophy, and for me, psychoanalysis is ultimately a tool to reactualize, to render actual for today's time, the legacy of German Idealism.[73]

Adrian Johnston, one of Žižek's best critical exegetes, puts it more soberly: "The chain Kant-Schelling-Hegel, knotted together vis-à-vis Lacan himself as this chain's privileged *point de capiton* . . . is the underlying skeletal structure holding together the entirety of the Žižekian theoretical edifice."[74] Lacan hence becomes a prism through which the "radical negativity and so on" of European thought circa 1800 can cast a light on Žižek's own present. With *The Sublime Object of Ideology*, that light is directed more brightly, and more aptly, at its immediate present than the author could possibly have intended.

What that light reveals is, among other things, that music played, if not a causal role, still a necessary and inevitable one in the late events of that year. In that moment, music became an ideal Real object, an object-cause of desire, one able like nothing else to entrain subjects to its radical absence, to teach them how to desire, to give them the chance to know and declare, "I know what the Other wants, and I can provide it." On its own, there's nothing especially remarkable about music playing such a role. In a provocative if problematic essay from the late 1990s on Schumann, Žižek himself imagines "music at its most elementary" as "an act of supplication: a call to a figure of the big Other (beloved Lady, King, God . . .) to respond, not as the symbolic big Other, but in the real of his or her being (breaking his own rules by showing mercy; conferring her contingent love on us . . .). Music is thus an attempt to provoke the 'answer of the Real' . . . the miracle of the Other stretching his or her hand out to me."[75] Such a figuration of music harmonizes astonishingly well with Bernstein's Beethoven, Rostropovich's Bach, and even Hasselhoff's own hyperreal self-presentation. There is, in a strict sense, little new here. Except the historical moment, one in which the actual physical coordinates of the world immediately surrounding those entrained, desiring subjects were literally disappearing, and when that world was readier than ever to reveal its inconsistency and insubstantiality, its stubborn nub of non-sense. In such a situation, music becomes Music. It shows the mercy, or confers the love or the outstretched hand, that the state itself was supposed to show, or at the very least withhold.

It seems fair to say Žižek is not—and, at the time of *The Sublime Object of Ideology*, was not—on the side of fantasy, but of traversal: of "traversing the radical fantasy" and coming to know, even on the level of the unconscious, the big secret of psychoanalysis, which for him was nothing less than the big secret of Hegelian dialectics. "All we have to do," he wrote in *The Sublime Object of Ideology*, "is experience how there is nothing 'behind' [fantasy], and how fantasy masks precisely this 'nothing.'"[76] This was Hegel's "absolute knowledge"—"nothing but a name for the acknowledgement of a certain radical loss."[77] By the late 1990s, Žižek would develop an elaborate playbook of the ways in which fantasy conceals this big secret. His "seven veils of fantasy" would lay out a series of structural inversions by which subjects are compelled to "misrecognize nothing," for instance the veil of passivity, masking the subject's fundamental hand in the scene, or the veil of coherent narrative, masking a deadlock or antagonism.[78] Such veils are not rooted in the depths of individual subjectivity, but "out there," omnipresent in the "purely material sincerity" of the world's "deluge of pseudo-concrete images"—the sociopolitical sphere, the culture-industrial complex, the theater of media.[79] And, of course, music.

Just after Žižek classifies "music at its most elementary" as an attempt to make the big Other appear without actually appearing, he adds a caveat: "Perhaps, musical modernity designates the moment when music renounces the endeavor to provoke the answer of the Other."[80] It is as curious a characterization as it is sweeping. But it also nods in the direction of an other music, one seemingly consonant with Žižek's own philosophical and critical designs. A music that might, for instance, expose the veils of fantasy for what they are, and reveal the Other behind them in all its inconsistency. Or a music that ceaselessly encircles what doesn't stop not writing itself, or that provides a stage for a certain "radical negativity and so on," a place where a Real continually fails to "take place." A vertiginous music, in terms not only of affect, but of language, style, material, form—one where "each pole passes immediately into its opposite," and where "each is already in itself its own opposite."

The reader will see me skirting around the "wild tangle" I left behind at the end of chapter 2: Beethoven's late style, or, rather, Adorno's "Beethoven's Late Style," a music about music, but whose disruptions, parataxes, and obscurities seem to unmesh the very consistency of the traditions and genres it receives, and even to attack its own fantasizing faculty. To describe such music as "modern" is, of course, too little. To describe it as modernist seems too much. But in Žižek's description of a Real where everything is already its opposite, there is an uncanny correspondence with the vision of modernism T. J. Clark gave in my introduction, and which I ought to excerpt again here:

> Positive and negative, fullness and emptiness, totalization and fragmentation, sophistication and infantilism, euphoria and desperation, an assertion of infinite power and

> possibility alongside a mimicry of deep aimlessness and loss of bearings. For this, I think, is modernism's root proposal about its world: that the experience of modernity is precisely the experience of the two states, the two tonalities, at the same time.[81]

It is—I admit it!—a stretch to say that Hasselhoff, Bernstein, and Rostropovich, in their various parades, are channeling the history of European absolute music circa 1800. If absolute music is historically nomadic, a "regulative concept," as Mark Evan Bonds put it, these 1989 performances come close to deregulating it entirely.[82] Far less of a stretch, I think, is the claim that the Europe of 1989 was permeated by an other music, far away from History's main musical stage, consumed by all matter of encircling nothing. But if fantasies can make things hard to see, they can also make things hard to hear.

5

DREI PHANTASIESTÜCKE (3)

If you had a bit of patience, and if you really wanted our impromptus to continue, I would tell you that, always, the revolutionary aspiration has only a single possible outcome—of ending up as the master's discourse. This is what experience has proved.

What you aspire to as revolutionaries is a master. You will get one.

—JACQUES LACAN, "ANALYTICON: FOUR IMPROMPTUS," DECEMBER 3, 1969[1]

"Did pop bring down the Berlin Wall?" "Did Bowie bring down the Berlin Wall?" "Did the Boss help bring down the Berlin Wall?" "How Springsteen helped tear down the Wall." "How David Hasselhoff brought down the Berlin Wall."[2]

In the quarter century since the collapse of East Germany, the uncountable reflections that flower the media landscape inevitably turn to music. And when they do, they waffle. Somewhere between the rhetorical questions and the pseudo-investigatory poses, one detects an uneasiness, less an anxiety than the fatigue of false consciousness failing to repress itself: Well, OK, *of course* music didn't really bring down the Wall, but isn't it at least worth asking? Wouldn't it be nice to imagine? "I know very well, but all the same . . .": the classic formulation of fetishist disavowal.[3] A short, initially puffy BBC video piece from 2009 embodies the maneuver perfectly. It starts out with a beguiling montage narrated by the journalist and former East German Oliver Fritz, who fondly recalls how "it was no coincidence that for three weeks before the fall of the Wall, David Hasselhoff's song 'Looking for Freedom' topped the West German charts and was quickly adopted by East Germans heading to the west. It was a rallying call and we heeded it."[4] The gauze of causality surrounding the Hasselhoff Thesis is then quickly chortled away in the panel discussion that follows (and from which Fritz is notably absent). But "all the same," the participants are perturbed, and each tries to make the case that music played some role. Paul Berman, writing in *Dissent* that same year about the simultaneous "rising and sinking of hearts" in that "age of revolutionary heartburn," does something similar. Reminiscing about "bohemian Bohemians" and "liberal dissidents," he also includes "the classical musicians" and adds that "never in history have classical musicians played so great a role in political events as in 1989, in one country after another."[5] People know that music—pop? classical? Boss? Beethoven?—did *something*, that it too "thrilled us, of course," that when "our hearts pounded in solidarity," it was somehow also a factor. But no one quite knows what that factor was.[6]

There is something untimely, and uncanny, about this waffling. It is as if the tensions structuring music's role in the heady days of the late 1960s were being therapeutically replayed twenty years later: '68 yet again as the fetish object. On the one hand, music here is the fantasmatic sound of revolution itself, of truth speaking to power, and power falling to pieces under the weight of truth's irrefutable audibility, equal parts libido and righteousness. On the other hand, it is the traumatic reminder of failure, and the disenchanting premise that this "society of the spectacle" wasn't so powerful after all—that the revolution, in merely appearing, failed to show up. Richard Taruskin, no great friend of '68, tries to have his cake and eat it too in a bitter *New York Times* polemic from 1995. Abiding the classic splitting of an ambivalent object into two objects, good and bad, he selects two musical examples, designates one properly revolutionary, and labels the other an imposter to the cause: "The true musical emblems of that glorious moment [in 1989 Berlin] were [not the performances of classical music but] the guitar-strumming kids in jeans atop the wall playing a music that would have landed them in jail the day before. They were the ones who symbolized *Freiheit*. What did Beethoven symbolize? Just packaged greatness, I'm afraid, and all that that implies of smugness and dullness and ritualism. Just what the revolutions of '89 were revolting against."[7]

This choice seems false to me, as does the notion that "either" music, the world of pop or classical, occupied a true revolutionary position. Or, rather, both pop and classical could be said to have played a factor in a successful revolution in which they themselves were not, discursively speaking, revolutionary agents. They were not, for instance, embroiled in what Lacan called the hysteric's discourse, in which an agent whose subjectivity is split tests and antagonizes a master, now in the position of addressee, demanding this master produce knowledge about the subject itself. Judging from the examples of Hasselhoff, Rostropovich, and Bernstein—and here one could include Bruce Springsteen's Weißensee concert in July 1988 or David Bowie's appearance at a three-day West Berlin festival in 1987—music seems woven perfectly into a master's discourse: a process of shoring up a sovereign, of suturing itself to an empty signifier, producing a split subject, and precipitating an excessive enjoyment in the form of an object of desire.

This isn't to say that Hasselhoff, Bernstein, and Rostropovich are themselves the masters here. Though each is marked more or less as phallic, a tool-bearing director of ceremonies (mic, baton, bow), I would argue that they are subjects of these ceremonies, and very much split subjects at that, lacking and desirous. Their master is the perfectly empty signifier "freedom." This seems appropriate enough; "freedom" is after all being held up to represent a provocatively *democratic* subject.

Here the words of the political theorist Claude Lefort, resonating amply with Ernesto Laclau and Chantal Mouffe, are apt:

> Of all the regimes of which we know, [modern democracy] is the only one to have represented power in such a way as to show that power is an *empty place* and to have thereby maintained a gap between the symbolic and the real. It does so by virtue of a discourse which reveals that power belongs to no one; that those who exercise power do not possess it; that they do not, indeed, embody it; that the exercise of power requires a periodic and repeated contest; that the authority of those vested with power is created and re-created as a result of the manifestation of the will of the people.[8]

If actual democratic government must work this way, music provides one among many cunning "theologico-political" supplements, means by which the empty place can be partially re-embodied, given back a bit of flesh. Here is where a Bach suite, a Beethoven symphony, or a hit song play a vital role: while they constitute a kind of knowledge and know-how on their own (of the tune, the score, the work, the rep, the canon), they also come to stand in for a kind of proper knowledge of "freedom itself," its seemingly inevitable articulation, what freedom really is. In the case of the Ninth, this articulation had already been partially made in 1971, when the Council of Europe selected the "Ode to Joy" as the basis for a "European Anthem."[9] But each of these very different musical texts aims to "anthematize" freedom, and to perform a consensus around it. Holophrasis becomes unisonance, what Benedict Anderson famously described as "a special kind of contemporaneous community" woven together by collective, ultimately un-locatable sound. In unisonance, "People wholly unknown to each other utter the same verses to the same melody. The image: unisonance . . . the echoed physical realization of the imagined community. . . . How selfless this unisonance feels! If we are aware that others are singing these songs precisely when and where we are, we have no idea who they may be, or even where, out of earshot, they are singing. Nothing connects us all but imagined sound."[10]

Here the stakes of the adventures of the signifier, the adamant suture between S_1 and S_2 (as explored in chapter 4) are clearer. It's not simply a matter of giving the moment some color, or even really of hegemonizing one signifier over another—of declaring "Looking for Freedom" more or less representative of the instant than "Ode to Freedom." It's more a matter of covering over a catastrophic breach opened up in the symbolic order, a gap in meaning created not just by the falling Wall, but by the contingency of those forces that put it there in the first place, a contingency that tumbles out into the open in one scene after another in late 1989.[11] The infamous televised press conference with East Berlin party boss Günther Schabowski is perhaps the most iconic such scene, with its unforgettable staging of a hapless bureaucrat, rifling through papers, searching for his master, finding none, scratching his head, and fabricating with a shrug an answer—and a wrong one: "sofort, unverzüglich" (immediately, without delay).[12] In this sense, Hasselhoff, Rostropov-

FIGURE 12. Günther Schabowski as anti-Hasselhoff.

ich, and Bernstein are Schabowski's antibodies. They are ushered in at a historical moment whose symbolic coordinates were hardly secure, in order to stage a composite image of knowledge, know-how, and mastery as all one and the same, as occupying the same—non-empty—place. They tune "freedom" to a unisonant frequency, but this is only possible by filtering out an abyssal noise, less the noise of Schiller's joy than of Schelling's terror, his admonition that "most people shy away from [*scheuen sich vor*] freedom."[13] In the face of such apprehension—an instinctive fear of a freedom that does not yet signify anything—the putty of reactionary thinking works well and swiftly: established codes, masterpieces, appeals to patriarchal authority in the form of the conductor, the soloist, the pop star in the sky. If the Wall has suddenly lost its hideous meaning, still it must not be allowed for even a second to become meaningless. Its significance must be immediately co-opted, transposed. It must, in this case, become an amphitheater for the inalienable right to free, post-partisan unisound, transforming a deadlock into the telos of a grand narrative in which totalitarianism and communism are, along with history itself, finally vanquished. There's stark political efficacy in these maneuvers. Their performative universalism sonically encrypts an ode to late global capitalism. It becomes consummate victor-written history, even as the history is still happening.[14]

• • •

Part of the critical power of Lacan's master's discourse schema is how it coordinates the master's agency as a wish, an effort, a desire. The master is already a

$$\uparrow \frac{\text{“freedom” } (S_1)}{\text{performer } (\$)} \begin{array}{c} \longrightarrow \\ \Diamond \end{array} \frac{\text{Bach et al. } (S_2)}{\text{“the people's enjoyment” } (a)} \downarrow$$

FIGURE 13. Performer as discursive master.

semblant, a wish to be master. Behind or beneath every master is a subject who lacks for something, and it is precisely this truth that any signification of mastery must conceal. It's no imaginative stretch to conceive the musical (and especially the classical) performer as a kind of lacking subject, $\$$: someone riven by text, work, score—the signifiers of the Other's demand. The long tradition of *Werktreue* is an elaboration of this, especially when understood as a cultural fantasy of a completely transparent—that is, repressed—subject: one who can play "very inwardly," so inwardly that they vanish.[15] (Rostropovich's own kenosis-fantasy is *Werktreue* taken to its inevitably theological conclusion.) It seems odd to speak of *Werktreue*, with its aura of Joachimesque reserve, in relation to these pageants, but the parabolic curve of fidelity doesn't apply to the musical work in this case; it applies to the master signifier. Only insofar as the subject vanishes not under "the Ninth," but under "freedom" does it achieve transparency, and each performer here at least tries to do precisely this. The old *Werktreue* ethic is split into two demands: "freedom" demands servitude from the music, but transparency from the performer. And a strange transparency, too, in that it isn't compromised by Rostropovich's beaded forehead and wobbly tone, or Hasselhoff's sloppy lip-synching, or Bernstein's failed attempt to still his heaving after the last bar's silence. These details stick not to the performer but to the performance, not to subject but to musical act. They help fill it out; they strengthen its compelling opacity.

Meanwhile, the performer-subject, as the "truth" of the discourse, remains open, unfilled and unfulfilled. "Freedom" persists as a stubbornly empty place, and the chosen music, with even the slightest pause for reflection, confesses its contingent status, its could-have-been-otherwise-ness. (Surely the thought crossed many a mind during the respective performances.) But here is where Lacan's schema is especially helpful. The adventures between "freedom" and Bach or Beethoven or Jack White et al. produce a knowledge, a discursive reality, that can be simultaneously believed and disavowed. One can know it very well, but all the same . . . What matters is that, "at all points homologous" with the play between S_1 and S_2, an unconscious register remains active, and this register operates through the axiomatic logic of fantasy. The void in the subject, which seeks closure through the master signifier, and then through its suture to so many binary signifiers, finds its end not in closure at all, but in the precipitate of their breakdown, the lack turned surplus that is *objet a*. In the case of the performers here, I would argue that the sublime ideological object takes the paraform of "the people's enjoyment."

This is adamantly not the same as the actual people, who shoot firecrackers and throw bottles, chat distractedly, nod off, snap photos, grab keepsakes, or look unself-consciously bored. Even en masse, "the people" is far too inconsistent and multiplicitous an object to grip the fantasizing subject. Rather, *a* is what occludes this inconsistency, while also eluding embodiment as an empirical object. It is not the fabric, but what lends it tautness—"that object," as Lacan puts it, "whose very reality is purely topological . . . that rises in a bump, like the wooden darning egg in the material which, in analysis, you are darning."[16] In this context, *a* is not, say, that "little piece of freedom" Hasselhoff chips off the wall and brings back to his *Baywatch* crew on plaques, nor is it necessarily what emerges in the moment of performance as the spectacle of the hooting throngs, the huddled half circle of auditors, the seated and rapt concertgoers. Rather, it is that prohibitive and prohibited enjoyment, that *jouissance*, that has them in its grip. *a* is what renders "the people" a single body capable of enjoyment, what Lacan calls an "enjoying substance" (*substance jouissante*), a body that "enjoys itself."[17]

This is the inversion, but also the inevitable precipitate, of "freedom" as Laclau's empty signifier, or Lefort's empty place of democracy. If theirs is a site that must be deprived of embodiment, carrying only the negativity of the sign itself—"the power of nobody," as Lefort puts it[18]—it finds its by-product in a kind of absolute "corporization," not simply an embodied something but an excess-of-body, body's obscene and ineliminable energic surplus. Eric Santner's development of the idea of "the king's two bodies," originally conceived by Ernst Kantorowicz, is especially useful here: the medieval and early modern king is double-bodied, inhabiting both a transient mortal form and an enduring immortal form whose "sublime somatic materiality" vouchsafes both monarchical authority and the passage of the royal line. With the modern transition from monarchy to biocracy and popular sovereignty, this second body gradually ceases to play a role. It "is no longer able to give some measure to, no longer able to figure, form, and distribute, this sublime somatic materiality."[19] But this "excessive semiotic—and somatic—vibrancy" persists. It can't be eliminated, and instead migrates out into the people, the "body politic," who must now each and all bear this "too-muchness" as their charge. Santner figures this too-muchness as "flesh," not in the sense of "the corporeal matter beneath the skin that normally remains hidden from view," but rather as the inevitable by-product "generated by the inscription of bodies into a normative social space in the first place, by this interlacing of entitlement and enjoyment that opens up the possibilities of distinctively human forms of wretchedness and joy, of misery and *jouissance*."

This, I would argue, is what Hasselhoff, Rostropovich, and Bernstein produce and "redistribute" as *objet a*. It is, I think, the unconscious aim of their performances, over and above any semiotic mastering of "freedom," or the curation of the "right music" for the moment. It is instead the need to produce and coordinate what an empty "freedom" cannot contain and what a music saturated with signifiers can itself only index or trigger: the enjoyment of the people as an excess fleshy vibrancy.

There's a certain pathos in reading this process through the schema of the master's discourse. What is being officially celebrated is, after all, the disintegration of a certain kind of master: socialism, as no less than (what many in the West regarded as) the last rotten remains of the sovereign's second body, its charisma now utterly disenchanted. But what these musical performances tear down on one register, they prop up on another. Sovereignty migrates from the king's body to the people's discourse. There it continues, with the help of music, to generate a charisma that can neither be destroyed nor sacrificed, but only transposed—an obscene (capitalist?) reallocation of surplus, if not quite a (socialist?) redistribution of wealth.[20]

If there is something axiomatic in this reallocation of the master's charisma, it would seem to correspond to the axiomatic nature of unconscious fantasy itself, as something "[not] to be proven or demonstrated per se, but . . . which generates all of the [field's] allowable statements."[21] Calling these performances fantasies suggests that they occlude any other possibility than the one in which their subjects are subjects of desire: entrained to a Real object, an object constitutively rather than empirically lost, and that paradoxically returns *through* being lost, as the sustained desire of the subject itself. The strange plenitude of desire substitutes for the plenitude endlessly promised by the non-appearing object.

But as Lacan puts it, the object itself is not the support of desire; only fantasy is the support of desire. The object must be coordinated, or, more precisely, given a dual coordination, which is what these performances do. On the one hand, they allow their subjects to determine their own place and the place of the other, by saying "I know what the Other wants, and I can provide it." Žižek opens his provocative if problematic essay on Schumann by imagining music "at its most elementary" as an "act of supplication: a call to a figure of the big Other (beloved Lady, King, God . . .) to respond, not as the symbolic big Other, but in the real of his or her being (breaking his own rules by showing mercy; conferring her contingent love on us . . .)."[22] There is something of this gesture at work here. These performances are obliging gifts to the Other, "acts of supplication" intended to provoke the Real Other to respond—a very different kind of *Darbietungsmusik* or "presentation music."[23] The performer does not present to the audience; rather, everyone becomes a performer. The actual audience disintegrates such that a "Real audience" can emerge, its chimeric inconsistency masked by a potentially infinite series of dispersed and concentrated big Others: "the people," "Beethoven," "Germany," "Europe," "History," et cetera. And in the process, fantasy performs its various inversions, its "reading awry" of whatever else the situation might have been. These performances actually do become revolutionary fantasies—but, as mentioned above, in a Copernican, pre-1789 sense. They become utopian—but in the mode of the quest-romance as Northrop Frye defined it: "the search of the libido or desiring self for a fulfillment that will deliver it from the anxieties of reality but will still contain that reality."[24] And they become liberation scenes. But hardly emancipatory ones: turning confrontationally toward the immediate future, their performers are nonetheless sprung into the deep past. They fly toward the present propelled by a spirit of impending restoration, bringing a fantasmatic past with them. Taken together, they are Benjamin's angels of history, their vector and function completely flipped around.[25]

On the other hand, these performances protect the subject. Their coordination of subject and Other preempts (or at least tries to preempt) any conscious recognition that "there is no Other of the Other," that *jouissance* is ultimately real—unlocatable, resistant to meaning, and radically disruptive to subjectivity, which is to say, properly traumatic. All semblances of immersion to the contrary, these performances are on the side of distance, however minimal; they provide "windows on the real," ways not of *being* immersed, but of *seeing oneself as* immersed. In this sense they are primarily visual events, not because they're so visually inventive or spectacular (they are far outdone by other proximate events), but because they tend toward the screen—the screen on which Hasselhoff plays back the VCR tape of "that whole night" for himself; the screens in the homes of French viewers of Antenne 2; the outdoor screens projecting Beethoven in the Breitscheidplatz; the screen of my laptop as I view all these events on YouTube. In the spirit of Lacan's definition of the signifier—that which represents the subject for another signifier—one could argue that the unconscious aim of these three performances was to screen their historical moment, to show it and hide it at once. Not to mediate it, to bring it to people, but to mediatize it, to register it within a symbolic order of like-representations, and to address it to that order—to make it "speak" not to speakers but to other representations. These performances were letters that could not but arrive at their destination, because their destination was an order of letters in which they were already instantaneously inscribed: the order of "1989," a phantasm covering over whatever that year was, or might have been.[26]

. . .

In his provocative essay on pop music in and around 1989, Joshua Clover argues that the historical moment's defining sound and sonic labor is inseparable from its Debordian "spectacularization." As a process, it "makes a fine bid" to collapse the distance between the actual political events and the "image-events" that enact their capture and expression. Clover sees in moments around 1989 "some sort of completion" of an ongoing process, whereby "history is now itself pop, and pop, history."[27] But this collapse is antithetical to anything like an avant-garde collapse of art into life. It is not a traumatic intrusion, a transgression, a breaking open. It's a screening over and screening out of what Fredric Jameson (with Lacan in mind) called "the Real of History."[28] Clover is a cannily agnostic theorist, refusing to get pulled into arguments about pop's greatness, even less its momentousness. He is the dyspeptic doppelgänger of all those giddy journalistic speculators, and certainly doesn't share Paul Berman's wide-eyed affirmation of all those empowered classical musician-politicians. He is instead deeply unsettled by the relationship between pop and history, and by the fantasmatic logic of what he calls pop's ensuing belle epoque, its "attempt to know itself *as* excess, as a superfluity which exceeds every container, which is liberation and infinitude, a cataract in the face of which meaningful action is impossible; an excess whose dark double is a world without actual events, without direction, without change."[29]

Though Clover doesn't engage Lacan much, he essentially argues for pop as the fantasy material par excellence, and indeed as a kind of master's discourse. To the subject's nagging "why," it offers up a charismatic "because I said so." This is pop's oldest move, as Clover quickly concedes; pop has always been the handmaiden of instant charismatic timelessness, the quick fixing of transcendence. What is new is, on the one hand, pop's pretensions: the videos screening the tanks, the protests and chisels, the world leaders, the ecstatic/bewildered confessions that (as the band Jesus Jones put it) "I was alive and I waited for this." And, on the other hand, the coincidence of these pretensions with a moment of what Carl Schmitt called "neutralization": "the foreclosure of an epochal contention that leaves behind a political and intellectual field, initially devoid of a primary, structuring antagonism."[30] Jesus Jones's "Right Here, Right Now," Scorpions' "Winds of Change," Billy Joel's "We Didn't Start the Fire," Roxette's "Listen to Your Heart": they all operate as S_2, as the agglutinating aids in "this effacement of narrative coordinates and conceptual distinctions."[31] They project for the subject "a coherent unified world that suppresses the fundamental contradictions and discontinuities that are always fissuring actual conditions." Pop history becomes "the disappearance of the edit, the cut. And this too bears an ideological payload, one that arrives even before the more expressly political messages. It is the spectacularization of coherence itself."[32]

Hasselhoff is nowhere in Clover's book, though he certainly supports its thesis; too much stunt, perhaps, and too little representation on the American charts. Clover doesn't mention Bernstein or Rostropovich, either, which seems reasonable enough. But their performances provide the beginnings of a strong corollary argument that 1989 is a watershed moment in the pop-ification of that historically inspired, multinational, and now largely corporatized industry called "classical music." This is essentially the argument Marius Carboni makes (entirely from a marketing standpoint) in a book on the significance of 1989 for the "classical music business." It was the year of Nigel Kennedy's breakthrough recording of Antonio Vivaldi's *Four Seasons* and Luciano Pavarotti's rendition of "Nessun dorma," which would become the unofficial television anthem of the FIFA World Cup the following year—also the beginning of the Three Tenors franchise.[33] (This is to say nothing of the classical-ization of pop, its own mortification into anthemic state statuary and always-already-advertisement.)[34] In each of these performances there emerges an inverse relation between the spectacle of eventfulness, the carnival of inauguration, and the "world without actual events" to follow. Which is another way of saying that, on the other end of Rostropovich's bow, Bernstein's baton, and Hasselhoff's microphone stands Francis Fukuyama's vision of "the end of history as such . . . the universalization of Western liberal democracy as the final form of human government."[35]

Fukuyama's famous/notorious thesis has been endlessly resaid, mis-said, and unsaid since its first publication in June 1989; by the early 2000s it seemed as if History had taped a "KICK ME" sign on Fukuyama's back, but already a decade later the thesis is finding footing again—a new and spectral (after)life?—in a drove of reassessments, some by Fukuyama himself.[36] Along with Clover, I'm far less interested in debating the claim's validity than in taking it as a symptom of its moment, something that might appear deluded in later contexts, but which maintains a strange integrity on its own, perfectly true and indisputable "in itself." It could be argued as a wonkier, more hubristic, but not fundamentally different operation than what Hasselhoff, Rostropovich, and Bernstein are doing: screening out and over the antagonisms and contingencies of the present; hegemonizing "freedom" (here qualified as "Western liberal democracy") and suturing it to a specific set of signifiers; fantasizing a situation of absolute, transcendental plenitude, "the disappearance of the edit, the cut . . . the spectacularization of coherence itself." The most important link comes not in Fukuyama's marquee headliner, which was always more stunned in its triumphalism than its attackers seem to remember, but in his essay's purgatorial close:

> The end of history will be a very sad time. The struggle for recognition, the willingness to risk one's life for a purely abstract goal, the worldwide ideological struggle that called forth daring, courage, imagination, and idealism, will be replaced by economic calculation, the endless solving of technical problems, environmental concerns, and the satisfaction of sophisticated consumer demands. In the post-historical period there will be neither art nor philosophy, just the perpetual caretaking of the museum of human history. I can feel in myself, and see in others around me, a powerful nostalgia for the time when history existed. Such nostalgia, in fact, will continue to fuel competition and conflict even in the post-historical world for some time to come. Even though I recognize its inevitability, I have the most ambivalent feelings for the civilization that has been created in Europe since 1945, with its north Atlantic and Asian offshoots. Perhaps this very prospect of centuries of boredom at the end of history will serve to get history started once again.[37]

The tearful, bangless-whimper pose hardly tempers Fukuyama's arrogance.[38] But it's not quite a pose, either. It is, from a fantasmatic perspective, not merely the end of the essay but its very axiom. It suggests an inverted reading of the essay's first and last pages. The official announcement of "the triumph of the West, of the Western *idea*" instead becomes a Hitchcockian MacGuffin of epic magnitude, its purpose to initiate a series of elaborate convolutions leading to a conclusion whose apparently accidental nature—note the aura of afterthought—was the goal all along, a kind of foregone conclusion: in this case, the unbeatable kick of an eonic melancholy, which is after all a kind of enjoyment. To imagine History as Fukuyama's *objet a* suggests that it was hardly done with for Fukuyama himself, but all too Real. So much so that that it needed a special kind of window to keep it at bay: the museum vitrine, in which the exhibited object's cracks and gaps invert into positive features in a spectacle of exemplary coherence. There are other, necessary ways to read the essay, obviously. But it seems important to shine a strong light on its thesis as an axiom of enjoyment, and as such, an enjoyment of what it does not have. It too must coordinate at all costs an ineliminable *jouissance*, itself the by-product of the equally ineliminable "empty place" of democracy that its author intends to hold up for all eternity. In the vacuum created by this "freedom," melancholy is no matter of loss. Affectively, it becomes fullness, a wealth of life. It might as well be joy. A few months later it will be, as the sound of Beethoven, Bach, and an improbable, invisible gospel chorus singing the words "I've been looking for freedom, still it can't be found."

PART TWO

NEW

6

FREIHEITSDRECK (1)

Frankfurt, September 6, the Alte Oper. A concert of "revolutionary works," three world premieres commissioned expressly to commemorate the two hundredth anniversary of the French Revolution. The second work on the program, by the Korean émigré composer and former political prisoner Isang Yun, is a *Kammersinfonie* dedicated to "the victims of freedom." The third, Rolf Riehm's *Les Chants de la Revolution sont des Chants de l'Amour*, maintains in its vast, complex program note that "the theme 'revolution' is a giant production site for generating rifts [*Entfernungen*]," and that his piece aims to "bring this to expression." But currently we are listening to the first work, *Befreiung* (Liberation), a "concert scene for speaker and ensemble" by the composer, dramaturg, and experimental rock musician Heiner Goebbels. We're about three minutes in. An amplified ensemble is playing sharp, syncopated pizzicati, winds are doubling a restless walking bass, a brush-struck drum kit is interjecting spasmodically. The unevenly perforated texture is filled in by the tinny, strangely menacing sounds of a sampler, its processed, backward-rendered *crescendi* emitting something between a chord and a fluorescent groan. Next to the conductor stands Christoph Anders, the front man for Goebbel's avant-rock band Cassiber. Rigid before the mic, he declaims a text by the young German writer Rainald Goetz with a combination of pitiless precision and splenetic disdain. The music, a grubbier, more dyspeptic reenactment of interwar cabaret, suddenly turns violent; a poor man's *Wozzeck* barges into *Dreigroschenoper.* Angular brass crunch out expressionist broken chords as an amplified, heavily distorted, vibrato-less violin enters, scraping out apoplectic over-bowed arpeggios; the drums and sampler engage in meter-canceling cross-rhythms. Over the whole paroxysm, Anders changes character. Full of an enigmatic disgust, he hollers at the top of his lungs:

EXAMPLE 2. Heiner Goebbels, *Befreiung* (Dreck!).

EXAMPLE 3. Paweł Szymański, *A Kaleidoscope for M. C. E.* (ending). © Copyright 1989 Chester Music Limited. All Rights Reserved. International Copyright Secured.

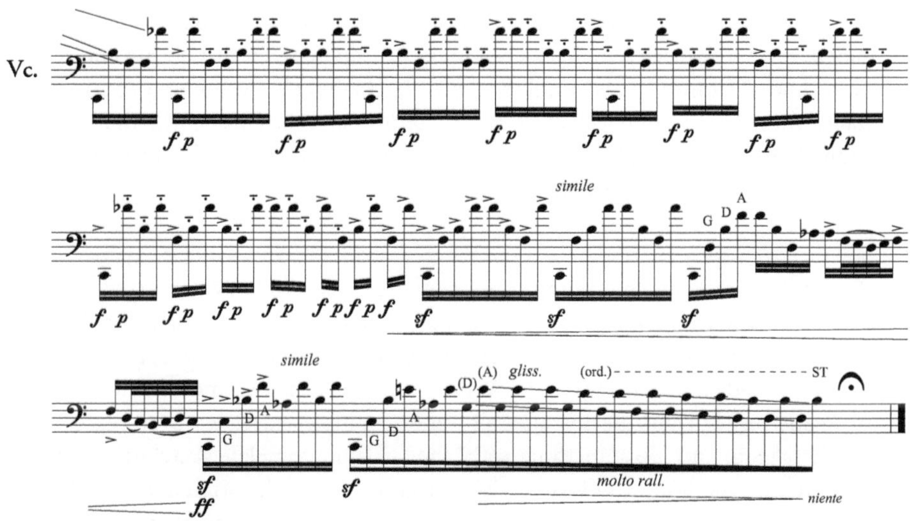

Nothing but *Dreck!*
Liberation!
The worst *Dreck!*
Liberation-*Dreck!*
Dreck!
All of it *Dreck!*
The whole lot, *Dreck!*

• • •

Wrocław, Poland, late December.[1] The cellist Ivan Monighetti, one of Rostropovich's last students and a champion of New Music, is struggling mightily to complete the world premiere of a fiendishly difficult new score by the Polish composer Paweł Szymański. The work is called *A Kaleidoscope for M. C. E.* ("E." being for "Escher"), and presents the performer with a ten-minute *moto perpetuo* gauntlet, fast, barless, *pesante e molto marcato sempre.* Gradually over the course of the piece, the music morphs from a kind of bad dream of 1970s pulse minimalism into a demented Bachian *Fortspinnung*, spinning out passages redolent of Bachian figurations, Bachian virtual polyphony, Bachian cadential formulae, and even Bachian rhetorical flourishes. So it's perhaps appropriate enough that the score ends its marathon with a dominant pedal on the low C string and a widely spaced, fully diminished seventh chord above, fervidly fanned out among the cello's four strings, and capped with a blustery scalar run. The entire passage is an almost exact conflation of the end of the fugue from Bach's first sonata for unaccompanied violin and the end of the prelude from Bach's fifth cello suite. But rather than arrive at a solid cadence in F, the piece remains locked in oscillation between suspension and seventh chord over the C pedal, until the score directs the cellist essentially to give up: *molto rallentando, decrescendo al niente, ordinario* to *sul tasto.* All the while, Monighetti is directed to execute a gradual downward glissando into absolute silence under a beatific fermata.

. . .

Amsterdam, June 14, an evening concert by the Concertgebouw Orkest, directed by Nikolaus Harnoncourt, as part of the annual Holland Festival. After a brisk and bright performance of Franz Schubert's *Overture im italiensichen Stile*, D590, Harnoncourt leads the orchestra in the world premiere of the two-movement version of *Rendering*, Luciano Berio's attempt—after multiple entreaties over years—to finally take up and "do something with" the far-from-complete sketches to Schubert's tenth symphony. In his notes, Berio claims to treat the original materials in a way analogous to modern fresco restoration practices, aiming at "reviving the old colors without, however, trying to disguise the damage that time has caused, often leaving inevitable empty patches in the compositions." Berio adds: "In the empty spaces between one sketch and the next, I have composed a kind of connective tissue constantly different and changing, always *pianissimo* and 'distant.'"[2] The result is something that sounds remarkably like a first draft of a Schubert symphony from around the end of the third decade of the nineteenth century: a statuesque dotted opening in bare octaves, followed by bustling strings in running sixteenth notes, propulsive, arching wind lines, sturdy brass chorales hairpinning in and out of a nestled background *piano.* But then, after just about two minutes, the sound of a celesta appears, and announces a sudden clouding of texture and harmony. The direction over the score reads *Molto lontano* (very distant), and while the running sixteenth notes continue in the strings, they are now surrounded by high violin harmonics and oboe unison *tremoli*, and loosen into multiple phrase lengths. The Schubertian soundscape gradually neutralizes into something at once inexpressive and equivocal—contemporary but paradoxically remote. Distinct solo figurations pop out of the haze, quietly self-automate, and tickle the memory: snatches of the vocal lines to "Gute Nacht," "Wasserflut," "Die Post," and "Der Leiermann" from *Die Winterreise* of 1827; themes from the B-flat Major Piano Trio and B-flat Major Piano Sonata, both from 1828, the latter written directly before Schubert began work on the symphony sketches. The running sixteenth notes in the strings soon quicken into soft *tremoli* and then trills, as do the proliferating figures in winds and brass. Everything eventually stills into a single cluster, trilling

EXAMPLE 4. Luciano Berio-Franz Schubert, *Rendering*/I ("musical cement," first episode) (© 1989 by Universal Edition A. G., Wien/UE 19311).

around F sharp, held by a long fermata, "yet more distant." Then, as the trill holds, a dissonant, extremely quiet brass-and-string chord. A long pause. A second chord for strings, in F-sharp minor. Another long pause. And finally the running sixteenth notes return, the strings crescendo, and both are met by rolling timpani and triple-stops in A major: "Schubert" is "back." Harnoncourt's appearance contributes to the festival's theme that year; two days later, another great pioneer of historically informed performance, Frans Brüggen, will enact yet another toggle between canonic masterwork and uncanny return in a concert entitled "Bach & 'Bach,'" leading his Orchestra of the Eighteenth Century and the Schönberg Ensemble in a concert of Bach and Igor Stravinsky. Berio, for his part, is not happy with Harnoncourt's performance.[3] The Concertgebouw was too good, too invested; they played Berio's "connective tissue" as if it really *was* Schubert; they made it sing.[4] Disappointed, Berio will take the score from Harnoncourt's hands and revise it the following year, adding a third movement and changing the performance directions from *Molto lontano* to *Molto lontano, non cantare!*—"don't sing!"

• • •

A rock-band front man, backed by an amplified ensemble commissioned to perform a piece about revolution, shouts into a microphone about freedom. A solo cellist heroically negotiates a Bachian polyphonic web. A composer, not without a certain chutzpah, doctors a symphony from a great master of Biedermeier Vienna. But not Beethoven—Schubert. And not quite Schubert, but unfinished Schubert. And not *that* unfinished Schubert, but another, irreparably unfinished Schubert. It would seem in these three moments that we have an initial answer—a retort, really—to an idiot question: when the Berlin Wall was falling down, and Bernstein wanted to inaugurate this patch of breathless present by staging a liberation scene with a piece of music, why didn't he choose a piece *from* the present, a new piece by a living composer? Why, when Rostropovich sat down at Checkpoint Charlie to perform his Freedom Scene, did he play Bach and not a new work? Or, to take the most seemingly absurd case: Why, when Hasselhoff pseudo-serenaded his thousands at the Brandenburg Gate, would the very idea of a piece by a living composer of New Music have been so utterly unthinkable?

The more robust form of this question: Was there at this moment something about the mode of production, the form of labor, the form of enjoyment, the greater ideological commitment of contemporary composition, such that the arena in which History performed itself publicly could not permit, better yet admit, its appearance? It's not like there wasn't enough of it. The internet databases for contemporary composition, which continued to spring up through the new millennium's first decade, make clearer every year how robust a field of productive labor it was and is. (As of this writing, for instance, IRCAM's Brahms Database documents information for more than six hundred world premieres from 1989, while national databases such as Austria's MICA turn up thousands of works for that nation alone.)[5] And, at least on paper, the world of contemporary composition would seem to check out with the brand of theater put on by Bernstein, Rostropovich, Hasselhoff. They wanted to stage liberation scenes; contemporary composition often fancies itself staging liberation scenes. They wanted to inaugurate the present with a sound-centered performance ritual; contemporary composition often claims to inaugurate the present with a sound-centered performance ritual. They wanted to draw a crowd; contemporary composition—well . . .

But as different as they each are, Goebbels's *Befreiung*, Szymański's *Kaleidoscope*, and Berio's *Rendering* all perform something of an about-face, almost a Situationist *détournement*, on precisely the fantasies enacted later that same year—a hijacking of the same materials, similar situations and signifiers, and a leading of them astray and into hazardous territory.[6] For Goebbels, Szymański, and Berio, no catastrophic breaches in meaning seem to get shored up, nothing arrives that will "deliver [the desiring self] from the anxieties of reality [while still containing] that reality."[7] *Nicht diese Töne.* Here, "freedom" is terror, a kind of inscrutable curse hurled in contempt at the audience. Here "Bach" is not held up as the integral Father restored to power, but staged as a kind of twittering machine constructed to self-destruct, propped up to fall down. Here a classical symphonic master's blessing is not summoned, but renounced. His message is declared unreceived, his rag-and-bone shop meticulously exhibited for all to hear.

But not necessarily to see: there is no filmic record of the premiere of *Rendering*, no concert footage captured and later packaged by Deutsche Grammophon. So far as I can tell, no TV crew came to the Alte Oper to document, better yet narrate for home viewers, *Befreiung*'s presumably irritating premiere. And any video of Monighetti's efforts in the first performance of *A Kaleidoscope for M. C. E.*, however heroic, has yet to show up on YouTube or anywhere else. Photos are hard to come by; testimonies and reviews are far and few; information on the internet, even on publishers' websites, is obscure and sometimes simply wrong. These are hardly forgotten events, it is recorded *that* they happened; there they stand in this or that registry. But their texture is elusive, semblances of their fullness missing. It's not clear if they *did* anything, if they "mattered," if they could be used to tell some grand tale, even a tale of the end of tales. They might even seem the antithesis of Joshua Clover's "image-events": little non-spectacularizations of incoherence that take place in a scene, a schedule, a system, whose raison d'être is to provide a relatively safe and reliable space for both their type of incoherence and their brand of non-spectacularization—business as usual. Here is neither History nor its End, but something aloof from either, and that might come under the proper name—a bit paradoxical in these contexts—"New Music."

7

MUSIC & NEW MUSIC (1)

The theory of modernity is little more than a projection of the trope itself.

—FREDRIC JAMESON, *A SINGULAR MODERNITY*[1]

But wait—*is* this "New Music"? To paraphrase the ethnomusicologist Philip Bohlman, "New Music" may be what we think it is; and it may not be.[2] Certainly it is not a reliable phrase. Unlike "contemporary music," "contemporary classical," or "contemporary Western art music," it comes preemptively subjectivized. It holds a claim, a desire, and is a bit tormented and shifty-eyed about it. Some attribute its original objects to the hypersensitive synaptic pathways of fin-de-siècle Viennese *Nervenkünstler*, and even if it's not true, it works: "New Music" is *nervous*. Starting with its orthography: why this anxious "N" and "M"?[3]

Read them sociologically, ethnographically, anthropologically, and you have one kind of answer, a very effective one, at work in more recent ethnomusicological endeavors but also in continental philosophy.[4] New Music testifies to a series of material conditions and the behaviors they afford and produce, leading to a series of specialized communities and a specialized form of "composerly" labor, a mode of musical production operating on a global scale but with roots deep in the European classical tradition.[5] Anyone involved in a conservatory or music department has an intuitive conception of the structure of this mode of production already, but it's still worth articulating in quick, explicit, materialist terms. It might be visualized as a Venn diagram whose seven circles comprise 1) agents who call themselves composers; 2) some sort of specialized training, often but not always at universities and conservatories, and following some kind of apprentice or studio model; 3) direct engagement (from unreflective adherence to ostentatious antagonism) with the concept of the musical work, often involving the creation of textual objects (anything from traditionally notated scores to written words to Max/MSP patches);

4) their delivery to a distinct body of often highly trained laborers for realization (occasionally including the composer in a different role); 5) engagement with Western classical instruments, frequently in provocative dialogue with technologies from other traditions and practices, or technologies that don't yet have a tradition or standardized use; 6) a substantial reliance on the economic model of the external commission (from performers, but more often from institutions such as the state, corporation, foundation, or festival); and finally, 7) the presentation of these scores in concert venues in which the works of the Western classical canon are also often presented, to an audience with a living memory of such works.

If this is New Music, then *Rendering*, *A Kaleidoscope for M. C. E.*, and *Befreiung* are, each slightly differently, New Music. But already there's something inadequate about this Venn diagram. It's not merely a matter of ungainliness. One could easily adopt a diagnostic model and require that, say, just four or five of the seven need be included (but which?). And it's also not simply that certain notable, but also more resistant and elusive, "ideologemes" are not included: it is hard to think of New Music without minimal ideological units such as "aesthetic autonomy," or "voice," or "métier," or, in one belated form or another, "genius."[6] But such units remain aloof from the practical considerations above: they are not, strictly speaking, material conditions, practices, or arrangements of bodies in space. Ethnographic and sociological orientations in the last two decades have rightly focused on the more ritualized, indeed theological forces that grip New Music as a series of otherwise provocatively secular institutions, para-institutions, dispersed communities: their belief systems, their inevitable reliance on certain forms of symbolic capital, their own idiosyncratic agons between prestige and independence, cosmopolitanism and identity.[7] It is no news that New Music too is a kind of Beckerian "art world"; that it is sustained by its own forms of distinction, habitus, and "feel for the game," à la Pierre Bourdieu; that in it circulates power, managed—never without some punitive, misrecognized violence—through Foucauldian disciplinary structures, which not only afford but promote and reward certain forms of self-fashioning over others.[8]

If there is also something inadequate in these approaches, it may have to do with what should be an eighth circle in my proposed Venn diagram: a circle that encompasses "none of the above." There is in the phrase "New Music" also a historically embedded naysaying, an anti-metabolic impulse that challenges absorption within even the most distributed, open network of practices and conditions. The commitment to the new would seem to have something to do with it: a revisionary intensity, a pledge, however collectively unconscious and un-predetermined, to interfere in the index or alphabet, the source code, from which "music" reproduces itself. (The lack of a capital "M" here marks the un-anxiousness of the perceived hegemon.) And here one is guided back to another reading of the phrase, at once more banal and more complex: "New Music" as a simple anglicizing of *Neue Musik.* Suddenly a vortex appears.

. . .

I want to take the reader down this vortex; we will move quickly past *Neue Musik* into some older and some newer theories of modernism and modernity, and into my own attempt, via Laclau and Lacan, to theorize precisely the vortex itself—that is, to conceptualize the role that a radical negativity has in the category "New Music," as a modernist music, a modern music, a musical subject split by the signifier "New." I will be building here on the work done in chapters 2 and 4 to theorize a negativity of the Real, a negativity produced by subjectivity and discourse while remaining inaccessible to them, their unrecoverable anterior ground. In returning to this complex of concepts, I will be developing a discursive theory of aesthetic modernism. By this I mean a theory oriented very seriously around the word itself, in the belief that this word alone—especially alone!—has the power to produce its own subjects and social links, to organize material conditions, practices, and bodies. In part I am responding to the last few decades' literature on aesthetic modernism in both music studies and more generally, and specifically to its expansionist aspect. While I hardly intend to counteract this trend, I do think the concept has suffered in the process—not the word, which is as powerful as ever, but the concept. Here I'm in agreement with Ian Buchanan, who has recently reminded us:

> We have become so accustomed to speaking about modernism as though it were a period in history when certain quite definite things took place, or more particularly, when a certain artistic style, or perhaps more strongly, a certain creative mode of production, held sway, that we have forgotten the basic fact that in the first instance "modernism" was and remains nothing more or less than a concept. It is a word that does a certain kind of intellectual work for us. Like all concepts, it is self-positing and self-referential . . . defined by its consistency, what it holds together, rather than what it refers to; in doing so, it unites the relative and the absolute. . . . Its relativity is its pedagogy.[9]

The signifier "modernism" ought to "hold together" ever more disparate historical and material objects, but it also ought to own up to its consistency, to the peculiar power with which it remains capable of enmeshing, indeed fabricating, those objects. As my language here implies, I will eventually come around to the claim that modernism is a kind of fantasy, or, rather, that fantasy provides it an unconscious consistency, one that covers for the failures it invariably encounters in the public sphere, where its struggle to hegemonize the discourse always falls short. This is, however, only one kind of modernism, discursively speaking. In part 3 of this book, I go on to develop another modernism, as a kind of counter-discourse—not a modernism of mastery and fantasy, but of analysis.

But back to the vortex. It has something to do with Germany, of course—with German music and with the German-speaking world's once-hegemonic power over the imagination of twentieth-century Western compositional history. It is a power that especially Anglophone musicology of the last three decades has done wonders to question, and in some cases to neutralize.[10] But it's not simply a matter of focusing on German agents, institutions, and behaviors; open up recent issues of the *Neue Musikzeitung* and you will find unceasing endeavors to chronicle the history of local German centers for New Music. Rather, the phrase *Neue Musik* testifies to an ongoing commitment to an embracing idea, a noumenon, something registrable in what used to be called the "history of ideas" as a persisting extrasensory object, spirit- and belief-like, resistant to any analysis of concrete practices and texts, but which nonetheless organizes a kind of sensible regime: the collection of all *works* of "New Music."[11] Alain Badiou's anti-anthropological conceptualization of the event could apply here; there is in the phrase *Neue Musik* something Pauline and epiphanic, a sedimented insistence on a pre-ontological opening, a new generic set, "a pure beginning, the inaugural or uncountable zero of a new time (a new calendar, a new order of history)."[12]

Such events inevitably give rise to—often exhaustive—reflection and debate on precisely *what counts* after this uncountable zero. Texts such as Paul Bekker's essay "Neue Musik" of 1919 or Theodor Adorno's *Philosophie der neuen Musik* from three decades later assume the status of primary documents. They come to appear in hindsight as concretizations of an otherwise unspecifiable antagonism, ways of polarizing a collapse of poles; Bekker, for instance, espouses a catholic, almost federal unity of peaceable collaborators, while Adorno (more famously) argues for a radical, atomizing, provocative self-isolation.[13] Secondary endeavors, such as the book-length studies by Christoph von Blumröder and Andreas Ballstaedt, restage both these antagonisms and their attempted mediation, on the one hand through a filling out of the historical field, and on the other through a rigorous conceptual analysis of framing terms and historiographical method (i.e., what is "new," what is "modern," what is "avant-garde," and why).[14] Such scholarly projects have a public life, too: witness the months-long series of concerts and talks put on in 2008 and 2009 by Stuttgart's Staatlichen Hochschule für Musik und Darstellende Kunst in cooperation with the Staatsoper Stuttgart. Pointedly titled "Was bleibt? 100 Jahre Neue Musik," the series appeared to have adopted a reflective and critical attitude toward its object of inquiry, asking, "What remains [of New Music]—of the historical memory, of the composers and works, of the centennial claim [*Jahrhunderstanspruch*] and mythos of New Music?"[15] But at the same time that it posed these questions, the series performed a kind of framing, silently preemptive answer. What remains? Arnold Schoenberg's *Second Quartet* (1908) and *Erwartung* (1909), and with them the supposed (Austro-German) break with tonality—*these* remain, the tacit causes of the event itself. They are, quite literally, its

Jahrhunderstanspruch, and must be perpetually re-inaugurated under any of a number of signs, including the festival's (rather rhetorical) question mark.[16] Somewhere between or beyond enchanting Badiouan event and disenchanting Bourdieusian analysis, "New Music" also counts as an empty signifier, a space of constitutive negativity constantly being filled in by (or sutured to) a growing corpus of concrete terms under constant debate. "New Music" remains, after its "first 100 years," a site of hegemonic struggle. With "contemporary music," one haggles over definitions. With "New Music," one enters a field of power and disputes a claim. The former is a matter of exactitude, the latter of fidelity.

. . .

Rendering, *Kaleidoscope*, *Befreiung*: are they *this kind* of New Music? There is certainly an argument to made, but it would seem quickly to beckon a third reading of "New Music": *modernist* music. Not simply *modern*, not the music of modernity, right-now music, in-style music, music à la mode.[17] But rather, as Björn Heile formulated it in the mid-aughts, music as the fruit of a long-enduring series of ethical and aesthetic problems and commitments—a *legacy*.[18] To weave the word "modernism" into the phrase "New Music" widens the field of power and disputation exponentially. This was not necessarily the case in 1989, at least in Anglophone music studies: Susan McClary's polemic on the "terminal prestige of the avant-garde" is arguably the denotative apotheosis of the word, exercising a deep confidence about the exact meaning of "modernism" in relation to music. It was, she argues, a coin of impossibly inflated value: on one side, the insignia of an academicized boys' club pledged to ideals of "autonomy, objectivity, abstraction, artistic liberation from bourgeois constraints, stylistic innovation, and progress"; on the obverse face, marks of an almost "criminal atrocity" toward race, gender, body, cultural responsibility, authentic creativity.[19] There is something admittedly fanciful about the notion that postmodernism was invented in order to provide a clear coordination of modernism, to know exactly what, when, who, where, how it was, its time of death (at which point its age and birthday), what it all really meant.[20] But McClary's article, and subsequent enterprises throughout the 1990s, certainly suggest an anxious need to put modernism in its place at all costs, often allying it with what was most hated—in some cases understandably—about the present.[21] In the midst of its well-needed and long-overdue critiques, musical modernism also precipitated its own object-cause of desire, a kernel of *jouissance* anchoring a fantasizing subject in place: I know who I am, and where I am, through enjoying (hating) you.

Since this moment a great complicating has happened. One scans the last long decade's scholarly work and finds a dogged prying open of the term, historically and aesthetically, to the point that, in the words of Ben Earle, "Recent commentators have been falling over each other in their haste to make more or less any late nineteenth- or twentieth-century music available to receive [the modernism] label."[22] Criticality remains the go-to tool, and here Heile's own assessment of "the dialectical critique advocated by modernism" opens an impressively functional neutral territory. But the term never stays in its Switzerland for long, and once it travels, it invades, executing a vast and sometimes incompatible series of programs that are constructive, affective, and attitudinal. For Daniel Albright, "Modernism" (note the capital M) is still heroic, "a testing of the limits of aesthetic construction," and the Modernist is one who tries "to find the ultimate bounds of certain artistic possibilities."[23] David Metzer, assuming a thoroughly post-heroic mode (and a post-Bekkerian spirit), appraises musical modernism from the other side of the twentieth century as a committed "inquiry" into certain musical "states"—a provocatively incomplete and un-completable project.[24] From an affective perspective, one finds Arved Ashby's ambitious edited volume on *The Pleasure of Modernist Music* identifying it with Lacanian *jouissance*—that is, precisely *not* pleasure, but rather that which the pleasure principle tries so desperately to protect against: an enjoyment of and in the Real, an impossible enjoyment, inductive of "pain and anxiety, even psychosis."[25] "Modernist" names a music that no longer masks anxiety as this or that feeling; the horror it induces is not a generic horror, not the horror of a monster, but rather of what the monster was invented to conceal. (The shower scene in *Psycho* [1960] is, in this sense, a consolation for its own music, a way of at least sourcing otherwise unbearable sounds: don't worry, it's just a knife.) Tamara Levitz, in her remarkable "revisionary account of modernist neoclassicism," identifies modernism with melancholia, with the introjection of the lost object and the "common ground" founded by a collective experience of such introjection. This melancholia actualizes an otherwise merely "stylistic" neoclassicism, turning what might have been heard as a flattening of the historical horizon into its opposite: "a vitalist art haunted by ghosts of the past—and brimming with promise for the future."[26]

Taken on their own, each of these formidable projects compels its reader to *have already known* modernism as a certain aspected negativity, a negativity set to work: it was about testing (Albright), questioning (Metzer), excess (Ashby), loss (Levitz). But I would argue that modernism only emerges as a conceptual consistency in negative form—that is, when all four appraisals are taken together, and subtracted from the power of the signifier that binds them. Something is, it would seem, left over. To some degree, this leftover is the central concern of what I might call musical modernism's scholars of attitude—those who aim to know and articulate not only what modernists did or do, but how they *felt* about what they did. Perhaps nowhere else does the term's elusiveness, its cirriform changeability, become most evident. On the one hand Richard Taruskin sweepingly maintains, in 2004, that the modernist artist's "divided consciousness" necessarily involves "detaching musical tradition from social and ethnic tradition, and regarding it exclusively as a matter of style and technique. . . . The modernist narrative, even though it is at bottom an instrument of social change, has always insisted on representing art as divorced from the social world, subject only to internally motivated stylistic change."[27] On the other hand, Alastair Williams can in the same year maintain that late twentieth-century musical modernism remains detached only in order to reattach: like "exhibits at the Tate, modernist musical artifacts cannot survive without support, yet their institutions can evolve and need not be governed by the curatorial attitudes normally associated with museum culture. Institutions, like music, are embodiments of human ideas and are therefore potentially mobile and subject to interpretation."[28] The two statements hardly contradict each other, and yet are worlds apart. For Taruskin, the modernist social divorce is ultimately Western music's most tragically wrongheaded and ideologically blind move, while for Williams it is essential to preserve its promise, and the humidity-controlled space of the museum is the central means of survival for a "sector of music" that fulfills "a vital aesthetic need" for the larger society of which it is a part-apart.[29]

A decade later, a similar inverse-valencing is still being rehearsed, now only pages apart in a single roundtable on "modernism and its others" in the *Journal of the Royal Musical Association.* Both Peter Franklin and Gianmario Borio emphasize musical modernism's criticality toward both its past and present, but the filling in of this criticality engenders very different attitudes. For Franklin, the musical modernist is still at heart a romantic, a distant member of Florestan's Band of David fighting against the Philistines, still trying "to escape from the vexing platitudes and embarrassing rhetoric of connoisseurship being loudly faked and broadcast by the bourgeois 'social' concert-goers who surrounded them," still laboring "to preserve, unsullied by the ill-chosen explanatory words of others, their profound sympathetic understanding of the tautologically ineffable 'depth' of [among others] Beethoven's music, which they sought thus to rescue from the audience that plainly and all too enthusiastically supported and funded its performance."[30] Borio preserves the dialectical armature of Franklin's points, but (not surprisingly) chooses entirely different colors and figures: not Schumann, and not the bruised and desperate fraternity of the *Davidsbund*, but rather the sober analytical appraisals of Enlightenment modernity and *Jetztzeit* by Jürgen Habermas, Adorno, and Albrecht Wellmer. For Borio, musical modernism is characterized most forcefully by a thoroughly modern self-reflectivity, its

> pursuit of the "new" . . . not an abstract principle with ideological nuances but one component of "time consciousness"; it is expressed in the historical distance that transpires in enquiries into the compositional techniques of earlier periods (undertaken by generations of composers), as well as in the theorizing with which the composer defines the issues he/she is faced with and above all in the creation of sound forms which stimulate new communicative dynamics. These sound forms character-

ize the *Jetztzeit* not simply for their novelty content but also as the expression of the general subjectivity captured at a given moment.[31]

Borio's musical modernist, like Williams's, escapes only to return, and is as helplessly committed to communication as to any kind of intervention in its protocols. Disdainful hauteur or dutiful reflexivity? Seditious incivility or civic-minded preservation? Transgression or inquiry? Melancholy or *jouissance*? In each case, a Real negativity must be aspected, valenced, given texture. In such a way, almost as if by a kind of dull magic, does modernism's recalcitrant "nothing" emerge as a positivity, a way of changing everything while saying "more or less" the same thing.

In the years that this terminological chiaroscuro is unfolding, a larger humanistic endeavor is afoot. And though there is only intermittent truck between music studies and what other disciplines are reassessing and reinventing under modernism, I think music studies can be seen as struggling with the same problem, and engaging in the same *kind* of endeavor. It is an endeavor in reprogramming, in finding ways to recode the signifier "modernism" after the old programs have, in one way or another, failed. In this context, the robust expansionist program of the "New Modernist Studies," beginning in the late 1990s, is indicative: expand horizontally! (transnational modernisms), expand vertically! (low modernisms, popular modernisms), expand temporally! (early modern modernisms, millennial modernisms).[32] By the beginning of the new millennium's second decade, volumes such as *The Oxford Handbook of Global Modernisms* and *The Cambridge Companion to Modernist Cultures* reveal such a program as thoroughly established. The program is positive in orientation—not in the sense of celebration and triumphalism, but of providing the signifier "modernism" with vastly more *stuff*—more world, more objects, more reach. A modernism that shouts a Penelopean "yes" ("I said yes I will yes"), in the process inverting the old Greenbergian asceticisms in favor of a conceptual consistency "attuned to all the vibrations of universal life: an art capable both of matching the accelerated rhythms of industry, society and urban life, and of giving infinite resonance to the most ordinary minutes of everyday life."[33] Each age remakes the periods it emerges from, goes the cliché, but it only makes sense to revise the modernist imaginary in the direction of the present—a *modernized* modernism, a modernism that looks more like a global, synoptic, digitally humanist "now."[34]

One anchor of this expansionist program in modernist studies is diaspora. It emerges in part from Raymond Williams's pathbreaking work on modernism in the 1980s, where immigration was a key figure, but it also revivifies in a previously under-thought way Baudelaire's classic formulation of modernity as "the transitory, the fugitive, the contingent."[35] On the forefront of modernist music studies, Brigid Cohen focuses on the figure of the émigré, the cosmopolitan, the refugee, not as an updated "cliché of the solitary Romantic exile," but rather as an actor in whom a "privileged knowledge" and an "extreme personal vulnerability" combine to produce the "need for multivalent community affiliations in the wake of unfathomable, humiliating experiences."[36] Here a Real negativity is valenced not as identity, but as "energetic exchange," formative of "multiple community affiliations—nearby and afar—[that serve] as lifelines through which many displaced artists [secure] a sense of identity and vocation in the midst of extreme life disruption."[37]

In this process, however, another, more venerable anchor remains: the new (not coincidentally the prow of the ship of New Modernist Studies). Modernism's heroic age is no longer taken for one's own, of course; Ezra Pound's "Make it new" and Harold Rosenberg's *The Tradition of the New* read not as calls but brackets, occasions for pause and reflection.[38] The *sensus communis* is that "new" is not, and never was, a program, and certainly not a solution, a path forward, but more a kind of paving—steamroller, not road. Moreover, as the literary historian Michael Levenson points out, the "agon of modernism was not a collision between novelty and tradition but a contest of novelties, a struggle to define the trajectory of the new"—a gaggle of steamrollers attacking each other.[39] The philosopher of art Peter Osborne, like many before him, emphasizes the sleight of hand in the very word, the fact that "new" as an object of speech deftly veils a temporal non-object. In his words, modernism "in its most general form" is "a collective affirmation of the modern, as such: an *affirmation of temporal negation*, an affirmation of the time-determination of the new. In its basic sense, modernism in art involves the application of this performative temporal logic of negation to the field of art: the project of the production of the qualitatively new in art or, more precisely, the production of an art appropriate to the qualitative novelty of the historical present itself."[40]

If "new" isn't what it used to be, it's because it isn't ever quite what it is. "New" is always an anamorphic "no," a "now" read awry, the warping of the insubstantial into dissembled *res extensa*. Angle it right and it becomes a vow, a suture, the bridging "commitment" Matei Călinescu wrote of when he famously called modernism "a conscious commitment to modernity, whose normative character is thus openly recognized."[41] But "new," after a century's booms and busts, remains modernism's standard discursive currency, even if that century's turn also entails a disenchanted awareness of its weakness, as precisely the weakness of any currency: to waver between content-less sign-for-something and useless sign-for-nothing, between the required mark of value and the most reliable mark of absolute contingency.

. . .

Even as the expansionism of the New Modernist Studies is developing steam (so modern!), a series of millennial aubades to modernism effect something like a contraction. Not necessarily a conservative one, appealing to some older set of signifiers for the modernist, but rather a general resistance to a valencing and filling in of the signifier's negativity. In books and articles by such authors as Fredric Jameson, T. J. Clark, and Susan Stanford Friedman, one finds a tenacious refocusing on the "no" behind the "new," on modernism as a mark of—sometimes for, sometimes against, always with—absolute contingency, something vertiginous, antagonistic, Real.[42] A 2001 quasi-manifesto by Friedman portrays modernism as, ultimately, a Žižekian collapse of polarities in which "each is already in itself its own opposite": "The lifeblood of modernity's chaos is its order. The impulse to order is the product of chaos. Modernism requires tradition to 'make it new.' Tradition comes into being only as it is rebelled against."[43]

In *A Singular Modernity* (2002), Jameson reluctantly admits the new as modernism's enduring master signifier. In his introduction, he even imagines "the quintessential modernist, passionately committed to the eruption of the genuinely, the radically, and, dare one even say it, the authentically New."[44] But already here, a dialectical skepticism creeps in. His example is Jean-François Lyotard, poster partisan of postmodernism. Unlike Levenson or Osborne, Jameson situates the signifier "new" not as modernism's fate, its ur-cause or inevitable effect, but as something discursively achieved, hard won through hegemonic struggle: "In the debates over modernism, a far more abstract notion of change has won out over all its rivals; and the victory was so complete as to render the new account commonplace and virtually self-evident. This is that well-known dynamic called innovation; and it is eternalized in Pound's great dictum 'Make it new': and in the supreme value of the New that seems to preside over any specific or local modernism worth its salt."[45] Here Jameson seems on the side of Laclau and Mouffe, and I'd push this connection further: in essence he appears to be claiming that, like "society," "the new does not exist," or rather, that "new" is an exemplary empty signifier, and the modernist is one who makes him- or herself the subject of this signifier. The work of modernism, its very history, could be seen as a kind of grand discursive battle within all registers of culture to hegemonize "new," to make "new" *seem* like fate, and to argue for the *proper* articulations—necessary, inevitable, exigent—between this empty signifier and (eventually all) other signifiers. This would hence involve repressing, or rendering invisible, the precariousness and contingency of such articulations, the ways in which they fall short of necessity, not just because of faulty connections, but because "new" is itself a perfectly unfulfillable gap, a constitutive failure of concrete designation.

Imagining modernism as such a battle necessarily entails a certain reflexivity. It wouldn't just involve arguments for why any -ism (cubism, futurism, imagism, surrealism, neoclassicism) ought be understood as the "true face," the minimal condition, of the new, or why the new is necessarily a matter of (to take examples from art history) flatness or objecthood or collage. It would also involve a propping up *of* the new as itself the very image of necessity, inevitability, exigency: "new" as modernism's unimpeachable call for "freedom" or "justice for all," and (to go to music now) "dodecaphony" as its concrete cause, its "environment" or "gender" or "economy," a sincere but ultimately arbitrary adequation. Modernism would be that site in which a subject hegemonizes the impossible signifier "new" by linking it to any specific set of aesthetic practices and concepts. Modernism's ideological component would involve efforts, conscious and unconscious, to veil the contingency of any such links and to suggest them instead as adequate to the truth of the new—again, the Aquinian formula *adaequatio rei et intellectus*. There's a curious irony when this formula is applied to aesthetic modernism. While it wages public war on so many regimes of representation, on a discursive register, it sneaks mimesis back into its practice. This hypothetical modernist silently performs fealty to a correspondence theory of truth, laboriously daubing up the canvas of the concept with a thousand little objects, hoping they will dissemble themselves into truth's image—modernist as truth's dutiful court portraitist. In Jameson's perspective, then, "new" is modernism's historical effect but not its conceptual fate. It might have been signified otherwise, because what it opens up, what it initiates on the stage of the aesthetic, is a radical contingency in the signifying operation itself. This is what allows modernism to persist at the heart of postmodernity. Lyotard and Gilles Deleuze are, for all intents and purposes, modernists of millennium's end, their epigones worshipping under a different sign. "The new fetish of Difference continues to overlap the older one of the New, even if the two are not altogether coterminous."[46]

On its own, this isn't a revolutionary reading of modernism, even whose most brisk and vulgar accounts begin with its venerable fractiousness, the tribalism of the -ismic. But Jameson's investigation is remarkably effective at listening for the hollows in the word itself, the ways in which "modernism" remains empty, not simply a field of warring programs but a constitutive void. Or, per Laclau and Mouffe, how modernism is not just the arena for "objective relations," however contentious, but also the site of antagonism, "the limits of all objectivity." This is of course its own venerable counter-tradition: House of Paz rather than House of Rosenberg, "Tradition against Itself" over *Tradition of the New*.[47] Books about nothing.[48] Jameson eventually comes around to Hugo Friedrich's epochal midcentury volume *Die Struktur der modernen Lyrik*, and its oft-cited deduction that, in modernist poetry, "negative categories predominate," and "—and this makes all the difference—these negative categories are definitional, not pejorative."[49] Jameson also rereads Adorno, whose "negative counterproposal" to a program of modernist innovation he finds "far more satisfactory: [Adorno] suggests, indeed, that we should think of the quintessential modern gesture as one of taboo rather than of discovery; or rather, that what look like innovations are, in the modern, the result of a desperate attempt to find substitutes for what has been tabooed."[50] Not Baudelaire's *nouveau*, but his *ennui*; modernism as a getting-nauseous, not a getting-hungry.

$$\uparrow\ \frac{\text{“new” } (S_1)}{\text{modernist } (\$)} \ \ \overset{\longrightarrow}{\Diamond}\ \ \frac{\text{school/style/technique } (S_2)}{?\ (a)}\ \downarrow$$

FIGURE 14. Modernism as a master's discourse (first pass).

Baudelaire is a key figure in Jameson's reflections; he stands for a resistance to modernism's positivities, an awareness that they are emergent patterns, imbrications, not the causing thing-itself. Before anything else takes place—goes Baudelaire's iconic assertion of demiurgic negativity—"[imagination] decomposes all creation." But even Baudelaire cannot stop here; he follows, famously, with a great "and," and delivers up a wildly compensatory program: if imagination decomposes all creation, then, "with the wealth of materials amassed and ordered according to rules whose origins can be found only in the deepest recesses of the soul, it creates a new world, it produces the sensation of something new."[51] Jameson doesn't cite this passage, but it speaks directly to a certain end-of-millennium reading of modernism, haunted by the suspicion that its subject was originally empty, born a ghost—that it spooks itself in the dark, and only then coaxes out stories to lull itself back into dream.[52] In such a reading, Baudelaire's sentence shudders at its conjunction. He writes it not only as a practitioner, but as an ur-critic and theorist of modernism. In doing so he enacts a kind of Damoclean primal scene, one that inquiries into modernism across the disciplines still have not worked through, and to which any future practitioner, critic, or theorist seems destined to return: the scene in which one decides whether the program following Baudelaire's "and" is aesthetic modernism's essential task, or its baldest betrayal, a flinching acquiescence to culture's pitiless refusal to take "no" for an answer—which is to say, its demand for desire, for fantasy.[53]

Laclau and Mouffe's hegemony schema provides one way of formalizing the Baudelairean conjunction: the linking of an empty signifier to all other signifiers, and the concealing of these links' contingencies. The Lacanian discourse of the master—which, as noted in chapter 4, is also a formal expression of the neurotic subject of psychoanalysis—takes this formalization considerably further. The differences aren't drastic at first: the modernist, as the locus of antagonism, can be taken as a kind of $\$$, a subject "sheared" by language. "New," as S_1, does the shearing. Held up by modernism as its first representative, its first master, it constitutes the quilting point of modernism's discursive existence, that which represents it for all other signifiers: "but is it New?" S_2 would designate these other signifiers: modernism's "knowledge," its epistemic life and history. It is not yet clear what *a*, as the precipitate of this process, would be.

There are further burrows in this formula, and they illuminate the history of modernism as a scene of constitutive negativity both discursive and extra-discursive. The upper two figures map the Aquinian truth operation from thing and intellect onto master and slave. "New" demands recognition *from* proper knowledge about it. Knowledge of modernism becomes the reservoir of all attempts to serve the new adequately, to deliver up to it what it "really" is. Out of this impossibility, an ever-increasing profusion of signifiers materializes modernism's notorious history of self-disidentification: the failed hegemony of all schools, styles, groups, appeals; the charisma of incompatible technologies or political causes; the pendulating between its detonations in the town square of the aesthetic and its retreats into absolute interiority. Modernism's pathos becomes the pathos of an enslaved master attempting, as Lacan put it, to *m'être à moi-même*, to be myself *to* myself, but also to be *maître à moi-même*, master *of* my self.[54] No knowledge ever proves adequate to its master, and "new" becomes as impossible a designator of stable content as the purely deictic "now."

$\$$, as discussed in chapter 4, is not simply "already there," lying in wait, but is constituted in the very process of signification. It emerges as the belated cause of these semiotic adventures, that "causal gap" that initiates a process of linking by inserting a cut. This deductive, sonar subject nicely echoes modernism's historical coming-into-being as a disciplinary subject; as Christopher Prendergast reminds us, modernism in its early moments "did not typically name itself as such but was characterized rather by a plurality of terms. . . . The homogenizing label 'modernism' was a later application, retrospectively conferred, partly with a view to imposing a seamlessly linear temporality on an allegedly unified field."[55] Like any subject of language, "modernism" designates something consistently inconsistent, always less unified than the word "new," which it holds up as its first representative. It is, in the schema of the master's discourse, the truth behind or beneath the "new": an (old) desire. And in this sense, modernism-as-$\$$ also returns us to the Baudelairean conjunction, which it clarifies. It suggests modernism as initially negative, and constitutively so. It is less a Mephistophelean "spirit that always negates" than a spirit already partly negated, and which subsequently puts this negativity to work. It is an imagination that not only "decomposes all creation," but that is always already decomposed, and for whom "the sensation of something new" is now a project, a way of maintaining (or promising) a subjectivity as something more than blip-and-ping.

The upper dyad S_1–S_2 articulates in formal terms something endemic to modernism's discursive existence, then, the cultural and semiotic "adventure" to which it is subject. It elucidates not simply the nature of an agon, a "contest of novelties," but also the stakes of that contest: on the one hand to be master, to assume the position of aesthetic hegemon, but also on the other hand how failure becomes not a glitch but a kind of support, something constitutive to the signifying structures in which modernism gets thought, written, and spoken. On the schema's upper register is, as Žižek would have it, the formalization of modernism's symptom, which is therefore open to a "symptomal reading." On this register, one can inter-

$$\uparrow\ \begin{array}{ccc} \text{“new” } (S_1) & \longrightarrow & \text{school/style/technique } (S_2) \\ \hline \text{modernist } (\$) & \lozenge & \text{modernity } (a) \end{array}\ \downarrow$$

FIGURE 15. Modernism as a master's discourse (second pass).

pret and decode things, can bring about "the 'deconstruction' of the spontaneous experience of [the symptom's] meaning" and reveal the contingencies of its construction.[56] But it is the lower half of the schema—$\$ \lozenge a$—that articulates something more elusive: the ideological grip this symptom has on the modernist subject, the way in which the modernist subject "enjoys its symptom," regardless of its meaning. The symptom may be read, taken apart, analyzed. Enjoyment is something else—less a *what* than a *that.*

• • •

What, then, of *a*, the Real object precipitated by the breakdown of S_1 and S_2? I wrote in chapter 4 of its function as a means of partially figuring a Real that never actually appears positively, but merely disrupts all appearances, as a blot, a stain, a warp—something simultaneously too little and too much for the signifier. *a*, as a constitutively rather than empirically lost object, doesn't provide satisfaction but rather causes desire, rendering as the promise of plenitude and wholeness what is otherwise a radical insubstantiality and inconsistency—or, in this context, "the transitory, the fugitive, the contingent." This was, again, not how Baudelaire defined modernism, but modernity itself, that to which the "painter of modern life" must necessarily pledge him- or herself. Taking its cue, I'd like to posit modernity as the fourth term in this schema.

I make this move for two reasons, both of which rely on the famous inconsistency and insubstantiality of the term "modernity" itself—reflexive attributes, permeating equally the term's definitions and the uses to which they have been put. They are both old stories, "modern classics." The story of modernity's inconsistency is the story of a splitting, and also a splitting off. Initially it is the trope of modernity's maddening fickleness, its evaluative duck-rabbiting into *either* a "good modernity" *or* a "bad modernity." Modernity as *pharmakon*, poison and cure at once, the utopia of instrumental rationality and its dystopian consequences.[57] I think here of Marshall Berman, still one of the most eloquent writers on this splitting, and his classic formulation that "to be modern is to find ourselves in an environment that promises us adventure, power, joy, growth, transformation of ourselves and the world—and, at the same time, that threatens to destroy everything we have, everything we know, everything we are."[58] If Berman's assessment becomes a kind of anthem for a decade sick on modernity (*All That Is Solid Melts into Air* first appears in 1982, and again in 1988), it undergoes a strong revision in the 1990s with an emerging attempt to rebrand modernity's inconsistency as multiplicity: modernity as a splitting off. In 1989, for instance, the philosopher Charles Taylor publishes *Sources of the Self: The Making of Modern Identity*,[59] in which he begins formulating a critique of what he will eventually call, in 1995, an "acultural theory" of modernity, whose paradigm case is the various "growth of reason": scientific, secular, instrumental.[60] Over and against this hegemonic Western conception, Taylor proposes a "cultural theory," which soon finds support in an explosion of "alternate," "alternative," "multiple," or "hybrid" modernities, all of which refute modernity as the big Other whose "inexorable march," as Dilip Parameshwar Gaonkar puts it, "will end up making all cultures look alike."[61] Instead, Gaonkar and others insist on the axiom that "modernity always unfolds within a specific culture or civilizational context." It affords everywhere and always the possibility of "creative adaptation," which is "not simply a matter of adjusting the form or recoding the practice to soften the impact of modernity; rather, it points to the manifold ways in which a people question the present. It is the site where a people 'make' themselves modern, as opposed to being 'made' modern by alien and impersonal forces, and where they give themselves an identity and a destiny."[62] While Gaonkar and others are far from giddy at the global effects of modernity, they nonetheless represent a move to resolve modernity's *traumatic* inconsistency—its unending toggle between salvation and doom—through a deft redistribution: "bad modernity" becomes the Western hegemonic "acultural" big Other, from which can take flight *infinitely many potentially good* modernities, all by contrast non-hegemonic and "cultural."[63]

Both this splitting and splitting off testify directly to the trope of modernity-as-insubstantiality. The warming corona around good modernity, bad modernity's leering grimace, the re-saturated sensoria promised by alternate modernities: all constitute effective strategies for giving light and hue (or hue and cry) to a modernity defiant of all concretion, all sense and sensibility. Here Berman again summons the trope most effectively, in the phrase from Karl Marx that gives his book its title. Berman took pains to clarify the line's context in *The Communist Manifesto*: it's not merely an auratic harbinger of transcendence or apocalypse, but a precise diagnosis of a bourgeoisie entrapped inside a cycle of endless technical revolution, the constant death and birth of instruments of production and their relations, ensuring an "uninterrupted disturbance of all social conditions [and] everlasting uncertainty and agitation." In such a situation, "all fixed, fast-frozen relations, with their train of ancient and venerable prejudices and opinions, are swept away, all new-formed ones become antiquated before they can ossify. All that is solid melts into air, all that is holy is profaned, and man is at last compelled to face with sober senses his real conditions of life, and his relations with his kind."[64] Modernity here designates an anti-object, in two senses: not a thing but a force, and a force moreover that liquidates all objects, generating a condition its inhabitants are ironically hard-pressed not to call—"modernity." At the same time, such a story finds its doppelgänger in arguably modernity's most canonical definition, itself built on negativity: "the belief," as the sociologist Peter Wagner puts it, "in the freedom of the human being—natural and inalienable, as many philosophers presumed—and in the human capacity to reason, combined with the intelligibility of the world, that is, its amenability to human reason."[65]

Jameson is more skeptical, noting that at any given point, modernity's founding moment is always somewhere else: in the Protestant Reformation of René Descartes's *Cogito*; in the conquest of the Americas or the French or Bolshevik Revolutions; in the Enlightenment or Galileo or Adam Smith; in Kant or Nietzsche or Freud or Weber; even in Lyotard or Deleuze.[66] Jameson's provocative synopsis—"some fourteen proposals," by his count—explodes what is already there in the coupling of liquidated object and liberated subject: a thing-less modernity, or rather modernity as an un-thinging, the voiding of preexisting objects under the pressure of a future always yet to arrive. *Extensa* without *res*.[67] "Progress" becomes one way of "objecting" this void and making it desirable; "freedom" becomes another. But—given that desire can easily turn into a kind of sublime agony—so too does the Schillerian-Weberian "disenchantment of the world," its own voids encaged in iron. "The trope of modernity bears a libidinal charge," Jameson writes as if describing the *objet a* itself. "It is the operator of a unique kind of intellectual excitement not normally associated with other forms of conceptuality."[68]

In the end, Jameson takes modernity to be almost synonymous with trope itself: a turning away, an otherwising, a "rewriting operation," all of whose attempts at positive identification (self-consciousness, reflexivity, et cetera) are "mere pretexts for the rewriting operation" itself. The very word "modernity" becomes a Kantian transcendental illusion, some *thing* that appears where there should be nothing.[69] Here we are, uncannily, at the core of what Žižek considered the hegemonic intellectual debate at the moment of publication of *The Sublime Object of Ideology*: the Habermas-Foucault debate, which in the early aughts still flourished under slightly different terms. The insubstantiality of Habermas's incomplete and un-completable modernity, practiced by rational transparent subjects in a public sphere, butts heads against Michel Foucault's inconsistency of endless "creative adaptations," by which subjects self-fashion their irreducibly specific substantialities.[70] Here we are, too, back at the same splitting that characterizes the dual trajectories of modernism studies in the new millennium, which arguably rehearse the same fork in the road as the discourse on modernity did a decade or more earlier: to toggle between an inconsistent multiplicity good, bad, or alternate, and an insubstantial negativity constantly re-staking its claim as the "break" that ends any historical moment and begins another.[71]

And here we are again, at Žižek's attempted intervention in *The Sublime Object of Ideology*, which turns out to be not so different from Jameson's a long decade later: namely, an attempt to argue that modernity, as a terminological plea for a kind of universal condition, be considered not some primordial "essence," an essential consistency or substantiality one embraces, denounces, refashions, or flees. Rather, modernity could instead be taken as a kind of radical "nothing" that grounds and engenders potentially infinite subject positions, infinite ways of relating the void in the subject to the self-occluding void of the "real object." This may have something to do with Jameson's special aversion to the notion of *multiple* modernities. The "singular" his title posits (he never overtly explains it) is not, as Žižek puts it, "the encompassing container of the particular content, the peaceful medium-background of the conflict of particularities." It is instead "the site of an unbearable antagonism, self-contradiction, and (the multitude of) its particular species are ultimately nothing but so many attempts to obfuscate/reconcile/master this antagonism." Modernity, in the singular or universal, "names the site of a Problem-Deadlock, of a burning Question, and the Particulars are the attempted but failed Answers to this Problem."[72]

In this sense, the most minimal formulation of modernity—"the break"—is already too Particular, already too much of an Answer, a way of putting in its place an un-placeable Real object. With the vital aid of the right modifiers, "break" cannot resist becoming the most basic fantasmatic armature of any future modernist program: a break *from* "the past," "tradition," "convention," "belief," "morals," "history"; a break *into* "freedom," "the future," "the self," "reason," "history," ad infinitum. In *Farewell to an Idea*, Clark fashions one of the more disenchanted definitions of modernity in recent memory: "'Modernity' means contingency," he writes, comparing the "blindness of modernity . . . to which modernism is a response" with "the hiddenness of the 'hidden hand'; or rather, the visibility of that hiddenness—the availability to individual consciousness of more and more 'information' (a ludicrous, lobotomizing barrage of same) pointing to the purposelessness of social action."[73] But such disenchantment, which seems to spare nothing in its "disabusal" (one of Clark's favored terms) of all positive definitions, still holds on to something. "Contingency" and "blindness" here let off some numinous air; "information" is almost purple with pathos; this "modernity" is nothing if not libidinous. Paradoxically so: it is the *signifier* of what neutralizes all fantasy and desire, but it is also, for Clark's modernists, and arguably for Clark himself, the *object* of desire. To write it, or say it, is to experience a kind of enjoyment.

. . .

I return to the Lacanian schema, and to the formula "modernist ◊ modernity," the modernist as the fantasizing subject of modernity as a Real object. In the remaining chapters, I will continue developing its consequences, but a few observations seem important to clarify in the final pages of this chapter. The first involves stressing how, in this formula, "modernity" ought not be taken as a piece of actuality, the neutral designator of a historical period or condition—modernity as "the world we live in," or the world we have left behind—but as a psychoanalytic object in the Lacanian sense: the impossible, constitutively missing object that supports a fantasy *of* the world. Saying that modernism fantasizes modernity also means that modernism is, quite literally, a "modern subject." But only insofar as such a modern subject is understood as the subject of a certain desire. Modernity is the *name* of that desire, and it is a desire to do nothing less than *make modernity appear.* This entails, simultaneously, that modernism would be an enjoyment of a modernity it does not and cannot "have"—an enjoyment of precisely modernity's failure to appear. Here modernity becomes a kind of eternal parapraxis, an act "whose explicit goal is [never] attained."[74]

This proposition entails four corollaries, which could be thought in pairs. The first concerns impossibility and subjectivity: if the modernist fantasizes modernity, this also means that impossibility plays a structural, constitutive role. But this impossibility, far from jeopardizing the modernist subject, gives it a peculiarly robust form. The second pair of corollaries concern the multiple and the singular. Insofar as modernity is conceived as a Real object, a cause of desire, the subjectivities it gives rise to—the modalities through which the non-existent can *appear*—are infinite and non-totalizable. This would be one way of theorizing the famous-notorious inconsistencies of modernism; all modernisms are "alternate." But this is only because their cause of desire is a "singular modernity"—singular here as the antithesis of essential: neither a substance (say, the quiddities of any given cultural practice), nor a prohibition that conceals a substance (i.e., the arcane knowledge of the "modern expert"), but an "impossible" with no alternate or alternative. These two pairs of corollaries can be understood to fit together into a kind of perpetual cycle: an impossibility that engenders subjectivity, a multiplicity engendered by a singularity that is "impossible."

This impossibility, as discussed above, comes out of the way fantasy positions the subject. It is an impossibility that paradoxically strengthens and undergirds the subject, rendering the object's not-having and not-getting, and the corresponding lack of satisfaction, as a kind of interval, a screen onto which the subject's own lack can project itself. Through desire, the subject itself becomes a kind of anamorph, a void angled into a semblance of the ongoing, the unending, the substantial, perhaps even the transcendent. From this perspective, Arthur Rimbaud's famous formula—"Il faut être absolument moderne!"—need neither be supported as possible nor dismissed as impossible, but understood as a way of making impossibility both *desirable and enjoyable*—a cunning failure.[75] (Along these lines, Bruno Latour's proclamation that "we have never been modern" becomes the support for why and how "we are nonetheless modernist.")[76]

To some degree, this cunning is behind modernism's problems with time, and particularly its obsession with the periodicity of the modern. Fantasy is precisely what unfurls “break” into “era” or “age,” what renders each a screen onto which an extensible image of the subject can be projected. The projection provides both subject and object a place they wouldn’t otherwise have. Modernism, in coordinating the modernity perpetually beyond its grasp, comes to know where it stands. And this dual coordination becomes a kind of defense against what is real in modernity. “Break” becomes a window on the libidinous plenitude of history from which the modernist departs. “Period” becomes a way of veiling modernity’s constant catastrophic breaking.

The multiplicities of modernism are to some degree its most established story, vying for prominence only with an older, more threadbare tale of modernism’s commitment to abstraction, to formalism, to autonomy. These two sets of tropes would seem to grind dissonantly against each other as they unscrew in opposite directions, the former toward an inclusive everything, the latter toward an ascetic nothing—a desire for “belonging and serviceability” versus a “disdain for the world,” as Clark puts it, or, for Raymond Williams, a “Futurist affirmation” versus a “pessimistic recoil.”[77] (At every stage of anything called modernism by one or another actor in the discourse, this dynamic has been in play; it is an incessant problem.) I would argue that the radical variability of modernism’s *appearances* is a necessary precipitate of its fantasmatic relationship to something radically non-appearing: the break to which it proclaims fidelity.

To formulate modernism as a desire to make modernity appear would entail an attempt to make modernity’s radical invisibility reveal itself; to represent through aesthesis its “anti-aesthetic” resistance to representation; to render the hiddenness of its hidden hand, the visibility of its hiddenness; to render this visible hiddenness as such, or as altogether something else.[78] The quixotic challenge of picturing the blindness of modernity—or sounding its deafness—is certainly related to those archetypal modernist strategies, their “deep and ruthless materialism,” their “absorption in the logic of form.”[79] But these strategies can also be understood, paradoxically, as fundamentally mimetic in nature. They are tacit confessions that “real” abstraction doesn’t exist. Or rather: abstraction becomes only one among countless strategies (including various hyperrealisms) at the adequation of not-thing and intellect, the production and staging for the senses of the break that modernity is ceaselessly fantasized to be. A useful model, given the formula of the master’s discourse, would be Oedipus standing before the Sphinx. But modernity, as the trope of re-writing itself, rewrites this scene, too: imagine a silent, imploring Sphinx (modernity) who has no answers to enriddle, and an anxious, desirous Oedipus (modernism) who veils through fantasy the unconscious knowledge that his own answers are pure fabrications, founding statements rather than found solutions.[80]

Imagining modernity as an answerless Sphinx is one way of hypothesizing its status as singular. It doesn’t conceal any positive truth that, as soon as it appears, inevitably prompts alternatives. Such a positive truth would count as a kind of "knowledge which knows itself," a knowledge in the symbolic, the regime of all substitutables, everything iterable, reiterable, and thus alterable. Instead, a singular modernity, as the anchoring other of modernism's endless fantasies, would operate in the negative: a Real that never stops "not writing itself," a nothing "always and in every case in its place," without substitute, unprovable, beyond all predicates, but nonetheless *effective*.

• • •

What would it mean to call modernism's fantasizing of modernity *unconscious*? Am I claiming that the modernist is someone who doesn't know he or she desires modernity? This hardly seems plausible. Isn't the modernist precisely the figure who dares to call out modernity by its name, who openly proclaims fidelity to it and often demands that we do so, too? The modernist as modernity's street-corner evangelist, its hocker, its "hectorer" (another of Clark's favored terms). But I wouldn't suggest that modernity itself—as anything positive—constitutes modernism's unconscious knowledge, a "knowledge which does not know itself." Instead, I'd argue that the formula "modernist ◊ modernity" designates that the impossibility of modernity, its status as a Real object of desire, provides modernism with its unconscious axiom.

It's here that the Lacanian schema of the master's discourse is at its most salient. S_1 and S_2 could be said to enact the register of modernism's "consciousness": its discursive life, its adventures in the symbolic, its endless ostentatious attempts to *prove itself*, in the sense of seeking recognition or achievement in the eyes of Modernity-as-big-Other; but also in the sense of deduction and demonstration, from the most seductively polemical rhetoric to the most scientific (or scientistic) displays of controlled experimentation, research, testing. Here, again, would be the register of what modernism *shows*, of what is readable in modernism—its ego, its symptoms, its semiosphere, as Yuri Lotman might have put it.[81] But all these self-presentations, each predicated on the possibility of failure and the threat of loss—egos are there to be bruised, symptoms are often first readable by others—are supported by a unconscious fundamental fantasy that is axiomatic. Which is to say: assured of failure and certain of loss. It is this assurance and certainty of impossibility that provides modernism its enjoyment, an enjoyment it cannot sacrifice without also sacrificing its very subjectivity. This suggests a revision of Călinescu's aforementioned formulation that modernism is "a conscious commitment to modernity, whose normative character is thus openly recognized." Modernism could also be conceived as an *unconscious* commitment to modernity, whose impossible character, now repressed, is thus secretly enjoyed.

8

FANTASY & FANTASY (3)

At this point, my preceding formalisms are heuristic, and still terrifically abstract. It will be my charge, as the remainder of the book unfolds, to bring them to bear directly on some specific situations, people, texts, and events, and to put them to some tests, or at least bring them to some trials. Even, at points, to fantasize their fullness, to put some flesh on them. But the ludic fumbling with schemata seems a necessary first step. After a half century of putting modernism in its place, declaring death and obsolescence or resurrection of part or whole in flesh or spirit (Lazarus as model, or the ghost of Hamlet's father, or Marx himself), no one is *waiting* for a new theory. Not least because those who dare to put one forward can seem foolhardy, insular, or, worst of all for modernism, restorationist.[1] If anything, those millennial aubades from Jameson and Clark, or Friedman's virtuosic staging of disciplinary bewilderment, might be best understood not as "new" theories but as novel realizations of an old practice: mourning, in this case a mourning—perhaps preemptive or wishful—of a situation of endless purgatorial theorizing.[2] Subsequent projects, particularly as mapped out by the New Modernist Studies, have arguably been far less interested in *a* theory of modernism and modernity than in a remarkable collaborative effort to map the relation between the two terms on a global historical stage. And this often involves knowing already—*having* to know already—what modernism more or less is, was, or could have been—for instance, that "modernism throughout much of the world is the consciousness of what is gained and what is lost when the lifeworld meets the forces of globalization."[3]

I am not so sure. It is a real befuddlement, more than any consolidating pretensions, that prods me to venture a theory—somewhat novel if not New—of musical modernism, and to do so in relation to a field of practices, beliefs, and texts at the epicenter of European culture, precisely the territory from which New Modernist Studies so eagerly departs. Moreover, I want to retain enough of this befuddlement in order to put it to use. Usufruct is not such a bad model here—a use that, initially at least, "serves no purpose whatsoever." Musical modernism may be what we think it is, but—given that the "we" of music studies consistently fails to resemble a big Other on this topic in particular—it may not.

The blessed befuddlement first came to me in the experience of this non-encounter, or "missed encounter," between those three performances by Bernstein, Rostropovich, and Hasselhoff, and what I am suggesting are their "dark doubles," these otherwise unextraordinary—one might even call them minor—works by Luciano Berio, Paweł Szymański, and Heiner Goebbels. That this missed encounter could tell us something about musical modernism might itself befuddle, given that many features of *Rendering*, *Kaleidoscope*, and *Befreiung* would seem to nominate them as poster children for a term I engage skeptically in these pages: postmodernism. The ostentatious bricolage, the intertextual "double-coding," the skewed and partial "return to tradition"; also the insinuations of parabasis, the scrambling of "the composer's voice" and of the metrics of historical near and far. Isn't this all taken straight from the table of contents in the Jencksian (and Jamesonian) textbook music studies has been using for the last few decades, guiding its utilitarian diagnoses of countless cases of "blank parody" and "death of the author"?[4]

Such diagnoses would admittedly prepare these pieces nicely for pacific existence within Jamesonian postmodernity, "an age that has forgotten how to think historically."[5] That is, *Rendering*, *Kaleidoscope*, and *Befreiung*, understood as properly part of the postmodern "plague of fantasies," would constitute eccentric, barely audible side acts in that spectacular "disappearance of the cut, the edit," that screening out and over of historical antagonisms whose main stage was occupied by Hasselhoff, Rostropovich, and Bernstein. Fukuyama would inevitably be the emcee: an announcer of the End of History as the End of Modernity itself, and the Beginning of New Eternity, a new kind of time in which, paradoxically, all other times are included, even *Neuzeit*, provided one cease believing it will lead anywhere. "The Assault of the Present on the Rest of Time," as Alexander Kluge put it.[6] In this epoch, equally blessed and nightmarish, capitalism and liberal democracy would reign over a lifeworld in ceaseless dynamic equilibrium, driven by uncountable "white lies" rather than a few oppressive "tall tales."[7] A world of consensus, continuous, plenitudinous, total. Modernity as break, broken. In its place, what Steven Connor calls "the perpetual present of postmodernism," a present that "is mapped, scheduled, dense with retrospection and forecast. The present (as of old) is all there is, but now it includes all time. There is nothing absent from this present, which makes it curiously spectral. This means in its turn that the present can start to age, to become old before its time. The present of postmodernism has come to seem like a stalled present, an agitated but idle meanwhile."[8] This is, I've argued, precisely what Hasselhoff, Rostropovich, and Bernstein were trying to do, consciously and unconsciously: to show this perpetual present coming into being by putting on a show, by making a spectacle of what Fukuyama, with less pomp and sensuousness but no less fantasy, proposed earlier that same year.

But what befuddles me is thinking that these pieces by Berio, Goebbels, and Szymański are also doing the same thing. They are, it would seem, trying very hard to do exactly the opposite: to make a show of antagonism, discontinuity, gap, void. To stage the break as something that happens within the work, or that might happen once the work has transpired, or—perhaps most importantly—that appears already to have happened, such that the work now has its work cut out for it. Another way to put this, drawing from the schematic play in the previous chapter: *Rendering*, *Kaleidoscope*, and *Befreiung* seem still to believe in modernity, or at least they wish for it and want it to appear, which is to say they act as subjects of a desire *for* modernity. In this they heed, before the fact, the first of Jameson's "four maxims of modernity": they "cannot not periodize."[9] No one has told them that History is over. They seem still in the grip of "a powerful act of dissociation whereby the present seals off its past from itself and expels and ejects it"; to paraphrase Schelling (whose *Ages of the World* Jameson cites in his support), they know what their past is precisely by treating it antagonistically, confronting it from a point of absolute difference.[10] That they cannot keep the past from returning in however broken or inoperative a form seems almost beside the point. The ejecting and expelling is the thing. Here are works in which "the past is created by way of its energetic separation from the present . . . an act without which neither present nor past truly exist, the past not yet fully constituted, the present still a living on within the force field of a past not yet over and done with."[11]

. . .

I make no claims yet about the efficacy of these stagings. Maybe they fail to fail, or execute poorly, and perhaps they do not carry any such conscious intentions to either succeed or fail in the first place. Certainly they are no "match" for the power of the Hoff. Perhaps postmodernism is only the minimal authority or subject-perch—"Hasselhoff's Crane," we might call it—from which to declare anything contrary to its program a delusion or, better, a citation. But I think *Rendering*, *Kaleidoscope*, and *Befreiung* could just as well serve as Connor's own imagined foils for the "perpetual present of postmodernism": subjects, or at least fantasists, of "modernism's present," which—note the participle—"was undefinable, a vertigo or velocity rather than a habitat. The presentness to which modernism was drawn was a hair-trigger affair, always on the brink of futurity."[12] It's not at all clear yet which present Berio, Goebbels, and Szymański subscribe to here, nor that there isn't a (postmodern?) sleight of hand in Connor's very distinction. The more robust distinction, it seems to me, is between two radically incompatible, but equally reality-building fantasies, one of which is ascendant, the other seriously on the wane: a fantasy of the grand and total suture versus a fantasy of the break. The former, historically, finds its master fantasist in Fukuyama. Following Joshua Clover's compelling pairing of Fukuyama with Jameson, I'm tempted to think of Jameson as a master fantasist of the latter scenario.[13] This would afford the chance to suggest, not so heretically, that one of the great theorists of postmodernism is what I would define as a modernist: one who fantasizes the break in the epoch of its decline.

But my schematic play introduces another significant befuddlement. I paint a picture of two radically incompatible fantasies: one of plenitude and restoration, repairing the break; the other of void and loss, insisting on the break, making it appear again and again. I appeal to a rich critical-theoretical tradition that supports such a picture, with Jameson as one discursive founder and Clover as one of his more visionary recent re-readers. They both narrate a transition—incomplete, overlapping, monstrous—of modernism into postmodernism, a fantasy of modernity-as-break being displaced by a fantasy of end-of-history. Clover's contention that the larger event "1989" means "one antagonism has ended and one has escaped" resonates well with this material. If "Looking for Freedom" seems here to enact the process whereby the antagonism that "produces narrative history [slips] away into the night," Goebbel's *Befreiung* enacts its return as a kind of phantasm, the contemporary aesthetic version of the horror movie monster. The screen imprisons the threat; we are jolted by the rattling and consoled by the bars.[14]

. . .

But something about this picture sits uncomfortably with me. It has something to do with calling the allegedly modernist machinations of Goebbels, Szymański, and Berio *fantasies*. It's not that they aren't; I will eventually come to argue that they are. But to do so here skips a step. A big one. It has to do with the psychoanalytic purview of unconscious fantasy, and, more broadly, with what—if I dare write such a phrase—psychoanalysis was invented to do. If psychoanalysis was from early on a torment for Marxists—equally for those who defended Freud and those who dismissed him—it has something to do with psychoanalysis's almost preposterously modest taking up of Marx's dare to change the world. (All the more outrageous, then, that it did this in the most bourgeois way possible, by asking the revolutionary-to-be to recline and do nothing—an unintentionally vicious parody of the general strike.)[15] Psychoanalysis had pretensions. From its beginnings, it claimed nothing less than the power to change the structure of one's soul—*Seele* was the word Freud often used—through the use of speech. This was not a matter of Freudian and post-Freudian metapsychology, of explaining to the world how psychoanalysis works or is supposed to work, or what the structure of the psyche or subject really is. It was a matter of deep pragmatism, of a new kind of clinic, what Foucault might have called a heterotopia, an "other space," temporally and functionally autonomous, "deviant" and "critical," but utterly tied to the world it breaks from.[16] In this clinical other space something was actually supposed to *happen*. A strange kind of auditor called an analyst was supposed to help a strange kind of speaker called an analysand to allow a postulate phenomenon called the unconscious to realize itself a bit. This unconscious, as a new kind of negativity, would produce certain effects: moments of gap, glitch, and non-meaning; episodes of fantasy, dream, hallucination; a relationship of transference. In sharp contrast to "everyday life," all these effects would no longer be dismissed as nullities, accidents, or embarrassments, but instead foregrounded and contended with.

Psychoanalysis was thus the invention of a new kind of social link, a new discourse, perfectly at odds with the discourse of mastery. It was not to be a discourse of suture and consolidation, but one of scission, un-knotting, de-compounding. As I discussed in chapter 2, Freud made unfailingly and repeatedly clear that "analysis" needed to be taken at its word, its aura of chemistry intact: it should lead to a kind of falling apart, a breakdown, the kind that keeps you *out* of the hospital.[17] In analytic discourse, the subject would no longer conceal its split-ness under the commanding force of master signifiers, but display this split openly and set it to work. In turn, master signifiers would no longer run the show, no longer serve as the agents of the discourse, but instead become its by-products—coughed up by the subject as *disjecta membra*, initially inscrutable, their myriad contingencies gradually placed out in the open. The analyst, meanwhile, would assume the place of agent, but of an un-mastering kind—the role of desire itself: a special kind of impossible, never entirely nameable or placeable, always less than a subject, and at the same time more Real.

In the process, fantasy too would take on a different role. Rather than providing the axiom of the subject's desire, it would gradually undergo a traversal. This traversal wouldn't be a matter of "symptomal reading," of decoding dreams to find out what they really mean, for instance, but of discovering the axioms that determine how one dreams, and what one dreams for—what one has been taught to desire without even knowing it. As Bruce Fink emphasizes, discovering such axioms doesn't really entail *understanding* them, since axioms don't ask to be understood. They don't get pushed around in a network of meaningfulness, and don't take other words' cues and orders; they cue and order.[18] So the very bringing of an axiom to consciousness *is* the central analytic work, since its consciousness is what begins to compromise an axiom's absolute efficacy. It becomes less powerful precisely by becoming more meaningful, more "mean-able." It becomes a way of realizing, without Žižek glaring at us, "to what extent, when we freely choose, our choices are predetermined."[19] Freud himself was (in)famously modest about the therapeutic limits of psychoanalysis from the start—the transformation of "hysterical misery into common unhappiness," as he put it at the end of *Studies in Hysteria*, his late thoughts on the possibility of a "cure" contract yet further from any promise of transcendence.[20] But the premise behind this analytic discourse was a utopian one. Not utopia-as-blueprint, as Russell Jacoby puts it, but utopia-as-iconoclasm: an imaginative, very particular "decomposing of all creation."[21] By temporarily un-mastering the subject, by traversing the subject's most fundamental, axiomatic fantasies, the psychoanalytic clinic proposed a radical negativity with the aim of changing the coordinates of the possible.[22]

• • •

A considerably different picture of these musical events in 1989 emerges if one takes the psychoanalytic clinic into play. The picture materializes first by analogy: instead of positing a contemporary moment charged with two incompatible fantasies, one affirmative and the other negative, let's imagine that *Rendering*, *Kaleidoscope*, and *Befreiung* are not fantasies at all, but clinics—heterotopian "other spaces"—in which certain subjects are temporarily un-mastered and their fundamental fantasies traversed. Their subjects are, respectively, Hasselhoff and Jack White's "Looking for Freedom," Rostropovich's Bach suites, and Bernstein's Beethoven Nine: all complex, composite beings, doubly or triply split. Those subjects' fantasies, as I've tried to argue, are yet more complex: intensely intersubjective, suffused with multiple subject positions, transmedial, coordinated at disparate but often conflated historical moments. These fantasies do not "belong" to their subjects in any simple way, but are part of a cultural fabric or screen—in more Lacanian terms, a semiosphere. This semiosphere is at once contemporary and historical, and capable of gripping any number of subjects. Experienced individually, these are nonetheless collective fantasies, and, in this case, fantasies *of* the collective.

In *Rendering*, *Kaleidoscope*, and *Befreiung*, if we pursue the clinical analogy, it is precisely these fantasies that are being analyzed, destabilized, traversed. *Rendering* becomes a clinic in which the fantasies of Beethoven's Ninth, and of Bernstein's Beethoven, come apart at the seams and cough up their axiomatic master signifier. *Kaleidoscope* becomes the heterotopian space in which a burdensomely patriarchal Bach no longer has to put on the *pater familias* sham, and instead turns to memories of children's toys. *Befreiung* morphs into an unforgiving couch on which "Looking for Freedom" can finally lie down, listen to its own words, and realize what it's actually been saying—that freedom "*can't* be found," not even here at the newly opened Brandenburg Gate. *Dreck!*

9

FREIHEITSDRECK (2)

Michel Foucault unfolded his now-canonical conception of heterotopia in a lecture entitled "Des espaces autres," given to the Circle of Architectural Studies in Paris in March 1967:

> First there are the utopias. Utopias are sites with no real place. They are sites that have a general relation of direct or inverted analogy with the real space of Society. They present society itself in a perfected form, or else society turned upside down, but in any case these utopias are fundamentally unreal spaces.
>
> There are also, probably in every culture, in every civilization, real places—places that do exist and that are formed in the very founding of society—which are something like counter-sites, a kind of effectively enacted utopia in which the real sites, all the other real sites that can be found within the culture, are simultaneously represented, contested, and inverted. Places of this kind are outside of all places, even though it may be possible to indicate their location in reality. Because these places are absolutely different from all the sites that they reflect and speak about, I shall call them, by way of contrast to utopias, heterotopias.[1]

Foucault goes on to give quite a few examples: cemeteries, movie theaters, festivals, prisons, brothels, colonies, a ship at sea. He considers this last example the "heterotopia par excellence," a "floating piece of space, a place without a place, that exists by itself, that is self-enclosed and at the same time is given over to the infinity of the sea."[2] Foucault meanwhile outlines six characteristics of heterotopias: their historical ubiquity and constancy; their functional uniqueness; their conflation of multiple incompatible spaces into one; their temporal autonomy, breaking absolutely with "traditional time"; their often restricted access; and, finally, their inextricable and intimate relation to the remaining space they leave behind.

Heterotopias are not in any simple sense places of escape, consolation, or even emancipation, neither Lands of Cockaigne nor Temporary Autonomous Zones. Rather, they often remain in great tension with the dominant worlds they depart from. They *cleave*, they break and bind at once.

Foucault eventually allowed his lecture's publication in 1984, and since then it has garnered considerable attention, always impending toward what he envisioned as the concept's fulfillment, a "systematic description" and study, a "heterotopology."[3] But the concept is admittedly extremely shifty, inevitably underdeveloped in the lecture's modest length, and its subsequent applications seemingly too hybrid and cross-purposed to cohere into anything like a discipline or subfield.[4] In any case I adopt heterotopia here as another heuristic, a way of suggesting that New Music, as an otherwise extremely heterogeneous field of labor and mode of cultural production, could be considered precisely such an "other space," one in which the more robust and hegemonic cultural fantasies of greater Europe—I would even venture to say its utopias—are analyzed, broken apart and broken down, eventually traversed. And, as a corollary, I'd suggest that these hegemonic fantasies first come to New Music *as* music. That is, it is in the medium, the form and format of (older) music, that these fantasies are made accessible to New Music in the first place. New Music encounters "joyful brotherhood" not primarily as a complex signifier, but insofar as it has a sound, a body, a coordinate in the symbolic order "music" that is, in this case, Beethoven's Ninth. There is initially something disappointingly Weberian about this proposition. It would seem to drag even the most florid and buoyant works of New Music back into an arena where the stolid work of modernity, the "disenchantment of the world," goes ever on, ever more out of the way. Give us something magical, says New Music, and we'll take away its shine.[5]

But here I think of Foucault's very first use of the term *heterotopia*, in his preface to *Les Mots et les choses*; there he identifies the term with literature, and a rather magical literature at that, the stories of Jorge Luis Borges. But after his iconic recounting of his confrontation with Borges's "certain Chinese encyclopaedia," Foucault emphasizes that heterotopias are not counter-sites to *reality* strictly speaking, but to *fantasy*, specifically the fantasies afforded by utopian thinking:

> Utopias afford consolation: although they have no real locality there is nevertheless a fantastic, untroubled region in which they are able to unfold; they open up cities with vast avenues, superbly planted gardens, countries where life is easy, even though the road to them is chimerical. Heterotopias are disturbing, probably because they secretly undermine language, because they make it impossible to name this and that, because they shatter or tangle common names, because they destroy "syntax" in advance, and not only the syntax with which we construct sentences but also that less apparent syntax which causes words and things . . . to "hold together." This is why Utopias permit fables and discourse: they run with the very grain of language and are part of the fundamental dimension of the fabula; heterotopias (such as those to be

> found so often in Borges) desiccate speech, stop words in their tracks, contest the very possibility of grammar at its source; they dissolve our myths and sterilize the lyricism of our sentences.[6]

Given Foucault's complex antagonism toward psychoanalysis, I'm reluctant to ascribe Lacan's direct influence to this passage, but the correspondences to his conception of fantasy and its traversal are uncanny.[7] Especially in their common figuration and logic: utopias, like fantasies, are essentially agents of continuity and consistency, the glue that holds the Other together, that suture words with things and words with other words. They are the grain of language itself, the smoothing of that grain. Heterotopias, like the psychoanalytic clinic, are sites that place pressure, sometimes enormous, on precisely these continuities. In them, consistencies fade, "the world" goes to pieces, smooth ground endlessly reemerges as brittle contingency—a central thesis of *Les Mots et les choses.*

David Harvey points out in *Spaces of Hope* (2000) that heterotopia becomes, paradoxically, a kind of escape for Foucault, a way of alcoving his thinking into concrete, readable, actually existing "other spaces" at precisely that moment in the late 1960s when utopia, as amalgam of good-place and no-place, is threatening to transform from a tool of social and political analysis into a hegemonic fantasy.[8] Something analogous is, I think, at work in mid- to late 1989: a moment of incontestable joy, ecstasy, intense relief, a rush of pain where numbness had been, which the larger culture industry nonetheless can't possibly co-opt fast enough. Emotions thawing, representations reifying. In this context, these works of Goebbels, Szymanski, and Berio provide another kind of paradoxical escape. There is little emotional relief here, but—hypothetically—something else. A freedom from "Freedom," perhaps: an undermining of a certain kind of logic and language, a desiccating of a certain kind of speech, a dissolving of otherwise omnipresent myths.

. . .

Goebbels's own account of the origins of his *Befreiung* speaks directly to this idea. His marvelously nasty shouting spree was the result of a commission from the Frankfurt Alte Oper for the Frankfurter Feste celebrating the bicentennial of the French Revolution. Goebbels "hesitated for a long time because the hackneyed revolutionary vocabulary seemed to render a differentiated historical treatment impossible, particularly at that time (before the end of the GDR, Romania, etc.). Every furniture company appropriated it ('The revolution is Franz!')." He only changed his mind when he "rediscovered the anti-liberal, polemic tirade from Rainald Goetz's dramatic trilogy *Krieg*," a text whose enormous "political tensions" Goebbels refused "to resolve for the audience . . . but [rather] unleash for individual confrontation."[9] (The choice of Goetz was clearly a provocation: the author had risen to fame in the early 1980s for, among other things, his appearance as a finalist for the famous Ingeborg-Bachmann-Preis. During his electrified live-televised reading in front of a staid jury and a restless audience, he proceeded to slit his forehead with a razor blade and bleed all over his typescript. He did not win.)[10] The provocation of simply choosing Goetz was in itself not enough for Goebbels; he also wanted to "oppose [the contemporary] theatrical convention which usually treats Goetz's rhythmic language merely naturalistically, deeming it necessary to give the characters a personality to provide psychological motives for good and evil, where, in fact, this serves only to protect us from establishing this distinction for ourselves."[11] In realizing his aim, Goebbels fused two of Goetz's characters ("Stammheimer" and "Heidegger"—a "Stockhausen" was left aside) into a single narrator who simply switches, without preparation or explanation, back and forth between a shrill strident demagoguery and a chill, affectless stream-of-philosophic-consciousness.

Here it would seem that Goebbels is adamantly opposed to fantasy, especially in the Žižekian sense: a filling out or "backstorying" of what is otherwise confusing, confrontational, and fragmentary, with the aim of rendering it all more coherent. (Žižek gives the example of Ernest Hemingway's aggressively short story "The Killers," which, when rendered into film, provides an expansive, eminently reasonable prequel to justify the protagonist's otherwise inexplicable acceptance of his own assassination.)[12] Goebbels instead treats Goetz's characters in a pointedly artificial way. On the one hand he provides a fulsome set of notes directing in the greatest detail the qualities of voice and tone that the speaker must adopt for each role; on the other, he does not personify these voices, does not attribute motivations, attitudes, or designs to them. They remain "unsourced," acousmatic: voices without characters, loudspeakers behind curtains.[13]

The music accompanying this schizoid speech reads as similarly split. While the score is none too subtle in its techniques, intertextually speaking it is a consummation of a decade's work in that quintessentially acousmatic genre, the German radio play, or *Hörspiel.* By 1989 Goebbels had become a master of the genre. His endeavors—all based on pitilessly analytical texts by the East German playwright Heiner Müller—display a progression, from the almost music-less *Verkommenes Ufer* (Unkept Shores) of 1984 through next year's fervid cut-up *Die Befreiung des Prometheus* (The Liberation of Prometheus), and on to 1989's five-part, seventy-five-minute-long *Wolokolamsker Chaussee* (Wolokolamsk Highway), based on one of Müller's *Lehrstücke* (teaching plays). This last work could be carelessly diagnosed as consummate late-1980s postmodern maximalism à la Kyle Gann; musically it moves without the least resistance from heavy metal to German folk revival to *Männerchor* to hip-hop, using as an *idée fixe* the insidious march from the first movement of Dmitri Shostakovich's Symphony No. 7 ("Leningrad") of 1941, which "occupies" the entire fourth part of *Wolokolamsker Chaussee.*

This promiscuity would seem to have something to do with Müller's "original" text, each of whose five sections treats as skeleton or host body preexisting texts from Kafka, Heinrich von Kleist, Aleksandr Bek, and Anna Seghers.[14] This is the kind of scenario that prompts readers of Müller to ask questions (rhetorical, of course) like, "Has there ever been a playwright more postmodern than Heiner Müller?"[15] But Jonathan Kalb takes pains to emphasize that Müller's approach is far less carnivalesque than clinical: "the point of his borrowing is [generally] to lay bare what he sees as hideous historical processes beneath lyrically beautiful literary surfaces."[16] If Müller "utilize[s] the postmodern indefinite," it is less in a spirit of sublime surrender than as a sharp tool for accessing "multiple meanings anchored at almost all times in specific historical inquiry."[17] The result is "a critique of the source artist's historical existence, not just of particular attitudes, manners, or opinions but of the original art's very basis for communication."[18] Goebbels remains creatively faithful to Müller in his own approach; as Philip Bohlman and Brian Currid lay out in their reading of the *Hörspiel*, he curates his musical choices surgically, and with cunning.[19] No choice is "correct": for instance, rather than setting the first part, which initially treats the Soviet army's retreat from the invading Germans, to the "Leningrad March," Goebbels employs the German speed-metal band Megalomaniax, who tangle awkwardly with Müller's crunchy-prosaic non-rhythms. But the misapplication is effective, perfectly illuminating. It rarely fails to hit on something real in the text, to stalk historical causes and press them where they hurt. The music and text are made to resonate with each other, to unearth something strange but true, while also remaining mutually estranged.[20]

This catechristic approach reaches a new sophistication in *Befreiung*. Part of this involves the performers, Frankfurt's cosmopolitan Ensemble Modern. Their slick and un-stumpable virtuosity was concurrently being deployed in performances of canonical post-serialists such as Franco Donatoni and IRCAM affiliates such as Hugues Dufourt; in *Befreiung* they come up against a very different sound that is crude, deskilled, raw, and synthetic at once. Another central influence is without a doubt Goebbels's prog-noise-avant-rock band Cassiber, still active at the time, and whose front man, Christoph Anders, originally performed *Befreiung*'s speaking role; it's not a stretch to assume it was written for him. At times the score intersects with tracks from Cassiber's album *A Face We All Know*, recorded in late 1988 and mixed a year later. The spasmodic time changes and driving keyboard ostinati, the muddied whole-tone collections, the insistent but cryptic, never-less-than-slightly-disgusted narrator come very close to songs like "Gut."[21]

But the score's archive unfolds backward in time, toward richer and more strategic intertexts. Frank Zappa, by 1989 long in Ensemble Modern's repertoire, constitutes a strain, as do jazz-band noir film scores from the late 1960s and early 1970s (a few passages are dead ringers for David Shire's scoring of the opening credits to *The Taking of Pelham One Two Three* [1974]). But influences cluster around two obvious models for Goebbels, both of them examples of explicitly politicized musical practice: the Sogenanntes Linksradikales Blasorchester (So-Called Left-Radical Wind Orchestra), which he helped found in 1976, and Louis Andriessen's De Volharding

(Perseverance), which served as its precedent. There are moments that call to mind Andriessen's eponymous piece, which gave his group their name, as well as his better-known follow-up, *De Staat.* At the same time, these intertexts all carry within them older source materials from between the two World Wars: 1920s big band on the one hand, and on the other Igor Stravinsky's neoclassicism and the *Neue Sachlichkeit* of Kurt Weill, Paul Hindemith, and Alban Berg (all of which point to Bach). A common link emerges in the *Kampfmusik* of Hanns Eisler and Bertolt Brecht; it haunts the score, and eventually comes to take it over in its penultimate section. The hard-bitten sound and hue of the music to *Kuhle Wampe*, for instance, and the *Solidaritätslied* itself, whose bracing *Vorwärts* reverberates in "Stammheimer's" repeated cries of *Fortschritt!* Eisler was an essential figure for Andriessen in his early conception of a political music, and a few years later he also became central to Goebbels, who would complete a sociology thesis in 1975 titled "The Question of the Progressiveness [*Fortschrittlichkeit*] of Musical Materials: On the Social Context of Compositional Measures in Pre-Classical Era and in Hanns Eisler."[22] (Eisler soon became a staple of the Blasorchester, whose first album, *Hört, Hört*, opens with distant whistled strains of the *Solidaritätslied.*)

But this intricate semiotic network is not allowed to bear any transparent message. The frenetic march that ensues also seems to drag in the world of Carl Stalling's Looney Tunes scores, with farcical depictions of ridiculous mechanisms and Sisyphean industry.[23] And Brecht's steely irony is displaced by Goetz's narrator, whose words quickly begin to eat themselves:

> Progress
> History
> The world in the balance
> Victory
> Dictatorship
> Dictatorship of the proletariat
> Revolution
> Attack
> Attack
> Score (*Partitur*)[24]

"Stammheimer" vanishes; "Heidegger" suddenly reappears. The remarkable formal tension leading up to this moment neither culminates nor dissipates, but simply snaps.[25] The score enters a default coda, a kind of abstruse non-space marked "Letting go." To sampled sounds of heavy iron tubes falling and rolling across a concrete floor—"the acoustic signature of demolition," as Max Nyffeler put it—we hear only the quiet tremolo of the strings and the unraveling thread of spectral keyboard samples. Above them, a calm, un-positionable voice we can hardly identify with, caught in a conceptual bind strangled of circulatory energy:

EXAMPLE 5. Heiner Goebbels, *Befreiung* (“Forschritt”).

The assault is the threat.
War of extermination of today against everything old.
Production of new material.
Thunderous noise.
Raging chaos,
Farthest peak.
Moment.
Our science.
The pure science of assault.
Science of destruction.
Science of extermination.
Now.[26]

In an essay from 1988 entitled “Prince and the Revolution: Über das Neue,” Goebbels writes about “the irritations and scruples which must accompany composing today—especially politically intentioned composing—if one is not, like a nineteenth-century genius, still going to sit in his little room, believing that through *Phantasie* he's capable of expressing what the world spirit [*Geist*] has bottled up in him." Goebbels cites Müller in support—"*Phantasie* is something very negative. People with phantasy are constantly threatened by the adversities of real life"—before directly addressing "composers with *Phantasie*," who "run the particular risk of losing contact with the interfaces of reality [*Schnittstelle*], of losing themselves not simply in private, free-floating thought, but in music that is no longer coupled to the reception structures and attention levels of the listeners, of the time."[27] For Goebbels and Müller, *Phantasie* is probably closer to Freud's "free imagination" than any structural Lacanian notion. But at the same time, it is precisely such *Phantasie* that occlude the antagonisms, the fissures, the *Schnittstelle* of contemporary reality, papering them over with narratives and images of identification, cohesion, and cohesive subjectivity. The *Freiheit* shouted in *Befreiung* is something else altogether. It is not to be trusted, worse yet identified with; it comes from an Other that is enigmatic at best, dangerous at worst, an Other whose antagonism is clear, but whose coordinates are not. Here, then, is one antipode of both Bernstein's customized Schiller and Hasselhoff's secondhand pop. History is not finished here, but stuck, caught in a *Dialektik im Stillstand* that demands discomfort and analysis rather than celebration.[28] And the historical subject, torn between two characters, each of whom spits out streams of foregrounded contradictions, is caught in an aporia—not unlike the "Hamlet-Actor" in Müller's *Hamletmaschine*, whose "place, if my drama ever took place, would be at both sides of the front, between the fronts, over them." Faced with this deadlock, he (perhaps like *Befreiung*'s split subject) chooses automation: "I want to be a machine."[29]

. . .

Molto ritmico (come una macchina) begins Szymański's *A Kaleidoscope for M. C. E.* His note for the premiere begins coyly, his pointed refusal to explicate his work couched as a grade-school object lesson:

> Freely scattered colored pieces of glass in the area of an equilateral triangle, being the base of a prism constructed of three mirrors turned to the inside, when watched from the perspective of the opposite base, they dazzle with its multiplied images—which of us has never surrendered to the magic of this simple toy? . . . What gives sense to the random setting of several meaningless glassy particles? Surely: 1) symmetry, and 2) multiplication. These two features make (always and exclusively) the sense of kaleidoscope and of (not always and exclusively) arts. They definitely don't constitute a sense of life, but—after all—it can be reasonable to suspend discussing this gloomy matter till a few-minute piece is over.[30]

A playful pedantry oscillates here with a kind of scientistic aloofness. Which of us has never surrendered to the magic of this toy? Maybe Szymański himself, who

EXAMPLE 6. Paweł Szymański, *A Kaleidoscope for M. C. E.* (opening). © Copyright 1989 Chester Music Limited. All Rights Reserved. International Copyright Secured.

conceals his own enchantment behind a forensic naming of parts. “Coming back to a kaleidoscope,” Szymański asks, “what happens if at the bottom of it—instead of glass—we place objects semantically detrimental, presenting (for instance, part of an image of a human face), or symbolizing (like a fragment of a sentence in some unknown alphabet or language)?”[31] The phrase “semantically detrimental” is an odd one, but continues to flesh out Szymański’s self-stylization as lab saboteur. Things are being mixed incorrectly, put in positions they shouldn’t occupy, performing operations they weren’t made for: a potentially disastrous experiment, in the service of a plaything. It won’t “come alive,” won’t “constitute a sense of life,” unless, like Frankenstein’s monster, it does.

Despite—or because of—the connection to Bach and baroque figuration, the ensuing work could be crudely described as postminimalist. Its modus operandi is one of gradually assembling and disassembling subtly changing pitch and articulation patterns over a bar-less, unwaveringly fast sixteenth-note grid. Canon, a venerable technique for Szymański, seems to play a role again here, though its effect over the first few minutes is more that of a fugal exposition. And Szymański’s “trick” (as Adrian Thomas calls it) of exchanging “notes or motifs for rests in different places as the canon circulates” helps align the score more directly between Steve Reich’s process pieces of the 1970s (*Drumming* and *Music for 18 Musicians* in particular) and György Ligeti’s “pattern-meccanico” scores of the late 1960s, with a good measure of his *Three Pieces for Two Pianos* from 1976.[32] There are quite a few moments when the piece would fit perfectly within the favored paradigms of the Bang on a Can All-Stars, not yet founded for another three years; *A Kaleidoscope for M. C. E.*'s opening anticipates Michael Gordon's string ensemble piece *Weather* to a T (and by nearly a decade).

In tension with these precedents, however, are Szymański's own revisionist directives and his "source material." Like his other two works from 1989, the orchestral score *A Study of Shade* and the tape piece *Through the Looking Glass II*, *A Kaleidoscope for M. C. E.* depends not merely on a visual metaphor, but on a doubly encoded screen or window: a surface that may simultaneously obscure and open up, veil but also give way. In all three works, some form of *insight* is woven into the work's conceptual metaphor. Something essential is going on in the background, or underneath, while a bewitching, potentially mystifying process of symmetry and multiplication unfolds in the foreground, or up above. The premise is essential to Szymański's work from the late 1970s on, in which he increasingly deploys "some ready musical structure as a basis" for a series of "transformations [that] may have nothing to do with this structure (which I call 'basic structure'). Basic structure may be constructed in one or another way, but we may abstract from it to some extent."[33] Szymański gives the generic examples of single melodies, canons, and so on, but he also cites two works that exerted an especially powerful influence on his approach, Lucas Foss's *Baroque Variations* and Helmut Lachenmann's *Accanto.* (Both works employ preexisting works in their entirety: the complete Mozart Clarinet Concerto for Lachenmann and, among other pieces, the first movement of Bach's E Major Violin Partita for Foss.) Though *A Kaleidescope for M. C. E.* doesn't seem to exploit an actual preexisting score, Foss is nonetheless a clear model. Like his *Phorion* of 1966, *A Kaleidescope for M. C. E.* at least *appears* to adopt wholesale a brilliant Bachian solo string toccata, whose incessant thread of steady sixteenth notes serves as a kind of grid, a historically locatable "basic structure" that can undergo all manner of anachronistic transformation.

In 1984, along with his compatriot composer Stanisław Krupowicz, Szymański dubbed "this kind of polystylistic music 'surconventional music' (musical convention plays the role of reality in this analogy; surrealism is impossible in music because music does not refer to reality)."[34] Szymański is, however, emphatic about this music's relationship to older styles, languages, and processes: this is neither a matter of return-to, nor of lofty critique, but of an intense and sustained intersubjectivity. His approach "doesn't mean that one should compose in the style of Mozart, but it is *possible* to go back to Mozart and find out one's own relative position."[35] Similarly, though Szymański's chosen structures may assume the gestures, ornaments, transitional patterns, affects, and harmonic and melodic progressions of older music, they are not themselves tonal or "neo-tonal." "As far as I am concerned," he writes, "the only reason that I use tonal elements in my music is the fact that until now I have not found a better way to make possible the distinction between the basic structure and its transformations. Therefore the 'new tonality' does not exist in my pieces. There is only the 'old tonality' in its very conventional

EXAMPLE 7. Paweł Szymański, *A Kaleidoscope for M. C. E.* (multiple bowing regions). © Copyright 1989 Chester Music Limited. All Rights Reserved. International Copyright Secured.

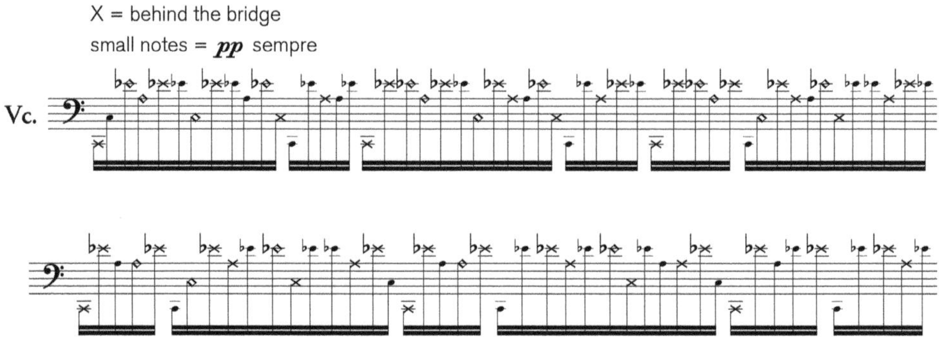

aspects, because it is only a medium and not the purpose. If anyone interpreted my music according to my established principles, he would not call it 'tonal' but 'meta-tonal.'"[36]

So Szymański's slightly creepy note to *A Kaleidoscope for M. C. E.* is entirely appropriate. It testifies openly to a kind of test-tube chemistry, an indeterminate toying with existing "nature" in which the specimen—in this case Papa Bach—is dis-identified with, and forced to undergo processes not necessarily immanent to its own integrity, not *in-*, but rather *sur-* and *meta-*. A neo-Baroque *Fortspinnung* is maintained, but obsessively and at an impossible pace, all the while shackled into an increasingly difficult executive frame as the cellist navigates unpredictable, terrifically hard shifts in dynamic and bow articulation.[37] Simultaneously, a Bachian "virtual polyphony" is promised by the quasi-fugal opening, and always seems about to appear. As the cellist's bow continues its mad biaxial leaps across all four strings and both sides of the bridge, the semblance of some tonal coherence continues to promise itself.

But both these parameters—the propulsive stream of articulations and the evolving pitch relations—undergo ever more intense estrangements until, near the very end of the piece, the music leaves behind the tempered space in order to glissando slowly and indeterminately up and down the fingerboard (echoing the climax of Berio's viola *Sequenza*, with its own fraught line to Bach). The virtual polyphony becomes unsustainable, no more capable of arrival than someone ascending one of Escher's staircases; and "tonality" becomes suspended, colloid-like, in a mixture of estranging intertexts (Reich, Ligeti, Foss) that liquidates its capacities for vector and closure. Or, to return to the work's concept metaphor, it is the kaleidoscope conceit itself, not any fractured contents, that becomes "semantically detrimental." It's only after this that the score produces, in its last seconds, the

EXAMPLE 8. Paweł Szymański, *A Kaleidoscope for M. C. E.* (glissandi). © Copyright 1989 Chester Music Limited. All Rights Reserved. International Copyright Secured.

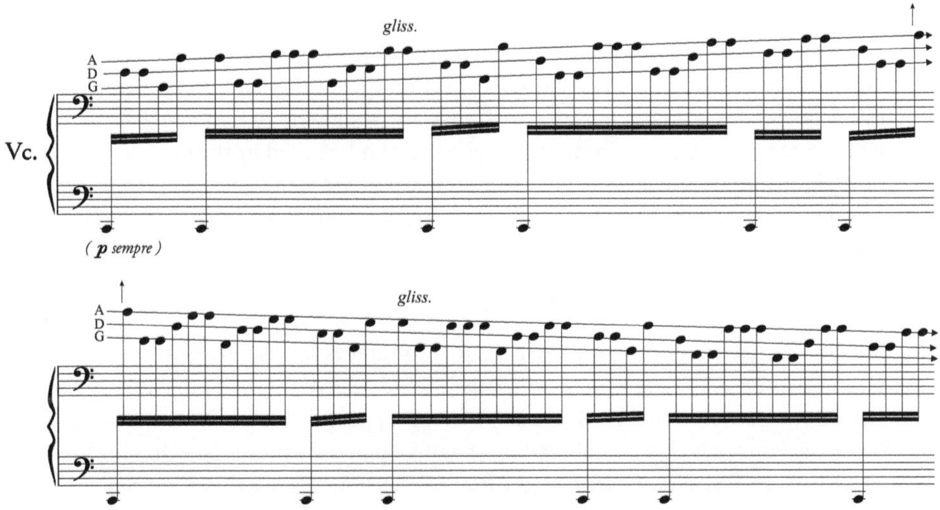

closest thing to an actual quote of Bach. The veil is removed, the meta-polyphony between "basic structure" and its irreducibly aloof manipulations collapses. One finally gets insight into the structure—and it doesn't work.

A Kaleidoscope for M. C. E. is a modestly scaled, poker-faced showpiece. In the context of a contemporary Polish scene already saturated with estranged baroqueiana, it's hardly European New Music's intervention of the year.[38] Rather, it's a particularly deft example of a hybrid style, cross-breeding the processes of pulse-oriented minimalism with the surrealistic inclinations of neoclassicism—Bach updated from sewing machine to early computer, cybernetic cyphering mechanism (and, via Ligeti, a highly problematic mechanism). But composed in earshot of Rostropovich's early-November stunt, it's difficult not to hear Szymański's score as a multiple annulment of Slava's Bach-fantasy. The Father is not only not restored to some kind of full presence, but revealed as constitutionally absent: *come una macchina*, and not a particularly well-assembled one—perhaps something more like the shoddy manual metronome that would have otherwise accompanied a student rehearsal of his music. Here, contra Rostropovich, Bach and the Wall are not so different: one crumbles, the other simply winds down. At the same time, one witnesses in *A Kaleidoscope for M. C. E.* a cunning if unintentional inversion of Rostropovich's conception of the performer. The dual premise of fidelity and servitude is (faithfully) preserved. But in *Kaleidoscope* it is "outsourced," handed over from the priest to the twittering machine. An anti-kenosis: perhaps the "Word of God" is still being delivered to this machine. But the listener will never know, because the machine itself "does not deliver," does not make good on its function.[39]

So far as I can tell, there's no record of Szymański's having witnessed Rostropovich's performance. But this is perfectly beside the point. There is already something deeply fantasmatic, almost Schindlerian, about the hypothetical scene in which Szymański catches Slava on the television and, piqued by the pseudo-magic of it all, promptly unsheathes his twin conceptual arms of "basic structure" and "surconventionalism" in order issue a severe correction.[40] And such a scene is in any case impossible in Goebbels's case, since *Befreiung* was written and premiered months before Hasselhoff's New Year's Eve performance. But Goebbels's score *was* a conscious intervention in a historically specific imaginary, and it was exactly this imaginary that would provide the myriad affordances for the realization of Hasselhoff's stunt. *Befreiung* was, if Goebbels is to be believed, a direct reaction to the "hackneyed revolutionary vocabulary" being appropriated by "every furniture company," and it is this confabulation of agitprop and consumerism that finds its apotheosis in Hasselhoff's extended fist as he belts out a song about looking for a freedom based on becoming a "self-made man" who rejects his father's fortune presumably in order to amass his own.[41] It's in precisely this context that *Befreiung* and "Looking for Freedom" become unconscious agonists in an arena where the meaning of signifiers such as "revolution" and "freedom" are being contested. But it's also here that one locates the difference between a hegemonic struggle and a more psychoanalytic scenario: *Befreiung* and *A Kaleidoscope for M. C. E.* don't appear to provide, or want to provide, an alternative content for an empty signifier currently dominating discourse. They are not strengthening, but rather weakening, the articulations that hold "Bach" or "Freedom" in a positive, semiotically coordinated place. One could even say they are forcing—or have pretensions of forcing—the recognition of "the precarious character of [such a] positivity, of the impossibility of any ultimate suture."[42] Which is to say, they appear to be engaged in a form of ideological critique.

And here, the intertextual complexions of the two works play a significant role. In both cases, an engagement with "Old Music" contradicts a facile diagnosis of pastiche postmodernism. There is little heteroglossian "surrender" to the semiosphere here, little cackling over the ruins of history. This is not Fredric Jameson's "parody without vocation," and hardly a "neutral practice."[43] The engagement is weighted, pointed, one might even say goal directed: "Eisler-Brecht" and "Bach" serve rather as sources of gravity, pulling their respective compositions toward them. The result in both *Befreiung* and *A Kaleidoscope for M. C. E.* is a strangely teleological formal arc. But what ensues is something of an anti-apotheosis: the gravity of the focal intertext pulls the music toward it not as moth toward light, but as sand down a funnel. There is a hole, an occlusion, where the object could or should have been. In this sense the focal intertext functions as a kind of *objet a*: a means of warping the field of activity, a "darning egg," which pushes and pulls the fabric of the music, but which, when sought, remains elusive. "It" is not *it*.

But it is difficult for me to see and hear this negativity as "blank," the creation of "a statue with blind eyeballs," in Jameson's memorable phrase. It is the larger context of the historical moment that creates this difficulty. In *Befreiung*'s case, its chronotopic straddling of both the noisy present—the West Berlin punk and experimental improvisation scenes—and "between the two wars"—the sound and swagger of Brecht and Eisler's own early-1930s agitprop—shines a crucial light on "Looking for Freedom," which comes retrospectively to resemble agitprop's ghastly farcical return—something so inadmissible that it can't get a mention in a book expressly on pop and the fall of the Wall. Presiding over its own "peoples of the world," "Looking for Freedom" becomes the most cynical of *Solidaritätslieder*, imploring them "forward! and [do!] forget." A musical contemporaneity of late 1989 reveals "Eisler-Brecht" as a strange site of contestation over a fantasy's logic and function. Either it finds itself reincarnated in the most ironic way—as recycled pop sung by a TV celebrity imported from the world's Number One Superpower, celebrating the demise of socialism by exhorting its listeners to become "self-made men"—or, in *Befreiung*, it finds itself rendered traumatic, unreliable, aporietic, a torrent of words and noises that will not "protect us from establishing for ourselves" whether what we hear is "good or evil."[44] Similarly, it is the historically coordinated signifier "Bach" that becomes the contested territory over which Rostropovich and Szymański agonize. For Rostropovich, it is a site of fantasy that props up simultaneously a desiring subject and a big Other. For Szymański, "Bach" becomes—along with the corollary fantasy of "the solo performer"—a site of estrangement, liquidation, analysis without synthesis. Desire yields to recognition of the fruitlessness of repetition, and the big Other (as both "Bach" and "tonality") emerges as unavoidably piecemeal and inanimate, a puppet in a bit of elaborate marionette theater.[45]

• • •

Berio's *Rendering* is generally easy on the ears. After all, it sounds for the majority of its 1989 two-movement version like *echt erste Wiener Schule*. But *Rendering* is also both the most explicit and the most complex example of the dynamics at work in *A Kaleidoscope for M. C. E.* and *Befreiung*. It is another heterotopian countertext, intervening in—and occasionally sabotaging—a dominant musical-cultural fantasy that grips a particular historical moment. "Schubert" is of course the moment here, and more specifically "late Schubert," heavy with its own considerable transferential baggage.

The baggage was arguably already brought along by the work's commissioners, the organizers of the Schubertiade Hohenems who approached Berio in late 1986.

Founded by the great baritone and Lieder singer Hermann Prey in 1976, the Schubertiade had by the mid-1980s become the world's most famous Schubert festival; it was also already something of a contradiction. On the one hand, it was an off-site of transplanted cosmopolitan sophistication, connecting the world's most prestigious classical musicians with an expert public willing to traverse significant distances to a tiny mountain town at the westernmost tip of Austria. On the other hand, it was an uncanny reenactment of, if not the actual Schubertiades of old, then the long ensuing tradition of their posthumous, highly sentimentalized recollection, in anecdotes and scenes like Moritz von Schwind's famous 1868 drawing: the scene of fleeing the city for the country, and fleeing as one of Schubert's "inner circle," embraced by a small, elect crowd of aesthetically high-minded friends of nature and song. From this perspective, the Hohenems commission could be seen as the latest and most prestigious in a series of especially rigorous attempts to access "Our Schubert"—by imagining what the composer might have done in order to complete his fragmented sketches for a "last symphony" (D.936a).[46] By the time Hohenems solicited Berio, these sketches had already been circulating through the European scene in at least four instantiations: first, in the form of an "in-the-style-of" completion by the British musicologist Brian Newbould in 1980; then in the East German musicologist and conductor Peter Gülke's 1982 performance version of the fragments; in composer Roland Moser's "fragmentary sound-picture" of the sketches for Schubert's "Andante" from the same year; and finally, in the conductor and composer Pierre Bartholomée's revision of Newbould's score in 1983. (Newbould would publish yet a further revision of his own version in 1985.) The summer of 1986 had seen the world premieres of two of Berio's period-faithful orchestrations of Austro-Germanic greats: Gustav Mahler's early songs and Johannes Brahms's Sonata for Clarinet and Piano, Op. 120, No. 1. Perhaps the Schubertiade's organizers had heard them and eagerly sought more of the same: something like what Newbould or Bartholomée had done, but on a more inspired, and distinctly more prestigious, level.

The score Berio eventually handed them was something quite different. Among other things, it was a refusal, either to "complete" or even "reconstruct" the sketches into an actual symphony. Instead, the score would issue a robust critique of "those operations of philological bureaucracy which sometimes lead musicologists to pretend they are Schubert (if not Beethoven) and 'complete the Symphony as Schubert himself might have done.'"[47] Berio chose rather to "restore" the sketches, setting himself "the target of following those modern restoration criteria" that do not conceal damage, decay, and "empty patches," but seek simply to repair what is already there, "reviving the old colors." At the same time, the score—initially a two-movement version completed in 1988 for Nikolaus Harnoncourt and the Hohenems Festival Orchestra under the title *Opus X*—was also a rebuke to purists such as Hartmut Lück, who felt that such sketches "are not intended for a bourgeois and auratic concert market, or to put it another way: the hubbub of our commercialized philharmonic events destroys these not only uncompleted, but also un-completable works more than it salvages them."[48] *Rendering*—as it was retitled for the 1989 world premiere of a revised version—managed to be something else altogether: less like Berio's recent orchestrations of old masters, and more a poker-faced, stricter, far subtler version of the middle movement of his 1968 *Sinfonia*, in which the scherzo from Mahler's Second Symphony, treated as a kind of *objet trouvé*, fructifies into an endless stream of associations sonic, semiotic, and conceptual.[49] No less than *Sinfonia*, *Rendering* became another of Berio's essays in "the art of commentary," a further assertion of "what I've done my whole life long: to indicate and examine a chosen, pre-given text from different sides. I believe that the realizations of historical facts which one can obtain from literary, poetic, or musical angles of view are unlimited; and I would certainly say that this consciousness is typical for my work method."[50]

The commentary in *Rendering* could be said to occupy three registers. The first is orchestration: Berio generally tries "to safeguard the obvious Schubert color," and in fact manages to (re)vivify Schubert's piano sketches with considerably more finesse and imagination than his predecessors.[51] The resulting score is not only less reliant on formulas copied from Schubert's completed symphonies, but also substantially more polyphonic, and replete with interstitial harmonic shifts and subtler textures not necessarily extant in the sketches, but clearly a result of imaginative inference.[52] The orchestra ceases to behave provisionally, to remain deferentially under-furnished, and emerges as something pliable, dynamic, "alive." So alive, in fact, that it drifts into other composers' orchestrational tendencies: Felix Mendelssohn's symphonic allegros emerge as potentialities in the first movement, and the second movement slips all too easily into the timbral and harmonic hallmarks of Brahms's and Mahler's symphonic slow movements. The result is very much a dialogue, not simply between "Schubert" and "Mahler" (or "Brahms" or "Mendelssohn"), but between Berio's safeguarding hand and his own associative memory. A recollective prowess and a ludic predisposition destabilize a philological endeavor, and render the orchestra something considerably more problematic than a simple meta-instrument, a secure line for the Schubertian transmission. It becomes instead a kind of unreliable narrator, always about to tumble into the uncanny valley.[53]

If Berio all too easily shows his hand as an orchestrator, he is provocatively passive in actually arranging the sketches, and here plays antagonist to the "completists"; this passivity becomes in Berio's hands a second register of commentary. In creating a symphony out of Schubert's materials, Newbould and his followers inevitably confronted a series of leaves that simply fail to make structural sense. In the first of the three movements, for instance, melodies, theme groups, and transitions lead into each other on the page but don't add up to an entire symphonic sonata allegro. If anything, they are defiant, tantalizing perambulations: a clear opening theme group leads to a disintegrating transition; material that appears highly developmental nonetheless produces an entirely new, perfectly Schubertian "wandering" theme, which undergoes extensive elaboration; and, after a page break, material that seems to transition from development to recapitulation instead moves straight into a coda. The completists' inevitable solution is to insert breaks and cuts where there were none, and to override Schubert's own incomplete (and sometimes inscrutable) formal evidence with their own conviction in formal conventions—to twist Schubert's arm while ostensibly playing his hand.

Berio, by contrast, reads the sketches almost like a machine: recalcitrantly, from left to right, top to bottom, recto to verso. This is done to particularly chilly effect in the opening of the second movement "Andante," whose first plangent strains are preceded on the page by a few banal, broken-off exercises, likely assignments from Schubert's lone meeting with the counterpoint teacher Simon Sechter just a few weeks before he died. Berio obeys the texts to the letter, scanning and sounding out each of the three counterpoint exercises before fading into the "Andante" proper. But Berio's scanning of the first movement produces especially confounding results. Parsed out into three larger sequences separated by two passages of "cement-work," the opening "Allegro" comes to sound like three thematically related attempts to write—to start?—the same movement: a kind of choose-your-own-adventure sonata, none of whose scenarios are played out in full. Unlike Newbould and Bartholomée, Berio makes no attempt whatsoever to assemble a recapitulation, or to conceal its lack, and plays out without interference the jarring transition from what *sounds* like the end of the development into the presto coda. The effect is disconcerting: as the bubbling coda twirls around with giddy abandon, one finds oneself scratching one's head. The coda is celebrating an achievement that, technically, has not taken place. Or is it remembering something the listener has forgotten, or that got lost somewhere on the way, in Berio's musical cement work?

This musical cement, the third register of Berio's commentary, is arguably the most discussed aspect of *Rendering*, beginning with the composer's own enchanting description of it as "a kind of connective tissue constantly different and changing, always pianissimo and 'distant,' intermingled with reminiscences of the late Schubert (the *Piano Sonata in B-flat*, the *Piano Trio in B-flat*, etc.) and crossed by polyphonic textures based on fragments of the same sketches. This delicate musical cement, commenting on the discontinuities and gaps between one sketch and another, is always announced by the sound of a celesta."[54] Berio is explicit about how this "connective tissue" works and what it does. But he is tight-lipped about what or how it *means*, and this perhaps explains why his subsequent listeners cannot resist the temptation themselves. A reviewer of the UK premiere hears in these connective passages the vapid friendliness of "a magical weaving together of

EXAMPLE 9. Luciano Berio-Franz Schubert, *Rendering*/II (opening) (© 1989 by Universal Edition A. G., Wien/UE 19311).

* Counterpoint exercises by Franz Schubert, dated Nov. 1828:

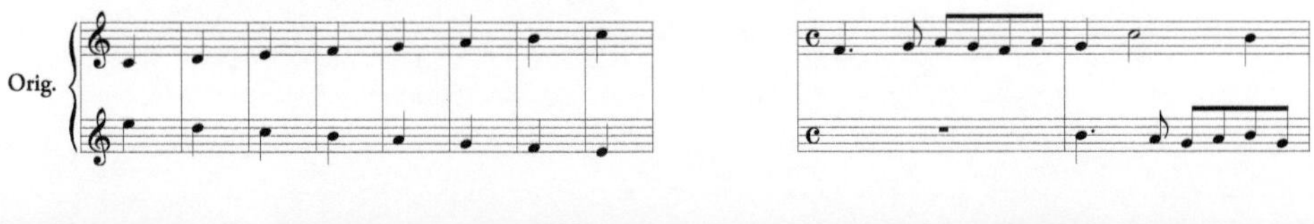

inspiration new and old," while David Osmond-Smith, 180 degrees away, labels them "a Brechtian *volte-face.*"[55] Another early reviewer feels himself "pleasantly lifted into another musical world[,] reminded of Tippett's haunting use of the celesta to mark transitions between natural and supernatural realms in his opera *The Midsummer Marriage*, and of Britten's not dissimilar use in *A Midsummer Night's Dream.*" But Wilfried Gruhn hears a fragmentariness "bemoaning the loss of an imagined image of beauty that can be called forth only in the inner mind, and for which Schubert's music is the ultimate paradigm." David Metzer, one of the most characteristically careful commentators on the work, maintains that Berio's cement is nothing less than the sonic result and representation of extensive processes of damage and decay.[56]

Such divergent hearings might suggest Berio's cement as an audible Rorschach test, engineered to provoke interpretation while itself renouncing any intentional meaning—a test in which every answer is right. But this is not quite the case, as evinced by Berio's response to the very first interpretation of the work, by the conductor Nikolaus Harnoncourt at *Rendering*'s world premiere. Berio was apparently disappointed with Harnoncourt's reading: he had "completely missed the basic idea and let the [Schubert] quotations 'sing,' having them played with vibrato and at far too slow a tempo. In this way they ended up suggesting dreams, interior quotations, a kind of peering in from outside, a 'love-letter' to Schubert."[57]

This litany is quite curious, given that the great majority of quotations Berio stirs into his musical cement come from Schubert's Lieder—mostly from *Winterreise*, but also a few moments from *Schwanengesang*; and the remaining quotations, from contemporaneous solo and chamber works, are unfailingly lyrical, strains born for quotidian humming and whistling. Yet it seems that Berio was interested precisely in the not-lyrical here, in liquidating or disassembling the lyric impulse, and with it the expressive, sympathizable, *vocal* subject, the one whose mental contents and emotional states might speak, and on whom the listener might eavesdrop. After all, this is *cement*, not a confession, and certainly not a symphonic version of those kitschy candlelit scenes of the composer at his desk, awaiting the moment of inspiration.[58] As mentioned in chapter 6, after the premiere, Berio took pains to revise the connective passages, including more directions like *non cantare* and *poco vibrato*, but also excising some of the more foregrounded Schubert quotations, or else adding further estranging elements (rests, timbral distortions, chromatic clusters and trills). The result is a contradictory situation: a gauze of songs that "don't sing," a profusion of earworms voided of their staying power, instead self-smothering into near indiscernibility.[59]

The "Wasserflut" quotation, appearing prominently in both of the first movement's connective episodes, provides a telling example. In Schubert's score, it comes from the piano's right hand in the first two bars of the song: a slow eighth-note triplet, E-B-E, scales an octave, falls back to B for a dotted quarter note,

EXAMPLE 10. Franz Schubert, *Die Winterreise*, D.911, "Auf dem Fluss" (opening).

droops down to a D-sharp eighth note, and repeats. Its shallow-breathed torpor is emphasized by a funereal left-hand tread, always slightly chafing in dotted eighths and sixteenths, and also by the meter: the phrase, in 3/4, nonetheless feels like a 2/4 phrase whose second beat is too long—spent by the effort to achieve the first.[60] The poem's first words speak of hot tears in cold snow, and the piano preamble testifies to an affective "gelid state": water stilling into ice as the chilling of the blood, the hibernation of the emotions. It is a figure quite literally seized by affect.

Berio preserves this right-hand piano figure in his connective tissue, and lets it virtually take over the second, larger episode. But he relieves it of its affective weight; a listless torpor is replaced by weightless proliferation. With unfettered ease, the figure migrates to all ends of the orchestra, played at pitch and rhythm by the lone celesta, or by four solo violins in any of a number of parallel-voiced harmonic clusters; sounded out in seven-voice canons at the minor second, or in alternating choral antiphony between strings and winds; augmented into dotted triplet half notes, or wedged into a solo flute line as an extremely quick series of grace notes before the beat. Its first or last or middle notes are altered chromatically, or turned into trills, or into high *sul ponticello* harmonics, or sutured at any point with bits of other quotations in the mix, whether "Ständchen" or "Gute Nacht," or the third movement of the B-flat Sonata or the first movement of the B-flat Piano Trio—or, toward the very end of the episode, harmonizing with the

EXAMPLE 11. Luciano Berio-Franz Schubert, *Rendering*/I ("Wasserflut" in migration) (© 1989 by Universal Edition A.G., Wien/UE 19311).

Fl.
Ob.
Cl.
Bsn.
Hn.
Tpt.
V.T.
Tbn.
3.
1.
Timp.
Cel.
Vl. I
solo
Vl. II
solo
Va.
sola
Vc.
DB

trumpet as it plays a line from "Einsamkeit": "Through bright, happy life / lonely and without greeting."[61]

In the process, this little figure from "Wasserflut" jettisons its origins in a burdened body, in the leaden hands of a heavy-hearted pianist brooding over a singer's impending words of woe. It enters a space of unfettered mutation where repetition—as the index of rumination and fatigue—becomes replication: body into sign, into a semiosphere seemingly without regulon. In a passage from *If on a Winter's Night a Traveler*, Berio's close friend and collaborator Italo Calvino recalls reading in a book "that the objectivity of thought can be expressed using the verb 'to think' in the impersonal third person: saying not 'I think' but 'it thinks' as we say 'it rains.' . . . Will I ever be able to say, 'Today it writes,' just like 'Today it rains'[?] . . . And for the verb 'to read'? Will we be able to say 'Today it reads' as we say 'Today it rains'?"[62] Such a musing—replete with its own semi-quotations of a century's worth of inquiry into the unconscious—captures something essential about Berio's cement: it is a music apparently without an "I," a music in which "*it* thinks" or "*it* sounds." And what it thinks or sounds in this case is something at odds with the lyric subject, unassimilable by it. In this sense, Berio's cement bears analogy to the Freudian and Lacanian unconscious: a space of constant and unlimited assemblage, ciphering, exemption from mutual contradiction, independence from any "reality principle."[63] And, perhaps most importantly, it is a space of drives—drives that, despite their fragile cacophony, remain silent, unspeaking, unsinging. If there is a subject here, it is a subject without a mouth to sing, what Lacan has called a "headless subject," an agent of untiring repetition and enjoyment.[64] Here the connotative surface of Berio's connective tissue—what it triggers associatively—testifies to something. It is quite logical that the "lyric I," the Schubertian symphonist-as-orator, metamorphoses into a sound closer to that of an orchestra warming up: the clangorous non-sense of the rehearsing multitude, a noise that "says" nothing but is instead a by-product of countless quasi-automatic repetitions, of individuals briefly acting like birds, or wind-up toys.[65] Berio had once called this cement-music a "no-man's-land," and it's perhaps not a coincidence that a similar soundscape forms the basis for his "musical action" from a few years later, *Outis*—"Nobody," Odysseus's alias as he is imprisoned by Polyphemus.

Especially in the context of its 1989 premiere, *Rendering* can be seen as a particularly complex counter-text, and a rather cunning one at that. It constitutes a twin intervention. It is, first and foremost, an intervention in a long-standing Schubert fantasy, a fantasy of "Our Schubert," which renders its object—even among all the Great Masters—an especially intense example of listener-composer transference.[66] In such a fantasy, an alienated "Schubert" is co-constituted along with an "inner circle," whose attention and care both redeem the composer's alienation and prop up the circle's sense of distinction, its status as the "few" identified by Schubert's first biographer, Heinrich Kreissle von Hellborn, when he writes that "Schubert in his totality is only known and appreciated by a few."[67] The phrase "in his totality" is essential: von Hellborn was speaking to the long-standing inaccessibility and ignorance of Schubert's actual music, to the status of especially the later works as "'outside' history and buried within it, the kernel of its eventual revision."[68] Of course, by 1989 virtually all of Schubert's music had been published, much of it recorded, and the late works, some unperformed until decades after Schubert's death, had ascended into the pantheon of masterpieces. But the mythos of Schubert as the quintessentially resurrectable composer, awaiting decades or centuries for his true delivery at the hands of the "few," was very much at work in the enterprise of completing this (third!) "unfinished symphony," and it certainly informed the original Hohenems request that Berio "do 'something' with Schubert." The fruit of this fantasy, *Rendering* also disrupts its operations. Its three registers of commentary all introduce an acute skepticism into the venture, emphasizing the artificiality and precariousness of the project: its potential to "slip" into the voices of other, later composers, its revelation of structural breaches and false or non-trajectories, its descent into nonsense, the babbling of automatic or "primary" processes. One hardly need subscribe to Metzer's claim that *Rendering* stages a process of "decay" in order to detect in it something ruinous, not quite human, zombielike. At the very least, it efficiently corrodes the premise of a Schubertian "lyric I," and with it the fantasy that one might successfully "enter the mind of Schubert" in order to access, predict, and embody once again his own "composer's voice."

In the process, Berio also subtly sabotages the nostalgic component of "Our Schubert," its staging of Schubert's music as an Arcadian emblem, a site of simpler, better, kinder, cleaner, more innocent times—or, as von Schwind recalled to his friend Ferdinand Hiller, the promise that "there could be no happier existence" than the Schubertiades of old.[69] The wispy diaphony of Berio's musical cement, with its anti-psychological image of oblivion, becomes a provocation to leave behind a performance of *Innigkeit*, and confront the social conditions that cursed these fragments to remain incomplete. The conditions, that is, of Schubert's death, the opposite of an Arcadia: a Vienna in serious political, economic, and infrastructural decline, full of distrust, filth, and oppression, where "no one takes in air that was not shortly before in the lungs of someone else."[70] Berio's connective episodes don't quite hold up Brechtian placards announcing that "Here the Master laid down his pen because he died of syphilis." But they inject a forensic chill into the incandescent textures of Berio's expert orchestrations, and are in this sense stark reminders of the merciless material conditions that encroach upon the disembodied, idealized voice being resurrected.

At the same time *Rendering* interferes in the smooth functions of the Schubert Fantasy Industry, it can also be seen—in the European musical landscape of 1989—as the antagonist of Bernstein's Beethoven. A far more radical act of editorial interference, Berio's score is its obscene doppelgänger. Both works stage an untenable

EXAMPLE 12. Luciano Berio-Franz Schubert, *Rendering*/II ("rallentando a poco a poco e morendo") (© 1989 by Universal Edition A. G., Wien/UE 19311).

symphonic form, the unfolding of a symphony fated to encounter a fundamental structural impasse, its symptom, so to speak. The Ninth's impasse famously produces a parabasis, the engendering of a vocal subject that transgresses the boundaries of the symphony in order to address directly the audience—"O friends! Not these sounds! / But let us strike up more pleasant sounds and more joyful!" *Rendering*'s impasses engender the opposite experience, something like the inversion of parabasis, if this were possible: an emptying of the stage and a fading of the subject altogether, as voice, line, narrative cohesion, a structuring aegis that would constrain desire and direct its flow. In *Rendering*, form doesn't mutate so much as disappear, its thematic and harmonic skein unraveling into a perfectly unsingable, supremely delicate noisiness. Something like a second-order Real emerges, and along with it a revelation: not only is the Other not what and where you thought (for instance, the message to rejoice in and under the signifier "Freedom," to become its subject), but there is no Other as such—just a quasi-cybernetic unconscious,

13
(tutti ppp) ♪ = 50
♪ = 40
Fl. 1
Cl. 1
Tpt. 1
Hn. 1
3 Tbn.
1.
con sord.
2.3.
ppp
Cel.
tutti
1 solo
Vl. I
Vn. II
Va.
arco
Vc.
DB

(continued)

EXAMPLE 12. *(continued)*

incessantly ciphering, creating random assemblages, unencumbered by the burden of protecting the subject with the veil of an "I." In this sense, the one moment when Berio's musical cement turns from noise back into signal is telling. In the second-movement "Andante," whose "expressive climate . . . seems to be inhabited by Mahler's spirit," Berio's second connective episode produces a near quotation from the Adagio finale of Mahler's Ninth.[71] Quite unlike *Rendering*'s other quote-infested interpolations, this passage is exceptionally transparent, held up to the ear with minimal interference. The appearance of the Mahler figure initiates a remarkable extended deceleration: *rallentando a poco a poco e morendo*, Berio's direction reads as he shifts from "quarter note = 84" to "quarter = 50," "40," and finally "30," *sempre ppp, immobile e lontanissimo*. The entire transition effects a reenactment of Mahler's famous *Adagissimo* coda—and, through it, one of the most extensive and culturally robust "revocations" of the finale of Beethoven's Ninth.

There is a delicious irony here. Listening to Berio's symphonic pulse stumble and slow, thinking also of the last time Berio "set" Mahler, it's not at all difficult to summon Bernstein's own well-known gloss on Mahler's coda in the fifth of his famous Harvard Norton Lectures, "The Unanswered Question":

> [The final page of Mahler's Ninth Symphony is] the very act of dying, of giving it all up. The slowness of this page is terrifying: *Adagissimo*, he writes, the slowest possible musical direction; and then *langsam*, *ersterbend*, *zögernd*; and as if all those were not enough to indicate the near stoppage of time, he adds *äusserst langsam* in the very last bars. It *is* terrifying, and paralyzing, as the strands of sound disintegrate. We hold on to them, hovering between hope and submission. And one by one, these spidery strands connecting us to life melt away, vanish from our fingers even as we hold them. We cling to them as they dematerialize; we are holding two—then one. One, and suddenly none. For a petrifying moment there is only silence. Then again, a strand, a broken strand, two strands, one . . . none . . .[72]

Much has been made of *Rendering*'s "rendition" of distance, its performance of its own remoteness from Schubert's time, his life, the unfulfilled aims of his own sketches.[73] But this obvious and intentional relationship ought not occlude another chasmic distance, a special form of non-relation, between Berio's score and its own immediate musical contexts. In channeling Bernstein's Mahler, *Rendering* also becomes the magnetic pole of everything Bernstein wanted his Beethoven performance to accomplish. It becomes the sound of what his "Ode to Freedom" could not possibly admit: that no loving father dwells above the starry canopy, that no narrator remains to tell us which tones.

10

FREIHEITSDRECK (3)

Befreiung, *Kaleidoscope*, and *Rendering* are my three snags in the discursive fabric of European composition in 1989; I pull them and other works, caught on the same signifying thread, follow. They create on their own a series of strange counter-networks, all linked by a common endeavor on the part of European composers to invite some "Other music" into the immediate heterotopian space of the work, and also the greater, more conceptual domain of New Music, and submit it to some form of analysis, un-tying, breaking apart, traversal. In figure 16 I've tried to construct some of these signifier networks along thematic lines, but ought to stress that the themes are very often emergent properties. For every *Rendering*, semaphoring its alienated bond to a canonical past, there is also a far less direct work such as György Ligeti's seventh piano étude, "Galamb borong," whose pidgin title mashes up Balinese and Hungarian roots to conjure a music from an island that doesn't exist—hence the étude's coexistence in two distinct networks, "Nowheres" and "Composer-as-Ethnographer."[1] These thematic networks, it might be quickly observed, confound many of the more venerable taxonomies of style and school active at the time (and far beyond it). The most recalcitrant serial procedures and shattered textures rub shoulders with refulgent neo-tonalities and fluid spectral envelopes (Franco Donatoni's *La souris sans sourire* versus Valentin Silvestrov's *String Quartet No. 2*, or Wolfgang Rihm's third *Musik in memoriam Luigi Nono* versus Philippe Hurel's *Mémoire vive*); severe, almost computer-programmable cohesion with the crassest, most willful eclecticism (Klarenz Barlow's *Orchidae Ordinariae* versus Poul Ruders's *Symphony No. 1*); sonorist swarms and neoexpressionist shards with shimmering drones and throbbing pulses (Gérard Pape's *Faces of Death* versus Gavin Bryars's *Alaric I or II*, or Hans Zender's *Furin no kyo* versus

FIGURE 16. Heterotopian networks in European composition, ca. 1989.

Gervasoni, *An, Quasi una serenata con la complicità di Schubert*

Schubert, 1817:
"Die Entzückung an Laura," D.577

Schnebel, *Schubert-Phantasie*

Riehm, *Schubert Teilelager*

Schubert, 1826:
Sonate in G-Dur, D.894

Schubert, 1825:
"Der blinde Knabe," D.833

"SCHUBERT"

Schubert, 1828:
Sinfonie in D-Dur, D.936a

Schubert, 1827:
Die Winterreise, D.911
("Der Wegweiser")

Berio-Schubert, *Rendering*

Schubert, 1826:
Streichquartett, D.810

Kröll, *Omaggio. 2. Klaviertrio*

Hölszky, *Hängebrücken, Streichquartett an Schubert, Nr.1*

FIGURE 17. "Schubert" network.

Iannis Xenakis's *Okho*); pop and punk with historical arcana or arcane numerology (Steve Martland's *Principia* versus Heiner Goebbels's aforementioned *Wolokolamsker Chaussee,* and Louis Andriessen's *De Materie* versus itself). Put another way, these networks link IRCAM with the BBC Proms with Donaueschingen and Witten—a virtual blueprint of New Music's institutional antagonisms in the late 1980s. University composition departments, even in the second decade of the new millennium, rarely see (and often unconsciously prohibit) such variety.

There are, for instance, at least five other works composed or premiered in 1989, besides Berio's, that "do something with Schubert"—odd, given this is hardly a Schubert Year. And what they do is notable. Without in any way resembling Berio's approach or sound, they each "render" Schubert distant, "far him away" in their own idiosyncratic manner. The twenty-seven-year-old Italian Stefano Gervasoni, writing for an eventual 1990 premiere in Milan's Nuove Sincronie festival, composes a musical essay in what he calls *trascurabilità*, or "negligibility." A "microscopic and anamorphic observation [intent on] giving and simultaneously removing a center," this negligibility can, under the right conditions, "transform poetically" from a "condition of 'lack' . . . into a state of 'fullness.'"[2] He titles the short chamber piece *An. Quasi una serenata con la complicità di Schubert,* its pre-title an elision of Schubert's 1816 Lied "Die Entzückung an Laura" (The Ecstasy of Laura), D.390. The new work, too, is an elision: redolent of the chamber works of his older compatriot Salvatore Sciarrino, Gervasoni's piece presents a depopulated, slowly evolving landscape of semi-automated, almost spasmodic pseudo-nature sounds (repeated constellations of jitters, rustlings, squeaks), which suddenly produce near the end a few measures of Schubert's song, the flute taking over the singer's word "Silbertöne" (silvery notes). The quotations go from longer (four beats) to shorter (one beat), each being stopped midphrase by a quarter-note fermata-covered rest for the whole ensemble; the effect is one of liquidation, a gradual erasure of the record.

German doyen Dieter Schnebel's *Schubert-Phantasie*, originally written in 1978 as one of the composer's *Bearbeitungen* (Arrangements) cycle and revised for a 1989 performance by its commissioner, the Frankfurt Radio Symphony, takes the notion of distance quite literally. A chamber orchestra, playing an "analytic orchestration" of the first movement of Schubert's late G-Major Piano Sonata, D.894, is placed behind a thick, widely spaced veil of orchestral strings Schnebel calls a *Blendwerk*, literally a "blinding-work," but more idiomatically rendered as a mirage, a deception, even a phantasmagoria. This *Blendwerk*, originally a product of the mid-1970s spectral turn, meticulously filters out and smudges together the overtones of Schubert's harmonies, while figurations from the earlier composition come and go in slow succession. On the one hand, Schnebel appears to be applying Schubert's own formal law—the sonata was originally billed as a "fantasie or sonata"—to the newer compositional supplement, and so his description of the Schubert applies at least as well to his own score: "Forms take on a vague shape, ramble off into the distance, approach again, dissolve into figuration, then suddenly condense into almost concentrated forms, thin out into wisps and immediately knot into almost crude clumps—only to relapse once more into bare perceptibility, dripping off into the void."[3] But on the other hand, the status of the *Blendwerk* is ambiguous: it is not simply a more contemporary imagination of "the void," into which "Schubert" now passes as "Music" did in Schubert's own day. The string-supplement is also at once a kind of structural analysis, a means of elucidation, and also an impediment to reception. The same device stages the mediation of the historical object and also the impossibility of it ever becoming immediate. If this "sound-screen" serves as "a kind of modern horizon onto which the Schubertian forms are projected,"[4] it is also a way of preserving Schubert's distance and, in the end, absence.

The annual Rheinische Musikfest (now the WDR-Musikfest) commissions no fewer than three composers to respond to its theme, *Begegnungen mit Schubert* (Encounters with Schubert), resulting in a trio of works that run the stylistic gamut of the late 1980s. The Romanian composer Adriana Hölszky writes a string quartet, *Hängebrücken an Schubert* (Suspension Bridges to [and also for] Schubert), which allegedly "deconstructs" fragments of Lieder and quartets ("Der Tod und das Mädchen" among them). Hölszky wants these "Schubert-fields" to sound "as if they were swimming in dirty water"; the work's first program annotator writes of "an encrypted attachment" in which the composer "seems to make clear to the hearer above all Schubert's absence."[5] Amid the extreme timbral and gestural fragmentation of writing, the quotations are barely detectible, if at all—the toneless rubbing of bows on strings to the rhythm of the second variation in slow movement ("Der Tod und das Mädchen") of Schubert's String Quartet in D minor,

D.810, is an exception. What instead ensues is a testing inscrutability: the name "Schubert" standing almost like a taunt over the most textually atomized music of the entire network. Constantly re-beginning after halting silences, its four players barely ever cohering into a collective phrase or movement, the music continually refuses anything remotely like Schubert's full appearance.

Georg Kröll's piano trio *Omaggio*, tonally and timbrally far more "traditional," works through different genres of Schubert's music, all three movements revolving around single characteristic gestures and/or figural constellations. But each movement promises a transformation it never quite realizes before coming undone, or to naught. Jörn Peter Hiekel writes of a first movement that "circles relentlessly, seemingly without aim, only to dissolve itself in the end," a second movement whose "intense urgency and energy . . . still nonetheless seem to end in a kind of dissolution," and a finale whose "relentless berserking quality" eventually "entwines itself with bleak ossification" before ending, "as do so many of Kröll's works, open."[6] The language resonates with precedents set already in the early 1980s, each an attempt on its own to commune with the nineteenth-century canon: Rihm's stylistic collisions with Schumann in his *Fremde Szenen* from 1982–84, also for piano trio; Ligeti's alien refractions of Brahms and Beethoven in his Horn Trio of 1982; even Bartók—or, rather, Ligeti's Bartók, also channeled in the Horn Trio—seems to make an appearance in the second movement. But Kröll also seems to take seriously the need to entrain to Schubert, or at least to a discursive tradition surrounding his music. In all three movements, for instance, Kröll seems to channel (Hiekel's trope on Carl Dahlhaus's trope on) Adorno's trope of Schubert's music as an "eccentric construction . . . every point equidistant from the center, [revealing] itself to the wanderer, who circles his way through it without progressing: all development is its complete antithesis, the first step is as close to death as the last, and in circling, the dissociated points of the landscape are scanned but never actually left."[7] Kröll's first movement achieves this effect most literally. As the piano unsystematically permutes a never-quite-tonal collection in steady running *pianissimo* eighth-note octaves, the strings repeatedly intone single harmonics on E, each lasting a long bow stroke. The music moves without going anywhere, least of all toward a citation of the Schubert song ("Der Wegweiser") whose opening lines give it its title: "Why then do I avoid the main roads . . ." The music's paralytic shimmer, combined with its nod to *Winterreise*, all but acknowledge that Adorno's "eccentric landscape" was "the landscape of death."

Rolf Riehm's *Schubert Teilelager*—something like "Warehouse for Spare Schubert Parts"—excises the accompanimental figures from another Schubert Lied—"Der blinde Knabe" (The little blind boy)—and projects them into a disorienting mega-hurdy-gurdy soundscape of antiphonal strings. The spasmodic choruses of ostinati-without-melody are decoupled from their means of attack, which are then applied at later points pell-mell. The threadbare postminimalist fabric thoroughly unravels by the end, leading to a shattered coda, pieces of pieces, before closing with a refractory, bathetic peroration that slows to an utter standstill. "It was my dream," writes Riehm, "to experience compositionally . . . the 'sadness that makes the heart flutter' . . . to express myself in the 'romantic guise' so typical for Schubert, without however even the slightest trace of falsehood." But this dream necessarily "takes place in the cynical present of the Federal Republic of Germany and not amidst the existential endangerment of Metternich's Vienna. . . . Today, authentic 'romantic feeling' is the story about itself, about hopes that circumscribed this topos but that have themselves long since worn out. At best, one can show something of the markers, but the carrier itself is gone."[8]

"The language of this Schubert is a dialect," Adorno writes in his centennial Schubert essay of 1928, "but one that has no native soil. It has the concreteness of a homeland, yet its only homeland is one remembered. Nowhere is Schubert further from the earth than where he cites it."[9] It's possible that Adorno's essay, and the discursive construction of Schubert it gave the German-speaking world, is perhaps closer to these composers than the actual Schubert works they engage.[10] Despite the Rheinische Musikfest's expectation of "encounters with Schubert," the new pieces seem less invested in bringing Schubert back than in using invocation and apostrophe to stage a kind of distance—not a suspension bridge, but a bridgeless chasm. They cite to separate, not to draw closer; they are each essays in unsummoning. Christoph von Blumröder writes about how "distance to the Romantics is one of the strongest overarching characteristics of the 'New Music' around 1910; abandoning this constant would mean essentially abandoning the concept 'New Music.'"[11] The music of this Schubert network, otherwise classifiable as textbook postmodern "music about music," is worth hearing with those earlier ears, as a music whose "concept" depends for its life on distance. Citation becomes another way—perhaps not so new at all—of again leaving the earth behind for the air of other planets.

. . .

The nodes of a Bach network test the stylistic categories more intensely. On the one hand, there are works mired—quite literally—in the German tradition, like the German composer Ulrich Leyendecker's *Streichquartett Nr. 3, Ricercar zur Kunst der Fuge*. Not unlike the commissioners from the Hohenem Schubertiade, the organizers of the Rheinische Bach-Collegium go looking for a creative canon collaborator: they solicit Leyendecker to take up the last uncompleted Contrapunctus from Bach's collection, leaving him free to finish it "in the style of," or to compose out a kind of bridge between his own music and Bach's. Leyendecker, concerned with preserving a "respectful distance," elects the latter strategy. The work adopts "ricercar" to the letter, and commences a kind of "searching out" of Bach; the score's initial marking, *cercando*, remains unaltered through the last bar. But

EXAMPLE 13. Ulrich Leyendecker, *Streichquartett Nr. 3, Ricercar zur Kunst der Fuge* (ending).

this searching unfolds within Leyendecker's "own" post-dodecaphonic language, its gestural string-writing strongly redolent of early atonal Anton Webern and Alban Berg (especially the latter's Op. 3 string quartet, though parts of the *Lyrische Suite*'s "Allegro misterioso" third movement maintain a strong hold on later passages). Eventually the score's pursuit becomes embroiled in another unofficially solicited work, Beethoven's *Grosse Fuge*, whose subject overlaps with the B-A-C-H theme introduced two thirds of the way through Bach's own Contrapunctus. "The ever-denser entanglement of the basic contrapuntal elements," writes Leyendecker elliptically, "leads to a formal trajectory turbulent in all its registers."[12] The work gradually reaches a moment of maximum textural saturation before suddenly breaking into fragments and grinding to a halt, ending in its last measure with a bungled triple- and quadruple-stopped cadence—D minor with a C-sharp/G-sharp fifth stuck in the spokes.

On the other hand, there are two considerably larger and louder works that absorb "Bach" into quite different traditions and temperaments. Unlike Leyendecker, the Danish composer Poul Ruders seems utterly unburdened by "the burden of tradition" and is already established by the late 1980s as an omnivorous, cosmopolitan maximalist with a Straussian sense of irony. And yet, he is still nervous about his first symphony, which he had to wait until the Brahmsian age of forty to complete.[13] Titled with a famous line from Goethe's *Egmont—Von Himmelhoch jauchzend . . . zum Tode betrübt* (Exulting to the Heavens . . . Grieving unto Death)—the four-movement symphony baldly announces its affiliations with nineteenth-century romanticism. But Ruders complicates this affiliation from the start. The opening "Presto jubilante" violently rewrites the beginning of Bach's Christmas Oratorio, "Jauchzet, frohlocket," blaring out shrill, exploded quotations in different keys, at different speeds and in extreme registers. In the middle section, marked "Triste," Ruders describes how "the lonely piccolo and piano" render "a popular, pre-reformation German Christmas Carol, but in a bleak context with low winds and strings. Thus the ancient concept of Yuletide as happy, a harbinger of peace for all mankind, collides with our knowledge of modern Christmas deprived of innocence." This affective and structural bipolarity afflicts the rest of the symphony, eventually yielding a manic third-movement scherzo of implosive compression (a mere two minutes long) and an apocalyptic finale Ruders calls a "maschera funerale," in which a "huge, chromatic cluster [is] slowly pared away over a time-span of seven minutes." The "facial features of the piece stiffen into a symphonic 'tundra': the heartbeat and changing colors of the first movement freeze into one, glacial entity." Pointedly, Ruders does "allow a door to open towards the very end by inserting, very *sotto voce*, a recognizable recapitulation of one of the [Bach] brass chorales from the first movement. Ending this way, with piano and solo violin revisiting the gentle German Christmas Carol, enables me to proceed from there in a future piece, when perhaps I will climb towards a lighter level. But [the] pessimism is there, and it's a fact, but never the goal."[14] Thus does "Bach" coordinate the entire symphony from first to last—its equilibrium and apogee, both equally unreachable.

Coming from a very different, but similarly omnivorous, orientation is one of 1989's highest-profile New Music events: the world premiere of Andriessen's remarkable hundred-minute music-theater piece *De Materie* in a production by Robert Wilson at the Holland Festival. The work, a chiseled neo-tonal and post-minimalist disquisition on the relationship between matter and spirit, would seem to constitute a exemplary postmodernist endeavor: ostentatiously eschewing any prohibitions on the past, it is "a labyrinth of quotations and historical references," as Yayoi Uno Everett puts it, "assembling musical and textual sources with virtuosic flair."[15] Moreover, the score manifests Andriessen's ongoing antipathy to sentimentality, identification, and psychologism—what Fredric Jameson might call a modernist fetish for "depth." *De Materie*, surely helped by Wilson's own coolly ambiguous (if not quite "blank") staging, maintains its poker face throughout. Despite Andriessen's intertextual labyrinth, the work's armature and attitude are beholden to his "two gurus," Stravinsky and Bach, "the world's two greatest composers."[16] Bach's presence is clear enough: the majority of the monumental opening movement is erected around the temporal proportions of the E-flat Major Prelude from Book I of the Well-Tempered Clavier, which are used as a structural scaffold. More explicitly, the B-A-C-H motto repeatedly signs all four movements of the score, pervading the first and third in particular. It returns, in "arguably [its] most profound and explicit quotation," at the close of the entire piece: a monologue in which an actress, "with restrained motion and frozen facial expressions," recites passages from Marie Curie's diary describing her agony over the death of her husband, Pierre. As she meditates over his coffined corpse—"pale and discolored lips," "little beard turning gray," "we kissed your cold face for the last time"—the first note of the B-A-C-H motto hangs in the air, the highest pitch of a luminescent chord for vibraphone, glockenspiel, piano, synthesizer, and harp. At the end of the monologue, the remaining three notes unfold above similar chords, and "the lighting on stage grows dark except to cast a momentary spotlight on the dejected widow as if to emphasize her utter solitude."[17]

In its final moments, *De Materie* concentrates its gaze on the mortal chasm between spirit and matter, which in a good modern ethos it affirms as constitutive, "irreparable" in Everett's words. And it would seem that "Bach," or at least "B-A-C-H," is summoned to fill that chasm. A "sort of guardian angel," as Andriessen describes him, Bach comes to serve as a fantasmatic suture, riven modernity's beneficent Band-Aid. But it's precisely here that Stravinsky emerges into the foreground, since it is arguably *his* Bach that Andriessen "receives." One hears in *De Materie* not just a return to Bach, but Stravinsky's Parisian neoclassical *retour à Bach.* And this aligns Andriessen's score with one of the more venerable tropes of pre-World War II musical modernism: Bach's husking, his mortification and rendition into an absolutely distant coordinate, such that a historical break can be installed and an eccentric return initiated—in Stravinsky's case, transformed into an entire aesthetic project. Modernism's Bach is its own book (I am tempted to imagine it a book about the history of *necroclassicism*). But suffice it here to think of Bach, despite Andriessen's reverence, less as a "Papa" than as a paternal function, an inanimate or dis-animated operand, what Lacan would call a "name of the father." The more depersonalized, the less face and more mask, the better. Thus does Bach become the great functor of abstraction, and also its signifier, whether this be "pure music," a "constructivist . . . geometry" whose "dryness and precision" lends it "an authority without artifice," or "a miraculously beautiful-sounding machine music, music of pulsating rhythm."[18] (This last quality forms the basis for Richard Taruskin's extensive argument, beginning in the late 1980s, that Stravinsky's machinic Bach became a performance prototype for the early music movement.)[19] The B-A-C-H motive, often intimating death throughout *De Materie*, induces in its last bars a strange conflation: Marie Curie gazing on her dead husband, Andriessen listening in on a mortified Bach, both of them partners of the dead, the former anguished, the latter consoled.

The moment resonates uncannily with its otherwise stylistically irreconcilable partners in this Bach network: Ruder's frozen "maschera funerale," ejecting only in its last bars a chill sotto voce artifact of Bach's jubilant oratorio; Szymanski's frenetic/failing Bach-omaton; Leyendecker's unfulfilled "search" for the completed fugue promised by Bach's own "carving" of his subject. Each of these works seems to find its own errant path back to a canonically modernist project of depersonalization. At the same time they suggest something rather compelling about this project: namely, that the artist might not depersonalize *himself* as a subject, so much as some *other*, now taken up as an object. And in this, these works remain inversions of Rostropovich's own Bach performance later that year. Bach, for these composers, is not a presence to be channeled by the evacuated vessel of the musician. Rather, Bach himself is emptied out, such that a place can be made for the younger composer, so that the composer "comes into his own," grandfathered into the canon through a "deadfathering out" of the progenitor.

• • •

All this freezing and fixing, husking and (death-)masking; this impossible-izing of various pasts, rendering them irrecuperably distant, or present but inoperative. One might—and I *do*—feel a temptation to force an identification here, to declare such aesthetic enterprises part and parcel of a much wider cultural pessimism gripping Europe as it saunters glumly toward the next millennium. Here Jürgen Habermas would seem already to have written the perfect caption; all one needs to do is fasten music as an aesthetic response to his famous 1984 jeremiad on *die neue Unübersichtlichkeit* (the new obscurity). What are all these out-of-grasp Schuberts and mortified Bachs if not expressions of a new condition in which "it seems as if the utopian energies have been used up, as if they had withdrawn themselves from historical reflection"?[20] Here, perhaps, is a music correspondent with—in the Aquinian sense, *adequate to*—the truth of Europe in its historical moment: a continent where "the horizon of the future has pulled itself back," and where "the future is negatively occupied [*negativ besetzt*]," consumed by

> a terrifying panorama of a world-wide threat to the interests of life in general; the spiral of the arms race, uncontrolled proliferations of automatic weapons, structural impoverishment of developing countries, unemployment and growing social imbalance in the developed countries, problems of overburdening the environment, and

> the nearly catastrophic operations of high technology are the catchwords that penetrate by way of the mass media into public consciousness. In Europe, the answers of the intellectuals reflect the same helplessness as do those of the politicians. It is by no means just "realism" when forthright "helplessness" more and more replaces attempts to find orientation determined by and directed toward the future. It may be that the situation is objectively obscure. Nonetheless obscurity is also a function of a society's belief in its capability and readiness to take action. At issue, then, is western culture's confidence in itself.[21]

Habermas's grim eloquence finds an aesthetic corollary in an article from that same year by Perry Anderson in the *New Left Review.* "What marks the typical situation of the contemporary artist in the West," writes Anderson, is "the closure of horizons: without an appropriable past, or imaginable future, in an interminably recurrent present."[22]

Such claims doubtless capture something essential to the prospective climate of 1980s Western Europe, not least a certain strategic apocalypticism aimed at provoking a shrinking welfare state to recognize the stakes. But there's something preemptive, conceptually and historically sloppy, about equating New Music (better yet the "contemporary artist in the West") with such a climate. Two problems arise in particular. The first is that such an identification forecloses the possibility that there might be a wing of culture engaged in something like an analytical position, a traversal of that culture's own fantasies. Instead, New Music is strong-armed back into a fantasmatic function. It becomes a mere servant of the contemporary imaginary, another modality by which Europe can see, hear, and confirm itself—in this paradoxical case, can see what the stultification of its own imagination *looks* like, or what its deafness to the future *sounds* like. This is one way (arguably Habermas's intention) of reading his curious phrase *Die Zukunft ist negativ besetzt*, especially if *besetzt* is taken to refer to Freudian "cathexis," *Besetztung*: the present is gripped libidinally by fantasies of bad futures, including the future of "no future." The present is getting off on the "terrifying panorama" it projects for itself.[23]

The second problem is that such an identification renders too consistent what is meaningful precisely in its inconsistency, in the tension it produces between apparent irreconcilables. The challenge is not, to my mind, to cleave the musical situation in two and divide the spoils—to declare Leyendecker a dusty modernist stuck in the 1920s (or 1820s), and Ruders and Andriessen the two faces of a cynical anything-goes postmodernism (one a leering grimace, the other a Mona Lisa smile). The challenge is to hear them together, to hear the common tone in their inconsistencies: Leyendecker *with* Ruders *with* Andriessen. Their respective endings, for instance: a desperate *deutsche Misere*, caught between Bergian liquidation and Beethovenian fist pounding; a gaudy apocalypse, haunted by Hector Berlioz at his most proto–Grand Guignol; a pearly stoicism, as bright, hard, and hopeful in its widow's lament as Stravinsky's *Les Noces* was in its aural haloing of a new bride. This way of hearing, beyond a historical correspondence theory of aesthetic truth, and also beyond the modernism-postmodernism divide, is stifled by the stylistic checklist. Something is going on here that fits neither into Connor's postmodernism as a "stalled present, an agitated but idle meanwhile," nor into Adorno's archetypal high-modernist claim for all art: "the ever broken promise of happiness."[24]

Die Zukunft ist negativ besetzt: it is worth returning to Habermas's phrase, because it's possible to argue that, at least as far as New Music is concerned, the opposite was true in 1989. In this heterotopia, the "future"—as fantasy, a collective bad panorama gripping the present—was being dis-occupied, de-cathected, traversed. Negativity was unquestionably at work, but a negativity at odds with the enterprise of projecting images, of fleshing out appearances and veiling antagonisms. For the moment, I would propose hearing these Schubert and Bach networks as part of a larger desire to unveil antagonisms, to submit the contemporary musical imaginary to acts of, as I put it in chapter 8, "scission, un-knotting, decompounding"—in a word, analysis. And, to return to the psychoanalytic analogy at the end of the preceding chapter, there is, I think, something utopian about this analysis. It is not a blueprinting of the perfect world, but a momentary unmooring of the coordinates that anchor and fate the present one. A forcing open of the temporal horizon, by corroding the images of the future that close it up. I wouldn't dare claim this strategy "worked." To suggest it is light hagiography at best. In truth, the marvelous, sad irony of spotlighting New Music in a moment of actual revolution is that it reveals how *little* these analytic traversals, this supposed forcing open of the temporal horizon, actually accomplished. (Or, rather, Günther Schabowski's parapraxis accomplished considerably more.) But I am less concerned with historical consequences than with historically specific desires and, if unconscious registers are included, intentions. Pessimism is only one modality in this music, tempting the hasty ear to hear the whole compositional field as the sound and spirit of foreclosure, the present as death-of-possibility sonified. But zoom out, and this pessimism gradually comes to sound like a side effect, a flinching or coping or trying out, only one among myriad manifestations of a deeper irresolution about the situation being engaged.

• • •

This uncertainty is perhaps best spotlighted by looking at the network of "revolutionary" works from 1989, of which Goebbels's *Befreiung* is only one node. Revolving around the goal of celebrating the bicentennial of the French Revolution, it is one of the largest, most politically and financially robust cultural networks of the year, connecting up composers not only with ensembles, presenters, and festivals, but with international corporations, state organizations, and occasionally—at least in name—the state "itself." *Befreiung* is, as I mentioned at the beginning of chapter 6, one of three bicentennial works (the others being by Isang Yun and

EXAMPLE 14. Mauricio Kagel, *Fragende Ode* (middle [chorus only] and ending).

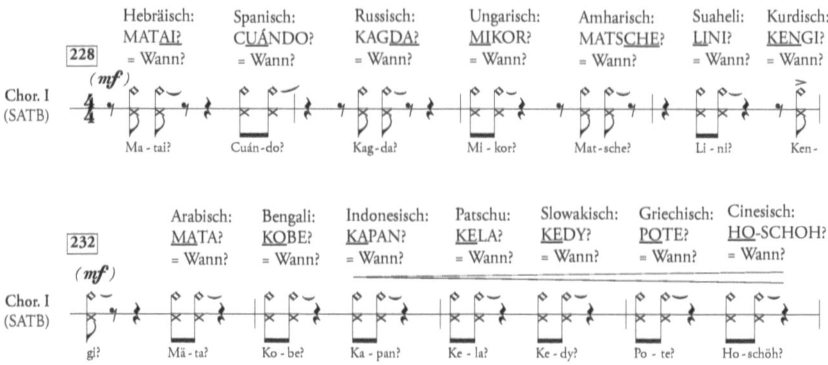

Rolf Riehm) commissioned by the Alte Oper Frankfurt for a concert as part of the larger Frankfurter Feste. But the Oper's most ambitious festival endeavor that year is a retrospective of the work of the Argentine expatriate Mauricio Kagel, and it is to be capped off by his own bicentennial commission. The result is *Fragende Ode* (Questioning Ode), a setting for double chorus, brass, and percussion of nothing more than the revolutionary motto itself, *Liberté, Egalité, Fraternité.* Kagel sets the motto in more than thirty different languages. The double chorus veers back and forth between singing and speaking—and laughing, whispering, and shouting—while the brass and percussion constantly flirt with martial topics, never quite hooking up. Kagel eventually adds a fourth word, "When?," cycling again through the dozens of languages in endless permutations of accent and declamation. A closing Adagio, increasingly unable to keep its tongue in its cheek, finally ends the piece in tense confrontation, half raspberry, half sad snarl—a long, grand pause, followed by a choked whisper: *Wann?!*

Stages all over continental Europe summon the composer-as-reflective-revolutionary: the Donaueschinger Musiktage, the Dresdner Tage der zeitgenössischen Musik, the Paris Festival d'Automne, Radio France. The Festival d'Avignon programs a *Guirlande révolutionnaire* in which they ask seven young composers from the Conservatoire de Paris to respond to the revolutionary song "Les malheurs du temps," a lilting ditty with vicious lyrics. The results include Jean-Marc Singier's *À gogo, de guingois* (Lopsidedness Galore), which submits the song's phrasing and pitch material to cyclic serializations, straitjacketed into cartoonish march rhythms and increasingly interrupted by prankish percussion before closing with repeated snaps of the whip. Stéphane Bortoli's *Tel qu'elle*, by contrast, is severe and somber, a "rigorous extension," "multiplication," and "augmentation" of the tune, which it treats as a (largely undetectable) *cantus firmus*; it ends by dwindling down in register and size until it reaches a soft, sluggish unison bass. The trajectory of Bortoli's score is echoed by the entire sequence of pieces, which begins with a work for thirteen players, and progressively dwindles down in numbers to a last work for unaccompanied contrabass, weaving into this revolutionary garland the contrary signifier of Haydnesque farewell.

At the other end of the spectrum, thirty-five-year-old Pascal Dusapin, already having a banner year, fulfills a wildly well-networked opera commission, with support ranging from the Fondation Louis Vuitton pour l'Opéra et la Musique to the Mission du Bicentenaire de la Révolution Française et de la Déclaration des Droits de l'Homme.[25] The result, an intensive collaboration with the writer Olivier Cadiot, is *Roméo et Juliette.* Though the work announces itself unabashedly as an opera, it takes more than a page from Berio's "musical actions," and from the (post)structuralist adventures of postwar European musical theater in general. Which is to say it's an extremely self-conscious opera, one about writing an opera, and it reenacts in theatrical terms its collaborators' incessant axiomatic questioning: "Why sing?" "Why sing opera?" "What is a text in opera?" "What is being told in opera?" "Why ought it be told in an opera?" Romeo and Juliet, in their failed "struggle to spin the perfect love," allegorize the operatic endeavor itself; they "[put] into crisis the relation text/music," its "global form" becoming the unfolding "history and future of lyrical and textual techniques" of the opera it is trying to become.[26] The work becomes "the story of a project: how to sing together with a single voice, how to come together and assemble, how to become a true (operatic) duo."[27] Here the dual themes of failed love and attempted opera summon a third, political revolution, which grips the work within a stark temporal frame. The fifth and central number, the orchestral tone-poem *La révolution*, becomes the wordless gap, a mise-en-scène become *mise en son*, around which the entire opera "revolves": a first part "in future tense," "prologue-beginning-morning-before," and a second part, "in the present and the past," "after-night-end-epilogue." This rigid chronologic doesn't appear to add up, however: a late, startlingly euphonious *coup-de-théâtre*, the only real *tutti* of the opera, leads only to a dispersal of voices and orchestra, and a slow dissipation of consolidating energies. "Romeo and Juliet finally sing exactly together—the perfect duo—but stammer to the point of aphasia." In the end, "everyone dies, some while singing, others in silence. Nothing has happened, the future is in the present, the end was the beginning."[28]

The Festival d'Automne, one of the most generous European stages for New Music, puts forward an especially ambitious program, "Creation in Music," consisting of no fewer than twenty-one new commissions, all officially marked as bicentennial affairs and many receiving further support from the French Parliament–controlled Caisse de Dépôts et Consignations, and from the private Fondation Total pour la Musique and Fondation Vuitton. Among the most prominent is Helmut Lachenmann's *II. Streichquartett, "Reigen seliger Geister,"* commissioned by Fondation Total "with assistance from the French state on the occasion of the celebration of the bicentennial of the French Revolution." The work takes its subtitle from one of Gluck's "greatest hits," the Elysian "rounds of the blessed spirits" from *Orphée et Eurydice*; and perhaps as a nod to the number's famous *obbligato* flute, the half-hour quartet charts a painstaking elaboration of what Lachenmann calls a *flautato* technique, in which the performer bows across a dampened, pitchless string. "Tones: grasped out of the air. Air: grasped out of the tones," Lachenmann writes in his program notes.[29] The work unfolds a remarkable—and, for Lachenmann, remarkably linear—metamorphosis. The weightless, seamless, barely audible air(s) of its opening bars gradually blossom into long pitches, single, then double-stopped, eventually bursting into manifold forms of tapping, plucking, snapping, ringing (figures 18a, b, c). It finally explodes into bacchanalian violence, *quasi Walzer*, *fff sempre*, all four performers striking their now wildly detuned instruments with plectra, before a coda returns to the quartet's opening but finds it unrepeatable: the pristine *flautato* is now perforated by shuddering, slack-stringed tremolos and exquisitely taut scratchtones, drooping slowly in pitch like sharp rock against glass.

The French state, now with the help of Radio France, also commissions Krzysztof Penderecki's *Symphony No. 4, "Adagio"* in celebration of the two hundredth anniversary of the Declaration of the Rights of Man. A typical fruit of Penderecki's neo-tonal turn away from the "avant-garde," it is a meditation "on the question of destiny and the dignity of the individual." It is also the most Wagnerian score of 1989. Quite literally: it seems to recycle extended transitional moments from *Der Ring des Nibelungen* and *Parsifal*, now channeled through what David Fanning sharply hears as the mediated Wagner of Eastern European symphonists of pre–World War I (Reinhold Glière, Nikolai Myaskovsky, Joseph Suk, Mieczysław Karłowicz, et al.); Dmitri Shostakovich of the war years is surely an ingredient, too, as is the "critics' music" from Richard Strauss's *Ein Heldenleben* (the symphony's own *idée fixe* comes perilously close).[30] But the form of the score is also striking: using a (post- or pseudo-) language of momentum, trajectory, climax, and coda, the symphony repeatedly fails to "symphonize" them. Angular fugatos, funereal perorations, nocturnal scherzos, celestial hymns: such genres and topics are repeatedly conjured, allowed to project possible paths, and then invariably cut short or neutralized. The symphony is placed in a perpetual holding pattern. But its tensions are not annulled; embedded, along with tonality itself, in its artifactual languages and forms, they are instead relocated. Rather than being allowed to produce developmental arcs and apotheoses—and with them a certain satisfaction—they are instead fed back into themselves, creating unending episodes of not-yet-coda and just-after-introduction. Here Wagner is again channeled: the incessant frustrations of *Tristan*. But Penderecki's symphony displaces those frustrations from a tonal plane onto a semiotic one. One pines not for the tonic but for the mythical generic signified, which (unlike *Tristan*'s tonic) never shows up, not even at the end.[31]

Maybe this is just another, pleonastic way of saying the symphony is really pretentious, a big orchestral bluff. It's not clear, at least to me, whether its negativity emerges out of some kind of sadistic semiotic cunning or a lack of formal skill coupled with cynicism; I'm inclined to think the latter, while the committee who granted the symphony a Grawemeyer Award in 1992 obviously felt the former (or a third option: the Pose of Great Seriousness). But I think this makes it all the more productive to hear Penderecki *with* Lachenmann. This is probably heresy for the latter composer's partisans: the *II. Streichquartett* is one of Lachenmann's most celebrated pieces, and arguably one of the most respected string quartets of the late twentieth century. It is also in some ways the strange antithesis of Penderecki's symphony: the work of a composer who also engaged in the early 1960s with extended techniques, alternative notations, and *Klangkomposition*, but who, unlike Penderecki, never "defected" from them and instead pursued their hyper-refinement to a point of extreme dialectical systematicity.

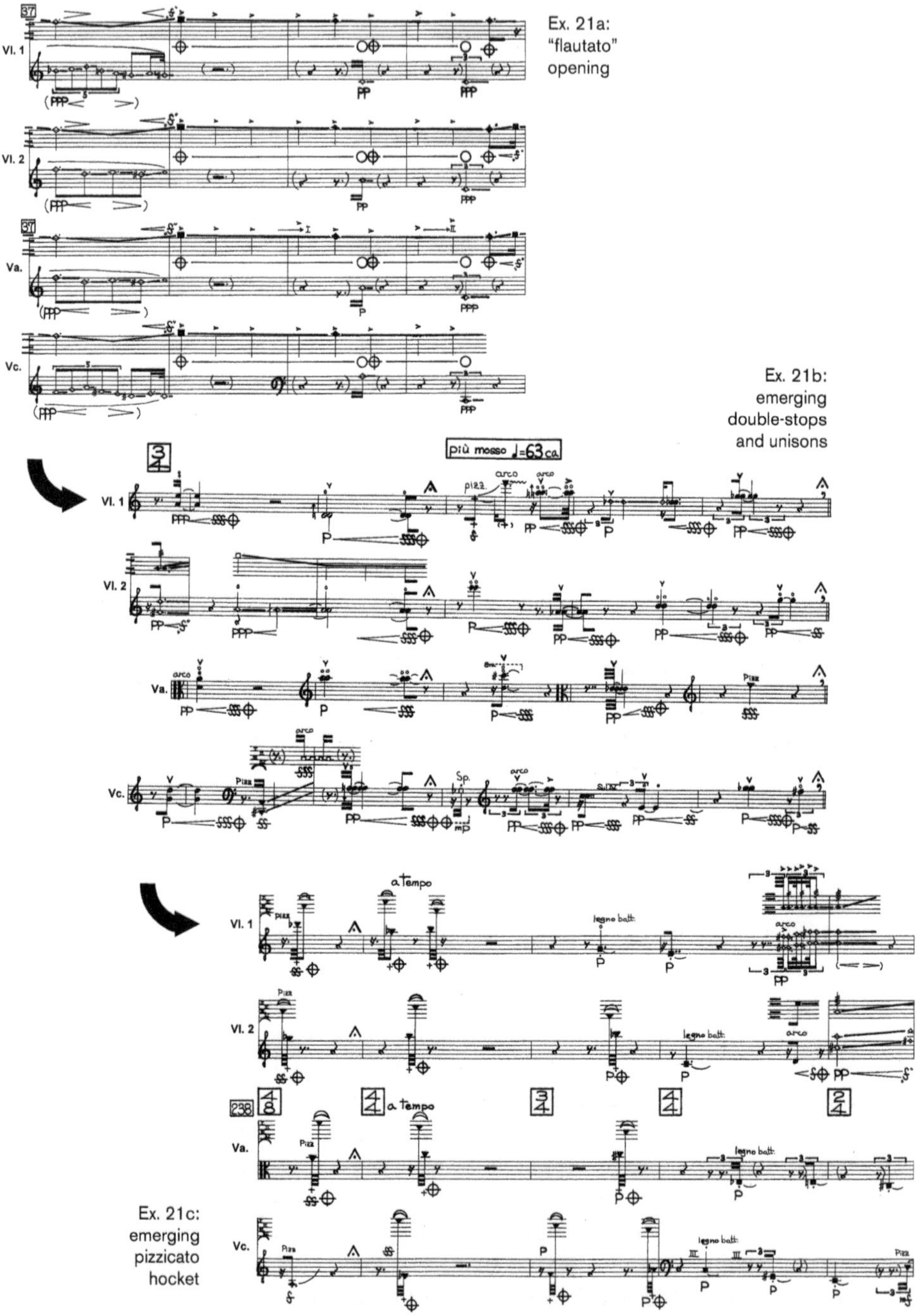

FIGURE 18a, b, c. Helmut Lachenmann, *II. Streichquartett, "Reigen seliger Geister"* (trajectory) (© 1989 by Breitkopf and Härtel, Wiesbaden, Germany).

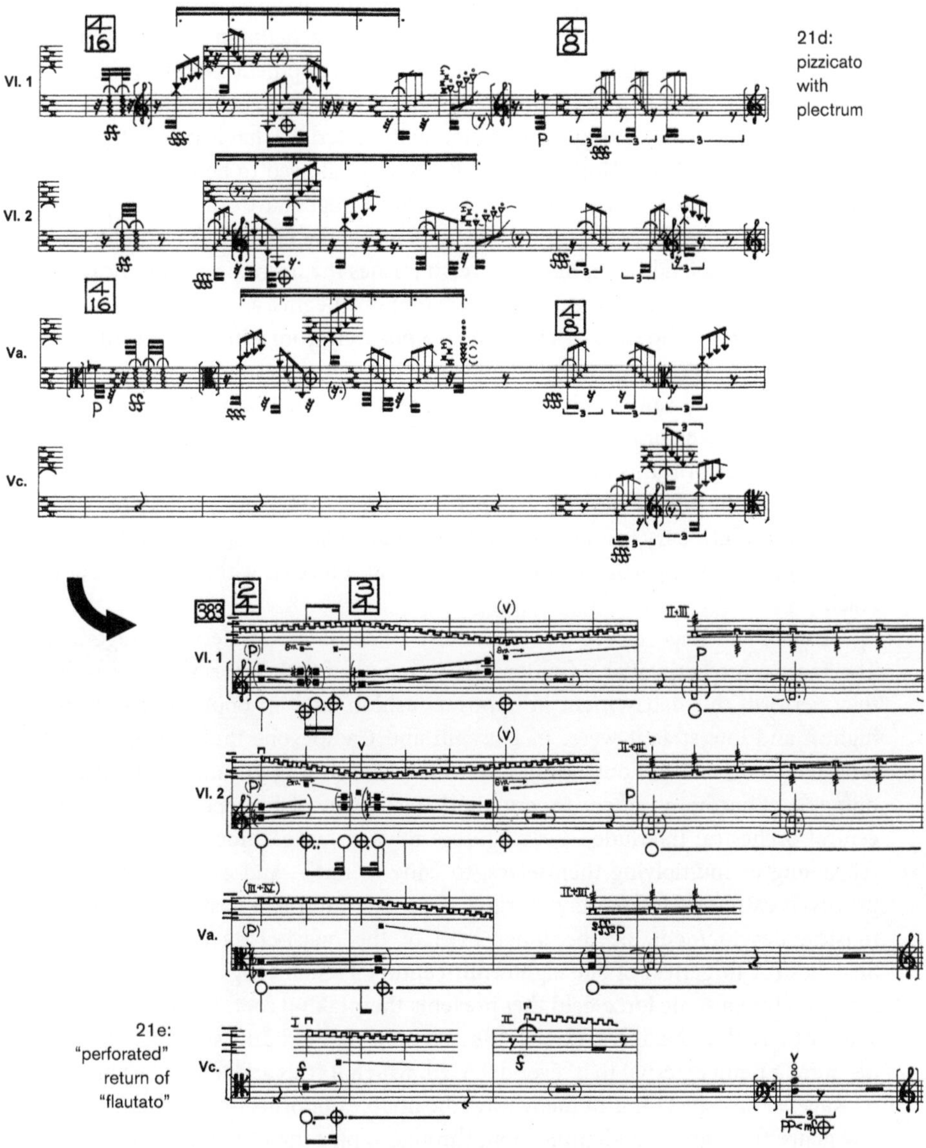

FIGURE 18d, e. Helmut Lachenmann, *II. Streichquartett, "Reigen seliger Geister"* (trajectory) (© 1989 by Breitkopf and Härtel, Wiesbaden, Germany).

Out of this polarity emerges another, more significant one: if Penderecki's symphony enacts (or suffers from) an unrelieved torpor, Lachenmann's quartet enacts (or, some could argue, suffers from) an unceasing development. Despite its forbiddingly abstract, often pointillist surface, the latter work is positively Brahmsian in its commitment to the developing variation of its material. It has learned Orpheus's lesson: never look back. Nothing, once iterated, is allowed to be repeated, while everything, as written, revises some facet of what it might have otherwise repeated. Everything changes as it flows, flows as it changes, the entire form unfolds as if in a single Olympian breath. But this breath pushes the form to a point uncannily close to that at which Penderecki's whole symphony begins, and where it remains: in standstill, in an end time or fallen time, a position from which the promissory notes of the musical past are declared invalid or unredeemable. Lachenmann and Penderecki do not simply presume a break with such a past as a means of securing their own autonomous "work-space" in which things will operate otherwise.[32] They perform this break; its *acting out* is what gives them their substance. Whether it is the prerevolutionary utopia at the tip of a dancing spirit's flute, or the incipient revolutionary rumblings of a Wagnerian endless melody, an "Old Music," in both generic and particular form, is broken and broken with, sounded out of reach.

Dusapin and Kagel can in this regard also be considered fraternal antagonists. Their works are both, after a fashion, debasements of their respective genres, but they perform this debasement in opposite fashion, and on opposite genres, the highest and lowest as it were. In Dusapin and Cadiot, one finds an opera that repeatedly fails to carry out a program, while also refusing to concede the goal of doing so, of becoming a "true (opera) duo." In so many of its scenes (including the central orchestral interlude), lyrical forces muster, by teaching or dreaming or rehearsing or multiplying themselves, to "sing as one"—and cannot. The entire process is extremely temporally charged, a constant future- or past-tensing of plot, musical development, or the inner lives of the quasi-characters themselves. Snatches (or forgeries) of late eighteenth-century French songs and marches are swept up into a sonic force field that prevents their taking root.[33] Time is burdensomely present in the opera, even as the present is methodically suppressed; genre becomes a point external to it, ever deferred, which it tries and fails to reach.

Kagel's *Fragende Ode* is in many ways the double opposite: the debasement of a low genre through over-identification, through a pushing of the genre's conventions to their limits. As Hans-Peter Jahn points out, Kagel was by 1989 a well-known saboteur of the occasional piece, having already achieved some notoriety for his previous "celebratory" commissions *Ludwig van* (1970) and the *Sankt-Bach Passion* (1985), both festive assignments he took on with a typical "mephistophelean meticulousness."[34] But the generic debasement of *Fragende Ode* is striking specifically in that it elects to celebrate Western modernity's (positive) archetype of radical political transformation with a piece of music that sticks to the present like gum on the sole of a rented dress shoe. The work is absolutely locked in place, turning the revolutionary motto itself into a "permanent litany" in thirty languages before reducing itself to just one word: "Mäta? Kobe? Kapan? Kela? Kedy?" and on and on, all mezzo forte, "with a just a bit of voice," each question separated by a slightly unpredictable length of rest. The over-identification with the occasional genre eventually turns the encroaching monumentality, with its perennial demand to stop the clocks, into something deeply anti-monumental: a strange (and quite Kagelian) mix of bureaucratic goofiness, sub rosa rage, and Sisyphean insistence. Unlike a proper monument, the *Fragende Ode* begins to tempt the listener to respond not out of solemn respect but out of irritation, as if a reply might end the piece and let time begin again. The work's title and theme undeniably render it yet another of 1989's multiple anti-Ninths, "Beethoven's bombast [replaced] with skepticism."[35] But Kagel also hits a particular nerve: embarrassing the very idea of the occasional piece by taking it *completely* seriously, he also shames the "occasional Ninth"; he turns it into a bad bureaucrat, submitted to review by HR.[36] If it was supposed to celebrate universal brotherhood, it technically hasn't been doing its job; it hasn't been asking the right questions, nor asking them in the right languages. It should be demoted, or at least put on probation.

• • •

In a generally favorable review of Perry Anderson's *The Origins of Postmodernity* (1998), T. J. Clark is nonetheless perturbed by the book's treatment of aesthetic modernism. Anderson is cogent and lucid in his outline, which was first articulated in the 1984 article cited above; he understands modernism

> as the outcome of a field of force triangulated by three coordinates: an economy and society still only semi-industrial, in which the ruling order remained to a significant extent agrarian or aristocratic; a technology of dramatic interventions, whose impact was still fresh or incipient; and an open political horizon, in which revolutionary upheavals of one kind or another against the prevailing order were widely expected or feared. In the space so bounded, a wide variety of artistic innovations could explode—symbolism, imagism, expressionism, cubism, futurism, constructivism: some quarrying classical memory or patrician styles, others drawn to a poetics of the new machinery, yet others fired by visions of social upheaval; but none at peace with the market as the organizing principle of a modern culture—in that sense, virtually without exception anti-bourgeois.[37]

Under such terms, modernism had long run its course by 1989. The bourgeoisie had, per coordinate one, long fulfilled and exceeded its program of industrialization, and simultaneously its own tortuous process of self-definition and hegemonization, of which modernist art was an essential part. As Clark puts it in his review, "Its endless riffs and deformations of the aristocratic legacy—the very legacy the bourgeoisie was struggling at the same time to turn to its own purposes—came to mean nothing, to have less and less critical force, because the bourgeoisie had abandoned the struggle, and finally settled (as it always wanted to) for purely instrumental reason."[38] Coordinate two—Anderson coins the apt phrase "charisma of technique"—also faded, as technique and technology were "routinized" and came, especially through television, to saturate the cultural field via the production of "perpetual emotion machines, transmitting discourses that are wall-to-wall ideology."[39]

The third coordinate would seem to bring us back to 1989 with special force—to Francis Fukuyama, to Joshua Clover's "disappearance of the edit, the cut"; for Anderson, modernism *and* modernity come to an end with "the cancellation of political alternatives." "The possibility of other social orders was an essential horizon of modernism. Once that vanishes, something like postmodernism is in place."[40] Again, I can well understand the temptation to hear and read works like those of Penderecki and Lachenmann, or Dusapin and Kagel, as the sound and spectacle of precisely this cancellation, its expression or symptom. Or mirror: could there be any more *reflective* scenario than this particular network of scores, all commissioned to celebrate one Revolution, all being written on the cusp of another, all dislocated from anything like revolutionary time, and preoccupied instead with the impossibility of revolution, its failure or failure-to-be? Really, it is too perfect.

But it *is* too perfect. It is an image, and as such, a forcing of music that clearly lives and breathes by its iconoclastic intentions and desires—that distrusts images, that wants to shatter and liquidate them, to sabotage and reconfigure its inherited symbolic—into a passive and harmonious role. Music-as-echo, "whose babbling voice would always answer a call but never speak first," whose "chattering tongue could only . . . parrot the last few words of the many spoken by others."[41] Anderson's three coordinates are themselves extremely compelling, and seem to me (as to Clark) quite right: at one historical moment, a moment bound up with modernism's "golden years," they signaled openings, political, technological, social, and economic; by 1989 they had long signaled a grand foreclosure, precisely the kind lamented by Habermas and Anderson himself. But, also like Clark, I disagree that these foreclosures brought an end to modernism. They couldn't. Modernism, in coming to name a series of clangorously inconsistent beliefs and practices oriented around a constitutive negativity, named a larger testing *of* foreclosure. Radical uncertainty—"a deeper irresolution about the situation it is engaging"—was not its justification but its cause, its axiom. The whiff of revolution on the horizon was a source of intoxication; so was the foul air of political standstill. Here I think Clark still makes the strongest case, when he finds modernism's "devices and features," but also its "purposes, problems and objects," virtually identical to those of Anderson's postmodernism. Both "stand in the same central, undecidable relation of ambivalence toward the main forms of modernity, of bourgeois industrial society."[42] Modernism, as the mythical anterior of postmodernism, was

> already characterized by a deep, truly undecidable doubleness of mind in the face of the main forms of modernity. And that doubleness was *constitutive*; since modernism is a name not for a stance of Left or Right insurgency or negation, but for a pattern of artistic practice in which modernity's very means of representation—the structure of symbolic production and reproduction within it—are put to the test of exemplification in a particular medium. That is to say, one can never be certain of modernism's "attitude" to the appearance and logic of modernity because modernism itself was never certain—because it could not have put modernity to the test in the way it did without bracketing overall "judgment" of what it took on until such judgment was given in the act (the whole structure) of representation itself.[43]

Taking issue with Anderson's third coordinate, Clark goes on to ask whether it is actually true that

> the end of effective political opposition to capitalism robbed modernism of one of its necessary supports? Had modernism not constantly (again, constitutively) lived precisely with such an ending? Did it not thrive, in France at the turn of the century, in the face of bourgeois society's most hideous positivity? And did it not feed deep, exactly in its pre-war heyday, on the worst kinds of Rightist vitalism, mysticism and racism? . . . In what sense were the years between the two great wars not already an ending—a crushing and freezing of revolutionary energies?[44]

If something similar is being felt in the Europe of 1989, however mistakenly or myopically, New Music offers itself as rather stark evidence. It presents a heterotopia in which its own modernity—or postmodernity; let's settle for "its now"—is being tested, in which its lifeworld's "very means of representation—the structure of symbolic production and reproduction within it—are [being] put to the test of exemplification in a particular medium." I don't think it such a leap to append to Clark's "very means or representation" the psychoanalytic concept of fantasy. Indeed, this concept is what brings with it an account of the "glue" of representation, of what makes an order of representations stick, to both itself and its inhabitants. Clark's "testing" resonates here too with the analyst's analyzing: a process of un-sticking, or of pushing on the seams and joints, of seeing how much pressure is required to pull things apart—or, more exactly, how much pressure is already being exerted to keep things *from* coming apart. The individual nodes in these New Music networks from 1989 all have a different answer; to push the analytic analogy, they all have their own orientation and practice, and relate to their analysands in a distinct style and tone of voice.

But they do all test, and appear to do so out of a deep and aporietic relation to what they take as their object: Berio's impossible "restoration," Gervasoni's elusive "negligibility," Hölszky's indecipherable "encryption," Riehm's empathic "exhaustion," and so on. In the case of the larger network, that object can be seen as a signifier—"Schubert," "Bach," "Revolution"—but only initially. These signifiers remain weightless without their sonic imaginaries, always historically embedded in some there-and-then, and at the same time libidinally embedded in the present's fantasy lives. So Dusapin's and Cadiot's opera tests "revolution" only through testing "opera," and does so in a process that telescopes itself back in time in search of concrete material, eventually locating it in the operatic soundscape of the late collaborations of Wolfgang Amadeus Mozart and Lorenzo Da Ponte, themselves always circling around the sonic imaginary of the coming revolution. (And with a similar ambivalence: the act 1 finale of *Don Giovanni* is exemplary, especially at the lines "È aperto a tutti quanti, viva la libertà!" [It is open for all, long live liberty!], accompanied as they are by a martial bombast at once seductive and cynical, brutal and joyous.)[45] Kagel tests "revolution" through the occasional genre, and through Beethoven's Ninth; Ruders tests "Bach" via the symphonic genre, and through its doubly coordinated "farewell" deformations in Mahler and Haydn, and then through Bach's Oratorio, and *then* through a pre-Reformation German Christmas carol; Schnebel tests "Schubert" through the modern(ist) genre of the "analytic orchestration," then the classical and romantic genre of the *fantasie*, and finally through the first movement of Schubert's own late G-Major Sonata. In each case, the new work's modernity *already has a way* of enjoying these same objects fantasmatically. "Bach," "Schubert," "Beethoven," "Mozart," "Mahler," "Haydn": each precipitates its own *objet a*, a libidinal prop in a canon of fantasies, each bearing aloft a desire that circulates constantly in the same concert halls and often on the same recordings, endlessly trotted out for occasions special and quotidian alike. It is this desire that the new works interfere with most drastically. They reconfigure a culturally robust object-cause of desire; within their frames, Schubert "names the site of a Problem-Deadlock," Bach a "Burning Question," Revolution a collection of "attempted but failed Answers to [a] Problem."[46]

In this sense, perhaps Anderson's concept metaphor itself is what occludes his view of aesthetic modernism. What these works bear witness to may not be *closure*, a shrinking and contracting of the political horizon, coaxing them like plants to effect their own mimetic dance. What brings them together in the same improbable Borgesian tableau is, I think, a desire to stage antagonism, in the sense Žižek, Laclau, and Mouffe use it: the limit of objectivity, the emergence of the Universal or Absolute not as an undivided One, but as a self-contradicting Two. To render this in Lacanian terms, they want to put the Real—"the impossible," the absolutely-resistant-to-signification—on stage.[47] In both cases, this antagonism, this impossible, is a ramifying one: it takes place *within* each of these works, and also *between* them. Lachenmann's "rounds" enact a seamless, unstoppable transformation (revolution?) of Apollonian tranquillity into Dionysian violence, seemingly showing each to be constitutive of the other. But simultaneously, the work becomes one term in a larger, "intra-opus" antagonism, with works like Penderecki's symphony as the other term: a piece in which impossibility is entirely recast, now as a fragmented, un-startable transformation, able to neither escape nor realize the revolutionary promise in the "ruined" historical materials out of which it constitutes itself.

So maybe here it makes less sense to speak of opening and closing. The dialectic seems to me much more one of flow and break, consistency and gap, smooth circulation and its choking or pinching. In contrast to other therapeutic clinics, which propose to help the subject "reach closure," the Lacanian clinic inverts the logic of open and closed. The fantasy is what brings a kind of symptomatic closure, what subsidizes the flow of desire, what systematically misrecognizes impossibility as an ever-about-to-be that never shows up. The traversal of the fantasy is what reveals—or at least allows the experience and recognition of—breaks or gaps. It is what happens when impossibility is no longer veiled, sealed off from the subject or imagined as something to be vanquished or annulled. The strange logic of this kind of cure is that identification with a certain structural impossibility—"I am that," as Lacan succinctly puts it—*doesn't* foreclose the subject's horizon, but opens it, drawing it sometimes catastrophically near.[48] This puts these musical networks in a surprising position vis-à-vis Anderson and Habermas. In affirming the priority of antagonism, they inadvertently spotlight the fantasmatic logic behind stories of "the new obscurity" or the "cancellation of political alternatives." Awkwardly, they make such proclamations look a bit more like wish fulfillments: the grim enjoyment that comes from declaring a failing form of hope definitively dead. The awkwardness comes from the fact that these failing forms of hope—or, better, hopeful failing forms—continue to saturate the landscape, claiming to be alive.

. . .

A last example, one that I think intensifies and focuses the scenarios outlined above. Amid all the "official" revolutionary works of 1989, each conducting their tests of contemporary representation under the interested eyes of festivals, corporations, radio, and ministries of culture, are two remarkable works that carried out their commemorative endeavors independently, out of "free will" or "inner necessity." Both are, in whole or part, "tape pieces," though this doesn't say very much to begin with. The first is *Mon 1789* by the East Berlin composer Georg Katzer, probably the most important figure in East German electronic music. The piece is a relatively small but bitter pill, premiered at a festival of electro-acoustic music in Bourges in July. Katzer would eventually fulfill a second bicentennial commission for the Dresdner Tage der zeitgenössischen Musik in October. *HEX*, for acoustic ensemble, opens with "La Révolution permanente," in which the mordant revolutionary song "Ça ira" (It'll Be Fine) is turned into a piano riff. Over it unfolds an increasingly turbulent chain of musical commentaries and disruptions, illuminating the two meanings of "revolution" (upheaval and rotation), and "out of the constantly new organization of the material emerges a kind of frenzied standstill."[49]

Mon 1789 is infused with a similar skepticism toward the meaning—and very possibility—of revolutionary time, and it also shares with *HEX* a biting approach toward (mis)appropriation. The work begins with Nietzsche's rendering of one of the richest, most difficult fragments from the pre-Socratic philosopher Anaximander: "Woher die Dinge ihre Entstehung haben, dahin müssen sie auch zu Grunde gehen nach der Notwendigkeit; denn sie müssen Buße zahlen und für ihre Ungerechtigkeit gerichtet werden gemäß der Ordnung der Zeit" (Whence things have their source, to that place must they also pass away, according to necessity, for they must pay penance and be judged for their injustices, in accordance with the ordinance of time).[50] Katzer, reciting the text himself, sets the aural stage meticulously: *VOOOH—hehr*, resounds the first word, as if falling (with the help of a little ring modulation) into a canyon. The tone is both stentorian and gawking, Katzer sounding slightly like a wide-eyed tourist in his own piece. Upon completion of the fragment, a more nasal, echoless Katzer enters channel right, da-da-da-ing the opening notes of "La Marseillaise." The long high fifth of the phrase locks in place as an old, clangorous recording of—at this point, what else?—Beethoven's Ninth barges in, the chorus harmonizing with nasal-Katzer to the words "Alle Menschen werden Brüder . . ." The two tunes are broken off by a rude enveloping crackle, which is itself broken off by the phrase (uttered with Gallic spleen) "La révolution est fini" (The revolution is done), in turn followed by a whispered "commence" (begin). This triggers an electronically manipulated accordion, spinning out a *moto perpetuo* as hectic and rigid as it is headless. In her excellent analysis of the piece, Martha Sprigge concedes that there is "no doubt that Katzer treats his original texts cynically, but he is also playful." The piece is full of black humor, Katzer's crack sense of timing and sharp ear for all manner of homophones harmonizing with his brutally smart montage technique.[51] The piece has no downtime, and nary a moment forfeits the opportunity to seize the listener's attention and laser it at some ghastly contradiction. Every positive value is reevaluated, often in a quick rush of noise or a clap of breathless silence. Schiller's "all men become brothers" soon hatches its evil twin, a passage from *Das Lied von der Glocke* in which the shout for "freedom and equality!" leads "women [to] transform into hyenas" and "tear the heart from foeman's breast." The Universal Declaration of Human Rights's "all men are equal," cycling through various language, eventually attracts the suffix *devant la guillotine*, before eventually admitting in a hushed chill that "some are more equal"—a phrase that initiates its new process of language cycling.

The work ends as the *Alle* from Beethoven's and Schiller's *Alle Menschen werden Brüder* is panned back and forth between right and left channels, gradually shortening to a vowel, and eventually forced down a kind of sonic garbage disposal. Through some deft manipulation and a last artless push, it morphs into the simulation of a snare drum and, finally, a machine gun. Sprigge suggests that the particularly surgical cut-up of the UDHR mirrors an increasing mobilization in East Germany of the discourse of human rights—an attempt to untwist the Socialist Unity Party's early reversal of "no socialism without human rights" into "no human rights without socialism."[52] But Sprigge also, and to my mind rightly, hears Katzer's work as more and messier than an ideological signal for recognition and redress. It is less a partisan in the hegemonic struggle than an arena: "competing claims to human rights are enacted aurally, [and] Katzer's layers become louder and louder, each fighting, and ultimately failing, to be heard."[53] Similarly, the dismal drain of the piece's ending performs less a denunciation of revolution tout court than revolution's dream of leaving the bad behind. It becomes a musicalization of Anaximander's sentence, and slingshots us back to the chasmic start of the tape itself. Caught in a strange loop, *Mon 1789* too must return to its source, and pay penance for its anger and humor, its fatal hauteur, by passing away "in accordance with the ordinance of time."

Revolution never appears as an actual signifier in the second work. But the work conjures it nonetheless, through the thick web of associations it weaves, the coincidental moment of its completion, and the well-known history and passions of its central author. The title of Luigi Nono's *La lontananza nostalgica utopica futura*, a "madrigal for multiple 'travelers' [*caminantes*] with Gidon Kremer," is not a simple one to interpret. It references a 1977 work for solo flute, *All'aure in una lontananza*, by Nono's compatriot Salvatore Sciarrino, who was the eventual dedicatee of the later work. Sciarrino claims *lontananza* is a seventeenth-century poetic archaism, connoting a "far distance" or "distant distance," but the Italianist Armando Maggi begs to differ; it is "a pretty simple and normal word in Italian," he says, and "has a melancholic connotation," implying "that a person is away from another. Distance between two lovers for example."[54] The remaining words, easy enough to render in English, nonetheless add up to a conceptual mind bender, for which Sciarrino himself provides a thorny exegesis: "The past reflected in the present (*nostalgica*) brings about a creative utopia (*utopica*), the desire for what is known becomes a vehicle for what will be possible (*futura*) through the medium of distance (*lontananza*)."[55] *Caminantes* alludes to a phrase that permeates—or, better, haunts—virtually all of Nono's last works: "Caminante, no hay caminos, hay que caminar" (Wanderer [or traveler], there are no roads, one has to wander).[56]

To my mind Sciarrino's chewy language courts sophistry, and the *Caminante* motto—condensed on its path from a poem by Antonio Machado to a cloister wall in Toledo where Nono first saw it—runs any motto's risk of triteness. But Nono's work reveals itself as an undeniably deep and complex meditation on temporality and place. It is, among other things, one of Nono's most open works—but very strategically and specifically so. Like much of his music following his *Wende* or "inward turn" in the late 1970s, it emerges through an intensive collaboration with its eventual first performer, in this case the violinist Gidon Kremer, who met Nono in 1987. While the larger process unfolded over many months, the bulk of the work's initial material emerged over a few days in February 1988 at the experimental studio in Freiburg's Heinrich Strobel Foundation, then part of Südwestfunk (now Südwestrundfunk, or SWR). There, Nono encouraged Kremer "to play for three, four, or five hours every day," producing "whatever sounds I wanted," but with an interesting caveat: "keep well clear of familiar territory and avoid works I already knew. This had to do with improvisation, which was something I had never learned. And so I simply played notes and looked for a possible binding force within them."[57]

The set of eight tapes that eventually emerged (sixty-one minutes in total) is a trove of Kremer's playing. Even with Nono's subtle processing of the sound, much of it still bears on playback the signs of contingency and precariousness the violinist felt, and which Nono encouraged: jittery *saltando*, *jeté*, *spiccato*; heady high-wire *cantilena*; unsteady bow pressure; arpeggios that smudge and fan out, searching for the right-wrong chord. But this intimacy and private play is only one register; it runs in constant counterpoint with a larger, impersonal record of the virtuoso classical violin. A kind of wavering historical big Other, it coalesces and disperses throughout the tape parts, adding a semiotic fragility to a sound already acoustically frangible. It's never clear when the brittle abstraction of string and bow will morph into the spectral apparition of "Paganini" or "Ysäye," or any number of nineteenth-century violin topics. At times Nono processes and multiplies the sound, producing clouds, swarms, and bands of bright bowed vibration—an apparitional mega-violin, sounding divine redemption and judgment at once. But the tapes also contain another, antithetical material: the sounds of the process of trying to find the materials of the piece. "An opening door, a passing train," Sciarrino recalls, "a falling pencil, the hesitant voice of the composer, key words fraught with meaning, maelstroms of sound (created by percussion instruments, or music stands being dragged along the ground?), a flourish of the violin, the closing door."[58] Through incorporating these "parergonal" sounds, "Nono made the working process itself, and thus the search for new sound possibilities, a fixed part of the tape."[59] To the two registers of sonic abstraction and historical archetype is added a third: the diary. A corollary triad of temporalities unfolds within it: the big time of "sound itself," the historical time of styles and canons, the quotidian time of personal experience.

A fourth might as well be added: the time of composition, understood here in a rather traditional way to mean the construction of an actual notated score for

Kremer—hence a combination of scaffold building, analysis, improvisation, notation, explanation. Here Nono remains true to his stylistic tendencies of the previous decade. On the one hand the score is saturated with "long, long notes of a kind that [Kremer] scarcely knew from other scores," and also with vast expanses of extremely high (and, in Nono's thick handwriting, virtually illegible) notes; often the music sinks below the horizon of the audible, with extreme dynamics such as *pppppppp*.[60] On the other hand, it is torn asunder now and then by Nono's signature outbursts: often marked *sfffff*, they are never prepared in the least; they simply happen, almost acephalic in their inscrutable intensity, and soon become a nerve-wrackingly reliable part of the landscape. As Stefan Drees points out, historical and biographical materials are embedded here, too, if far beyond earshot. Nono "harvests" some of the intervallic content from the *scala enigmatica*, allegedly "invented" by Giuseppe Verdi used in his "Ave Maria" from the 1889 *Quattro Pezzi Sacri*; likewise does Nono's *Varianti. Musica per violino solo, archi e legni* from 1957 serve as a lender of both material and techniques.[61] But these sources, techniques, and notational elaborations do not necessarily lend the score any fixity. It remains an extremely unresolved object, full of what Trent Leipert calls Nono's "unsettled unisons"; lines and points never coalesce into phrases or figures, but instead open on all sides to indeterminate silences and fermatas increasingly incapable of marking a beginning or end.[62] The score's many micro-intervals, sometimes down to one sixteenth of a tone, allegorize the score as a whole: written but unwritten, variable, a "searching for itself / or searching for the sound / varying it every time."[63]

This sense of contingency reaches a new, almost transfiguring intensity when the tapes and score are combined. The work is "open," but not in a conventional way. Strictly speaking, it obeys time's merciless arrow: the score's six *leggii* or "stands" are to be read in order, and the eight magnetic tapes (or, today, tracks of the digital master) are to be played back through from start to finish. In this sense the work's openness isn't primarily a matter of the *actions* of the performers. There's no strategic splicing and dicing, no "random access" of the materials, and likewise, no calculated recomposition of new sequences or creation of a new overall form. The performers are still mastered by a rather traditional "time of work." But the "time of the materials" is something else altogether, and here the performers have considerable agency. It is an agency rooted principally in perception, cognition, listening. As the composer and frequent tape performer for *La lontananza* Christopher Burns puts it, "I'm thinking 'here's what [the violinist] is doing right now; here's what's available on the eight tracks at this moment; given that situation, which of those tracks should we hear, with what dynamics, and positioned where in space?'"[64] Simultaneously the violinist, her written parts full of semi-indeterminate breaks and fermatas—including the breaks between the six *leggii* themselves—is listening to tapes, constantly reassessing her decision to reenter, fall silent, wait, transition to the next part. As Burns notes, space becomes an essential factor in performance as well. Adding to the sonic theater of the eight loudspeakers placed throughout the hall is Nono's request that the *leggii* receive their own music stands, to be placed on the stage or among the audience, "irregularly and asymmetrically, *never near each other*, but in such a way as to permit free although *never direct* passage between them, the player searching them out. They can also be 'complicated' with 2 or 4 empty music stands in order to make the passage way more varied and imaginative, the players even suddenly getting lost or coming to a halt."[65]

The violinist thus plays the part of an actual *caminante*, wandering with a tense arbitrariness from spot to spot, buoyed by an extremely changeable soundscape composed—in the work's early performances—of the violinist's own doubles, triples, quadruples, and so on, all of which may at any point become more real to listeners than he himself. There is an air of unreconstructed romanticism about this, of the kind that made some of Nono's pre-*Wende* partisans squirm. Commentary on *La lontananza* is full of reverent proclamations easily at home in the Germano-Austrian nineteenth century: Luigi Pestalozza, for instance, declaring that "time, in Nono's music, is always 'distant, future, and nostalgic,' perfectly audible, yet far from any inert or static closure within our own (not just musical) time. It is projected forward on an ideal, ethical, thoroughly utopian scale."[66] Or Kremer himself, almost awestruck, reminiscing on how Nono "would sometimes say to me, almost in passing: 'What comes, will come—what doesn't come, won't come.' . . . The openness which he felt at all times and in every situation is something one might be disposed to dismiss as fatalistic, but for me it expressed Gigi's courage, his readiness to be taken to the very limits of 'non-being.'"[67] This is a long way from Robert Morris's *Box with the Sound of Its Own Making* (1961), another enterprise in Klein bottle–like sonic self-documentation, but whose acid artlessness runs reverie off the road at every turn.

But despite the sometimes apostolic aura and reception of the piece, there is something deeply uncomfortable, merciless even, about *La lontananza*. Over the course of its eventual hour-long length, the initial whiff of Schumannesque yonderness gives way to an almost sadistic denial of both orientation and direction. None of the work's rich trove of sources—the Verdi scale, the quasi-quotations from the violin rep, the conversations in the studio, to name just a few—is allowed to unfold in one place. Instead all are cut short, relocated, swept up into the gently relentless flow. Out of the subtle or "inner" infinity of the work's built-in indeterminacies emerges a dissonant, often jarring polyphony, not just of voices but of times and locations. None provides the least sense of tonic, better yet cadence—a sharp irony given the work's framing of its voices as *caminantes*, literally walkers. In this temporal-spatial atonality, everyone is a listener, beginning with the two performers, and none is allowed to rest, to take root in any here or now. In the violinist Miranda Cuckson's view, they temporarily take on the condition of those "displaced by war: emigrants, refugees, 'alien' residents."[68]

These valences suggest another interpretation of Nono's title, diverging somewhat from those of both Sciarrino and Drees. The word and concept *lontananza* could be conceived less as the work's "medium" and more as a kind of universal negative function, applicable to all its main parameters, beginning with the three words that follow it in the title. Taking into account Maggi's comments, *lontananza* might be better described not as a state or condition, but the result of a kind of intensity: not "distance," but something more like "away-ness." Thus nostalgia, which might otherwise be allowed to swaddle the listener in fully realized visions of unrecoverable pasts, is—pushed away; future, which stokes the listener's desire for its realization, at least as a stable image, is—pushed away; utopia, as a perfected "now" modernity eventually couldn't imagine without exiling it into the future or past, is—pushed *yet* further away.[69] "Revolution," as the work's ghost signifier, is perhaps the epicenter of this negativity, so much so that it doesn't make it into the title even upon revision. But it is "there." The always acute author and critic Tim Rutherford-Johnson hears in *La lontananza* a precursor of Derrida's portmanteau "hauntology," in which a perpetually absent presence (in Derrida's case, and appropriately here, Marxism) gives way to the ineliminable half- or not-quite existence of ghosts and specters. According to this logic, the declaration of an end or foreclosure—say, the death of socialism—seals its fate as an endless return.[70] Similarly, Nono's "fragile sounds, erratic conception and unpredictable realization [suggest] an aesthetic echo of Derrida's warning that the end of history will be unsatisfactory and untenable."[71] The notion of Nono's work as an impossible "echo" of what was not yet written captures something essential to its desire: to be always before or after, behind or beside or in front of the fixing and freezing of its own coordinates, of what secures its existence, its "being-there." Instead it insists on a *Nichtdasein*, or, with Freud, a *Fort-dasein*.

There are some well-established ways of measuring the proper historical distance between a work like *La lontananza* and one like *Mon 1789*. The most obvious, certainly in the "musicological 1989," would have been to appeal to something like aesthetic orientation. Nono's chill, forbidding, deadly serious abstraction is modernist, as is his romance with state-of-the-art technology, while Katzer's coarse, leering cut-up is postmodernist, as is his hyper-allusionist collapse of historical time.[72] There's some truth here, but problems, too. Katzer's is no blank parody, no "play of random stylistic allusion."[73] It's one of the year's most readable instances of New Music, flirting with vulgarity. Its signs and signals pelt and sting the listener, their convictions intact even as they are twisted into monstrous new meanings. If the piece can't make up its mind, it doesn't gloat about this fact; it believes in the problem, it seems to *want* a solution it also won't supply. And Nono's work too collapses time, and plays ostentatiously with multiple pasts. As the bits and pieces—flotsam? rubble? dreams?—of these material histories collect and disperse, "abstraction" becomes an untenable label. This work is as haunted by the referential myriad as any of Alfred Schnittke's polystylistic parades (more than few of which Kremer participated in). The epithet "autonomous" seems especially tinny here: *La lontananza*'s skin is too permeable to the atmosphere, its subject position too wavering and hallucinatory, its rejection of communication too ambivalent to be a heroic commitment.[74]

More difficult to counter is the political-historical distance between the two works, or at least the political reality of their two respective regimes. The story that could be told (and has, in relation to other figures): Nono, in Freiburg and West Berlin, mourning the impending death of socialism from the other side of the Curtain, strategically retreats inward and re-cultivates his utopianism as *Sehnsucht* via a series of neoromantic, indefinite, but still "difficult" projections of political futurity. Katzer, actually living through this impending death as an increasingly unbearable everyday, enjoys no such distance, and is not himself *sehnsüchtig*, addicted to longing. Instead he maintains a practice of (only slightly) encoded provocation, rich and politically readable in its materials, means, and significations.[75] While Nono casts out into the far distances, where the air is cool and thin, Katzer draws everything perilously near, where it heats up and sparks. There is a crude but, I think, not false political assessment to make here: Nono, knowing that the socialist horizon is closing, wants to open it back up in a nonexistent future, one potentially derivable from a never entirely accessible or exhausted past (embodied by, among other things, an hour of eight unfathomably rich tapes that can never be played all at once). Katzer, living less in view of a closing horizon than a crumbling facade, becomes a kind of proto-accelerationist. He hacks at the facade with the sharp tools of parody and passionate cynicism, not necessarily knowing what lies behind it, but that it nonetheless lies, and lies badly.

But are these negativities so opposite? In application, perhaps. But in constitution, I am less sure. And I am drawn more to the latter, to what they have in common: a rather relentless determination, contra Habermas, to "dis-occupy" the future—in short, to prevent certainty. Call this certainty closure, in which case they enact their own irreconcilable acts of opening. Call this certainty the smooth, fantasmatic circulation of "reality," in which case these works enact breaks, gaps, a choking or pinching of the flow. To choose either set of oppositions over the other seems a shortchanging of the way antagonism presents itself within each piece, and in the tension between them. But they do nonetheless bear out a patterning also at work in the other revolutionary pairings above. Either a standstill puts pressure on the present, forcing it to budge, or else an incessant flux puts pressure on either side of that same present, daring it to hold, to produce a bearing, an anchoring place, good or no. In either case, the very possibility of a revolutionary time, a path linking past, present, and future, is put in grave doubt. Katzer turns the path into a strange loop, in which freedom and terror constantly generate one another: no "there," only a constant, outrageous "here." Nono eliminates the path altogether, and one must simply walk: no "here," only a perpetually indefinite "there."

This seems to me neither a parody of an obsolete modernism, nor a postmodernism which increasingly emerged as just such a parody. Rather, it seems a manifestation of a modernism that never stopped, however deluded or ineffective its persistence might have appeared at any given historical moment. By 1989, the repertoires eventually designated by such terms as "early," "late," "heroic," and "high" had become a repertoire of practicable modalities, part of an *ars combinatoria*. But I think it would be a serious miscalculation to spy the arts of play and replay and call out "pomo!" And not even because one could argue *other* works as more "authentically" postmodern. (I suppose one could.)[76] Rather, these works seem deeply invested, in a way quite independent of their sometimes blank miens. They want. This is not a canonic trait of postmodernism. They want, even if they know not what. In this sense they operate more than a bit like the sounds on Nono's eight tapes, at once perpetually re-available and ultimately unfathomable in their totality. These works could all be seen as playing back these tapes, trying to find in them the right sounds: the sounds of a foundational beginning again, a stopping and starting, a breaking and breaking open. In this sense they *are* looking for an opening, if a paradoxical one—a kind of absence, a not being there.

Dusapin's and Cadiot's opera, for instance, is terrifically self-conscious of its ultimate precursor in genre negation, *Pelléas et Mélisande*, Claude Debussy's own attempt to not-write an opera, to both extend and destroy the Wagnerian horizon (here the Berio of *Un Re in Ascolto* could be said to play for Dusapin the part of Debussy's Wagner).[77] Kagel's *Ode* is electrified by Schoenberg's speaking choruses, with their currents polarized between collective and invective. Imagine *Die Glückliche Hand* without its *Mann*, *Weib*, and *Herr*, its "six men and six women" stuck mocking the audience instead. Schnebel's *Phantasie*, summoning Schubert, also summons Webern's founding "analytic orchestration" of the Ricercar from Bach's *Das musikalische Opfer*, and precisely its own aporias (is it a revivification or a mausoleum?). Andriessen's musical disquisition on matter begins exactly where *Le Sacre du Printemps*'s "Danse sacrale"—which it quotes—stopped, pounding mere body in search of some fleshier spirit (and it ends where *Les Noces* ended). In Penderecki, Ruders, and Berio, one finds three very different ways of beginning again the modernist symphony that cannot finish itself; Mahler's Ninth remains behind (or still ahead) of them all. David Metzer's claim that musical modernism at century's end is characterized by "modes of inquiry"—that it constantly mines its own traditions of testing for unfinished business—seems true enough.[78] But it stops short of conceiving that testing as axiomatic, that is, as only one of a panoply of strategies for saying "no" before knowing what to say. I would argue that these works, in returning to some of musical modernism's "foundational tests," are returning to moments that were themselves gripped by Clark's "deep, truly undecidable doubleness of mind in the face of the main forms of modernity." That undecidable doubleness doesn't seem to have gone away. It is there, loud and clear, in Katzer's gawping rendition of Anaximander, which comes to speak for many such musical "sites of confusion," as Sprigge so well puts it.[79] These sites on some level understand their confusion, like their loss, not as empirical but as constitutive. They know their "source" *as* a kind of "passing away," and turn this knowledge into a kind of performance.

• • •

In an iconic essay from 1964, Jean Laplanche and Jean-Bertrand Pontalis postulate that the fundamental psychic fantasy—the origin of fantasy itself, as it were—is the fantasy of origins: an attempt on the subject's part to fill in, flesh out, or cover over the radical contingency of his or her own birth.[80] Adrian Johnston illustrates with a line from Georges Bataille: "This infinite improbability from which I come is beneath me like a void."[81] Fantasy conceals this void beneath "me" in part through the construction of an "I." It is this "I," not so distinct from the Cartesian *cogito* itself, that is capable of being *there*, at the subject's birth, or even its conception, looking on—a pure gaze. Žižek thinks of this as the "basic temporal paradox" of fantasy, a kind of "time loop" that cunningly short-circuits mortality: while the flickering subject may come and go, much to its horror, the gaze remains, as something utterly immaterial and consistent.[82] Under its adhesive force, everything, even an image of ruin, or of the subject's own death, holds together. What occurs under this gaze becomes an answer to "the enigma of the Other's desire": a way of organizing the scene that tells the subject what the Other wants and how to provide it. But this perhaps already gives too much agency to "the content." The fantasy is, at its most schematic, only this gaze, this emptying axiom that can accommodate any scenario, that can transfigure any content.

In terms of content, I doubt too that many of these works' many commissioners—the venues, festivals, performers, cultural ministries, radios, et cetera—were all that surprised at the results. Their gazes were accommodating. I would even wager that, on a concrete level, they wanted more or less what they expected, and they got it. Even a cursory acquaintance with Riehm's or Hölszky's music would have clued in the organizers of the Rheinische Musikfest to expect "encounters with Schubert" that might test the very premise: missed encounters, or encounters with the dead, dismantled, or otherwise debased. The BBC Proms surely knew of Ruders's bipolarities, his horror-show humor and black melancholy, and the Rheinische Bach-Collegium could not have more perfectly set up Leyendecker to "fail" in his "completion" of Bach's last contrapunctus. Radio France had heard what Penderecki did to Christmas in his previous symphony, and could reasonably presume the Declaration of the Rights of Man would suffer a similar darkening.[83] And the Festival d'Automne—if not the Fondation Total and French State—was doubtless familiar with Lachenmann's aesthetic and political preoccupations, not least from his 1986 row with the SWF

Baden-Baden Symphony Orchestra, which had refused to play his companion piece to their performance of Beethoven's Ninth: a work called *Staub* (Dust).[84] All this impossible-izing of various pasts: in some ways, business as usual.

For the moment, however, I want to train my own gaze at a higher, more mythological plane, which is no less influential for all its abstraction: the plane on which Europe, as an official if precarious unity, but also as a mythic or "imagined community," is directing the enigma of its desire at one of its own most mythic constructions, the Composer. Where, after all, would the Composer be without Europe? Here's where the signifier "revolution" plays such a vital role. It becomes a signifier of birth, indeed conception, in this case the conception of the modern democratic state and, after a fact, of modern Europe itself. On this plane, Europe can be seen commissioning the Composer to produce an origin fantasy: a scene and a gaze capable of explaining to Europe where it comes from, why it exists, what it wants. And, at the same time, a scene and a gaze capable of concealing "this infinite improbability from which I come." If this seems a melodramatic way of putting it, it's also not *so* off key. Bernstein, Rostropovich, and Hasselhoff are what Europe got when it didn't have time for commissions, when it needed its origin fantasies in a real pinch. But what it really wanted was perhaps closer to Beethoven's *Chorphantasie*: a musical fantasy capable of patching up a break it was simultaneously celebrating, the sonic staging of an "obscure conceptual vacancy" finding its consolation in "music's vacant sign of freedom."

Instead it got a mass of wild tangles. An autoimmune attack on the fantasizing faculty, a profusion of disruptions, parataxes, obscurities, "strangely opaque features," each trying in its own way to compromise the capacity to keep things patched up. In this sense, the cultural arena of European New Music here seems to resemble a hypostatization of "Beethoven's Late Style," not just in its collective endeavor to create a knotty, analytical "music about music," but more so in its refusal to capitulate to a desire, on the part of its parent culture, to tell that culture what it wants, and to show it where it comes from. In the guise of Anaximander, New Music here sides with Schelling, not Schiller: it insists on the unrecoverable ground, "the beginning [that] cannot know itself." Ask the Composer to respond to the pressing enigma of origins, and you will get back a metallic *VOOOH—hehr*, declaring that the origin is a hole, a vortex, an anterior void beneath. Ask the Composer to tell you what he or she wants of you—*Che vuoi?* as Lacan puts it—and you will receive a petulant question: *Wann?!*

PART THREE

AGAIN

11

REPETITION (1)

Berio, Goebbels, Szymański; Gervasoni, Hölszky, Riehm, Kröll, Schnebel; Ruders, Leyendecker, Andriessen; Dusapin, Kagel, Lachenmann, Penderecki, Katzer, Nono. I have argued that they are repeating something. What are they repeating?

Here it wouldn't be a bad idea to offer a compressed recapitulation, because the question, as I see it, operates on multiple registers. Certainly they are repeating "themselves." This is banal artistic fact, but worth remarking on, since few better metrics for historical change exist for the historian of the arts. Dusapin uses similar pitch matrices and virtually the same melody as the one in *La Révolution* in his Second String Quartet, "Time Zones," written during roughly the same period as the opera. Szymański's *Kaleidoscope* is finding new ways and instrumental contexts for continuing a (yes) kaleidoscopic processing of Baroque polyphonic idioms, one that dominates his compositional output in the 1980s. Lachenmann, even as he is painstakingly and systematically reinventing his approach to writing string quartets (after 1971's *Gran Torso*), is still making use of his tried-and-true *Zeitgerüst* or "time-scaffold," an elaborate, serially derived temporal network of on-off switches (to put it reductively) used for regulating an indeterminate polyphony of sounds and playing techniques. In the first part of *De Materie*, Andriessen is repeating a gesture—a repetitive gesture, the hammered *tutti fortissimo* chord followed by a long silence—that tattoos numerous works after 1976's *Hoketus*. Whatever else Berio's *Rendering* is, it is also, as I remarked above, a sleeker, more doleful, far more poker-faced repetition of his *Sinfonia*. Place "the measure of the distance," as David Osmond-Smith puts it, not just between *Rendering* and Schubert, but between *Rendering* and *Sinfonia*, and one might learn much about what happened to New Music between 1969 (when the five-movement version of

Sinfonia was completed) and 1989. At the other end of the spectrum, Schnebel's *Phantasie* repeats itself, a minimal revision of a 1978 work *about* revision—indeed, one of a massive two-part cycle of scores, each critically reencountering a "great work" from the canonical past, called *Re-Visionen*.

I concede that "repetition," gathering all these works together under its rather meager signifier, really makes hash out of so many hard-won categories for the historical and theoretical analysis of music. Here are styles, techniques, procedures, quotations, genres, works themselves, all mashed together in a Borgesian tableau that is perhaps not quite what Foucault was celebrating in the preface to *Les mots et les choses*. Still, it's quite un-parochial, like calling fugue a form, and makes for terrible textbooks. But this collection of repetitions does clarify one thing: any rhetoric of "break" here, of whatever the opposite of repetition might be, would have to remain deaf to a past these works are carrying constantly with them. It is an "immediate past" already much more than immediate, opening onto an unprecedentedly rich terrain of artifacts and attitudes near and far.

Schnebel's *Phantasie* awakens another register of repetition, one that stands a little firmer. Schnebel's work was among a generous number of scores, including pieces by Wolfgang Rihm and Kurt Schwertsik, commissioned for the 150th anniversary of Schubert's death in 1978. One could argue that this became the last year that European composers—and commissioners, performers, and festivals—needed a "Schubert year" in order to "do something with Schubert." The New Music landscape, which previously had only seen a peppering of pieces (Ernst Krenek's 1923 completion of the *Reliquie* Sonata, Anton Webern's *Deutsche Tänze* orchestrations from 1931, Lachenmann's *Variationen* from 1956), gradually began to sprout *Schubertblumen* everywhere. By the time of 1989's "Schubert" network (the 161st anniversary of Schubert's death, or the 202nd anniversary of his birth), doing things with Schubert constituted an industry: repetition as reproduction, if not of skills, then still of something not entirely at home with the New in New Music, a bit too close to a "reproduction of submission to the rules of the established order, i.e., a reproduction of submission to the ruling ideology for the workers."[1] I am being slightly cheeky quoting Louis Althusser here, but as all these Schubert pieces accumulate, the chafing of false consciousness intensifies as well. As they speak to a distant, broken Schubert in their irreducibly distinct languages of brokenness or breaking or distance, their individuality becomes ostentatious, the apparatus behind each compositional "voice" increasingly gaudy; they come to resemble melancholics showing up to the same party all wearing the same improbable spangled leather poncho. But the awkwardness of this accumulation ought not override—and doesn't contradict—the fact that the great majority of these works take a negative stance toward their chosen master signifier and all it represents. In one way or another, they present dissolution scenes, asserting Schubert's return on one plane—the signifier, and the iterables (scores included) they pull with them—while they make him go away—be lost, or even *get* lost—on another.

Something similar could be argued for the "Revolution" network, which certainly pings awake the explosion of "revolutionary" works of New Music beginning roughly a quarter century earlier. Quite a few of the composers in the later network were involved, no less—Andriessen, a major actor in the Dutch collective music-theater piece *Reconstructie* (1969); Berio, again with *Sinfonia*, which bragged of its use of French 1968 protest graffiti; and certainly Nono, from 1964's *La fabrica illuminata* through the 1969 LP *Venezuela in questo momento di guerriglia*, with its *Musica-Manifesto n. 1*, whose second part, "Non consumiamo Marx," also used Parisian graffiti, far louder and clearer than Berio's.[2] (New Music would of course continue to signify "Revolution" throughout the 1970s and 1980s; Nono, wasting no time, set parts of the *Capitalist Manifesto* in 1971's *Ein Gespenst geht um in der Welt*.) Here would be a strange repetition indeed, as so many of the earlier works are not commemorating an old revolution but cacophonizing (and in some cases wishing to foment) an impending one. *La lontananza*, like its contemporaries, appears unspeakably distant from such earlier works: no more shouts in the street, but instead the restless banter of great artists shut away in a soundproof state-subsidized *Experimentalstudio*. There is something poignant in this repetition's measure of the distance. Like Søren Kierkegaard's Constantin Constantius, returning to Berlin to relive those experiences that had provided such a wild kick the first time, these later works suggest that there is "no such thing as repetition." As an extremely variable network, they even seem to confirm this discovery "by having it repeated in every possible way."[3] But the historical context does not trump everything. There is a braiding of different and same, and something difficult to grasp is nonetheless repeated: an implosive intensity, one that announces its strategic negativity by embroiling itself within historical situations and objects, and hastening their coming apart and coming open. In this sense, Nono's (or his ghostwriter, Lachenmann's) exhortation of 1959 still holds here: a plea for "the constructive violence of the revolutionary, who deliberately provokes the destruction of existing forms in order to replace them with new ones which are in the process of development."[4]

And Bach? One could look again to the 1960s, to allegedly postmodern classics like Lukas Foss's *Phorion* and George Rochberg's *Nach Bach*, but really, in this case it is much less as a matter of delimited coordinates than a vast field, stretching back as far as one would want to argue and blanketing all historical attempts at partition: if to Igor Stravinsky, then also Schoenberg; if to Wagner, then Brahms, or Verdi, or César Franck.[5] If one argues, as I would, that in this 1989 network too one finds a similar implosive intensity, a negating apart and open, then such a strategy doesn't begin with Stravinsky's *Opus Dei*, his "daily mortifications of the past,"[6] but with Beethoven's late works and, as Daniel K. L. Chua puts it, "the notorious

B-A-C-H motif that threads its way through the late quartets [as] a kind of historical task."[7] It is arguably first there that Bach becomes not simply a point of return or recollection, a father to a prodigal son come home, but a consummate figure of anti-resurrection, a mausoleal presence initiating a sequence out of M. C. Escher: dead hand authorizes living hand to write this deadness into the work.

Bach, however, raises a third register of repetition, which I briefly developed toward the end of previous chapter, and which I want to develop more now. Andriessen repeats Stravinsky, Kagel Schoenberg, Ruders and Berio Mahler. To expand an example, one can hear Dusapin repeating Berio, and quite concretely: the recursive melos, searching, finding, and re-finding itself; the protean harmonic stream, rhizomatic, non-atonal, growing without exactly going; the conversion of genre into a mise en abyme, rendered directly as a sonic hubbub of half-sung, half-spoken opera-rehearsal-within-opera. So: a repeating of some of Berio's more defining ways of working with repetition. But one can also hear Debussy. Though perhaps "hear" is not the right word. Yes, the two operas share a demurring Gallic melancholy, at once lyrically restless and strangely static. But they also share something negative, a relation to what is not, strictly speaking, repeatable. While Berio could be said to constitute Dusapin's partner in a Bloomian scenario of precursor and ephebe, Dusapin's relation to Debussy doesn't strike me as one of mimetic rivalry, of Dusapin trying to not repeat what could so easily be repeated. Rather, it seems a kindredness with what Debussy's opera, in its Bartlebean legion of self-diminutions and turns away, thought itself turning *toward*. "I found myself using, quite spontaneously too, a means of expression which I think is quite unusual," Debussy wrote Ernest Chausson while starting work on the opera, "namely silence (don't laugh). It is perhaps the only way to give the emotion of a phrase its full value."[8]

This silence need not be restricted to matters of text-setting any more than Debussy's own agon with Wagner be considered distinct from a "means of expression": the anxiety of influence becomes another form of expressive silence, of giving "the emotion of the phrase its full value" (here read "work" for "phrase"). Agonism becomes one among multiple paths toward antagonism, toward the making manifest of an ineliminable negativity, a recalcitrant not-ness with no positive object.[9] Here would be a fourth and last register of repetition: the repetition, or the attempted repetition, of an ontological lack, of what was never there in the first place. This path is already embedded in Maurice Maeterlinck's play, which attracted Debussy not only with its words, but with its "whole system of aesthetics and metaphysics," and which seems inextricable from what pushed Pierre Boulez to call the opera "a kind of mirror in which a whole culture can see itself transfigured."[10] That "system" was what made *Pelléas* too modern for Joseph Kerman, precisely an opera overwhelmed by a "purposelessness" in which no one really exists at all—neither entirely "comes to life" nor truly dies.[11] A foundational opera about nothing, then, looking one second far back to Gustave Flaubert's silences (his "book about nothing"), and the next second ahead to Samuel Beckett's silences, to his "unnullable least"—arguably one of the most eloquent formulations of antagonism.[12]

Each of these registers enacts repetition rather honestly—that is, not as a mystical moment of full re-presentation, but as an impure iteration, an ad hoc mashup of same-with-difference and different-with-stubborn-same. The first three registers would seem to coincide well with psychoanalytic forms of the (unconscious) Other, of the signifying chain "at all points homologous with what occurs at the level of the subject": the ego, or S_1 (composers repeating "themselves"); knowledge, S_2 (composers repeating, or "caught up" in, signifying chains that continue to circulate in the cultural "air"); and the imaginary other, what Lacan formulates as "i(a)," *l'image de l'autre* (composers repeating, or agonizing to not repeat, their precursors).[13] These three registers also enact a deepening and widening of the horizon, away from the intimate present as a repeated self-identification (the ego insisting, in the here and now, on its own reality, as what it is and what it sees); through the collective experience of culturally dominant forms (the zeitgeist, the "doing things with Schubert," the writing of "revolutionary" works); and toward the confrontation with, or channeling of, more distant Others who threaten or loosen the bonds of the ego (Berio and Debussy for Dusapin, Frank Zappa and Hanns Eisler for Goebbels, Stravinsky and Bach for Andriessen, et cetera). The move is one from persona to depersonalization, from immediate to proximate to distant to mythical.

And in this sense, it is the fourth and last register, the repetition of what was never there to begin with, of a negative object, that pulls these other registers more properly into the psychoanalytic domain. Here we are back at Žižek's paradoxical writing of the Real, his unending attempts to encircle that which "doesn't stop not writing itself." Lacan eventually considered this encircling the form of repetition most proper to psychoanalysis: a repetition in the Real, an impossible repetition, and better, a repetition of the discovery that there is "no such thing as repetition," repeated, in the course of analysis, "in every possible way." Kierkegaard was Lacan's precursor here, as the latter, perhaps suspiciously, was all too ready to admit.

12

REPETITION (2)

Aristotle's elaborate theory of the four causes, one of the cornerstones of Western philosophy, ends up producing two strange little remainders, exiles from the domain of causality proper.[1] On the one hand there is something called *automaton*, often translated as spontaneity; on the other there is *tyche*, alternately rendered as chance, fortune, fate.[2] *Tyche* happens to beings with reason and intention, while *automaton* happens to things—horses, rocks, tripods are some of Aristotle's examples. *Tyche* is to some degree an elevated form of *automaton*, a meaningful breach in meaning.[3] But both involve the notion of something *happening without cause*. In the eleventh seminar of 1964, Aristotle becomes another of Lacan's "silent partners," as Žižek calls them—which is to say, someone to be smartly but blatantly misread, repurposed with wile, such that afterward, Aristotle becomes a bit hard to read on the matter without a certain transference.[4] Lacan's initial remarks on the distinction between the two terms are, unsurprisingly, oblique: "First, the *tyche*, which we have borrowed . . . from Aristotle, who uses it in his search for cause. We have translated it as the encounter with the Real. The Real is beyond the *automaton*, the return, the coming-back, the insistence of the signs, by which we see ourselves governed by the pleasure principle. The Real is that which always lies behind the *automaton*, and it is quite obvious, throughout Freud's research, that it is this that is the object of his concern."[5]

How to square this with Aristotle? With a few threads in place, things begin to assemble into some kind of sense. *Automaton* is repetition in and of the symbolic. It is still in fact a spontaneity involving things, but now those things are letters, the chain of signifiers circulating in the unconscious, that render it "structured like a language"—*comme une langage*, Lacan says, implying with *langage* rather than *langue* that this language is artificial, even cybernetic.[6] Dead letters with a spectral life of their own, these *automata* come and go, jostle, smush together into silly or monstrous assemblages, and occasionally even fall out of the mouth, as awkwardly and surprisingly as if they were a horse, or a tripod. Something like *automaton* is of course there in Freud. On the one hand, it appears in concepts like the "recent and indifferent material" with which dreams have their way, and in the thing-like alienness of fantasies and "imaginary situations" that always return, unsolicited, to excite and trouble one's thoughts.[7] But it also engages Freud's larger concept of *Wiederholung*, repetition, which Lacan reads quite literally: a hauling back up. Lacan compares this *Wiederholung* to a *tirer au sorts*, a drawing of lots. One doesn't pull just anything out a hat; one pulls out, *spontaneously*, what was placed there *by chance.*[8] And never a "pure chance": *automaton* accounts for how the game is rigged for the subject of the unconscious. As the subject of the signifier, of what it is iterable and hence properly repeatable, the subject is enchained to a pseudo-spontaneity in which the only accidents that happen are those already scripted, already written into the chain. The pleasure principle, Lacan suggests, can be understood as precisely the attempt to keep drawing the same lot from the hat, and to studiously avoid others. Its frequent failure is in some sense due to these unconscious chains having their own lifeless will, persisting and insisting "by themselves," *auto-matos.*[9]

With *tyche*, Lacan conceptualizes a radically other repetition. Not a repetition of the signifier, the iterable, the spectral intention of the dead letter, but of what is produced *in between* such repetitions. A gap, a not-sign, a not-iterable, the surplus of any intention. As the repeatable repeats itself, so emerges in between its iterations the paradoxical repetition of what was never there to begin with. This would be, for Lacan, a repetition in and of the Real, that which "resists symbolization absolutely." It would involve a gap that paradoxically fills up the differential negativities of the sign, stopping them in their tracks, or a surplus of results that nonetheless manifests itself as a deficit of intention.[10] These two repetitions might seem independent of each other, but Mladen Dolar warns that they can't be parsed into two independent domains: "they only exist intertwined," they give rise to each other, and could even be considered in the singular as a repetition that "keeps splitting itself."[11] If the Real can be understood here strictly as an effect of the signifier, as something shaken awake by its introduction, it is nonetheless crucial to understand that the Real is not the signifier's *opposite*, since the very concept "opposite" is native to the signifier. This is precisely what makes the premise so strange. *Tyche*, as Dolar formulates it, introduces

> a difference different from difference itself; a difference different from the symbolic difference, while emerging in its bosom, yet not accountable for in terms of the symbolic. It cannot be assigned an identity or a trait. It insists through repetition, be it by something as dramatic as the recurrence of trauma or so (seemingly) light-hearted as the mechanism of the comical. *Tyche* is the good and the bad fortune of the

> signifier. The final essential point is this: *tyche* and *automaton* form an opposition, but which should not be understood as a binary opposition (and the binary opposition was at the heart of the symbolic). *Tyche* is not an entity to be opposed to *automaton*, but this doesn't turn it into a non-entity. Hence, the conceptual couple forms a two which cannot be counted for two, nor reduced to a one.[12]

Here is where Søren Kierkegaard displaces Hegel in the Lacanian cosmology. If Hegel stands for dialectical repetition—a repetition capable of *progressive* negation, of displacement and cancellation, passage and transition, departure—Kierkegaard stands for a kind of repetition that "cannot be submitted to dialectics precisely by not being a negation of negation."[13] Rather, this Kierkegaardian repetition always drags in on its feet what dialectics would have gladly left behind: a bit of Real "stuck to the sole of its shoe."[14] It refuses to remain countable, to adhere to the dialectical command "Be one or none." It always emerges as a zero-plus . . . , or one-minus . . . (Here again might be Beckett's "unnullable least," which Dolar cites near his article's end.) Dialectics needs the iterable, because only what can be repeated can be stopped. The Kierkegaardian repetition of the non-iterable, this unending insistence on repetition's impossibility, liquidates dialectical movement from the inside.[15] It counters a dialectical insistence on the *break*, founding the very possibility of departure, with an anti-dialectical *antagonism* that cannot technically return because it never left the scene. This could sound like a philosophy of foreclosure, but such a conclusion contradicts at least Lacan's own. Kierkegaard kept things open, so he thought. It was the Hegelian system that sewed them up, and Lacan was unambiguous in applying to the latter the logic of fantasy—Hegelian dialectics was an uncountable antagonism veiled by an ongoing chain of zeros and ones. "Hegel's entire dialectic," Lacan declared in his abandoned 1964 seminar on "the names-of-the-father," "is designed to fill this gap [between universal and particular] and to show, through a prestigious transmutation, how the universal can manage to be particularized through the path of scansion brought on by *Aufhebung* [sublation]."[16] Kierkegaard worked through this "prestigious transmutation," essentially traversing Hegel's fundamental fantasy and revealing *Aufhebung* as the concealing name of what was "non-dialectizable," as Lacan put it: the Real object, the object-cause of desire as precisely what is produced through *tyche*. In traversing the dialectical fantasy, the object emerges from under fantasy's veil as what it always was, and what "does not mislead" [*ne trompe pas*]: the object of anxiety.[17] Not least Hegel's own.

This is, undoubtedly, another of Lacan's strong (and in this case quite rash) misreadings.[18] And there is a sticking point. We know when *automaton* happens, and where: here, where the sign repeats, now, when the iterable is iterated. How do we "know" *tyche*? When and where does this bit of Real, this Real object, appear, and what is its manifestation? In the eleventh seminar, Lacan refers to *tyche* once as "the encounter with the Real," but he is careful to qualify it elsewhere: it is a *missed* encounter, a *failed* encounter. The Real can't "show up," it *is* not, it has no ontic status; it is not a metaphysical or gnostic beyond-of-letters, undergirding the shimmer of being, or spreading out, firmament-like, over the world of phenomena. It is an emergent property of the scene, and the psychoanalytic session becomes for Lacan an ideal stage on which to track its truancy. In "this misunderstood concept of repetition, I stress the importance of the ever-avoided encounter, of the missed chance [*chance manquée*]." This "function of missing, of misfiring—which happens all the time [*toujours*] in the analytic repetition—sustains itself through nothing but the marking of a point X, the place of rendezvous, place of *tyche*."[19] Beckett, again.

. . .

Che vuoi? What do you want?

In the analytic session, the question is never that easy to answer, and much harder to stop. It constantly repeats itself, in words but also silently—as a hesitation, a look or looking away, a provoking, by silence, of the silence itself. It begins to toggle back and forth between analyst and analysand, turning into the shortest and most artless of Beckett's plays, their own unnullable least-ing.

On one level, there's a simple enough way of stopping this process. The question must be heard as coming from the analyst, and being answered by the analysand: I want help. And here Lacan, like Freud, had a pretty clear and modest conception of the clinical *aims* of analysis from early on: analysands will likely experience some relief from their suffering by clarifying the nature and logic of their symptoms; coming to recognize their resistances and, in unsettling them, bringing to consciousness their dreams, fantasies, and repressed memories; and articulating the truth of their desires.[20] In the unending factionalized tumult that is the history of psychoanalysis, it's worth noting how canonic these aims remain even today.

But this last condition—the truth of one's desire—already introduces a complicating reflexivity into the process. Desire is, as Lacan endlessly repeated, a lack. It is, moreover, a communicable lack: one catches it from others, from reading their own cues that they too lack for something.[21] And it is in the arena of desire, bound up in the still-radical concept of transference, that the question *che vuoi?* stops stopping and begins again. It becomes an unstable echo, getting longer with each reiteration: "What do *you* want?" "Well, what do you want from *me*?" "Well now, what do you *want* me to want from you?"[22] There, where "the subject expects an oracular reply," a stepping up of the big Other and a filling in of the gap created by the desire behind the question, the oracle persistently abstains.[23] *Che vuoi?* becomes an invitation into the oracular hollows of desire. The ever-avoided encounter, the missed chance, and the rendezvous with the X become points of arrival, where the analysand's desire for help becomes thoroughly reflexive, a plea for help with desire.

Behind this restless little question of want looms the larger question, not of aims, but of ends. What comes of this "marking of a point X" that remains ever empty, ever fails to come to pass? How does one stop a process committed to the unstoppable, enchained to an anti-dialectical insistence on the never-ending repetition of the impossibility of repetition? The question haunted Freud, if in considerably more practical terms. In an essay from 1913, he recalled how at the beginning of his practice "I used to have the greatest difficulty in prevailing on my patients to continue their analysis," but that this difficulty "has long since been shifted, and I now have to take the greatest pains to induce them to give it up."[24] Freud revisits these greatest pains in the canonic late essay "Analysis Terminable and Interminable," offering no anesthetic but instead a sober, deeply ambivalent last word on the possibility of an end: yes, perhaps, in some cases, but often, one must admit, no.[25]

The question continued to haunt, and there is an argument to be made that the history of psychoanalysis—at least, as a history of exhaustive and exhausting self-differentiation, fulminating with life and decline at once—that *this* history is one of so many irreconcilable attempts at "the sense of an ending." Certainly Lacan's "return to Freud," his swaggering series of breaks in the early 1950s with various big Others (the Société Parisienne de Psychanalyse and the International Psychoanalytical Association) and his eventual founding of the École Freudienne de Paris, all revolved in one way or another around the controversy of ending: ending sessions, ending analysis.[26] "Ego psychology," arguably the hegemonic image of psychoanalysis mid-century, quickly became Lacan's *bête noire*: encouraged by the work of Freud's daughter Anna, and seeking a "synchronization" of Freud's concepts, their recalibration into a "self-consistent system," ego psychology was for Lacan pure fantasy, quite literally.[27] It sought the most spurious of stopping places: identification, the image of the Other, the analysand's identification with the analyst. In this sense it became for Lacan a perversion of the (already false) Hegelian dialectic itself, a little enactment of the "prestigious transmutation," the closing of the gap between the analyst's pseudo-universality and the biographical and symptomal particulars of the analysand. In this dystopian scenario, the end of analysis witnessed the re-completion of ego, a becoming-of-self as new self-image, a whole-ing of truth not via immanent dialectic but imposed fantasy: the fantasy of becoming another person.

The Lacanian clinic, as is now well-chronicled, went the way of unbecoming, initiating a process that "tends in a direction that is the exact opposite of identification" and is ultimately guided by the analyst's own "desire to obtain absolute difference."[28] Here the distinction between *automaton* and *tyche* illuminates what could be seen as the central partition of Lacan's practice. On the one side, there is a psychoanalytic *aim* beholden to the logic of *automaton*, tracking iterable objects (dreams, memories, fantasies, concrete and readable symptoms) in a spirit of, if not quite dialectical, then at least progressive movement toward a relief of symptoms and a self-excavation. Here the model is anamnesis, the maieutic method of

Socrates—the repetition of the act of discovery, of what one didn't know one already knew. The analysand arrives at an "assumption of his history," a recognition that "his unconscious is his history—in other words, we help him complete the current historicization of the facts that have already determined a certain number of the historical 'turning points' in his existence."[29]

On the other side of this clinical partition, unfolding simultaneously, one finds a psychoanalytic *end* beholden to the logic of *tyche*, tracking Real objects, objects that perpetually avoid their appointment with the signifier, that bring about its "good or bad fortune," its welcome surplus or unwelcome failure. Here it is less Socrates than Kierkegaard who provides the model: a pure or empty-handed repetition, of what cannot be retrieved and reinserted into its proper place in the chain of one's history.[30] A repetition of what cannot be mastered, and of one's own un-mastery. Dolar reminds that Hegel is, in the broadest strokes, of the Socratic line when it comes to anamnesis; knowledge moves by making "for itself" what was already "in itself." In Kierkegaardian repetition, knowledge is replaced with—or, better, sutured to—irony, as a return to what dialectics cannot cancel out or supersede, and in fact keeps producing.[31]

Despite an older tendency to periodize Lacan—to show, for instance, that "early Lacan" was all about the symbolic, and "later Lacan" about the Real—these two registers persist throughout Lacan's work from the early 1950s, their form, respective priority, and interrelation in a state of constant recalibration.[32] In the talks and seminars of the early 1950s, for instance, Lacan adamantly asserted that the end of analysis entails "the advent of true speech," a putting into words the truth of one's desire.[33] But already here, this recognition doesn't necessarily bring about a catharsis, and certainly not a moment of positive identification in any traditional sense. Quite the opposite: it initiates a coming apart of the subject's anchoring identifications, an almost chemical ana-lysis of the very materials, the "gear," of the subject's self-image and construction. As Lacan puts it in the first seminar, "What is at issue at the end of analysis [is] a twilight, an imaginary decline of the world, and even an experience at the limit of depersonalization."[34] Lacan holds on to this scenario of subjective *Götterdämmerung* through the end of his work, constantly revising its dramaturgy. It appears in especially vivid form in the seventh seminar of 1960 ("The Ethics of Psychoanalysis"), where "the true termination of an analysis" comes with a real existential crisis, a bringing of the subject into a state of almost infantile helplessness. Alluding to Freud's work on anxiety, Lacan claims the analysand "should reach and know the domain and the level of the experience of absolute disarray [*désarroi absolu*]." Disarray, but not necessarily angst, which "is already a protection, not so much *Abwarten* [an abiding or deferral] as *Erwartung* [waiting for something]. Anxiety develops by letting a danger appear, whereas there is no danger at the level of the experience of a final *Hilflosigkeit* [helplessness]." This final helplessness is infantile, not a state of summoning, of supplication and appeal, however inarticulate. Rather, it is a state of certainty, "in which man is in that relationship to himself which is his own death . . . and can expect help from no one."[35] Lacan maintains this dynamic of dis-identification, disarray, and transition in the eleventh seminar, insisting on the possibility, at the end of analysis, of a "crossing of the plane of identification," brought about by "the maintenance of the distance between the I—identification—and the [*objet*] *a*." It is also in this seminar where Lacan finally makes explicit the "traversal of the radical fantasy" as "the beyond of analysis," a beyond that "has never been approached," but that must nonetheless persist as a postulate. In an oeuvre of retractions and formulations, this constitutes what Bruce Fink considers the only one of Lacan's "utopian moments" he never recanted later on (unlike, say, "true" or "full speech").[36]

By the mid-1970s, Lacan comes to a more formal account of the end of analysis, involving a triad of co-constitutive conditions or situations. But all three affirm the priority of *tyche* over *automaton*, repetition of the gap over recovery of the memory. Truth emerges not as hauling up of what was always there, but as a (repeated) encounter with what never was. The fundamental fantasy, as the axiomatic frame for the subject's desire, is traversed, and as it "capsizes," the subject loses its "foothold of desire," along with the coordinating assurance of its "window on the Real."[37] This entails a corresponding "subjective destitution," a *désêtre* or "dis-being," in which the subject's imaginary identifications are unmoored, experienced in all their weightless contingency. The very metric for gauging the subject's relations to others, its capacity for similarity-to and difference-from, falters. The "big secret of psychoanalysis" is placed in the open, and assumed: there is no Other of the Other; the Other is, like the subject, split and also lacks. Hence the analyst too suffers a kind of destitution or dis-being; he or she is expelled from the position of having some secret knowledge about the subject and is reduced to a "mere surplus, a pure *objet petit a*, the cause of the analysand's desire."[38] As these two forms of illusory plenitude and security break apart or dry up, the subject comes to perhaps the only form of identification Lacan ever endorses: an identification with its own symptom. "Symptom" here designates not a specific manifest behavior (a conversion symptom, for instance), but the subject's own unique means of experiencing the impossibility of *jouissance*, and the ensuing behavior produced by attempts to come to terms with this impossibility. As Colette Soler points out, this moment becomes an ultimate retort to the "mirror stage": rather than taking on an "ineffable identity" provided by the Other, and "affirmed by the ecstatic 'you are that,'" the subject takes up its own imageless, "incurable" lack, its inimitable way of enjoying what it doesn't have, and exclaims—perhaps also ecstatically—"I am that."[39]

. . .

Even admitting Lacan's controversial attempt to bring this process down to earth through his formalization of "the pass," there persists in his "end of analysis" a perfectly uncomfortable mix of apocalyptic prophecy and magician's sleight of hand.[40] Behold, the world as you know it will end! But—behold, nothing will change! Perhaps the most astonishing trick is that it is not an end at all. It changes, and with it also the subject's relation to the repeated impossibility of repetition, the unstoppable tracking of truancy. The triad of destitution, traversal, and symptom-identification prepare the analysand—by default, if not design—to become an analyst. "There is only one kind of psychoanalysis," Lacan says in *Seminar XI*: "the training analysis—which means a psychoanalysis that has looped this loop [the traversal of the fundamental fantasy] to its end. The loop must be run through several times. There is in effect no other way of accounting for the term *durcharbeiten* [working through], of the necessity of elaboration, except to conceive how the loop must be run through more than once."[41]

Despite Lacan's lifelong commitment to training professional analysts, the end of analysis doesn't entail a professionalization of one's new knowledge, but rather the possibility of a new kind of social link, one practicable far beyond the heterotopia of the analytic clinic. As I discussed in chapter 4, Lacan schematizes this link in his seventeenth seminar on the discourses. If "the other side of psychoanalysis" is the master's discourse, then psychoanalysis must be its inverse, a discourse of not-mastery, a paradoxical way of employing the practice of language, as what "dominates" society, in order to weaken and neutralize domination from the inside. Here the negative prefix is especially important. The discourse of the analyst isn't one of anti-mastery, which Lacan schematizes as the hysteric's discourse, a discourse of antagonizing the master, pushing the master's self-justification to and past the point of failure (the protester could be seen as one model, the hypochondriac another).[42] Nor does this link require the authorization of the master, which Lacan presents as the university's discourse, committed to rationalizing a master who remains repressed beneath the disinterestedness of knowledge (the textbook here is, indeed, the textbook example). The discourses of both the hysteric and the university emerge through a half turn in each direction of the master's discourse, with which they share an occlusion of antagonism; as post-Saussurean language schemata, they model its movement, and show how an ineliminable negativity is set to work in structurally distinct ways. But an essential part of this work is repression, represented by each discourse's "truth," figured in its lower left-hand corner. In the university discourse, "knowledge" represses its authorization by a master who need know (and often does know) nothing; in the hysteric's discourse, the hysteric represses a desire ultimately indifferent to the knowledge it demands from the master; in the master's discourse, the master represses its own status as a split subject, constitutionally lacking.

In this sense, each of these three discourses models an unstoppable repetition whose intensity is, if anything, egged on by its founding repression. The hysteric's desire, the authority of knowledge, the man behind the master's curtain, all obey

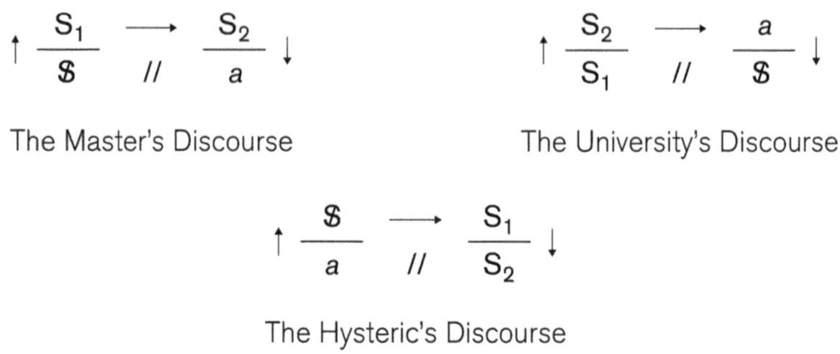

FIGURE 19. Discourse schemata of the master, university, and hysteric.

what Eric Santner calls an "immunological dialectic," a paradox whereby the "defense mechanisms [discourses] used to protect against a primordial exposure—to 'cover' [their] nudity—serve in the end to redouble this exposure. . . . Something falls through the cracks of the dialectic and keeps returning to its place to initiate the whole process again, indeed to endow it with the aspect of a *repetition compulsion.*"[43] But this repetition is compelled by repression, and by its masking: something structurally impossible in the scheme is covered over, rendered fantasmatic by the discourse itself. It becomes an empirically lost (or assumed) object, which the discourse in turn endeavors to recover—simply through the act of speaking itself. It seems "ordinary language" was following Socrates's maieutic method already, all by itself, *auto-matos.*

As Lacan formulates it, the analyst's discourse is no less immune to antagonism, nor does it involve a liberation from compulsive repetition, which is the fate of any discourse: to endlessly re-secure the coordinates and spacing of a certain spoken situation. Moreover, it still has truck with the master signifier, and is in fact designed to produce it—again and again. What makes the analyst's discourse constitutionally different than the other three is that it does not repress its antagonism, nor occlude the impossibility it engenders. Instead, it makes these the basis of its social link.

This begins with the place of the speaker or agent. It is now occupied, not by the analyst so much as the role the analyst tries to play in his or her "desire to obtain absolute difference": the *objet a.* It is the discourse's first manifestation of impossibility, since it requires on the analyst's part a kind of self-annulment, or unnullable least-ing. This would seem to correspond to Lacan's claim that *being* an analyst is impossible. One can only occupy the role for someone during a finite period; one can only *be* a subject, and the analyst is, during the treatment, not (or not quite) a subject.[44] In this sense, the analyst plays the part of *tyche,* a bit of Real endlessly reproduced by the repetition of the iterable, the "refuse and leftover of knowledge," as Dolar puts it.[45] And this explains the role, in the lower left-hand position, of the

FIGURE 20. Schema of the analyst's discourse.

discourse's "truth," S_2: it represents *automaton*, unconscious knowledge in the symbolic. This knowledge is, as Lacan stresses, opposed to anything like scientific knowledge; it is a "disjoint," "mythical" knowledge, replete with assemblages, chains of sense and nonsense formed "spontaneously" over time.[46] The analysand may repress such knowledge, but the discourse doesn't. Rather, the analyst is guided negatively by it, encouraging its errant anamnestic paths while tracking what remains unsaid, and prompting its saying.[47] So "truth" here is no longer veiled, as in the other discourse. It is simply not enough. It remains valuable only insofar as its signifiers continue to suffer a "good or bad fortune" at the hands of *tyche*. In this way, the left side of Lacan's model presents Dolar's non-binary opposition, a "conceptual couple [forming] a two which cannot be counted for two, nor reduced to a one."

Continuing the inversion of the master's discourse, the formula for fantasy—$\$ \Diamond a$—is shifted from its repressed position, as what the master disavows, into the upper register. And it is reversed: no longer a split subject fantasizing its mute object of desire, but a "conscious" object of desire failing to be coordinated within the frames of the subject's fantasy. In the master's discourse, fantasy constitutes and controls the scene by remaining unconscious and axiomatic, its staging of impossibility enjoyed by the subject. In the analyst's discourse, the fantasy is gradually un-earthed, excavated but also cut off from its gravitational source. It begins to produce less anchoring enjoyment and more unexpected effects. It ceases to function as a projection, a source of enduring consistency for the subject, and begins instead to sputter, to manifest as gaps, glitches, impasses, sudden turns and discontinuities. As the fantasy enters the ego's arena of words—Lacan's *entrée en je* as a "getting into the game" [*jeu*]—it suffers the signifier's fortunes.

Essential to this process is its product, or rather, its by-product: S_1, the master signifier, now in the discourse's lower right-hand corner. S_1 is arguably the most equivocal of the discourse's figures, in large part because the *production* of master signifiers would seem to be a contradiction in terms. Once signifiers are "masters," *they* produce, *they* constitute unmoved movers, absolute causes. As such, they remain masterly only by means of their place, which is never entirely within the symbolic. Though they be words or phrases (actual or chimeric, like the "unicorn signifier" *Poordjeli*), they arrest signification's movement.[48] Rather than remaining open to potentially infinite displacements in an always contingent process of meaning-making, master signifiers retain something of the materiality and opacity of the imaginary. A bit like an unrecognized glyph in a digital text document, they remain unselectable, incapable of being copied and pasted into new contexts. In this sense their power is proportionate to their senselessness: the more isolated they remain as a "minimal form of inscription," the more efficiently they organize the signifying networks around them.[49] They are, as Lacan puts it in *Seminar XX*, stupid, a bit of "funny business" (*la bêtise*).[50] Ask a master signifier what it is, and it responds, with a vacuous, angelic smile, "I am what I am."[51]

This stupidity empowers precisely through tautology. The master's discourse displays it openly, a resounding "Because I said so" with no rhyme or reason. But it exists indirectly in the hysteric's discourse, too, via interpellation (master remains master so long as the hysteric antagonizes it as such), and in the university's discourse, via concealment (master remains master so long as its knowledge designates it silent authorizing Other). In the analyst's discourse, however, this tautology is disrupted through how a master signifier is manifested: coming out of the mouth of a split subject who doesn't understand it.[52] Fink notes that "in the analytic situation, a master signifier presents itself as a dead end, a stopping point, a term, word, or phrase that puts an end to association, that grinds the patient's discourse to a halt."[53] The analysand often wants to dismiss such moments, precisely as stupidity, *bêtise*, a failure of cognition or imagination. And on some level the master signifier itself "wants" this, too—to fill the silence with its own reiteration, to tautologize the gap out of existence. But Lacan contends that analysis must hold such moments open. It is there where the radically new emerges.

Here Kierkegaard is again summoned to the scene, this time in the form of his favored trope, irony. The image is certainly ironic in the everyday sense: the subject coughing up its most intimate master, whom it does not recognize—an anamnesis inducing sudden amnesia. But it is also ironic in the sense Kierkegaard prized it: as "a non-Hegelian, an anti-Hegelian negativity," as Dolar puts it, "a negativity which would not be merely a passage and a transition." Such a negativity, like dialectics, "bores holes into knowledge," but unlike dialectics, it allows such holes to stand. Passages and transitions emerge, but one remains there. The Hegelian seal between "what is reasonable" and "what is actual" is broken, introducing a gap that is not *permanent*, but *recurring*, the absent twin constantly being reborn alongside new knowledge.[54]

In this sense, the master signifier, as spoken by the analysand, becomes the quintessential "conceptual couple [forming] a two which cannot be counted for two, nor reduced to a one." There is on the one hand the production—spontaneously, via *automaton*—of a new piece of "unknown knowledge" that is not new at all, but old, and that is now hauled back up from the unconscious where it was originally placed "by chance": S_1, now rendered as a piece of language and allowed to "get in the game" of the symbolic, S_2. On the other hand, there is the rendering, along with this old and unrecollected signifier, of what was never there in the first place, something completely new: the signifier's contingency, its tychic fortune, a precariousness whose unthinkability was what kept the object hidden and unspeakable in the first place. Fantasy is here what maintains this unthinkability. The master signifier, as a piece of old unknown knowledge, is made manifest only by simultaneously manifesting a new knowledge beyond anamnesis, never before known—that it is no longer a master. Here, it might seem, is Kierkegaard's own owl of Minerva, an appropriate inversion of Hegel's: if knowledge only takes flight at dusk, truth takes flight at dawn, a dawning of the limits of knowledge. Lacan contends that psychoanalysis ceaselessly repeats this new truth. It is, as Dolar puts it, only in this repetition that it "has the capacity to transform the past and to produce the new."[55]

13

REPETITION (3)

" . . . there stirs here everywhere an apocalyptic dissatisfaction with subjectivity itself and the older forms of the self." Fredric Jameson is here talking about aesthetic modernism at the turn of the twentieth century.[1] But—to slip into the mode of Žižekian rhetorical questioner—is not Lacan the quintessential apocalyptic dissatisfactionist of subjectivity? Is his clinic not an exemplary modernist heterotopia, a quite literal "other space" in which the more robust and hegemonic cultural fantasies of the European bourgeoisie—even its utopias—are analyzed, broken apart and broken down, eventually traversed? Certainly Lacan's long-evolving conception of the end(s) of analysis, and his extension of their effects into the meta-clinic of social discourse, bear an uncanny likeness to so many of modernism's most canonical categories. Perhaps more than a likeness: a parody, or a daemonization.[2] Those (there are many) who are piqued by either Lacan's attitude or modernism's, or both, would find this an easy equation to make: the disdainful hauteur, the extreme difficulty bordering on opacity of the writings and seminars, the hubristic prioritization—now utterly scandalous in a therapeutic context—of truth over happiness, or, rather, truth *at the cost of* happiness. It is an almost too-perfect rehearsal of modernism's bipolar stance toward style, its utter effacement or total transfiguration of surface.

But attitude needn't direct the diagnosis; it's there in the operations. Subject loses coordinates of its reality and experiences the crumbling of its symbolic order; subject's capacity to cultivate and regulate desire is disrupted, or outright sabotaged; subject's self-placement in relation to the other (as individual, group, tradition, history, law, nature, and of course language) is unmoored; subject assumes the "big secret" that there is no Other of the Other, no absolute guarantor of the symbolic order's consistency. Destitution and radical helplessness, identification with the symptom, the endless repetition of the gap, the void, the missed encounter. We are in the territory of a modernist poetics here, where "negative categories predominate" and "are definitional, not pejorative."[3]

What would Hugo Friedrich have made of the Lacanian session? I wonder if he wouldn't have found it a strange kind of modernist performative verse, whose improvisatory character didn't diminish the presence of Friedrich's own clinical categories for modern poetry, but strengthened them, made them more "real": "disorientation, disintegration of the familiar, loss of order, incoherence, fragmentism [*sic*] . . . brutal abruptness, dislocation, astigmatism, alienation."[4] And then there is the Lacanian clinic's twofold problem of ending, which was also modernism's, not least Samuel Beckett's: How will this ever end? How will this ever-ending ever stop? If modernism can be understood in the most general sense as a response to modernity, a testing of its modes of representation, then Lacanian psychoanalysis is a testing of Jürgen Habermas's classic formulation: the latter's "incomplete project of modernity" is pushed to its limits by a ceaseless *projection of incompleteness*, a practice of "subjectivizing oneself indefinitely . . . with no reason for stopping."[5] It is uncanny to read T. J. Clark's brazen assertion, back in 1982, that "the fact of Art, in modernism, *is* the fact of negation," in the context of Lacan's last great scansion, a year before his death in 1981: the dissolution of the École freudienne de Paris, the school he had founded upon his "excommunication" from the International Psychoanalytic Institute.[6] As Clark goes on in his article about medium, think of speech and letter; as he writes of gap and silence, think *tyche* and scansion. What is Lacan's subject but a captured lack, made over, endlessly, into form?

> The very way that modernist art has insisted on its medium has been by negating that medium's ordinary consistency—by pulling it apart, emptying it, producing gaps and silences, making it stand as the opposite. . . . [Modernism] presents itself as a work of interminable and absolute decomposition, a work which is always pushing "medium" to its limits—to its ending—to the point where it breaks or evaporates or turns back into mere unworked material. That is the form in which medium is retrieved or reinvented. . . . Negation is the sign inside art of [a] wider decomposition: it is an attempt to capture the lack of consistent and repeatable meanings in the culture—to capture the lack and make it over into form.[7]

Lacan's emerging fame in the 1970s and 1980s, particularly in the academy, seems inextricable from his (dubious) status as a canonical postmodernist; he is still sometimes carelessly bound together with that 1960s "slogan of the decade," the "death of the subject."[8] But very few—with the exception, in an odd moment, of the ever-canny Raymond Williams—have considered Lacan as a modernist, as someone who could not stop thinking about the subject and about language as its (and his) "medium," and whose relentless testing of its wiles suggests something almost like faith in its indestructible, virtually absolute status.[9] The Lacanian field is not, I think, what psychoanalysis looks like when it finally receives or is overtaken by postmodernism. It is what modernism, losing its hegemonic grip on the arts, begins to look like when it migrates (back) into psychoanalysis, when the linguistic turn invites the human psyche to become as pushable, as testable, as absolutely decomposable as paint.[10]

. . .

In the course of this book, I have been moving toward—or, better, cycling progressively around, in my own scansions and digressions—the postulate that we are seeing and hearing in much European New Music in 1989 something like an analyst's discourse in the Lacanian sense. This would be the heuristic claim. It was initially afforded through propinquity—by taking a "found object" from that same year, Žižek's strong (mis)reading of Lacan in his *The Sublime Object of Ideology* (1989), laying out some of its theoretical and analytical possibilities, and fashioning from them a lens, a tool, a "critical apparatus" for reading a musical world contemporaneous and geographically proximate, but otherwise utterly aloof.[11] The usual justification for such heuristic approaches is that, regardless of their historical "truth," they produce interesting results, create new affordances, bear forth happily unanticipated thought-fruit; I would hope to have done this, and I think there is much more to be accomplished in the directions suggested here. The enclosure of the psychoanalytic clinic—an ambivalent one, endlessly provocative of intense debate—is a durable allegory for the heterotopian "other space" of European New Music, a space that was still in 1989 as autonomous a musical scene as any the world had ever produced, for better and worse. It was also a space into which subject after subject from the past seems to come, recline, speak, and fall apart. Here is where one might speak of a "deep resonance," but I think this cheats a bit, tacitly chalking things up to the grand historical Om.[12] I have so far been identifying an isomorphism: an equality of forms that, nonetheless, do not *generate* each other.

But at the same time, in my cycling and scanding I've also tried to shift Lacanian psychoanalysis gradually from a place of mere "good fortune" into a more reflexive domain, where its constitutional likeness begins to compromise its tool-being, its capacity for instrumental manipulation. Here I recall Shoshana Felman's classic essay "To Open the Question," in which she investigates the notorious cupola between literature and psychoanalysis.[13] Felman doesn't dare assume the possibility of a *rapport sexuel*, but she does conceive literature and psychoanalysis as two bodies, one of language, the other knowledge, and she seeks to destabilize their master-slave dialectic, both through reversal (psychoanalysis "submitted" to literary methods) and implication (a literal in-folding, bringing mutual enlightenment, but also displacement). With music it clearly isn't so easy—it's not at all apparent whether music is a "body," it seems hasty to speak of reversals—and I have no intention in the remaining few chapters of arguing for a larger conceptualization of the cupola between psychoanalysis and music in general.[14] But Felman makes a striking move midway through her essay, when she writes of how literature

> deconstructs the fantasy of authority in the same way, and for the same reasons, that psychoanalysis deconstructs the authority of the fantasy—its claim to belief and to power as the sole window through which we behold and perceive reality, as the sole window through which reality can indeed reach our grasp, enter into our consciousness. Psychoanalysis tells us that the fantasy is a fiction, and that consciousness is itself, in a sense, a fantasy-effect. In the same way, literature tells us that authority is a language effect, the product of the creation of its own rhetorical power: that authority is the power of fiction; that authority is, therefore, likewise a fiction.[15]

While one might now take issue with the strength and sweep of this 1977 claim, I'm compelled by something in it that pushes past isomorphism, and even a bit toward an Om. Felman invokes literature's "language effect," its "rhetorical power," in such a way that it casts a shadow back onto something like its pure medium, material indifference, pushable testable decomposable stuff. It is an uncanny moment, there in that late-1970s bastion of deconstructive intensities, *Yale French Studies*, to see something resonating to roundly with an assessment like Clark's, just a few years later in *Critical Inquiry*, of a "wider decomposition" in culture for which "negation is the sign inside art," "an attempt to capture the lack of consistent and repeatable meanings in the culture—to capture the lack and make it over into form." I am not prepared to make the argument that deconstruction is what modernism looks like when it migrates into the heterotopia of the academy, and when it takes literature and philosophy as its subjects to test. But Felman's alignment of deconstruction with (psycho)analysis as mutual projects is noteworthy. She identifies them both as engaging in a structurally specific negativity, one that links an analytic agent to an Other through a discursive structure, and which performs the gradual negation of the other's mastery—as a mastery of frame or form—such that the very armature of mastery is undone, such that no new master comes.[16] Not a hystericized deposing of the king, but a dismantling of the throne. It is a discourse that, temporal at heart, nonetheless has no future, or, rather, no *image* of the future, no *authorizing semblant.* Instead it proposes to unearth the axioms that it believes determine the past and control the present, and that, finally being unearthed, no longer need determine a future newly opened. Felman even goes so far as to contend that the traversal of fantasy is the common essence of this negativity, and that a tychic tracking of the missed encounter, the text's or subject's own never-was, is the way out of the foreclosure brought on by fantasy itself.

If I have a more robust claim to make, it is that the isomorphism between the Lacanian clinic and European New Music—one rooted in a discursive logic, a structuring of the dynamic between speaker/musicker and listener, but also between composing subject and historical or artifactual subject—is not a mere fabrication of the book, created to produce meaning effects, but also anchored in its cultural and historical moment. But this moment is *long*. And strange. It is strictly speaking *not* a moment of beginning, or of ending, which is to say it interferes with the idea of periodicity itself, with the very possibilities of break, span, and supersession. If anything it is their undoing, a moment which is no moment. It emerges through the buckling of such categories, their "impediment, failure, crack"—the glitch or parapraxis in the periodizing unconscious. It presents as antagonism, a stumbling of the dialectic, the breaking down of the mechanism of break. To go all the way back to chapter 2, it is what happens—not necessarily *with* the composition of Ludwig van Beethoven's late works, but when their wild tangles, their self-attacking profusions of fantasy, are prevented from sinking into obscurity and instead mediated by a kind of discourse, a form of social link, and when that discourse gradually takes root, struggles hegemonically, becomes political. Musical modernism becomes analogous to the analyst who heard the slip that would otherwise have gone unnoticed; or, better, it becomes the clinic in which what would have sounded like nonsense must now *mean*.

Paradoxically, this glitchiness is what allows this moment-of-no-moment to constantly return, to appear in its own right as historically indestructible. "The more the signifier signifies nothing," Lacan says in his seminar on the psychoses, "the more indestructible it is."[17] When I wrote in chapter 11 of a "fourth register" of repetition, of Dusapin's repeating of Debussy's generic silence as a repetition of what was never there to begin with, it was this moment I had in mind, as the repetition of an indestructible null set. Here the word "resonance" no longer seems like such a cheat. This is modernism as a hollows, an acoustic situation. A void to which the modernist comes, anticipating echo, and calls, not *OM* but *NO*.

• • •

Jameson seems to read the Lacanian project as a—potentially—emancipatory one, a continuation or uncanny return of "the great modernist evocations of subjectivity as so much longing for depersonalization, and very precisely for some new existence outside the self, in a world radically transformed and worthy of ecstasy."[18] In its call for "a twilight, an imaginary decline of the world, and even an experience at the limit of depersonalization," Lacan's enterprise would seem to constitute another of Jameson's "great new and original modern philosophies . . . that [carry] aesthetic modernism forward." All these philosophies "involve or project, in their very different ways, methods of radical depersonalization," and in this sense they find a common area—a paradoxical atrium, one might say—in the enclosure of the psychoanalytic clinic, a place where the invitation to be subjective, to "turn inward," turns quickly into one of the twentieth century's more "self-punishing and depersonalizing" disciplines, a doppelgänger of phenomenology for the unsuspecting, non-philosophizing everyman.[19] Jameson reads depersonalization as perfectly counter to the Frankfurt School's universally pejorative conception of the term: for them, depersonalization signified a long, slow, "tendential reduction in the possibilities of human praxis," the reifying and shattering of what is most human in the individual.[20] In Lacanian psychoanalysis, Jameson detects an inversion, and one he thinks essentially modernist: ego is *already* reification, the first, the most oppressive and effective defense against the possibility of the new. One must, like Rimbaud or D. H. Lawrence, sleep and exile oneself in bottomless nights, or let oneself be carried by a wind blowing the new direction of Time.

Jameson holds up the angels in Rainer Maria Rilke's eponymous 1907 poem as exemplary in their hatred of psychology, of the ego as the bourgeoisie's most insidious residence:

> . . . Otherwise they'll come
>
> at night to you to test you with a fiercer grip
> and go like someone angry through your house
> and seize you as if they'd created you
> and break you out of your mold.[21]

Common to all these modes of modernist depersonalization, Jameson contends, is their emancipatory intention. Though they might initially look like inward turns, calls to a subjectivity "new, deeper, richer," it is "on the face of it perverse" not to hear them as exhortations to break the category of subjectivity altogether. As such, "they evoke a momentum that cannot find resolution within the self, but that must be completed by a Utopian and revolutionary transmutation of the world of actuality itself."[22]

Here Jameson returns us to Perry Anderson's "third coordinate of the modernist conjuncture," the "imaginative proximity of social revolution." It was "the haze of social revolution drifting across the horizon of this epoch," Anderson writes, that "gave it much of its apocalyptic light for those currents of modernism most unremittingly and violently radical in their rejection of the social order as a whole."[23] So the "apocalyptic dissatisfaction with subjectivity" is not hyperbole. It is literal: it is the expression, the pressing-out, of a world-ending immanence, "already indwelling and stirring convulsively within the present." This expression "does not posit mere individual affects and faculties, but imperiously demands whole new kinds of human beings fit for a world poised on the edge of some thoroughgoing metamorphosis."[24]

The *passage* from one world to the next, the *transition* from one kind of human to the next, a *newness* departing from what could be left behind through radical negation. It shouldn't at all surprise that Jameson (like Anderson) is holding on here to the dialectic, and that his modernism takes a Hegelian-Marxist form. But Lacan, at least the anti-dialectical, Kierkegaardian Lacan, fits awkwardly into it. Or rather, he would know how to place Jameson's portrait of modernism: a master's discourse. As Jameson and Anderson conceive it, modernism's call-for-the-new coordinates its S_1 in the position of discursive agent. "New," as master signifier, is also *in the position* of master. It assumes the function of an absolute demand. It mobilizes the aesthetic regime's means, its knowledge and know-how, in the production of a Real object, a surplus enjoyment—an impossible modernity, ubiquitous, incipient, always "poised on the edge of some thoroughgoing metamorphosis," some imminent manifestation.

This is modernism as a master's discourse, and—as I postulated at the end of chapter 7 (see figure 15)—it could also be read as a formalization, after Matei Călinescu, of the fundamental modernist fantasy, which the discourse's upper register disavows: its unconscious commitment to a modernity whose impossibility it axiomatically enjoys. "Commitment" here could be another way of designating fantasy as "not something to be proven or demonstrated per se, but something that generates all of the [field's] allowable statements."[25] But herein lies the sleight of hand in the master's discourse: the fantasy's unconscious foreclosure of possibility—its assurance of failure and certainty of loss, as I'd put it in the earlier chapter—is occluded by a projection of a radically open horizon and an infinite possibility. In short, this Jamesonian or "master modernist" holds up the ecstatic master signifier—"New!" or "Revolution!"—only so long as it remains capable of producing the revolutionary horizon as an impossible object, an object of enjoyment. This scenario would seem to correspond with Lacan's comments on Hegel in his abandoned seminar of 1964. The discourse performs precisely that "prestigious transmutation," that filling of a gap between universal and particular, that allows a fantasmatic foreclosure of the new to manifest as a dialectic utterly beholden to it. The split subject of the master's discourse enjoys a tychic repetition of the missed encounter, the bit of Real produced in its non-appearance, while the discourse's "ego" stages a dialectical performance: a pantomime of repetitions *forward, progressive* negations, acts of true cancellation and true beginning. Revolution as a break and breakthrough rather than a turning in place.

In a passage redacted from the published versions of the seventeenth seminar, Lacan allegedly proclaims that "the best thing to do to bring about revolution is to be not anarchists but analysts."[26] It's not clear why the passage never made it into Jacques-Alain Miller's preparation of the seminar's transcripts, but its absence is poetic: Lacan's own call for revolution could only take the form of a missed encounter. After all, the "revolutionary aspiration has only a single possible outcome—of ending up as the master's discourse."[27] In the same acrid exchange in which Lacan proclaims his famous "What you aspire to as revolutionaries is a master. You will get one," he confesses that he, "like everybody," is "liberal only to the extent that I am anti-progressive. With the caveat," he continues,

> that I am caught up in a movement that deserves to be called progressive, since it is progressive to see the psychoanalytic discourse founded, insofar as the latter completes the circle that could perhaps enable you to locate what it is exactly that you are rebelling against—which doesn't stop that thing from continuing incredibly well. And the first to collaborate with this, right here at Vincennes, are you, for you fulfill the role of helots of this regime. You don't know what that means either? The regime is putting you on display. It says, "Look at them enjoying!"[28]

The redacted passage holds to the same logic. The call for the new, as a call to revolution, is a call for masters—whether they be old or new—*to return to a position of master*, which, despite all upheavals, remains fastened in place. Hystericizing the master—playing the helots, allowing the master to point and shout, in accusatory glee, "Look at them enjoying!"—only protects the throne, as it were. The place of authority holds, and according to the logic of fantasy, the place is the thing. As such, "Revolution!" enacts the same ego-subject split as outlined above, and now as an etymological split as well: an ego-discourse in the symbolic demands revolution as break, an apocalyptic ending and beginning of worlds. Simultaneously an unconscious fantasy in the Real demands a revolution as turn, accomplishing—as I quoted in chapter 4—"its own revolution in the other sense of doing a complete circle."[29]

The analyst's discourse, as the implied "other side of mastery," is structured to counteract this dual process. Lacan conceives it as a kind of loop that brings analysands to their analytical "end," but also then past, into the position of analyst. This loop initiates an awkward, un-opposite counteraction: if it breaks the master's vicious *circle*, it is not through a full stop but through the repetition of a disruptive *cycle*, which, always moving forward in time, never ceases returning to an antagonism, in the process throwing off a bit of Real, an absolutely new beyond the recollectable or immanent. Here one sees the long reach of Schelling, a rendering of Schelling's refusal to "bring the beginning back," to "return into nothing, into boundless freedom," into a kind of method in itself.[30]

. . .

Contra Jameson and Anderson, what would the "analytic modernist" look like? We might begin to answer on a formal level, deriving the schema itself by turning the master's discourse two clockwise quarter turns. The schema is suggestive: the modernist, as a split subject, and modernity as its Real object always about to be, are transposed from the unconscious "into the open." Modernity retains its status as a Real object, and also as the surplus precipitated by an aesthetic knowledge and know-how inscribed in the symbolic other. Hence modernity remains the tychic

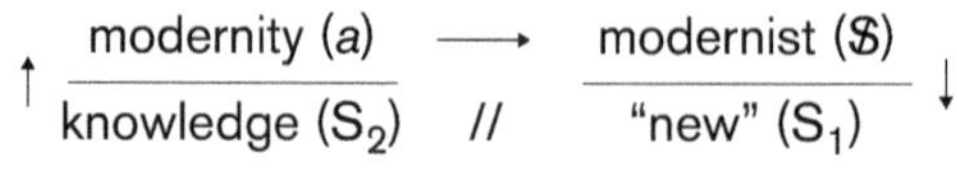

FIGURE 21. Modernism as an analyst's discourse (first attempt).

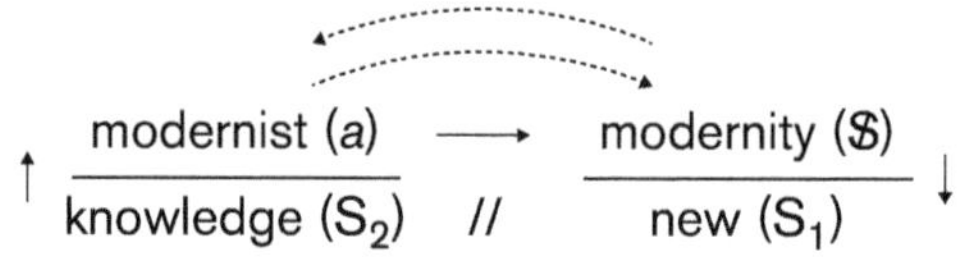

FIGURE 22. Modernism as an analyst's discourse (second attempt).

leftover constantly being reproduced by the symbolic's *automaton*, its signifying insistence. This impossible modernity, always striving toward "absolute difference," tests the fantasizing modernist, resisting all attempts to coordinate and enjoy its impossibility, all desires for absolute unity or harmony (a *rapport sexuel*). In the process, the modernist is brought to cough up its master signifiers, the axioms that anchor its fantasmatic framing of the world. Articulated, rendered in the symbolic, they emerge as double entities, "conceptual couples [forming] a two which cannot be counted for two, nor reduced to a one": *old* masters, coupled with a *new* contingency that unmasters them.[31]

I think this model goes some way toward schematizing the "other side" of a master-modernism. But it misses two essential characteristics. The first involves what I, along with Clark and Jameson I think, take as a constitutional desire of our mythical modernist: to *be* the analyst, to assume a position of agency in the analytic endeavor. To be the one who tests, the catalyst or instrument of an untying of subjectivity that may, in the end, nonetheless be one's own. So I would propose a transposition, not of Lacan's figures, but of the particular terms occupying them: *a*, the position of analyst, is also the position of modernist. Modernity is now rendered a split subject.

This transposition speaks to the peculiar salience of the analyst's discourse, specifically that it effects not a mere change of places, but a fundamental shift in roles. To imagine an analytic modernism would seem to entail the modernist divesting him- or herself of either the thrall of fantasy or the pall of analysis *as a role*. But this transposition also speaks to Jameson's contention, with which I still agree, about modernism's "apocalyptic dissatisfaction with subjectivity": namely that its endeavors in depersonalization were initiated *by* modernist subjects themselves, who were the first to come undone. One can understand Lacan's claim for the de-

$$\uparrow \; \frac{\text{modernity } (a)}{\text{knowledge } (S_2)} \; \begin{array}{c}\longrightarrow \\ // \end{array} \; \frac{\text{modernity [the past] } (\$)}{\text{“new” } (S_1)} \; \downarrow$$

FIGURE 23. Modernism as an analyst's discourse (third attempt).

ontologizing of the analyst (one cannot *be* an analyst) as another in a long line of modernist claims, from Rimbaud's *je est un autre* to Beckett's "not I." The analytic modernist would be one who actively takes up his or her unnullable least-ing, a self-desubjecting in service to *another* subject's desire.

This raises the second missed characteristic: the status of modernity. If modernity is for the master modernist an object of desire coordinated by fantasy, then it strikes me that its role, more than just its place, would be inverted in an analytic modernism. This would entail another divestment, now of modernity as eternally deferred future, irrecuperable past, or ever-elusive present—all means by which the utopian nowhere finds its coordinates in fantasy. Modernity would come to play for the analytic modernist a paradoxical role: the past. Not simply a past to be mined, not the past as a grand psycho-archaeological site, as Freud's Rome.[32] Rather, the analytic modernist would address this past as *split*. The analytic process would be one not only of anamnesis, but also its opposite: the ceaseless tracking of what remains unproduced in the past, what has consistently failed to appear there, what cannot be hauled back up because it was never there to begin with. Utopia as a radically *emergent* form. Simultaneously, the past would be repeatedly brought to speak its own signifiers of self-mastery, its means of repressing or veiling the ineliminable negativity that constitutes it. As such master signifiers are spoken, the new is spoken with them, an irreducible surplus endowed with a subtractive power: to de-authorize the sovereign sign. All master signifiers spoken in analysis are in this sense *alte Meister.*

Whatever details it loses, there is a handy way to condense all this. A master modernism, dominating discourse with its calls for the new, fantasizes the future as its (Real) object. An analytic modernism, dismantling domination through its desire for absolute difference, takes the past as its (split) subject.

14

REPETITION (4)

Only in theory, I think, do these "two modernisms" exist so cleanly, so separately. In historical reality, where all Archimedean points tilt and tumble, they are hopelessly implicated in one another. But for the moment, the theory seems to capture something crucial: a mode of modernism that is *hilflos* rather than heroic, that excavates and de-authorizes axioms rather than attempting to fill them in, and that makes subjective destitution, fantasy traversal, and symptom identification its horizons, rather than its forms of foreclosure. If Rilke's home-invading, subject-seizing, mold-breaking angels symbolize for Jameson a modernism that seeks a master and calls for revolution, one might locate something like an analytic modernism in another Rilke scene, from *The Notebooks of Malte Laurids Brigge* just a few years later (1910):

> I sit here in my little room, I, Brigge, who am twenty-eight years old and completely unknown. I sit here and am nothing. And yet this nothing begins to think and thinks, five flights up, on a gray Paris afternoon, these thoughts:
>
> Is it possible, it thinks, that we have neither seen nor perceived nor said anything real or of any importance yet? . . .
>
> Yes, it is possible.
>
> Is it possible that in spite of inventions and progress, in spite of culture, religion and worldly wisdom, that one has remained on the surface of life? . . .
>
> Yes, it is possible.
>
> . . . Is it possible that all these people know very precisely a past that never was? . . .[1]

The passage—which Eric Santner calls "a confession of a kind of subjective destitution or nullity, one that allows for a *new thinking*"—is no more or less invested in the signifier "new" than are Rilke's angels.[2] But the nature of that investment is radically different. No angels are called, and none come. Incipience, overwhelmingly present, emerges not through a progressive, dialectical negation—break, break-in, breakthrough, a hauling back up of the immanent—but through suspension of movement, voiding and repetition, repetition *of* void. "Yes, it is possible" is a sublimely empty response, an unnullable least-ing of the very category of the answer. (Rilke was an avid reader of Kierkegaard.)[3] It is also an ideal instance of the analyst's oracular speech in the psychoanalytic session: a registration of the analysand's lack, often by little more than echo, which does not fade the discourse, but intensifies it. Dolar calls this an "ethics of echo," an attempt "to make oneself an echo, to turn into echo: perhaps this is the best antidote against the nostalgia of the lost origin and the helpless effort to recapture by memory what has always already eluded us, and from which we are irretrievably cut."[4] Such an ethic has an interesting implication for the schema of the analyst's discourse, especially as applied to the artist-practitioner: *a* and $ are not so distinct, nor need be. The self-annulling of the artist-as-analyst becomes a means of testing a past that is the artist's own, a "language" that the artist too "speaks," a subject that in some sense the artist already is. The analysis is really more a self-analysis, and in Rilke's case it would have taken place not long after Freud's own around 1900.

Hugo von Hofmannsthal's fictional Lord Chandos underwent his own "imaginary decline of the world" at virtually the same time. An iconic moment in the fin-de-siècle Viennese *Sprachkrise*, Chandos's letter to Francis Bacon is a true "end of analysis," a testament to subjective destitution and fantasy traversal more eloquent than any of Lacan's own accounts:

> In brief, this is my case: I have completely lost the ability to think or speak coherently about anything at all. First I gradually lost the ability, when discussing relatively elevated or general topics, to utter words normally used by everyone with unhesitating fluency. I felt an inexplicable uneasiness in even pronouncing the words "spirit," "soul," or "body." . . . Rather, the abstract words which the tongue must enlist as a matter of course in order to bring out an opinion disintegrated in my mouth like rotten mushrooms. . . . Everything came to pieces, the pieces broke into more pieces, and nothing could be encompassed by one idea. Isolated words swam about me; they turned into eyes that stared at me and into which I had to stare back, dizzying whirlpools which spun around and around and led into the void.[5]

The rotten mushroom—which ought to join Aristotle's catalogue of automated objects—is a particularly effective articulation of the master signifier *as spoken by the analysand.* It may as well be a horse or a tripod. It is a source of surprise, even of horror, but also of infinitesimal, irreducible newness.

. . .

If New Music has a Chandos Letter, it is Schoenberg's monodrama *Erwartung*, Op. 17 of 1909. But what a different letter it is. Hofmannsthal holds to Denis Diderot's paradox of the actor; how else to account for his exquisitely controlled and refined articulation of a character who cannot write, who has lost his language? Whatever language he lost, Hofmannsthal got.[6] Schoenberg's method is closer to Lee Strasberg's Method: he seems to want to *become* the fabrication of his librettist Marie Pappenheim: *die Frau*, a woman in the throes of her own end of analysis. Torn from terror to terror, vacillating violently between hallucinations and associations, metaphors and metonymies, she undergoes her own absolute subjective disarray, her lines aggressively paratactic, more triple dotted than any script until Beckett's *Not I*. Like Beckett's play, she is a floating systole, mouth as muscle, voice as spasm. With the loss of her lover, she does not merely lose a cherished object of affection; she suffers the loss of his gaze, which fantasmatically framed her entire world. To lose *this* is to suffer that world's "imaginary decline," to experience a "capsizing" of the fantasy, the privation of her "foothold of desire" and "window on the Real." *Die Frau* experiences a radical subjective destitution.

But, as Elizabeth Keathley suggests, the process is a transitional one, if hardly "progressive": a shifting of positions, from one of Freudian *Erwartung*—overwhelming anxiety in the presence of an imminent threat, anticipation of danger, "fear *before* something"—to one of *Abwarten*, an abiding, a waiting-and-seeing.[7] In this sense the libretto is quilted in place by two large arcs. The first moves from the beginning of the text, through a constant stream of reminiscences and seismographic starts in the score's first three scenes, to a passage early in its fourth and last. It is a desperate moment, emblematic of Žižek's "music at its most elementary"—an "act of *supplication*," a call to the big Other to respond, an attempt "to provoke the 'answer of the Real.'"[8] The discovery of the lover's lifeless body only reinforces a demand for the help he might have given, and the entire passage rotates, vortex-like, around a notorious nine-note *fff* "scream" chord as the *Frau* cries *Hilfe!* (Help!):

> You . . . you . . . it's you . . .
> I was looking for you for so long . . .
> in the wood and . . .
> *(tugging at him)*
> Are you listening?
> Say something . . . look at me . . .
> *(bending right over, horrified)*
> Good God, what is it? . . .
> Help!
> *(She runs off a short way.)*
> For God's sake! . . . Quick!
> Can no-one hear me?
> *(looking about in despair)*
> He's lying there . . .
> *(back beneath the trees)*

EXAMPLE 15. Arnold Schoenberg, *Erwartung*, monodrama in one act, Op. 17, mm. 189–93 ("Hilfe!") (© 1916, 1950 by Universal Edition A. G., Wien/UE 13612).

Wake up . . . please wake up . . .
Don't be dead, beloved . . .
Don't be dead, I love you so much . . .

The second arc extends over the latter two thirds of the text, and seems to usher in—hardly an emancipation, and even less an assertion of the *Frau*'s newly won autonomy, but at least a speaking out loud of the lover's status as absolute master. Which is to say, a piece of old unknown knowledge manifested simultaneously with a truth never before known: that the master is no longer a master. In this sense, the transition is one from absolute appeal in the face of immediate danger—*Hilfe!*—to "the experience of a final *Hilflosigkeit*" in which "there is no danger."[9] There is instead a new registration of contingency, in the form of questions that waver precariously between rhetorical and actual:

> There is nowhere for me there. . . .
> I lived isolated from everything,
> a stranger to everything. . . .
> . . . What am I to do here alone?
> In my unending life . . .
> this colorless, boundless dream . . .
> because my boundary
> was where you were . . .
> and all the colors of the world
> were in your eyes. . . .
> The light will come for everyone . . .
> but for me, alone in my darkness?

There is even, if one wants to go by the Lacanian letter, an implication of symptom identification at the very end. *Die Frau*, having found, recognized, and conversed with her dead lover, makes no move whatsoever in the direction of a coming to terms, a healing acceptance that might bring some form of *closure*. Instead, she goes on searching: "Ich suchte . . ." The turn is often taken to signal delusion ("Doesn't she know he's *right there*?"), but it can also be read otherwise: as a taking on of the lack itself, and of the labor and fidelity it entails.

The last bar of the score would seem to support such a reading. If Schoenberg's "scream" chord marks the end of the first arc with an eviscerating punctuation—Time has stopped! Only the Now!—the second arc is famously brought to a close with its rhetorical inversion: a *ppp* saturation of the tonal, timbral, and registral fields, and certainly the most chromatic ending to any written work of music in Western history up to that point. Completing the aggregate, rising and falling to highest and lowest at once, smudging together all instrumental colors into the closest approximation of white noise a pitched orchestra can create, it is the kind of moment that tempts an analyst to have discovered the very image in music of the Lacanian Real. While this wouldn't be right—the Real does not "appear," we are talking of the imaginary here—nonetheless the ending mimes the concept insofar as it pushes the symbolic to a point of failure. It is not a simple matter of whether the ending signals radical closure or radical openness—something endlessly debated since the work's premiere—but of a disruption of the musical symbolic's capacity to sustain the very space between these two concepts. So that space either collapses—the "pure nonsense" thesis—or, like Jorge Luis Borges's noun-less society overrun by verbs, it multiplies. A double pair of new interpretive affordances emerges: on the one hand, the ending annuls the very capacity to end, through total saturation (of the chromatic), or through total evacuation (of the tonal orientation); or, on the other hand, the ending revolutionizes the logic of completion itself, through foreclosure (nowhere left to go), or through radical expansion (a new system, a symbolic-to-come). Here it is not *die Frau*, but a musical symbolic order, music as language, as big Other, which looks on in horror and speaks of how "everything came to pieces, the pieces broke into more pieces, and nothing could be encompassed by one idea." The "pieces" here, as I think they also are for Chandos, are not words, so much as the coordinates that allow differences to hold, that cut into a Real and allocate a void—the subject's own Archimedean gaze—and a corresponding field of objects. The last measures of *Erwartung* stage, in the imaginary but *also* in the symbolic, the disappearance of all such cuts, the "limits of all objectivity." Which is to say they stage antagonism.

It is an especially cunning place to *end*: there, where tonality's pretensions to dialectical thought must make good on their claim, their capacity to depart and arrive, to issue a true negation of the negation and a transition to *something*—there appears something that "cannot be submitted to dialectics," something that stultifies the capacity for thinking progressively. So it seems wrong to call this moment a culmination of what has gone before. It is arguably more an accumulation, not of something, but of a countless procession of nothings, bits of surplus, missed encounters, repetitions of the impossibility of repetition. The score to *Erwartung* is, like any piece of notated music, a perfect example of *automaton*, the blind insistence of dead letters. It is a mortification of spontaneity, and demands musicians' constant revivification. But it is also a demand, or at least a plea, to repeat the sign. And this plea lies in extraordinary tension with the music that the score "contains": a music following the law of anacoluthon, unceasingly inconsistent, self-unfollowing, the apotheosis of Schoenberg's short-lived moment of "radical athematicism." This is, one might say, as radical an attempt at tychic music, music that untiringly repeats the impossibility of repetition, as had ever been produced within the European notated tradition. If anxiety is a constant, unexpellable presence in the score, its function seems to be precisely this: to serve as the "causal gap," the *béance causale*, of the music's catastrophic desire. It is not the radically athematic music that precipitates the dread, but the other way around. A postulated dread, already operating as the work's axiom before the curtain rises in the title itself—"Be worried!," it essentially announces—functions as a kind of Real object whose effects are rendered in the form of a music utterly incapable of repetition. Which is to say that despite the score's many madrigalisms, its crickets and moonbeams, its primary object of mimesis is what cannot be imitated, or even iterated, in the subject.

This suggests how "expressionism" might be understood as the proper name, the coinage, for one among multiple aesthetic strategies around the turn of the twentieth century for engaging in something like an analyst's discourse, an

EXAMPLE 16. Arnold Schoenberg, *Erwartung*, monodrama in one act, Op. 17, m. 426 (last page) (© 1916, 1950 by Universal Edition A. G., Wien/UE 13612).

"analytic modernism"—for "keeping it Real," as it were. Lacan's schema bears further fruit if we follow it through its other figures. Positing Schoenberg as the discourse's agent, *a*, articulates his role as a very particular object-cause of anxiety: he is not here playing a master of musical theatricality, a showman engaging in an extreme modernization of well-worn tropes of fear, topoi operating in both the symbolic and imaginary; this would be precisely Richard Strauss's position, and the most Grand Guignol moments in *Elektra*, premiered only months before Schoenberg began his score, were surely ringing in the latter's ears. Schoenberg's agency in *Erwartung* is, obviously, different. But in a very specific way: rather than exploiting the capacity of established tropes to successfully signal, and to generate a pleasure in meaning-making, Schoenberg breaks and confounds their efficacy, adding actual noise into signals of noisiness. The process works, or at least appears intended to work, reflexively: there is a likeness between what the tropes *signify* and what their malfunction *engenders*. The score could, in this sense, be seen as an extraordinarily extended series of executive failures: the failure of the iterable to repeat itself, to read the script on which it is written.

"The script" is a particularly—modernist?—way of describing "the past," which is how I'd also suggested one could read the status of $\$$, the split subject, in the schema of the analytic modernist. And it is in the position of analyst that Schoenberg pushes this past to "go off script," to break in myriad and indeterminate ways, and to reveal what it lacks, what it never had and can't "bring back up." Here reappear, *Walpurgisnacht*-like, all of Schoenberg's famous Oedipal battles with tradition; this past is *his* past, it is what constitutes him, what he hauls back up when he spontaneously draws its lots. But it takes on a different character when placed in the position of other in the schema. Its "associations" begin to fan out on either side of the category "trope," becoming more or less coordinated in time and place. On the more coordinated side are Schoenberg's "little others," his semblants, quite literally repeatable passages from preexisting scores: Kundry's scream in act 2 of Wagner's *Parsifal*; countless moments in *Salome* and *Elektra*; an instant late in the "Der Abschied" from Mahler's *Das Lied von der Erde*, shortly after the funeral march; even Webern's *Fünf Stücke für Streichquartett* play a role. On the other side of the spectrum, one can identify a gradual shift from an embodied, artifactual past to something more epochal and conceptual: generic others of the kind Carl Dahlhaus found essential interlocutors for the score (opera, chamber music, the fantasia, recitative); and "big Others," the symbolic order and its alleged laws: tonality, harmony, thematic composition, the quilting points of a "Music proper."[10] In each and every case, these *automata* break script, repeatedly fail to iterate; unrendered *automaton* renders *tyche*, the music's constant return to what it continually fails to produce. If anxiety emerges here, it is in part as a constant inability to discern who or where the master is in these past signs. In this sense, tonality, arguably Schoenberg's biggest Other in these "transitional" works, is only a stand-in, a semblant, for what is really at stake: mastery, the demonstration that the tones are being authorized by a master.

The "product" of this analytic discourse, S_1, is just the opposite: a mastery separated from the subject that articulates it. Rather than shoring up their subject's lack, master signifiers are brought forth as an uneasy coupling of failure and surplus, "a two which cannot be counted for two, nor reduced to a one."[11] Kundry's scream fails Wagner's script just as it fails the vertical and horizontal "laws" of tonality, appearing instead as an unrepeatable, unresolvable nine-note chord extended to thirteen times Wagner's original length. Whatever else it may be, *Erwartung*'s ending also suggests itself as a failure of Strauss's *Salome* to execute its own ending; King Herod's order of execution is stayed by the chromatic cloud, and Salome, bloodied corpse-lover by her side, can continue searching for eternity. Webern's *Fünf Stücke*, shown by Ethan Haimo to have served as a precedent and precursor to *Erwartung*'s athematicism, are metastasized to operatic proportions; and so on.[12] The "Hilfe!" chord is in this regard the emblematic master signifier, now divested of its status *as* master. It carries the memory of Kundry in act 2, but also of Tristan in act 3 and Elsa in acts 1 and 3, and indeed the entire Wagnerian "aesthetics of the scream" as a kind of natural sign, the very sort that could transform the failure of Romantic opera into the birth music drama—as prestigious a transmutation as the invisible hand of dialectics could produce.[13] (One could go further, into passional song and myths of the birth of music proper; Schoenberg's scream would gladly let the process continue.) In the Wagnerian scream is the promise, or the historical fantasy, of a music that knows no alternatives, a radically exigent—which is also to say, non-contingent—music which could only emerge *as such*, which both *appears* and *is*. In Schoenberg's "Hilfe!" this exigency is undone, or rather cleft: on the one hand one hears a spasm, an image of seismographic shock or struck nerve, the involuntary stupidity of the body in excess of the laws of tonality, and on the other one hears a collection of pitches that, in the ear of the historical moment, are the very sound of contingency. They could have been otherwise, they might next time be otherwise, why *weren't* they otherwise? The music does not let on. The Wagnerian master signifier isn't just estranged, nor simply superseded or modernized. A phantasm of necessity, it is split in two: into actual emergency and mimetic bungle, a chord aware of its own precariousness. As a precipitate of ana-lysis, it lets slip the catachrestic aspect of all music, the way in which it inevitably fails to name, in which the tones "do not go into their concepts without leaving a remainder," to paraphrase Adorno's account of negative dialectics.[14] *Erwartung*'s cries for help to some extent become Music's cries for help, at least as Schoenberg may have heard them during the work's frenetic genesis: Can it exist without being the effect of a fantasmatic cause—expression, body, law, language? These push toward a larger question: *Ought* this music be helped? Or be

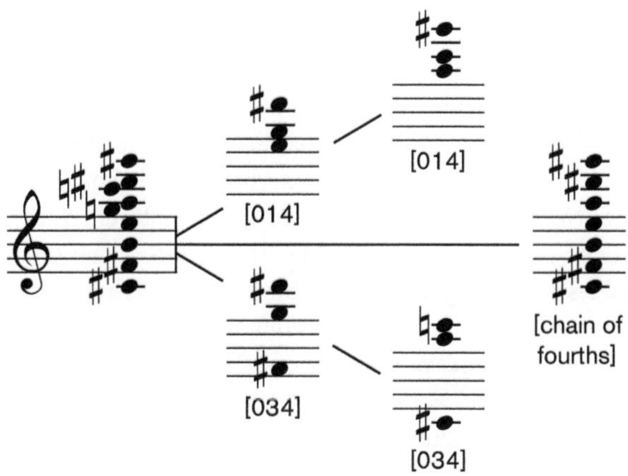

FIGURE 24. *Erwartung*, breakdown of "Hilfe" chord.

allowed to become helpless? All evidence suggests that such questions pursued Schoenberg at the time like the furies.

As any analyst of twentieth-century music will tell you, the nine notes of this scream chord are hardly contingency pure. They are, like a vast majority of the score, permeated by what Schoenberg would eventually consider an example of a *Grundgestalt* or "basic shape," and what American music theory would formalize as the major-minor trichord (set classes [014] and [034]).[15] The top six notes of the chord comprise two interlocking iterations of the set, E-G-D sharp and A-C-G sharp. The C sharp and F sharp that form the chord's lowest two notes can each substitute in for a pitch in one of the two sets in order to register different [014] sets (F sharp-G-D sharp and A-C-C sharp). And of course apart from these four iterations, there is the chord's bald presentation of stacked fourths (five if perfect, seven including the augmented fourths at the top of the chord).

All of which is to say, the chord reads not just as a split between expressive exigency and symbolic contingency, but also as a kind of knowledge, S_2. Read in the context of the analyst's discourse, such knowledge would constitute another kind of *automaton*: not conscious but unconscious, a knowledge "at all points homologous with the subject," but subject to repression, misrecognition, disavowal. In relation to the subject's conscious knowledge—in this context, the past's reproduction of its symbolic as what "makes sense" (Wagner sounds thus, Strauss thus, et cetera)—its unconscious knowledge takes on a character of disjunction, a mythical "it is so": pure figuration and random assemblage, chains that obey the letter and not the sense, a "mad cohesion." Late in his career, Lacan conceives of it as an "acephalic" knowledge, knowledge without a head. To conscious speech, this manifests as its disjecta, those moments of "impediment, failure, crack."

This knowledge completes the schema in a way that speaks to both Schoenberg's place here as analyst, and to the perfervid scene of *Erwartung*'s composition—426 bars of the most complex and inscrutable orchestral music ever written, composed in fourteen days in a summer study in Steinakirchen am Forst in central Austria. The two are, I think, inseparable. The origin scene, oft-recounted, certainly harmonizes with images of mad cohesion, pure figuration, random assemblage. But its mythic aura—its insinuation that mad cohesion equals mad *genius*, a sublime submission to higher powers—is one the schema dispels, or at least interferes with. If Schoenberg occupies the analyst's position of *a*, he *is* in something of a submissive position; he is attempting to stop being a subject, and to play the role of Real object. In this, he is performing Jameson's good work of depersonalization, precisely as a modernist, that is, in the service of an apocalyptic dissatisfaction with what the contemporary image of subjectivity affords him. Jameson's skepticism about "inward turns" is extremely apt here. The phrase implies a reaching for what one already has, whereas Schoenberg is performing something closer to a self-ousting, an expulsion of what was lying ready to hand.

What the schema suggests is that this process is co-constitutive of *another* knowledge that is not his own—the unconscious knowledge of the analysand, in this case "the past," Schoenberg's array of Others little to big. This knowledge is unconscious in that the past doesn't seem to know it knows it, even as it constantly produces it—as [014] sets, among other things, more than it ever knew possible. They are turned back toward the subject now, brought to bear on its conscious discourse. They disrupt its repeated signs with their own, which cannot but appear to it as impediments, mistakes even. Kundry, and Wagner, and the half-diminished chord, knew more than they knew. But bringing such knowledge to bear on the discourse is not the analyst's only aim, nor the end of the analysis. As a kind of pure technique, a savoir faire driven by its own mad logic, the *Grundgestalt* is indeed what Schoenberg knows. "Oh yes, he does know," Paul Verhaeghe writes of the analyst, "but he can't do much with it, as long as he takes the analytical stance. That's why this knowledge can be coined with the idea of *Docta Ignorantia*, i.e. 'learned ignorance' as it was called by Nicholas of Cusa in the fifteenth century; he has wisely learned not to know, and this opens up a way for the other to gain access to that which determined his or her subjectivity."[16]

So S_2 stands as a negative knowledge, the quintessential modernist "blind technique." Headless but not heedless: it remains powerful only insofar as it continues to drive "the past" to produce a truth beyond its knowledge, to produce what it does not know. This returns us once again to *Erwartung*'s "impossible" ending. It comes shortly after what has since midcentury often been taken as the consum-

$$\uparrow\frac{\text{Schoenberg }(a)}{\textit{Grundgestalt }(S_2)}\ \xrightarrow{\quad}\ \frac{\text{“the past” }(\$)}{\text{“tonic”/“scream,” etc. }(S_1)}\downarrow \qquad (S_2\ //\ S_1)$$

FIGURE 25. *Erwartung* as an analyst's discourse.

mate example of the score's repressed, unknown knowledge: its quotation of Schoenberg's early song "Am Wegrand" (By the Roadside). It is almost too perfect. The song seems to emerge as the source—the *tonal* source—of the work's *Grundgestalt*, its major-minor trichords doing what they can to anchor in place a highly precarious D minor. In a true moment of the signifier's good fortune, *die Frau* seems to stumble on the song's opening lines, "Tausend Menschen ziehen vorüber" (A thousand people pass by), and the music is shaken, automatically, "all by itself," into recollection.[17]

But readers of this moment, understandably caught between the dual registers of reference and motive, generally fail to chart the trajectory of the entire passage, and also its material surface, specifically its orchestration. The *sound* of "Am Wegrand" actually precedes the appearance of its words, so at least as a staging of reminiscence, music is the moment's madeleine.[18] Schoenberg orchestrates the penultimate bars of the piano's wordless coda with whimpering bassoons and haggard violas, and at a considerably slower tempo than the song's original *bewegt*; the result is a nod to the trope of the desultory waltz that peppered the soundscapes of fin-de-siècle Vienna, and of which Schoenberg and Mahler were already known adepts (musical example 18, first system). This gives way to the song proper, whose orchestration summons another trope: the submission to dubious enchantment, an implied intoxication signaled by a heady, diaphanous swell of tremolo strings, burbling winds, and arpeggiating harp and celesta (musical example 18, second system). Isolde's transfiguration scene at the end of *Tristan*, hovering in its world-breath, is arguably the model, but Schoenberg's assignment of the song's melody to the clarinets in their highest, most pinched register reenacts an equally well-established means, by 1909, of ironizing the model. My point in bringing up these two instances is to suggest that Schoenberg took pains here to place anamnesis not on the side of revelation, but *on the side of appearance*—a "true apparition," to be sure, recalling a moment lived, but still mere manifestation, a manifesting of mere-ness. And this mere-ness emerges no less by taking signals of mastery and cultural hegemony—music of waltz *kings* and *masters* of transfiguration—and gently ironizing then, cleaving them into impossible appearance and unworkable reality. Which is to say: treating them as fantasies to be traversed.

This might explain why, at the song phrase when *die Frau* might have sung the corresponding lines in "Wegrand"—"Longing fills the domain of life"—she instead expresses a bewildered alienation: "but I don't recognize you." Reading *Erwartung*'s

EXAMPLE 17. Arnold Schoenberg, *Acht Lieder*, Op. 6, no. 5, "Am Wegrand," mm. 21–25.

anamnesis as its true end—*this* is what it was waiting for!—means suppressing these nuances, not to mention catering to a line of "redemptive" interpretation Schoenberg found exasperating.[19] But more importantly, it relegates what comes after it into the status of a reflective coda, when I think nothing could be further from the truth. Keeping in mind Schoenberg as anti-Hofmannsthal, the Strasberg to his Diderot, we might imagine the line "but I don't recognize you" being sung by Schoenberg himself, and aimed directly at the song. The music soon moves past reminiscence, and into the last, radically un-recollective bars: an assertion of a beyond of anamnesis, where the lover's status as *die Frau*'s mirror ("You are that") is seemingly renounced for an identification with an incurable lack ("I am that") and the enjoyment this not-having brings. Schoenberg cannot resist performing the same transition: with the recall and dissolution of the song, the last "rotten mushroom" of the *alte Meister* falls from the score's mouth. The preexisting symbolic order's "language of closure" is staged as inoperative. Historical tonality cannot end the work, the work must end historical tonality, end its capacity to end. Which of course entails a going-on. The useless insistence of the tonic nonetheless engenders a situation seemingly fatal to the premise of making works. Its last veil of fantasy lifted, a new know-how is now stuck wondering how to search for something other than D minor. This suggests a new formula: *Grundgestalt* (S_2) // "D minor" (S_1)—post-tonality and tonality in an "impossible relationship," or, possibly, tonality as post-tonality's fantasy, its object-cause of desire.

EXAMPLE 18. Arnold Schoenberg, *Erwartung*, monodrama in one act, Op. 17, mm. 410–13 (quoting "Am Wegrand") (© 1916, 1950 by Universal Edition A.G., Wien/UE 13612).

. . .

Left in shambles, but also in incipience, Lord Chandos closes his letter in a wonderfully awkward spot: not quite apologizing to Bacon for the fact that "no more books by me have been arriving 'to make up for the loss of our companionship,'" but at least giving the reason for the silence: "It is that the language in which I might have been granted the opportunity not only to write but also to think is not Latin or English, or Italian, or Spanish, but a language of which I know not one word, a language in which mute things speak to me and in which I will perhaps have something to say for myself someday when I am dead and standing before an unknown judge."[20] Here, I think, is something important. Yes, certainly, here—throughout the entire letter—is also as iconic a portrait as one will find of aesthetic modernism as a crisis of language, a coming apart of the symbolic order that galvanizes not only the subject's psyche but its body, its very capacity not just for pleasure but for enjoyment.[21] And, as I've tried to argue, this *Sprachkrise* reemerges postwar in (among other places) the Lacanian clinic, now no longer just the tormenting, self-induced privilege of a few high-minded artists, but an open invitation, available to any Parisian with disposable income and enough schedule flexibility for a variable-length session. But *here*, in Hofmannsthal's last sentence, is also an insinuation of the what-may-come, of a learning to live and work in this new unthinkability, which has reduced a man to infancy, to being one who does not *yet* speak. It is in this sense also an insinuation of that "beyond of analysis" Lacan tantalized his seminar audience with in 1964, a beyond that "has never been approached."[22]

The history of modernism provides an extraordinary retort to Lacan's utopian beyond. Not only has it been approached, it has been entered, occupied, colonized a thousand times over—by the efflorescence and clangor of claims, beliefs, and practices emerging from, and maintaining fidelity to, the knowledge *that* one has lost one's language. This history has been so successful, so clangorous and efflorescent, that it still manages to convince that it is the essence and entirety of modernism, its true self as span and period. This is, of course, exactly what modernism as a master's discourse would do: repress the antagonism ($\$$) from whence it comes under the sign of an absolute break, which then founds the possibility of dialectical departure (S_1); formalize this departure through the construction of a body of conscious, conjunct knowledge (S_2); fantasize the impossible surplus of this process (a) as an ever-deferred horizon, the necessity of certain concrete projections and possibilities; and then, often with the help of a Lyotardian *grand récit*, disavow its status as fantasy.

Schoenberg is here again a *locus classicus*, now of a discursive transformation: from the striver for "complete liberation from all forms, from all symbols of cohesion and logic" (Schoenberg to Ferruccio Busoni, 1909), to the discoverer of "something which will guarantee the supremacy of German music for the next hundred years" (Schoenberg to Josef Rufer, 1922).[23] It is a transformation from knowledge (or desire for knowledge) that the big Other doesn't exist, to a need to show this big Other what it wants. *Erwartung* is an exemplar of this transformation in discourse; its history shows how a work whose catastrophic self-analysis left its composer and protagonist radically helpless was able to become a fortress of order for which one could find "the key." In this sense it's also a history of how Freud's definition of analysis—a "breaking up" and "separating out"—gave way to an opposite definition, quite in line with the ego psychology of Heinz Hartmann, Ernst Kris, and Rudolph Loewenstein that Lacan would spend his career disdaining. A definition of analysis as image consolidation and identity confirmation, indeed a kind of mirror stage. An *Erwartung* in pieces comes to the analyst seeking help, and is Humpty-Dumptied back together again, shown not only the truth of its desire—as a "desire for conscious unity . . . by means of a single central idea"—but that it *has already realized this desire.*[24] Again and again the ritual is performed in a process that yields as its precipitate something hardly recognizable in what I've read above: the picture of an incipient or latent master, a Father of Music-to-Come, fated for eventual stellification through the creation of something "*entirely* new." An anti-Orpheus, as it were. There is perhaps no clearer example of this process than Charles Rosen's reading, in 1975, of *Erwartung*'s last bars: "The saturation of musical space is Schoenberg's substitute for the tonic chord of the traditional musical language. The absolute consonance is a state of chromatic plenitude. . . . The saturation of chromatic space [is] a fixed point toward which the music moves, as a point of rest and resolution."[25] Rosen's claim performs a wonderful return of the repressed: it turns out Schoenberg couldn't leave "Am Wegrand" by the roadside after all. Its D minor, now Argus-eyed and all-toned, meets him at the work's end, *automaton*'s revenge on *tyche*, the master's revenge on the analyst.

15

MUSIC & NEW MUSIC (2)

That metaphysics is no longer possible becomes the ultimate metaphysics.
—THEODOR ADORNO, *MAHLER: A MUSICAL PHYSIOGNOMY*[1]

"Nearness to Mahler was like a wall." Composer Michael Denhoff's confession provides the title to a trio of panels "on the relationship of New Music to Gustav Mahler." The discussions are taking place in Hamburg, in early September, as part of the vast *Gustav-Mahler-Fest 1989*, also the first year of the city's own Gustav Mahler Association.[2] In his opening keynote on "the sloppiness of tradition," Hans Wollschläger sets the tone. This festival will be an opportunity for reflection—for gauging the measure of the distance, for meditating on the elusive and ambiguous nature of historicity, for taking stock of a complicated legacy. For thinking—in a phrase that permeates the giant "Report of the International Gustav Mahler Congress" that emerges from the festival—about *Mahler today.*

In terms of New Music, this gives rise—and the reader surely saw it coming, long before the "heterotopian networks" figured at the opening of chapter 10—to a Mahler network, or at least a good portion of it. Like the Schubert network I discussed in chapter 10, it emerges partially out of unrelated, stylistically disparate works, some of which explicitly cite or allude to the composer—the second movement of Berio's *Rendering*, for example—and others that stage pointedly Mahlerian scenes or tropes. Günther Bialas's orchestral *Ländler-Fantasie* is refracted through a century's worth of Mahler prisms (Alban Berg, Karl Amadeus Hartmann, Hans Werner Henze), themselves held up to Mahler's own Schubert prism. Mauricio Kagel's *Osten* (East) for salon orchestra, reimagining a klezmer street scene (and furnished with authentic tunes), re-presents the classic Mahlerian conundrum of simultaneous sincerity and parody, homeliness and exile.[3] Helmut Lachenmann's hulking *Tableau* gathers under its pitiless analytical gaze a wide variety of traditional orchestral tropes—among them Mahlerian horn calls and searing unison string lines—but scrambling their semiotic signals in a search, "step by step, after forms of illusionless communication."[4]

But like the web of "revolutionary" works I explored in chapter 10, the bulk of this Mahler network is the result of deliberate effort: European cultural institutions are trying to get The Composer to fantasize on their behalf, indeed, to produce collective ontogenetic scenes in music. *Chorphantasien*, as it were, in which "Mahler" (or "Schubert" or "Bach" or "Beethoven") takes the place of "Music" as a production site for "vacant signs" that fantasmatically cover over a subjective void. "Mahler" becomes a point of occluded origin, a dark ground, precisely so that "Mahler *today*" can become, not a theme but a process or program of recovery. Suture "Mahler" to "today," such that this "infinite improbability from which [we] come" no longer lies beneath us "like a void."[5] "Mahler today" transforms "Europe today" into a sensual material event; it brightens its obscurity, fills back in what the concept emptied out.

But, unsurprisingly, this isn't quite what happens. The eight commissioned composers are not with the program. Instead, they each find their own way toward a staging of Mahler's music as distant or inoperative or unrecoverable; or as recoverable, but only as ruin or riddle; or as too close, but "like a wall"; or as simply impossible to situate at the *right* distance.[6] In the process, Mahler's music becomes, quite literally, a subject for analysis, a subject whose claims to continuity are to be broken down or broken apart—even as its own "ego" already symbolized images of breakdown, ruin, catastrophe, spectrality. Such is the case with Denhoff's *Nachtbild* (Night Picture), for instance. The gestures and soundworld of Mahler's various battle musics (the first movements of the Third and Ninth Symphonies, the first and last movements of the Sixth), already full of fragmentation and poker-faced parody, are resubmitted to similar processes, their rubble rubbled and surveyed anew. The work allegedly emerged out of a dream analysis on Denhoff's part: Mahler's "signals and syllables," haunting the younger composer's worsening sleep, were worked through until they could be assembled into a "time-stretched reconstruction whose shape—associative, vegetative, eruptive, seemingly unordered—nonetheless followed its own atemporal dream-logic." The result is "simultaneously mirage, travesty, puzzle-picture, likeness, and photo-negative."[7]

Detlev Glanert's *Mahler/Skizze*, meanwhile, could not have had a more unabashedly Romantic purview. It emerged from Glanert's experience standing at Mahler's neglected and overgrown tombstone, reflecting on recently deceased friends and the transience of life. But while the piece, compared to Denhoff's, mines a more pastoral geography, it also tests it. Mahler's own orchestral interventions into nature, caricatured from the start, are now returned to a rawer state—not just wind and thunder machines, but, more prominently, stones and water. They begin to counter their (intended) effect in Mahler's symphonies. Rather than binding the orchestral fabric together, they pull it apart, recasting a single high tone on violin or repeated minor triads on celesta as the wind-strewn, insentient equals of the clacking rocks. Returning evocations of Mahler's various night musics, his own attempts to enchant the darkness, are constantly brought back to this point of harshly illuminated pre-music; their studious spectrality is re-exposed as so many mere bumps in the night, eventually yielding "the scaffolding of a piece of music that never was."[8]

In the case of Thomas Jahn's *Background*, the entire work becomes a methodical never-was-ing of a concrete historical artifact: measure 206—otherwise known as the famous *fortissimo* nine-note "scream chord"—in the Adagio from Mahler's unfinished Tenth Symphony. Jahn submits the chord to a strenuously gradual analytic procedure of reconstruction and disassembly, moving mostly from *ppppp* to *p* and back again; the entire chord appears only twice, *subito fortissimo*, rolled upward and then downward on—of all instruments!—piano.[9] The process undoes the galvanic rhetorical power of its chosen object. A moment of neuro-sonic shock, seemingly unparseable and immediate, is transformed into an attempt "to compose nearness and distance through the passing of time."

Jahn writes of the score as a "memory process," a "hearing back in time" through which "the background as a symbol of spatial and temporal distance changes its meaning. In memory it becomes nearness and presentness and points beyond."[10] But at the same time, the work seems intensely ambivalent about its charge. In relation to the actuality of its chosen artifact—all too available to hear, of course, live and on recording—it becomes an almost perverse endeavor, as much an undoing of contexts, effects, and affects as a coming to terms. It takes its hypothetical listener not *back* to Mahler's anguished scream—which was in any case already the product of its own anamnesis—but *past* it, to a point where it is no longer operative as a reaction, or even a protection.[11] Again, not a moment of *Abwarten* but *Erwartung*, not "fear *before* something," but a strange helplessness in the face of an impossible object, one placeable neither "here" nor "now," but only sideways, anamorphically. In *Residua*, the East German composer Walter Zimmermann ends up constructing another, very different essay in sonic absencing: "melodies that I know from my childhood" are "deeply encrypted and displaced through mirroring processes . . . filters, magic squares"; these techniques are deployed in a constant attempt to "redefine [an] original . . . that should never become graspable. One could say that the whole is like a series of variations in which the theme has been lost [*ist abhanden gekommen*]."[12]

There is something strange about these recitals of lost objects, or this composing out of the losing of objects, being framed by a discussion otherwise obsessively focused on history and historicity. Almost all the composers work hard to perform their historical awareness. When moderator Klaus Hinrich Stahmer misunderstands composer Babette Koblenz's cautious skepticism about the historicist ethic—"Doesn't this view feed a kind of 'escapist' thinking?"—she is quick to correct: composing itself, just as much as this Mahler fest, or the recent Schubert anniversary, or the coming Mozart anniversary "already casting its shadow," is also an essential form of receiving history. It's not just a matter of "compositional technique or reception theory [*Wirkungsästhetik*]." The "historical phenomenon" is concretized in composing, both materially and temporally—"an essential instant [*Moment*] of compositional work."[13] And the musicologist Constantin Floros takes pains to stress how "tremendously" music has developed since the—so he insinuates—ahistorical and technocratic composition of the 1950s and 1960s. In the majority of these commissions, we're hearing "a totally different music . . . an unbelievably expressive music, a music borne of emotion." Jahn's *Background*, for instance, is "a piece of limitless sadness."[14]

Here, perhaps, the strangeness of the entire scene is crystallized. As European composers are "rediscovering" history, they are simultaneously crafting myriad mechanisms for obscuring it; as they talk of recovering it, they compose its being or getting lost. They do not simply designate history—per Jameson—as "the Real," and step aside as it continues to "not write itself." Instead—per Žižek—they insist on having a hand in this process, each developing concrete technical means by which to "encircle [or] locate the empty place of the Real." The Real "cannot be inscribed, but [they] can inscribe this impossibility itself, [they] can locate its place: a traumatic place which causes a series of failures."[15] These failures are subtle but algorithmic; they seem to be what renders a work a "sketch," a foreground a "background," an original "residua," an otherwise consistent image "mirage, travesty, puzzle-picture, likeness, and photo-negative." There is in all this an odd inversion of Freud's classic formulation on melancholy, in which the ego, having suffered the loss of an object, sets one part of itself "over against the other, judges it critically, and, as it were, takes it as its object."[16] By contrast, the "limitless sadness" hovering around these works seems inextricable from a re-finding of the object. As if its proximity were unbearable, its distance a consolation, its loss a form of wish fulfillment. In the midst of this bruised, twilighted talk, even the moderator Stahmer begins to grow weary:

> Some of the pieces on this program seem shaped by an abyssal sadness and resignation . . . a skepticism bordering on general fatigue. In Mahler's work too there are many passages in which the music disintegrates [*zerfällt*] and loses itself in the infinite. But Mahler also often—perhaps even more often—presents the foil to this in his music: the fanfare, the breakout, the breakthrough, sometimes even the reaching of the goal. Can one simply no longer write this way today? Is then only *Weltschmerz* still possible in music?[17]

• • •

This is Hans-Joachim Hespos's cue. So far he's been sitting there entirely silent, but now he takes out a piece of paper and recites a written statement, apparently in the role of one mysterious UPEX:

> UPEX in Hamburg—in an explosion the likes of which no one has ever seen, the future breaks out all around him, and Mahler: out of the scraps of empty longing and depraved egocentrism emerge mountainous piles of fear and lies, debris obstructing the new horizons, blocking new thought. That now, 100 years after the premiere of his first symphony, [Mahler] is newly arrived in Hamburg, a boy scout being repeatedly and warmly celebrated as a master from the past, underscores the desolate state of contemporary German music making, unable to climb out of its touchy-feely mush, its false tradition and private haze. Spiritual ennui finds no purchase on the current horizons. No acts of fantasy, of courage. For this UPEX has only laughter. What would happen if dull affirmation were frightened awake, if the idols, rusted solid, were knocked over, if actual *per*formances [*AUFführungen*] finally made things clear, if the symphonies were played straight into the ground [*zu Dreck zerspielten*], their stacked layers uglified until the ear was blinded? . . . Would not the Unknown then appear, a full-to-bursting new light [*Leuchtung*], shimmering through, uncomprehended, from behind the thin cracks of misunderstanding . . . and why Mahler. And not Chaplin, Hitchcock, Varèse, Ives, someone else NOW[18]

And with that, Hespos gets up and walks out, slamming the door behind him.

In both its own context and in the larger scheme of things, it is an overdetermined moment. It feels slightly stale, redolent of a factionalism already dated by the early 1980s. Into a more or less genial community of melancholic, self-conscious, historically sensitive postmodernists strides a naive, brazenly unreconstructed modernist crying blue murder—calling for the burning of the libraries, the smashing of idols, the merciless hauling back and hacking open of Jürgen Habermas's retracting "horizon of the future." Here is Perry Anderson's revolutionary modernist, insisting on the capacity to imagine utopian futures through the violent charisma of technique. Here too is Jameson's, in whom stirs everywhere "an apocalyptic dissatisfaction with subjectivity itself and the older forms of the self."[19] Nor is Hespos so unlike Clark's modernist, attempting "to capture the lack of consistent and repeatable meanings in the culture"—that shimmering, misunderstood, full-to-bursting new light of the incomprehensible Unknown—"and make it over into form."[20]

But the timing is off. It's tempting to voice the anachronism in the contemporaneous language of late-1980s and early-1990s theory. Perhaps it is a hyperreal Baudrillardian simulacrum of the musical modernist circa 1910, for instance. Or better, perhaps it's a postmodern performance—the rantings of an impotent, pastiched father, say, huffing and puffing and putting on a charade of strength like Dennis Hopper's character in *Blue Velvet* (1986), while the speechless panel, like Kyle MacLachlan, watches safely from the closet of impending post-history.[21] Certainly Hespos presents a strong parody of the Hegelian dialectic. His diatribe crafts an absolutely negatable world, where present actuality, full of waste and mush and rust and haze, counts for zero, and the unknown future, always breaking through with ear-blinding brightness, counts fully for one. In this vision, repetition takes the form of the hardest break, the complete negation of the negation, the furious cancellation of the past. But Hespos's speech also casts the remaining composers in this Mahler network as consummate Kierkegaardian ironists. They revel in the negative, yes, but in contrast to Hespos, their negativities "cannot be submitted to dialectics."[22] They are not negations of negations, they do not progress and cancel out, and seem constitutionally incapable of departing for anywhere else. Instead, they stage musical situations of zero-plus . . . or one-minus. . . . They counter the scenario of break-and-start with the spectral surplus of the sketch or mirage, the unnullable least of residua or background. They seem less interested in Hespos's messianic Unknown, sure to appear once the symphonies are adequately played into the ground, than in what continually fails to show up, a repeated non-appearance, a persistent getting-lost of the original. Only this, their works and words imply, "has the capacity to transform the past and to produce the new."[23]

It is, as I have been constructing it, a perfect—maybe all too perfect—confrontation between two irreconcilable ways of conceiving the musically new: an analytic modernism butting heads with a master modernism. In this rather insular encounter, far away from the year's main musical stages, and out of which emerge few new masterpieces, new schools of thoughts, or shifts of stylistic paradigm, a nonetheless remarkable distillation emerges. It presents the antagonism between two radically different discourses, which is to say, two ways of putting antagonism to work, of mobilizing the Real, formalizing it as a distinct kind of impasse engendering its own roles and effects. To put it less abstractly, what we are seeing in this little out-of-the-way European New Music fracas, staged unintentionally but with surprising clarity, are the two antagonistic forms of continuing to receive Beethoven's wild tangle. For Hespos the monstrous Hegelian, that tangle represents a call for radically new "acts of fantasy, of courage," for "less lack of fantasy, thank God, than ever before," such that an unbearably un-fantastic present will be shamed into disintegration under its weight.[24] For these "Kierkegaardian composers," that tangle offers an invitation to traverse fantasy altogether, to deploy its own profusions and opacities to unmesh the fantasizing faculty itself.

It's a bit too easy to dismiss Hespos's brief filibuster. Its explicit fear of emotion—but also, even more, its implicit hatred of the very categories of gender and identity—makes me think again of Susan McClary's attack on American academic modernism earlier that year. Milton Babbitt said some pretty bad things, but he was no cackling UPEX. At least Babbitt masked his alleged contempt behind a university discourse; if its repressed truth was the master (S_1), still its agent, its semblant, was knowledge (S_2). Discursively speaking, Hespos/UPEX gives us the "purer form," the historical precedent to a university modernism, and it deploys a discourse that seemed increasingly untenable by 1989. I might put it this way: UPEX is the id to PhD Music's ego, the heaving European Hyde to Babbitt's Jekyll.

And yet—as I survey again the heuristic panopticon of figure 16 (see chapter 10), I begin to sympathize with UPEX, to hear, even if for a second, what he hears. As I insinuated near the end of chapter 10, there *is* something eventually unsettling about what the figure suggests, and what is increasingly confirmed as one zooms in on one network after another. When taken in as a larger field of cultural production, there is a niggling *consistency* to all these analytic endeavors, all these attempts to unmesh cultural-musical fantasies and speed along their traversal. It's not so much a consistency of "content," whether it be material, style, or technique. As would be expected of the New Music of 1989, the content of these works is unprecedentedly variegated; virtually no form of commentary—mine certainly included—seems up to the task of giving the differences their full value and nuance. It is, rather, a consistency of frame, perhaps even, in the expanded sense, of dramaturgy, of *plot.* The frame is temporal. If I assume the blinkered gaze of UPEX, I find myself utterly unsurprised by yet one more piece where the origin gets lost, or the opera fails to take place, or the restorer declares the historical artifact beyond his capacities and gives up. Of course Bach will be a broken machine. Of course the revolution will not happen. Of course the utopian imaginary will be dis-occupied. When the European composer is asked to do something with Schubert, there can be little doubt that this something will accord with Adorno's late Beethoven. Schubert himself will now become the landscape; the landscape will be "now deserted and estranged"; the composer will "no longer [gather it] up . . . to form a picture."[25]

But if the composer won't provide the picture, he *will* provide the frame, and within that frame, any scenario, any "content," will be transformed—transfigured, even. This is not the power of analysis; this is the power of fantasy. It is the consolidating power of the empty axiom capable of giving consistency to any scene, teaching the subject how to desire, providing a protecting "window on the Real." Its fabricating potency is perhaps best seen by tracing the threads that hold the larger networks together. It lies not just in, say, Adriana Hölszky's own proclivity for constructing suspension bridges that continually collapse before "reaching" Schubert; it also lies in the very choice of festival title, the signifier "Encounters" providing the place whose emptiness Hölszky will then maintain and encircle. The two nodes work together beautifully. It lies too in the commentary, not just in Hölszky's own wishing that the Schubert quotations would sound "as if they were swimming in dirty water,"[26] but the eagerness of her interviewer to listen and record, and then to craft a reverberant note around her oracular proclamations, pointing to some inscrutable historical or personal trauma always just outside the bounds of the note itself. It lies in Harry Vogt's formidable festival book essay, desperate to weave together New Music and Old by casting Schubert's whole oeuvre as "a creative work of mourning [*kreative Trauerarbeit*], music about (the loss of) music. We are, in a roundabout way, reaching Schubert's central motif, the theme of death, which also plays an important role in the compositional reflections of our day."[27] All these "purely material sincerities" find their most structural expression in the concerts themselves, whose constant alternation of contemporary works and Schubert originals come (as I suggested in my introduction) to resemble Freudian *fort-da* games. A spectral "Schubert," always already lost, always having been or about to be or never quite being, is constantly countered by the appearance of the "real thing"—the original Schubert work—its fleshy vibrancy seemingly restored to full presence. All but one of the six "encounter" concerts in the *Rheinische Musikfest* end with Schubert. Schubert completes them, and they in turn prop up a completed Schubert.

Here it seems like more than just a clever reversal to say that the traversal of fantasy has become the fantasy of traversal. And it implies that what we are bearing witness to in so many of these 1989 networks is less an analyst's discourse than a master's discourse—one in which the signifier "Loss" has ousted the signifier "New" in the place of master signifier and the role of agent. In which case Harry Vogt technically has it wrong. All this "music about (the loss of) music" is not a "creative work of mourning"; it is a cunning work of melancholy. Its goal is not the goal of mourning, not the "proper" and painful *letting go* of the object. Rather, as a kind of fantasy, its goal is to maintain the object at all costs *as a lost object.* And thereby to allow the subject to "maintain itself at the level of its vanishing desire, vanishing inasmuch as the very satisfaction of demand deprives it of its object."[28]

This, at least, is what I imagine the "desolate state" of European New Music might look and sound like through the eyes and ears of cackling UPEX. In many ways it's modernism's oldest curse. Clark calls it the "bad dream of modernism," and finds it at work in Cecil Beaton's famous 1951 *Vogue* spread using Jackson Pollock's abstractions as the background for models sporting the season's newest evening wear.[29] The pathos comes not from anything so simple as abuse or misappropriation. It's not, or not merely, that Pollock "deserves better," that his art has been wronged. It's actually the pathos of seeing the parent culture take the work to the letter. In Pollock's case, it involves seeing the fashion and magazine industries exploit untold new affordances in his un- and dis-figuring, watching as they excitedly put his patterned patternlessness to work, his catastrophic de-perspectivizing in perspective. We are back at the "Baudelairean conjunction" I discussed in chapter 7. Allow the modernist imagination to decompose all creation; allow it to traverse cultural fantasies, to initiate an imaginary decline of the world, to leave its subjects in absolute disarray. By all means! But if the labor is to have a future, culturally speaking, then losses will have to be turned to gains. Privation will have to become desire, and find a support in some kind of fantasy. Objects will have to be Real-ized, turned into object-*causes.* And "with the wealth of materials amassed and ordered according to rules whose origins can be found only in the deepest recesses of the soul," a "new world" will have to come into being.[30] Pollock's "no" will have to be read awry, anamorphosed into "new"—even the newest dinner gown will do. There is, I think, something piteous in this. If it is a form of domination, a quite literal way of "mastering modernism," still it is not a violent one. It is only a matter of a few slips, a discursive half turn. At some point, usually before it ends, analysis has to stop.

This makes me think again on Berio's *Rendering*, and its near quotation of the *Adagissimo* coda to Mahler's Ninth. At the end of chapter 9, I mused that it might be a nod to Bernstein's Harvard Norton Lectures of 1973, specifically his morbidly sentimental account of the final page: its terrifying, paralytic slowness, its "near stoppage of time," its "spidery strands" vanishing from our fingers "even as we hold them." It was "the very act of dying, of giving it all up."[31] Bernstein had already formulated the trope in a well-known 1967 piece in *High Fidelity* magazine, where Mahler's final works granted him "the honor of having the last word, uttering the final sigh, letting fall the last living tear, saying the final good-by" to nothing less than "*music* as he knew it and remembered it, to the unspoiled nature of tonal beauty, to faith in its future—good-by to all that." Mahler "was unable to live through [the] crisis [that followed]," he "had to die" before completing another symphony, his destiny was "to complete the great German symphonic line and then depart."[32]

This is hagiographic kitsch, certainly. But also *grand récit*, grand narrative and tall tale, not simply a Mahler fantasy but a music fantasy with Mahler as its object. "Mahler Nine" becomes a resistant, numinous image "set to work within a signifying structure," as Lacan put it. Through its operations, a dying adagio turns into not just a dying symphony and a dying composer, but a dying genre, a dying century, a dying tradition, and, eventually, the death of Music Itself. The crumbling of the pantheon. The flight of the gods. And in Bernstein's case, the story is told to us by a man cragged of face and voice, terrifically televisable, his tone lachrymose but burnished. Swaddled in endless undoubt at the power of his own words, he becomes a surrogate music-father on whose knee we hear of Papa Music's demise. It is a fantasy of the loss of language, which is what makes its seductive fluency so strange and awkward. At least in relation to Mahler's Ninth, the fantasy was arguably coined with Paul Bekker's verdict, in his 1921 Mahler monograph, that the Ninth is not only a symphonic farewell, but an actual bringer of death: "[The Symphony is] an attritional song, not really created for the ears of this world, it tells of the afterlife. Mahler himself died because of it. His instinctive urge for the truth had been met. He had seen God in that final revelation that it is given to us to encompass with our eyes here on earth: God as death. The unwritten subheading of the Ninth Symphony is 'What death tells me.'"[33] And this fantasy would soldier on past Bernstein, achieving something of a (kitsch?) apotheosis with the biologist Lewis Thomas's famous 1980 essay "Late Night Thoughts on Listening to Mahler's Ninth Symphony." The author's shocked lucubration would identify the *Adagio*'s end not just with the death of music, or death as concept, but with a nuclear holocaust, the death of the human race: "Now, those cellos sound in my mind like the opening of all the hatches and the instant before ignition."[34] Recounting the unbearable speculations about whether it will be forty million lives, or eighty million, or two hundred million, Thomas has a striking response: "If I were sixteen or seventeen years old and had to listen to that, or read things like that, I would want to give up listening and reading. I would begin thinking up new kinds of sounds, different from any music heard before, and I would be twisting and turning to rid myself of human language."[35]

The plight of Lord Chandos reverberates across these fantasmatic visions, this is clear enough. The inspired imaging of the complete loss of "the ability to think or speak about anything at all," of everything "[coming] to pieces, the pieces [breaking] into more pieces," of nothing any longer able to "be encompassed by one idea"; the paradoxical pathos of testifying with poetic eloquence to "the opinions [disintegrating] in my mouth like rotten mushrooms." But there is here too an echo of Chandos's knowledge—"not without a pang—that I would write no more books either in English or in Latin," for the single reason that "the language in which I might have been granted the opportunity not only to write but also to think is not Latin or English . . . but a language of which I know not one word, a language in which mute things speak to me."[36] When Vogt writes of death as Schubert's "central motif," he seems to have something similar in mind: it is not just a matter of *Trauermusik*, nor even *Trauerarbeitsmusik*, music that makes an occupation of mourning. It is, rather, "music about (the loss of) music." And what is strange, in the instance of both these Schubert and Mahler networks, but especially the latter, is how uncanny the scene is. On the one hand are contemporary works, each staging in their own way the impossibility of recovering origins, of repeating precedents, of gathering up the landscape of the past to form a picture. And on the other hand are, at the same moment, enduring stories about how Mahler's own music, as that same origin and precedent, that same past landscape, was *already staging its own past as dying, breaking into pieces of pieces, getting lost—abhanden gekommen*, as Walter Zimmermann put it in a nod to Mahler's famous Lied. On a concert stage, Berio restages Bernstein's staging of Mahler staging Chandos, and the music, trying and failing to restore "Schubert," instead turns to another music that was, already in its own moment, trying and failing to restore itself.[37] At the same time, in a special 1989 double volume of *Musik-Konzepte*, Peter Oswald abstracts "Mahler's late work" as "far-reaching critique of all preexisting forms of speech—dissolution of organic appearance as consequence of radical disillusioning—simultaneously, unleashing of new formal impulses, not however in order to domesticate the chaotic power of drives, but to throw light on a dissociative logic."[38] Berio's music and Oswald's words ought be placed on the same discursive plane. They are each staging a break; in them both is embedded Jameson's "theory of modernity [as] little more than a projection of the trope itself."[39]

Oswald—who would over the next two decades become one of the more influential figures in European New Music—could just as well be describing any of the contemporary works in this Mahler network. His tone here could not be more analytical, or further from Bernstein's tremulous tale of letting go. But the scene is, I think, the same, and it suggests that New Music in Europe has by this moment become a closed circuit, perhaps even a black box, inside of which persists a process of repeating what was never there to begin with, of encircling that place where something "doesn't stop not being written." Inside this box, I imagine modernism sharing a fate not unlike that of Schrödinger's cat, both dead and alive at the same time.[40] In modernism's case, the box simultaneously conceals the traversal of fantasy and the fantasy of traversal—on the one hand, the analytic unmeshing of the musical fantasies that support the cultural reality surrounding it, and on the other hand, the self-enmeshing kitsch of a *Trauerarbeitsmusik* that can't stop losing what it invokes and enjoying what it loses. All the while, on the concert's second half, the loss is recouped. My sense is that these are the terms of European musical modernism in 1989. Together they constitute its antagonism, its paradoxical double state. We can open the box, separate the terms, resolve the antagonism, but only at the cost of fantasizing it, veiling it, blurring it. The antagonism is, I think, the clearer picture.[41]

. . .

"But supposing He does not come." This book is almost done, and at some point in its trajectory, Hans Pfitzner's slight may have changed its meaning: it is no longer about Mahler, but about Adorno. And perhaps it is no longer a slight, but, for some readers, an irritation or worry. How has a book on radical negativity in postwar European composition managed to leave out Adorno? Why rely on Žižek and Lacan, neither of whom spare a word for Berio et al., when European New Music has its own court philosopher of the traversal of fantasy, the affirmation of antagonism, the tireless maintenance of the fact that objects "do not go into their concepts without leaving a remainder"?[42]

I'll risk glibness and counter that I haven't left Adorno out; I've *kept* him out. I've repressed him, and a discourse partially founded on its own theory of repression has helped me do it. I did so for numerous reasons, some of which carry more credibility within a scholarly context, some less. If I suggested in my introduction that the book would unfold a bit like an actual psychoanalysis, then perhaps it appears to work out nicely. Adorno "slipped" into the book's very first pages—its "first session"—seemingly a result of happenstance or a few parapraxes, and now, after a long and complex process of evasions and substitutions, condensations and displacements, he returns, full of meaning.

And how, here, could he not? Here, in a discussion of Mahler and New Music, where critics like Oswald are essentially providing abstracts for Adorno's 1960 Mahler book, and where composers like Berio, Lachenmann, Kagel, Denhoff,

Glanert, and so on seem to be musicalizing so many of that book's beguiling poetic descriptions of a music that "draws fatally back into itself," whose "hands retain nothing but ruins and a dubious flattering solace," and whose "subject cannot detach contemplative love from the irrecoverable."[43] I struggle to find a better articulation of musical modernism as a master's discourse—in which "loss" has displaced "new" as master signifier—than Adorno's ambiguous proclamation that the impossibility of metaphysics "becomes the ultimate metaphysics."

Adorno's "musical physiognomy" of Mahler is justly acknowledged as one of the great composer monographs, at once an acute critical and philosophical reappraisal and a literary documentation of a long-enduring love. This is not just a description, but a truly double role, and it yields an especially antagonized and symptomatic text. Adorno himself called it his "jungle book," and confessed to Hans G. Helms that he'd never "known so little" about what he'd just written.[44] There is here a foretaste of Adorno's famous last line in "Vers une musique informelle," written the following year, that "the shape of every artistic utopia today is: making things without knowing what they are."[45] And there is an argument to be made that the Mahler monograph initiated Adorno's late theory of utopia, developed most extensively in the two tomes of the 1960s, *Negative Dialektik* and *Ästhetische Theorie.* But the Mahler book is a messier affair, both more and less than theory. Interspersed among its more severe moments are passages as purple as Adorno ever wrote. They too summon kitsch, or maybe they're performative of Mahler himself, matching his dialectical banalities with prose husks of middlebrow literary convention. "Only as memory does life have sweetness, and precisely that is pain," is hard to scan without feeling a pang of Hallmarkian triteness. "Mahler's music," Adorno writes in Proustian pastiche, "passes a maternal hand over the hair of those to whom it turns." There are, as in Mahler, moments of sublime bathos: "The earth that has grown remote to itself is without the hope the stars once promised. It is sinking into empty galaxies. On it lies beauty as the reflection of past hope, which fills the dying eye until it is frozen below the flakes of unbound space."[46] Such lines gather up an overwhelming melancholy by book's end, and dare me to read it as other than a prolonged—and intensely enjoyable—"metaphysics of loss." "The leave-taking music cannot break away," Adorno writes. "The long gaze is fastened on the condemned."[47] But it is hard for me to see how this long gaze is not also a fantasmatic one, how the condemned is not simultaneously the object-cause of a desire dead set on eternally taking leave, which is to say, on never breaking away. It is jarring to see, in this poet philosopher of European musical modernism, such a brazen affirmation of breaklessness.

If it is easy to read the text this way, it also misses something important. As usual with Adorno, the argument is subtler. In his own account of Mahler's Ninth, for instance, there is everywhere talk of breaking. But it's not simply a breaking from the past, or a breaking *of* the subject, or a musical "portrait" of such breaking.

Rather, the symphony seems to be breaking from the very language in which the past, or subject or portrait, *could* be formulated. The opening *Andante comodo* exhibits an "omnipresent antithetical quality" that "makes a development, as a sphere reserved for colliding opposites, superfluous; thus the liquidation of sonata form by the New Music is initiated by Mahler's Ninth."[48] The second movement, a monstrous *Ländler*-scherzo hybrid, is not simply a dance of death, but of dead music—an "exemplary case of musical montage" characterized by "decomposition and lopsided reunification," "irreconcilable and obtrusive negativity," a "collage picture made from deformed clichés: it pillories reified, petrified forms."[49] The ensuing *Rondo burlesque*, another post-Beethovenian gross fugue turning inward counterpoint into ghastly spectacle, "stumbles on the fact that fugues can no longer be written"; it is a "virtuoso piece on despair" in which "the life of tonality is at stake"; it loses the wager.[50] Precisely this, Adorno writes in a centenary address to the Vienna Mahler-Gesellschaft that same year, makes it "the first work of the New Music."[51] It's in this context that the closing "farewell Adagio" fails to take leave. Shot through with the opening motto of Beethoven's *Les Adieux* sonata, it has nonetheless lost the *language* of goodbye. If it cannot "detach contemplative love from the irrecoverable," it's "not because it wants to appropriate, to assert itself," but because, like Lord Chandos, "the language in which [it] might have been granted the opportunity not only to write but also to think [*farewell*]" has been, or is being, lost.[52] This leads to a paradox. The "first work of New Music" is new precisely in its incapacity to take leave of an Old Music that had set the terms for how one "speaks" the musical act of leave taking.

In his Gesellschaft address, Adorno himself made the connection to Chandos. While "the disharmony between the aesthetic subject and reality had been the posture of the musical spirit ever since Schubert," Mahler's achievement was in allowing this disharmony "to modify the formal language of music. . . . The soul thrown back on itself no longer feels at home in its traditional idiom." But "unlike Chandos, Mahler did not conclude that the only solution was to fall silent. Instead, by attributing to the traditional words and syntax of music intentions which they no longer possessed, he signaled his recognition of the rupture. The inauthenticity of the language of music becomes the expression of its substance."[53]

Certainly such thinking provides uncanny counterpoint with figures from the Lacanian account of the end of analysis: the traversal of fantasy, the destitution of the subject, the identification with the symptom. Mahler's Ninth is for Adorno an imaginary decline of the world, an unmeshing of the fantasmatic fabric—"a fully composed-out disintegration and collapse," ending with a "leave-taking [movement]" that "dissolve[s] into particles which make no pretense of unity."[54] But throughout Adorno's account of Mahler's last works, there persist suggestions of more than occasional correspondence; something like a discourse emerges. Mahler continually appears as an agent of disintegration, renunciation, self-annulment. He still carries the poise and relentless negative power of a subject, but without the ego's semblance of autonomy. He is instead compelled by a kind of mad technique, stringent and nonsensical at once: "Mahler's technique centers on the principle of composing logically, in a manner free of caprice and indifferent to effects and at the same time [transcending] logicality."[55] He is a purely negative subject, generative of and receptive to the truly alien. His "self-denying identification with the Other . . . no longer knuckles under at the behest of the sovereign subject which insists that things must be so and not otherwise."[56] Similarly, Mahler directs his negativity at "the idea of music which evokes transcendental meaning"; this idea *is* his own past, the tradition from whence he comes, but his composition "adapts itself to this with figures of disintegration and by renouncing the ambition of integration."[57] In "abandoning the sovereign power to posit form," Mahler stages "the Western idea of unified, internally coherent, as it were systematic music" as "no longer viable."[58] Instead, out of this false unity emerges a stream of unsubdued "particularities and individuals," a "procession of the liberated, which in the midst of unfreedom necessarily sounds like a procession of ghosts."[59]

I read these figures as something like an analyst's discourse. They bear on each other systematically, working collectively to set a radical, ineliminable negativity in unending motion. Adorno's Mahler is an agent, but a self-annulling one, harnessing the power of a subject without the fantasmatic support of the ego. He is guided by stringent technique, a kind of mythic, disjunct knowledge; it helps him to train a disintegrative gaze on a tradition, a past, defined by its appearance of transcendent unity, but which he reveals as constitutively split. And this process yields a spectral procession of particulars, formerly subsumed by system and, in their invisibility, essential to its continued operation, but now liberated and exposed, at once dead and alive. If this is Adorno's formula for the birth of New Music, it is an idiosyncratic birth, indelibly marked by repetition. It is inseparable from Old Music, from its death and dying. It is mired in tradition and convention, unable to take leave from them, even to properly pronounce "farewell." But this repetition is also tychic: Adorno believes it constantly productive of the infinitesimally new. It is both recollective and anti-anamnestic, and even as it dredges up the old, it tracks in its own past those places or moments of never-was, where something consistently fails to appear and can't be hauled back up. If there is originality in Mahler's late music, it "has little to do with the traditional meaning of the term." It involves a simultaneous production of Old and New, uncannily close to the production of master signifiers, at once repressed and un-recollectable, in the analyst's discourse: "Familiar phrases carried by the gradient of musical language are lit up [*leuchten auf*]: someone who says something familiar, but behind which his life stands, says something more and other than what he says."[60]

That this thoroughly Janus-faced New Music looks backward and forward at once seems obvious enough. But it's striking that Adorno seems unable to accommodate both gazes within a single text. In the same year as the Mahler monograph and centenary address, Adorno gave a talk in memory of his publisher Peter Suhrkamp entitled "Music and New Music."[61] With the exception of its discussion of electronic music, little in the talk is qualitatively different in argumentative logic from the *Philosophie der neuen Musik* of a decade earlier. The later text is a distillation: more lucid, more mature, less defensive. But it also presents another distillation. While Mahler goes unmentioned, the Mahlerian account of an analyst's discourse reemerges in extreme form, almost a (Mahlerian?) parody of itself. New Music—and here Adorno seems to treat the composer and the music as virtually substitutable—is presented as a kind of Real object, *a*, an agent of radical self-depersonalization, a "bracketing out of the subject" seeking absolute difference with the Other it engages.[62] Bearing witness to "the world of Auschwitz," this bracketed-out subject "burrows into a world of its own" in a "splenetic mood of dogged blindness"; only with "mute utterance can it articulate itself."[63] Its absolute intolerance of any positivity is incorporated "into its own intentionality, as a possible self-annulment."[64] At the same time, this agent remains fundamentally analytical, ensuring "the pure elaboration of the material in hand in all its aspects which has accompanied music throughout its subjective phase ever since it liberated itself from ritual."[65] This "pure elaboration" is undergirded by a special kind of technical knowledge, S_2—on the one hand "the most rigid technical control, technique being understood here in the radical sense of realization, not in the comfortable sense of the manipulation of allegedly tried and true means," and on the other hand, "the disappearance of all syntactical and grammatical paradigms, of all lexical tokens, forces [the music] unremittingly to generate connections from within itself, connections which no longer emanate from elsewhere."[66]

This scenario's breathtaking negativity does not lead to solipsism, however, nor even to autonomy. New Music remains, for Adorno, desperately beholden to its Other: "The new musical language is encoded as the positive negation of the traditional one." But this negation takes the form of splitting—Old Music is constantly revealed to a barred subject, $\$$; "its assertion that this is what music is and how it should be" must be shown to be lacking. It must be made to slip, to "[betray] itself in constant stupidities and incongruities" that are not just mistakes but founding parapraxes, constitutive of its subjectivity.[67] "The bourgeois musical tradition had always contained an element of incongruity," Adorno writes, but it—and in many cases its historians—attempted to veil these contradictions under various fantasmatic guises (not least, *Geistesgeschichte*).[68] New Music, in sharp contrast, "may well be understood as the effort to do justice to all that the sharpened ear of the composer finds unresolved or antinomial in traditional music . . . the challenges which remained unresolved and which left flaws behind in the music".[69] This process in turn precipitates the tradition's master signifiers as contingencies; the "semblance of naturalness" is revealed *as* semblance, "the very notion that tonality is natural is [exposed as] an illusion"; their irrationality laid bare, such signifiers are broken of

↑ "a possible self-annulment" (*a*) ⟶ "all that is ... antinomial in traditional music" ($\$$) ↓

"the most rigid technical control" (S_2) // "the semblance of naturalness" (S_1)

FIGURE 26. (Adorno's) New Music as an analyst's discourse.

their conciliatory spell.[70] In the process of laying bare these contingencies, however, New Music's negativities invert their valence. Against a musical horizon constantly threatening to close, they consolidate into a "permanent, albeit Sisyphean effort to open people's ears, to penetrate the anthropological sound barrier."[71]

The tone of such words—"a tone of menace," as Adorno puts it—befits the Lacanian clinic far less than it does the Hesposian rant.[72] And I can easily imagine Hespos standing by Adorno's vision. It is pitilessly, unwaveringly antagonistic. It describes a music that remains close to its past, not in order to invite it in as a "boy scout being repeatedly and warmly celebrated as a master from the past," but to rend it to bits, "play it into the ground," "uglify" it, as Hespos put it. But it's harder to see Hespos having much patience for Adorno's talk of late Beethoven. And if Adorno's conceptualization of New Music as a proto-analytic discourse has an origin, a moment of coining, the Beethoven essay is it. An account of how the quintessential composer of bourgeois subjectivity desubjectivizes both himself and his tradition, it imagines subjectivity as both the agent and also something like a Real object, collapsing all meaningful polarities. It erupts, but also petrifies; it "forces extremes together in the moment," but also acts "as a force of dissociation," tearing the works "apart in time"; the power of subjectivity in late Beethoven, and in late works of art in general, becomes "the eruptive gesture with which it exits them."[73] This agent is guided by a severe and technical truth, a "formal law [*Formgesetz*]" that determines the relationship between subjectivity and convention, and whose ultimate engine is "the thought of death."[74] And this formal law compels the composing agent to treat tradition as a split subject, antinomial to the core. The precipitate of this process is a music both dead and alive. I struggle to find a better—more elegant, but also more physical and material—articulation of how an analyst's discourse simultaneously produces "dead" master signifiers and a "living" recognition than Adorno's account of convention here:

> Conventions become expression in the act of their own naked self-representation. . . . [His] style . . . seeks not to cleanse his musical language of formulas [*Floskeln*] but, rather, to strip the formula of its semblance of subjective control. Once released and lifted out of its dynamic context, the formula begins to speak for itself—yet only in the moment when subjectivity, escaping, rushes through it and suddenly illuminates [*erleuchtet*] it with its intention; hence the crescendi and diminuendi, which, seemingly independent of the musical construction in Beethoven's final works, often send tremors through it.[75]

It is as if no time had elapsed between such lines, written in 1937, and Adorno's claim more than two decades later that, in Mahler, "the inauthenticity of the language of music becomes the expression of its substance." Even the "lighting" of the two scenes is the same: if subjectivity "illuminates" in Beethoven, it "lights up" Mahler. In Beethoven's brittle objective landscape, subjectivity is the light that "alone can set it aglow [*erglüht*]."[76] In Mahler's disintegrating, thing-like language, it is those "unspeakable experiences that flash through [*durchzucken*]."[77] Searching for a "motto for Mahler," Adorno settles on a line from Stefan George: "die Lichter, die aus deinen Wunden strahlen" (the lights that beam from your wounds).[78] *Erleuchten, aufleuchten erglühen, strahlen, durchzucken*: each carefully chosen word, of which there are surely more, figures an unfigurable newness, the new as a Real effect, equally beyond the imaginary and the symbolic.[79] And it is an effect produced by failure—the failure of material, of the imaginary and symbolic, to master themselves. "And why Mahler," asks Hespos in his fit of pique, having just commanded the appearance of a "full-to-bursting new light [*Leuchtung*], shimmering through, uncomprehended, from behind the thin cracks of misunderstanding." Clearly he hadn't read his Adorno. Or, more likely, he had read him all too well, had internalized his trope, and now spoke it as his own, a kind of second nature, an image set to work within a signifying structure.

• • •

The question I want to end this book with—a question that necessarily remains open—involves this second nature, this image. It is, as I read it, a fantasy of the traversal of fantasy. To a vision of the very fabric of the world coming undone, it fastens a pure gaze beyond all undoing; it presents a picture of subjective destitution to a subject anchored and protected by that picture. The gaze, even as it conjures scenes of the death of desire, its fading and transcendence, is a desirous one. My question is whether musical modernism as I have tried to formulate it here is always fated, over any historical arc, to turn from iconoclasm into graven image, unpicturing into picturing, denaturing into second nature. It is an almost inappropriately visual question to put to some of the stranger sounds the world has known. But the late, anti-messianic appearance of Adorno, with all his summoning of dead and brittle landscapes glowing and flashing and beaming forth, has put pressure on a certain medium specificity.

Some of the pathos of the question comes from trying to give a psychoanalytic account of modernism—which is to say, an account of a modernism radically skeptical, like Freud and Lacan, of the very concept of fate, deeply convinced that if the upper gods had fled and could not be bent, then surely the lower ones could.[80] Fate is always a matter of pathos; it always takes the poor soul by surprise; it is always a sign of getting old, of historical processes coming, or grinding, to a temporary stop. In this, the modernism I've been describing here—a "late style" by any definition—would not be new. Tragic, perhaps—modernism, not only defying fate but wanting to destroy it, inevitably takes on a heroic cast—but not new. The pathos is one of the oldest there is. "All the new thinking is about loss," Robert Hass writes in "Meditation at Lagunitas." "In this it resembles all the old thinking."[81]

But some of the pathos comes from the weird aura being given off by European New Music in late 1989, an aura that is, if no longer new at this point, then at least unique. It is the aura—perhaps, yes, a glow, a beaming forth—that comes from a paradoxical community of the dispersed, the broken apart and defabricated, the anti-unisonant. Not a "lonely crowd," the solipsistic musician citizens of disenchanted modernity, trapped in the cages of their own idiosyncratic knowledge.[82] And also not Jean-Luc Nancy's "inoperative community," pining for "a lost age in which community was tight and bound to harmonious bonds," an original social body capable of "[playing] back to itself, through its institutions, its rituals, and its symbols, the representation, indeed the living offering, of its own immanent unity, intimacy and autonomy."[83] With the possible exception of Penderecki, I'd be hard pressed to describe the composers I've engaged in this book as nostalgists, even those, like Berio, whose voices occasionally quiver with sentiment. They are theorists and practitioners of loss, some quite inspired, but not of recuperation. Their crafts, often of tormenting complexity, are honed to stage non-appearances, and to repeat this staging—to make non-appearance a sustainable resource. This is their cathexis, their occupation. Though they show themselves again and again to be obsessed with history, history doesn't quite know what to do with them. Certainly it didn't in 1989. Though individual works may end up in articles, anthologies, textbooks, even their own monographs, collectively they will never be *of* their musical moment, whether at its most notoriously "important" (Bernstein), or at its most gloriously insipid (Hasselhoff).[84] While the latter still echo in the year's boomy historical theater, musical modernism occupies another acoustic altogether—the stubborn tinnitus of history's inner ear, perhaps. It might be argued that these works' non-relationship to their moment is the direct result of their ethics of traversal. In "tearing apart in time" the armature of fantasy, they end up lacking "a shared perception of the situation. Without this binding agent, gestures dissolve without a trace into nothingness, lives have the texture of dreams, and uprisings end up in schoolbooks."[85] This is what the Invisible Committee thinks is so desperately important about fantasy. This is what they think is lost when it is lost: the capacity not only to be history, but to make it.

• • •

I am looking at the Facebook wall of a young composer born in 1989—Marek Poliks, getting his PhD at Harvard University, studying with Chaya Czernowin. His work, what I know of it, I wouldn't hesitate to call New Music; the fact that he confesses elsewhere to "slowly disentangling himself from music" altogether only seems to support my sense of what the label might still mean.[86] On his wall he is irked and impish, and posts:

> Hey composers
> No one wants to hear your Beckett piece[87]

. . .

Now I am looking at a picture, a complicated one (figure 27). It zooms in on another of the heterotopian networks from chapter 10 (figure 16) and is a fantasy if ever there was: an image of impossible, chimeric consistency, a literal fabrication. Its graded curves and strands weave together a collection of objects that, by any stretch, are problematically put in one place. I've tried to be methodical: the picture is first and foremost a map of some string quartets "from 1989," composed or premiered in part or whole that year; they are represented by dark diamonds. But I've also tried to extrapolate from these quartets a number of distinct sub-networks, which I see and hear as immanent to the works themselves: networks of explicit quotation and allusion (hollow circles); networks of broader musical influence (asterisks); "topic" networks, as in figure 16 (dark solid circles); and networks of school, style, and -ism (light solid circles). This last network betrays a crisis of conviction on my part. I place the labels ("modernism," "dialectical composition," "new romanticism," et cetera) in quotation marks to reflect not only the contingency of their disputed usage in textbooks, articles, and reviews, but also my wavering belief in their legitimacy. They are historiographical fantasy's low-hanging fruit, ways of hastily parsing the mess so that we can know what the big symbolic Other wants, and then provide it. But in fact most of the other networks are easily opened to debate, too. The influence networks, while constructed around works on historical record as being important to their "influencees," still inevitably reflect my own fallible intuition and limited aural diet. The topic networks are an actual fantasy construction, dependent on my own creative associations. Even the choice of 1989 quartets themselves ought provoke questions. How is it that quartets from West and East Germans (Wolfgang Rihm and Paul-Heinz Dittrich), from Frenchmen and Ukrainians (Nicolas Bacri and Valentin Silvestrov), Muscovites and American expats (Alfred Schnittke and Stephen Montague), mingle here so freely, at the end of a book whose cover features the symbol of what so forcibly kept them apart?

My best answer to this question lies in the networks involving quotations and influences. There are many, and most of those represented in the figure test any overarching thesis. This goes especially for the citations: they range from the warhorse to the obscure, from traditional Chanukah melodies (Berthold Goldschmidt's Quartet No. 3) to sixteenth-century Polish motets (Henryk Górecki's Quartet No. 1) to minimalist orchestral scores from the 1970s (Stephen Montague's Quartet No. 1).

Epic works like Dusapin's forty-minute Second Quartet ("Time Zones") seem constitutionally allergic to any musical quotation whatsoever, while scores like György Kurtág's eleven-minute *Officium breve in memoriam Andreae Szervánsky* desperately invest every bar with the greatest intertextual intensity. But listening—and reading—for influences, the larger map produces some common nodes.

They are at first not *so* surprising. Luigi Nono's remarkable and only quartet *Fragmente-Stille, an Diotima* is an undeniable pole, its "inward turn" and airy hermeticism still magnetizing the New Music landscape almost a decade after its 1980 Bonn premiere.[88] Some quartets actually sound like it—the cavernous pauses, the diatonic and chromatic clusters caught in scurrying tremoli, the stagnating tension of long, cut-off chords built on fourth, fifth, and tritone. Beat Furrer's slight Second Quartet is a revision through diminution, while Rihm's Eighth is a hyperbolization, Nono as high-temperature slapstick. Other quartets act like Nono's: Hölszky's *Hängebrücken,* Dusapin's aforementioned Second Quartet, and Paul-Heinz Dittrich's Third Quartet (*Nacht-Musik*) all assemble themselves as a train of fragments whose mutual isolation only bolsters their continuity; they appear to have learned well the lessons of Nono's *campi,* his open "fields" and islands and archipelagos of activity unfolding in constantly interrupted waves (*onde*).[89] For Dittrich, lines from Novalis's poetry—his *Hymnen an die Nacht* provide the quartet's subtitle—model a structure "paratactically strung together and interlocked," equally incapable of wholeness or disintegration.[90] Dusapin formalizes Nono's fragments through the conceit of twenty-four time zones, but preserves Nono's dialectic of break and continuity. His "inscriptionist" ethos, too: while Nono infests his quartet with lines from the late poetry of Friedrich Hölderlin, and Dittrich with lines from Novalis, Dusapin increasingly settles on Beckett's 1946 novel *Mercier et Camier.* Beckett's death is announced at the end of the eighth "time zone," while the thirteenth—dedicated to Nono himself—is prefaced by a line from Leonardo da Vinci and concluded with another from *Mercier et Camier.* The quartet "joins the ranks of 'personal diary' quartets," and Richard Toop is reminded of "Adorno's comment that [Alban] Berg's *Lyrische Suite* was 'latent opera'."[91] Adorno's image works for Dittrich and Hölszky as well, and certainly for Nono; they do not simply embed texts in their scores, but repress them. They are there, but only for the performers; they are there, but only to *not*-perform; they "leave their mark" only by being passed over, silenced, unshown. Even effaced: Rihm writes that his Eighth Quartet "should carry a title. It should be called 'Drawings, pages.' But that's not what it's called. The title is struck through, overpainted, crosshatched out, blackened in, scratched away, scraped away."[92] At one point the players write the phrase "Con amore" in the air with their bows.

Given this trope of the repressed text, it makes sense that Berg's *Lyrische Suite* of 1926 would also exert a certain gravity here. By 1989 European scholarship had long since processed Douglass M. Green's 1976 discovery that Berg's score was an

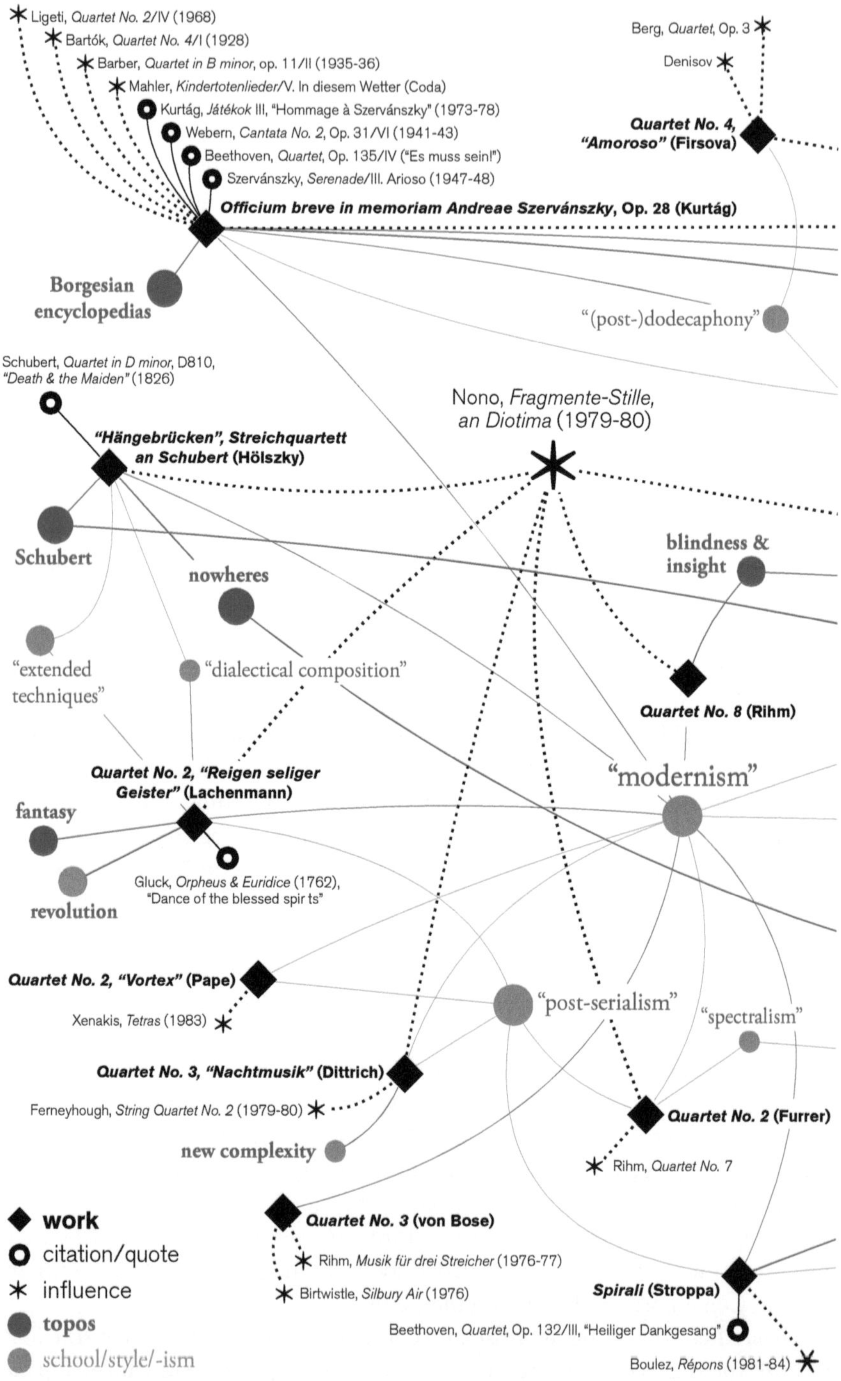

FIGURE 27. "Lyric Suites" network.

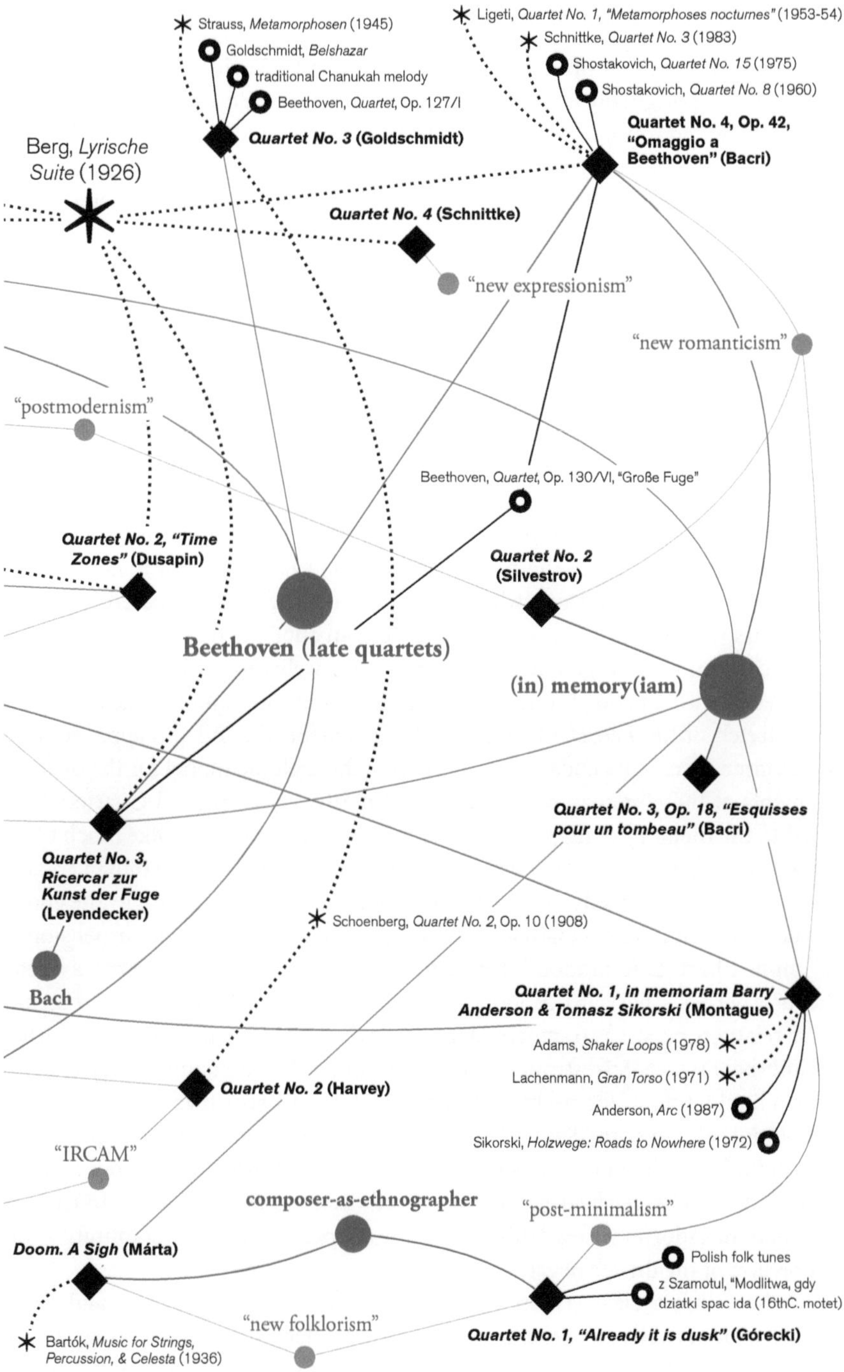

Strauss, Metamorphosen (1945)
Goldschmidt, Belshazar
traditional Chanukah melody
Beethoven, Quartet, Op. 127/I
Quartet No. 3 (Goldschmidt)
Ligeti, Quartet No. 1, "Metamorphoses nocturnes" (1953-54)
Schnittke, Quartet No. 3 (1983)
Shostakovich, Quartet No. 15 (1975)
Shostakovich, Quartet No. 8 (1960)
Quartet No. 4, Op. 42, "Omaggio a Beethoven" (Bacri)
Berg, Lyrische Suite (1926)
Quartet No. 4 (Schnittke)
"new expressionism"
"new romanticism"
"postmodernism"
Beethoven, Quartet, Op. 130/VI, "Große Fuge"
Quartet No. 2, "Time Zones" (Dusapin)
Quartet No. 2 (Silvestrov)
Beethoven (late quartets)
(in) memory(iam)
Quartet No. 3, Op. 18, "Esquisses pour un tombeau" (Bacri)
Quartet No. 3, Ricercar zur Kunst der Fuge (Leyendecker)
Schoenberg, Quartet No. 2, Op. 10 (1908)
Bach
Quartet No. 1, in memoriam Barry Anderson & Tomasz Sikorski (Montague)
Adams, Shaker Loops (1978)
Lachenmann, Gran Torso (1971)
Anderson, Arc (1987)
Sikorski, Holzwege: Roads to Nowhere (1972)
Quartet No. 2 (Harvey)
"IRCAM"
composer-as-ethnographer
"post-minimalism"
Doom. A Sigh (Márta)
Polish folk tunes
z Szamotul, "Modlitwa, gdy dziatki spac ida (16thC. motet)
"new folklorism"
Quartet No. 1, "Already it is dusk" (Górecki)
Bartók, Music for Strings, Percussion, & Celesta (1936)

encrypted chronicle of his doomed affair with Hanna Fuchs; Green also discovered that Berg originally conceived his quartet's last movement as a setting, complete with added soprano voice, of Baudelaire's dark verse "De profundis clamavi" from his *Fleurs du mal.* But Green's work only proved what people had long believed about Berg's "esoteric" score—that Adorno's claim of operatic latency was more than mere critical flourish, and that its quotes from Wagner's *Tristan und Isolde* and Alexander Zemlinsky's *Lyrische Symphonie* were already "crying from the depths."[93]

Strikingly, those 1989 quartets that actually sound like the *Lyrische Suite* tend not to overlap with the Nono group; they are overtly effusive and *espressivo*, seemingly disinterested in developing new techniques or solving problems of construction, and confidently embedded in significantly earlier—read: pre–World War II—musical landscapes. Alfred Schnittke's Fourth Quartet, commissioned by the Alban Berg Quartet and ostensibly written in Berlin while the Russian-German composer was on a fellowship there, eschews the overt polystylism for which he had become known since the mid-1970s, but the gestural, textural, and timbral profile of Berg's quartet is overwhelmingly present. The Moscow-based composer Elena Firsova's Fourth Quartet takes the Bergian subtitle "Amoroso" and begins with a consummate Bergian technique, parsing a twelve-tone row into three tonal triads each with an added tone; its quarter-hour duration unfolds like an oneiric time stretch of the *Lyrische Suite*'s fourth movement, the "Adagio appassionato." That same movement's coda seems to provide the melodic model for the opening moments of the Ukranian composer Valentin Silvestrov's Second Quartet, dedicated to the memory of his parents. This only seems appropriate: like much of his work from the mid-1970s on, Silvestrov's expansive score is a gargantuan coda in itself, a "postlude" outside or after music proper, capable of inhabiting "the end of music, in which it may remain for a long time."[94] Full of "Romantic suspension[s] of implied harmonic motion," it nonetheless "fatally unmoors [them]," as Peter Schmelz writes. "Forward motion staggers, unexpectedly zigging and zagging; tonal relations persist as fragmented memories."[95] It is fitting that all three quartets (Schnittke, Firsova, Silvestrov) end in a kind of double dissolution: they enact at once a liquidation of themselves and a liquidation of Berg's own act of structural dissolution, the *Lyrische Suite*'s "liquidation of the sonata," as Adorno put it—its concluding viola "not even allowed to expire, to die. It must play on forever except that we can no longer hear it." "If, after Beethoven, no finale was able to close in affirmation," Adorno writes, "this one simply adopts the principle of infinity as the expression of the finale's negativity."[96]

It's here that a clear stylistic division—between "Nono quartets" and "Berg quartets," or between an allegedly waning "late modernism" and a waxing "neoromantic postmodernism"—starts to seem suspect. Or rather, it obscures a bigger picture, a longer *durée*, in which Nono and Berg are not so much antipodes as distinct, emblematic ways of engaging the same problematic, the same antagonism. This only becomes clearer when Beethoven's own late quartets are figured into the larger network. Their presence is already summoned indirectly through Nono's *Fragmente-Stille*, whose citing of performance directions from the "Heiliger Dankgesang" of Beethoven's Op. 132 quartet is only one of its nods to its purview; the city of Bonn commissioned the score for its thirtieth Beethovenfest. Citations among 1989 quartets are, if not ubiquitous, still telling: Berthold Goldschmidt's Third Quartet, baldly quoting the opening E-flat major chord of Beethoven's Op. 127 quartet, studiously straddles the line between Schoenberg's First and Second Quartets—which is to say, between late (neo)romantic tonality and its letting-go. On the other hand, Ulrich Leyendecker's agonized paraphrase of the *Grosse Fuge* pulls Beethoven onto the other side of the post-tonal and dodecaphonic breach. Quartets by Marco Stroppa (*Spirali*) and Nicolas Bacri (*Omaggio a Beethoven*) embody as irreducible a stylistic divide as existed in 1989 Paris. When Stroppa writes his score—"a tribute to the slow movement of Beethoven's Quartet, Op. 132"—he has just been appointed head of Music Research at IRCAM. The work, "for spatially projected string quartet," features extensive state-of-the-art live electronics; its Beethoven remains a "latent chorale . . . never directly perceived" until the very end, and then only in outline, almost a mirage.[97] Bacri composes his *Omaggio*, meanwhile, while head of chamber music for Radio France. His score supports the profile of a staunch traditionalist, and zags freely from the idiom of Bartók's middle and Shostakovich's late quartets to that of Schnittke's Third, from 1983. Its extensive quotations from the *Grosse Fuge* are even more brazen than Schnittke's, but like the latter's quartet, Bacri's *Omaggio* embraces Beethoven only to tear him apart—Beethoven's own "impossible finale" is made (yet more?) impossible, and ends the second movement in an apoplectic whirl.

The challenge, though, is to hear past the citations. To hear Dusapin's otherwise quoteless score, for instance, as embroiled in the same self-undoing dramaturgy as Nono's *Fragmente-Stille*, or Berg's *Lyrische Suite*, or Beethoven's Op. 130/133. When Dusapin writes in his score's preface that "the string quartet alone can 'serve' a music where the lines, the networks, the flow of musical energy focus on the mechanisms themselves and the complexity of their relationships," he identifies the genre itself as a compositional summa. I cannot but recall Beethoven's "new manner of voice treatment," his own understated way of envisioning the entire string quartet genre as a new utopia of making. Dusapin conjures his own such utopia in the form of "two principal ladders, each with over a hundred notes," which "cross and uncross" in endless fructifying combination as the quartet unfolds. But when Dusapin's own quartet collapses at the end—"freezing into a rotary movement so fast that it exhausts itself," as he puts it—I cannot help but think of the *Grosse Fuge*, and how Beethoven ends up actually "treating" his "voices."[98] *Ein wüstes Gewirr*, a "wild tangle," "the negation of music itself" *as* music itself.[99]

This line from Beethoven to Berg to Nono to Dusapin and his contemporaries is, as I said above, fantasmatic. But whose fantasy? It is, at the least, a shared one, a kind of social, historical, and aesthetic glue, a way of binding subjects and objects across time. I myself am pulled in. But this fantasy binds together scenarios of pulling apart and coming undone. A composer turns inward, "cries from the depths," chronicles a dissolution of self; the work becomes a site of overwhelming potential meaning, wildly reverberating with unspoken, unsung, even unseen inscriptions ("overpainted, crosshatched out, blackened in, scratched away, scraped away"). A quartet's lyric drive, its capacity for sustaining lyric continuity, is constantly broken; the possibility of making the work a work—of bringing its processes to a point of completion or even closure, of being able to realize its demands, claims, or wishes—is put in radical doubt. It suffers a necessary "de-completion": much is left undone or unsaid, and what is said is said at night, from below or within or underneath. The expressive and constructive event never entirely comes to pass; it is held in mind, in mouth, in hand, until a right future—which, the work makes clear, may never appear—appears.

In the process, individual dissolution becomes a collective dissolution, a dissolution of genre; the practice of the string quartet itself becomes a parapraxis, an "act whose explicit goal is not attained." (If the Schubert network in chapter 10 framed a fantasy of insurmountable distance, perhaps this quartet network frames a fantasy of irreversible entropy, an incapacity to live up to the genre's utopian claim to order.) I recall Mikhail Bakhtin's elusive notion of "genre memory."[100] In these 1989 quartets, it seems as if the individual author, placing his own travails and torments—effusive or encrypted—at the center of the endeavor, paradoxically fades into what Bakhtin called "great time," a time in which "great memory" forgets absolutely nothing. In such time, as Ilya Kliger reads Bakhtin, genre itself becomes the remembering agent; it "contains everything that ever was in the domains of nature and culture both, allows us to break out of the confines of the present with its practical exigencies and linearly ordered time and to experience the past as non-identical, forever open to re-articulation."[101]

But in the case of these string quartets from 1989, the past is a kind of mise en abyme. What is being re-articulated is not a positive feature of "tradition," but rather a kind of syncope. "Only memory, and not oblivion, can move forward," Bakhtin insists.[102] Well, yes. Then perhaps what keeps musical modernism "alive" is also *what keeps it from moving forward.* In these quartets, an oblivion that cannot move forward is encased by a memory that *can*, the memory of this or that style or hybrid of styles, this or that precursor or precedent, forever open to re-articulation.

I can think of few better examples, not only from 1989, than a moment late in Helmut Lachenmann's Second Quartet, also discussed back in chapter 10. Near the end of its relentless journey from heaven to earth, from air to tone to the most walloping violence—and just before it tries to return to its beginning—the score arrives at a moment of extraordinary equipoise. Out of the wildly detuned quartet emerges "an expansive sixteen-note 'song' [*Gesang*]," but it emerges as a kind of shadow melody, one after another of the ensemble's sixteen open strings left resonating only after a brutal tutti pizzicato attack.[103] The delicate, almost alarming strangeness of the tones—unforeseeable by even the performers themselves—is only intensified by the blows that precede them. They are less a song than an aural corona to a song eclipsed.

A shadow song emerges at a similar point late in Nono's *Fragmente-Stille*, embedded in the viola, broken apart by long silences and set harmonically askew by the other players. In this case it is an actual preexisting melody, "Malor me bat" (Suffering beats me), often used as a tenor in fifteenth-century Netherlandish polyphony. In Nono's setting it silently bears another Hölderlin inscription—"Wenn ich trauernd versank . . . das zweifelnde Haupt" (When I sank myself in mourning . . . my doubting head)—and an encrypted memorial, to Nono's late friend and mentor Bruno Maderna, who had likely introduced him to the song.[104] Lachenmann's renowned and complicated closeness to Nono, full of rifts and reunions, suggests a biographical bond between these two "suspended songs," some combination of homage and revision, love and contest.[105] But I am more interested in the impersonal—perhaps even depersonalized—connection, the one that leads back to Berg and Beethoven. It is an almost automated connection, seemingly coming from the genre itself: genre-as-*automaton*, as the drawing of lots, the hauling back up of what was placed there by chance. The string quartet ends in dissolution, not simply by wish or accident, not only because it wants to, but because it has no choice. And before that dissolution, it sings a cavatina, not only because it has something to say, but because this is how it goes—"Es muss sein!" Some kind of Real, that which "doesn't cease not to inscribe itself," must nonetheless be placed, encircled, staged. A refractory history of retrograde progress, modernism with a song in its heart: Lachenmann's shocked shadow *Gesang*, hearing back to Nono's broken *Tenorlied*, hearing back to Berg's secret Baudelairean lament, hearing back to Beethoven's oppressed [*beklemmt*] cavatina. Reverberating through them all, the voice that wants to show itself hiding, the voice that wants less to speak than to choke.[106]

. . .

I don't know enough about Marek Poliks or his music to say how he feels about Beckett. But what I do know makes me read his post as something other than mockery. Impatience, disbelief, perhaps a—modernist?—desire for distance from the source. I imagine Beckett's Krapp listening to the old tapes of himself, and can hear musical modernism today, whatever has become of its tendencies toward un-becoming, grumbling something similar: "Just been listening to that stupid bastard I took myself for thirty years ago, hard to believe I was ever as bad as that."[107]

I'm tempted to think of *automaton* as modernism's "stupid bastard"—the persistent, humiliating recognition, on the part of those stuck on the new, that its handmaiden failure can be pulled out of a hat—or replayed like an old reel of tape. "When Beckett talks about failure," Ned Beauman writes in a deliciously dyspeptic essay from 2012, "he's often talking about how language can't withstand the weight of the meaning you want to put into it, and in that sense his unintended ubiquity [today] is ideal: What better argument for the feebleness of determinate meaning than the tawdry afterlife of 'fail better'?"[108] Certainly I read in Poliks's line a tiredness with "tawdry afterlife."

Getting rid of the tawdriness, finding a way to fail better than the now-corporate phrase "fail better," is modernism's unending labor. But there is no getting rid of the afterlife. It is unavoidable. Modernism, as a tradition of remembering oblivion, a ceaseless re-reception of what was never there in the first place, is still living it. I do not see—or hear—an end.

NOTES

INTRODUCTION

1. The complete festival brochure for Musikfest Berlin 2011 is available at http://archiv2.berlinerfestspiele.de/media/2011_1/musikfestberlin_3/downloads_3/11_mfb_broschuere.pdf.

2. See Theodor W. Adorno, *Mahler: A Physiognomy*, trans. Edmund Jephcott (Chicago: University of Chicago Press, 1992), 122–43.

3. On the Austrian political-cultural milieu surrounding Mahler's Eighth and especially the premiere of the composition, see Karen Painter, "The Aesthetics of Mass Culture: Mahler's Eighth Symphony and Its Legacy," in *Mahler and His World*, ed. Karen Painter (Princeton, NJ: Princeton University Press, 2002), 127–56.

4. Theodor W. Adorno, "122," in *Minima Moralia*, trans. Edmund Jephcott (London: Verso, 2005), 190. Jephcott renders the last phrase "most recondite insults," which I find less effective. I thank my colleague David Levin for the suggested alternative.

5. Christian Wildhagen, *Die Achte Symphonie von Gustav Mahler: Konzeption einer universalen Symphonik* (Frankfurt: Peter Lang, 2000), 224; cited in Julian Johnson, *Mahler's Voices: Expression and Irony in the Songs and Symphonies* (Oxford: Oxford University Press, 2009), 181.

6. Theodor W. Adorno, *Minima Moralia*, 223.

7. Michele Bertaggia, ed., "Conversation entre Luigi Nono et Massimo Cacciari," in *Verso Prometeo*, ed. Massimo Cacciari (Venice: Ricordi, 1984).

8. Cacciari's quasi- or outright purloined words—at one point the phrase "questo debole / messianische Kraft"—make clear reference to the philosophical thought of his and Nono's contemporary Gianni Vattimo, in particular his notion of *pensieri debole*, or "weak thought." For an excellent exploration of the concept, and of the intellectual network around it, see Trent Leipert, "Feeling in the Cracks: Subjective Binds in European New Music" (PhD diss., University of Chicago, 2014), 61–113.

9. The passage, from James Joyce's *Ulysses*, occurs at the beginning of the chapter "Oxen of the Sun," generally regarded as the novel's most difficult, but also one of greatest feats of inconsistency made consistent: the chapter's transition from Latin prayer through more than thirty different styles and authorial "voices," and eventually into what Joyce calls a "frightful jumble of pidgin English . . . Cockney, Irish, Bowery slang and broken doggerel," is framed as the nine-month gestation and birth of a human fetus. See the letter from March 13, 1920, in James Joyce, *The Letters of James Joyce*, vol. 1, ed. Stuart Gilbert (New York: Viking Press, 1957), 138–39.

10. This point is made with particular eloquence by Raymond Williams in his essay "Metropolitan Perceptions and the Emergence of Modernism," in his posthumous collection *The Politics of Modernism* (London: Verso, 1989), 43.

11. Theodor W. Adorno, *Philosophy of New Music*, trans. Robert Hullot-Kentor (Minneapolis: University of Minnesota Press, 2007), 7–10.

12. Mark Wollaeger stresses this point in his introduction to *The Oxford Handbook of Global Modernisms*, ed. Wollaeger and Matt Eatough (Oxford: Oxford University Press, 2012), 12ff. For an especially ambitious recent effort to revise modernism's imaginary, see Susan Stanford Friedman, *Planetary Modernisms: Provocations on Modernity across Time* (New York: Columbia University Press, 2015).

13. J. P. E. Harper-Scott, *Edward Elgar, Modernist* (Cambridge, England: Cambridge University Press, 2006). Harper-Scott has since issued something of a palinode in the form of *The Quilting Points of Musical Modernism: Revolution, Reaction, and William Walton* (Cambridge, England: Cambridge University Press, 2012).

14. T. J. Clark, "Clement Greenberg's Theory of Art," *Critical Inquiry* 9, no. 1 (September 1982): 154.

15. T. J. Clark, "Modernism, Postmodernism, and Steam," *October* 100 (2002): 165–66.

16. Michel Foucault, preface, in *The Order of Things: An Archaeology of the Human Sciences*, 4th ed. (London: Routledge, 2004), xiv: "This book first arose out of a passage in Borges, out of the laughter that shattered, as I read the passage . . ."

17. Samuel Beckett, *The Unnameable*, in *The Beckett Trilogy: Molloy, Malone Dies, The Unnamable*, ed. Patrick Bowles (London: Picador, 1979), 326.

18. Morton Feldman, "Predeterminate/Indeterminate" (1966), in *Morton Feldman Essays*, ed. Walter Zimmermann (Kerpen, Germany: Beginner Press, 1985), 49.

19. Hugo von Hofmannsthal, *The Lord Chandos Letter: And Other Writings*, trans. Joel Rotenberg, introduction by John Banville (New York: New York Review of Books, 2005), 121. The *Chandos Letter* is as celebrated a piece of early literary modernism as can be, with canonical treatments in Allan Janik and Stephen Toulmin, *Wittgenstein's Vienna* (New York: Touchstone Press, 1973), and to a lesser extent in Carl Schorske, *Fin-de-Siècle Vienna: Politics and Culture* (New York: Vintage Books, 1961), 1–25.

20. For an apt account of the *recusatio*'s political and cultural efficacy as an intensely codified, readable, and "high-profile act of denial," see Kirk Freudenburg, "*Recusatio* as Political Theatre: Horace's Letter to Augustus," *Journal of Roman Studies* 104 (February 2014): 105–32. I don't mean to suggest that there was something modernist about the *recusatio* genre, but more the opposite: already installed in the "hearts" of modernist endeavors and discourses explicitly dedicated to the new and emancipatory was the possibility, or more precisely the affordance, of adding prestige to the hegemony. As Freudenberg writes,

"The oft-repeated refusals of the Augustan poets to take on projects that, they claim, exceed their talents are informed not just by aesthetic principles that derive, most obviously, from Callimachus, but by the many high-profile acts of denial that were performed as political art by the emperor himself" (110).

21. Ernesto Laclau and Chantal Mouffe, *Hegemony and Socialist Strategy* (London: Verso, 1985), 122.

22. Though neither Lacan nor his seminar editor Jacques-Alain Miller capitalizes the term "real," in this book I will be following the orthography used by the majority of post-Lacanians, Slavoj Žižek, Adrian Johnston, Tom Eyers, and Anna Kornbluh among them.

23. McKenzie Wark, *The Beach Beneath the Street: The Everyday Life and Glorious Times of the Situationist International* (New York: Verso, 2011), 93–94.

24. Tom Eyers, *Lacan and the Concept of the "Real"* (New York: Palgrave Macmillan, 2012).

25. Jacques Lacan, *The Seminar of Jacques Lacan, Book I: Freud's Papers on Technique, 1953–54*, trans. with notes by John Forrester (New York: W. W. Norton, 1991), 66.

26. Alain Badiou, *The Century*, trans. Alberto Toscano (Cambridge, England: Polity Press, 2007), 32.

27. See in particular Jacques Lacan, *The Seminar of Jacques Lacan, Book XI: The Four Fundamental Concepts of Psychoanalysis*, trans. Alan Sheridan (New York: W. W. Norton, 1981), 53ff, especially 55 and 128ff.

28. Sigmund Freud, *Totem and Taboo: Some Points of Agreement between the Mental Lives of Savages and Neurotics* (London: Routledge, 2004), 166.

29. T. J. Clark, "Modernism, Postmodernism, and Steam," 172.

30. Franz Kafka, "20," in *The Zürau Aphorisms*, trans. Michael Hofmann (London: Harvill Secker / Random House, 2006), 20. Original German: "Leoparden brechen in den Tempel ein und saufen die Opferkrüge leer; das wiederholt sich immer wieder; schließlich kann man es vorausberechnen, und es wird ein Teil der Zeremonie."

31. The notion of the repeatedly failed repetition—the repetition that persists *because* it is in some sense failing to realize itself—inevitably raises the concept of the Freudian death drive, which becomes in Lacanian psychoanalysis the drive tout court. In his recent *Freud*, 2nd ed. (New York: Routledge, 2015), the philosopher and psychoanalyst Jonathan Lear argues that the death drive—distilled in Freud's famous thesis that "the aim of all life is death"—exploits some problematic logic; see pp. 162–63.

32. Françoise Meltzer, *Seeing Double: Baudelaire's Modernity* (Chicago: University of Chicago Press, 2011), 1.

33. Jürgen Habermas, "Modernity—An Incomplete Project," *Critique* 37 (1981): 950–67.

34. Steven Connor, introduction, in *The Cambridge Companion to Postmodernism*, ed. Steven Connor (Cambridge, England: Cambridge University Press, 2004), 10.

35. Francis Fukuyama, "The End of History?," *National Interest* 16 (Summer 1989): 1–18. For recent sympathetic reappraisals see Francis Fukuyama, "The Future of History," *Foreign Affairs* 91, no. 1 (2012): 53–61; and Francis Fukuyama with Jacques Attali, "The Beginning of a New History," *New Perspectives Quarterly* 31, no. 1 (2014): 20–24. For a representative neoliberal reassessment, see also Cato Institute Senior Fellow John Mueller, "Did History End? Assessing the Fukuyama Thesis," *Political Science Quarterly* 129, no. 1 (2014): 35–54.

36. Sigmund Freud, "Project for a Scientific Psychology," in *The Standard Edition of the Complete Psychological Works of Sigmund Freud*, vol. 1, trans. and ed. James Strachey

(London: Hogarth Press, 1966), 352ff. The Strachey *Standard Edition* will henceforth be abbreviated *SE*. See also Adrian Johnston, *Žižek's Ontology: A Transcendental Materialist Theory of Subjectivity* (Evanston, IL: Northwestern University Press, 2008): "And yet this illusion itself, once generated out of the Real, becomes something efficacious, operating as a *proton pseudos* (a "lie" that becomes a quite tangible, self-fulfilling prophecy)" (44).

37. T. J. Clark, *Farewell to an Idea: Episodes in a History of Modernism* (New Haven, CT: Yale University Press, 2001), 8.

38. Eric Hobsbawm, *The Age of Extremes: The Short Twentieth Century, 1914–1991* (New York: Vintage, 1994).

39. Ibid., 585.

40. Ibid., 516–17. See also Joshua Clover, *1989: Bob Dylan Didn't Have This to Sing About* (Berkeley: University of California Press, 2009), 135.

41. Arthur Rimbaud, "Depart," in *A Season in Hell and Illuminations*, trans. Bertrand Mathieu (Rochester, NY: BOA Editions, 1991), 147.

42. Bruno Latour, *We Have Never Been Modern*, trans. Catherine Porter (Cambridge, MA: Harvard University Press, 1993), 9.

43. See Hans Ulrich Gumbrecht, *In 1926: Living on the Edge of Time* (Cambridge, MA: Harvard University Press, 1997); James Chandler, *England in 1819: The Politics of Literary Culture and the Case of Romantic Historicism* (Chicago: University of Chicago Press, 1998); and Michael North, *Reading 1922: A Return to the Scene of the Modern* (Oxford: Oxford University Press, 1999). At present, the book-on-a-single-year is unquestionably a scholarly and now popular genre, as evinced by dissertations on the one hand, and popular titles on not only 1492 but 1493, 1776, 1916, *and* 1959 on the other. See the rather tongue-in-cheek listicle "How to Sell Your Book: Make It About a Single Year," *New Republic*, September 8, 2013, http://www.newrepublic.com/article/114614/single-year-book-titles.

44. See James Quail Davies, "A Musical Souvenir: London in 1829" (PhD diss., University of Cambridge, 2005); Hugh Macdonald, *Music in 1853: The Biography of a Year* (Woodbridge, England: Boydell Press, 2012); Joshua Clover, *1989: Bob Dylan Didn't Have This to Sing About*; and Tamara Levitz, *Modernist Mysteries: Perséphone* (Oxford: Oxford University Press, 2012). For an important progenitor of the genre in music, see Marie-Noëlle Colette, François Lesure, et al., *La musique à Paris en 1830–1831* (Paris: Bibliothèque Nationale, 1983).

45. Hans Ulrich Gumbrecht, *In 1926: Living on the Edge of Time*, ix.

46. See in particular Jay Bernstein's remarkable review, "Social Signs and Natural Bodies: On T. J. Clark's *Farewell to an Idea*," *Radical Philosophy* 104 (2000): 25–38. Bernstein expanded his account of late modernist painting in *Against Voluptuous Bodies: Late Modernism and the Meaning of Painting* (Stanford, CA: Stanford University Press, 2006).

47. Jean Laplanche and Jean-Bertrand Pontalis, "Parapraxis," in *The Language of Psycho-Analysis*, trans. Donald Nicholson-Smith (New York: W. W. Norton, 1974), 299.

48. Paolo Virno, *Deja Vu and the End of History* (London: Verso, 2015).

49. See IRCAM's partially state-subsidized "Brahms" website, begun in 1996 through the work of Marc Texier in particular, and brought to a (hopefully temporary) halt in 2007: http://brahms.ircam.fr. At the other end of the spectrum, see http://www.composers21.com, a completely independent labor of love founded by Dan Albertson with the design and maintenance help of Ron Hannah and Romeo Talenti. Many European countries also main-

tain their own national databases, which remain some of the "deepest," presenting records for works and composers who truly leave no other trace in international libraries, scholarship, or even the World Wide Web. See Austria's "Music Austria," the *Musikdatenbank* maintained by MICA, the Music Information Center Austria, at http://db.musicaustria.at/.

50. Robert P. Morgan, "Secret Languages: The Roots of Musical Modernism," *Critical Inquiry* 10, no. 3 (March 1984): 442–61.

51. Pietro Cavallotti, *Differenzen: poststrukturalistische Aspekte in der Musik der 1980er Jahre am Beispiel von Helmut Lachenmann, Brian Ferneyhough und Gérard Grisey* (Schliengen, Germany: Edition Argus, 2006). See also the excellent work of Christoph Neidhöfer, for instance "Inside Luciano Berio's Serialism," *Music Analysis* 28, nos. 2–3 (2009): 301–48; and Christoph Neidhöfer, "Bruno Maderna's Serial Arrays," *Music Theory Online* 13, no. 1 (2007): 1–45.

52. Jacques Lacan, *The Seminar of Jacques Lacan, Book XI: The Four Fundamental Concepts of Psychoanalysis*, 53–54.

53. See chapter 4, "Encounter: Breton Meets Lacan," in Margaret Iversen, *Beyond Pleasure: Freud, Lacan, Barthes* (University Park: Pennsylvania State Press, 2007), 61–72.

54. Jean Laplanche and Jean-Bertrand Pontalis, "Parapraxis," 299–300.

55. Mladen Dolar, "Which Repetition?," (October 2013), unpublished manuscript existing in PDF form. Dolar explores similar issues, in particular Lacan's reading of Aristotle's *tyche* and *automaton*, in "Tyche, clinamen, den," *Continental Philosophy Review* 46, no. 2 (August 2013): 223–39.

56. György Ligeti, "Form in der Neuen Musik," in *Gesammelte Schriften*, vol. 1., ed. Monika Lichtenfeld (Mainz, Germany: Schott Musik International, 2007), 185–99.

57. Milan Kundera, *The Book of Laughter and Forgetting*, trans. Michael Henry Heim (New York: Penguin Books, 1981), 164–65.

58. Cited by Walter Benjamin in *The Arcades Project* (Cambridge, MA: Harvard University Press, 1999), 228. I was directed to the passage from Fredric Jameson's own quotation of it in *A Singular Modernity* (London: Verso, 2002), 157–58.

59. Jorge Luis Borges, "The Wall and the Books," in *Labyrinths: Selected Stories and Other Writings* trans. Eliot Weinberger (New York: New Directions, 1964), 188.

60. Stephen Decatur Smith, "'Even Money Decays': Transience and Hope in Adorno, Benjamin, and *Wozzeck*," *Opera Quarterly* 29, nos. 3–4 (2013): 212–43.

61. Michel Foucault, "Des espaces autres" (1967), in *Dits et écrits*, vol. 2 (Paris: Gallimard, 2001), 1571–81. Translated by Lieven de Cauter and Michiel Dehaene as "Of Other Spaces," in *Heterotopia and the City: Public Space in a Postcivil Society*, ed. Michiel Dehaene and Lieven de Cauter (London: Routledge, 2008), 13–29.

62. Jacques Lacan, *The Seminar of Jacques Lacan, Book I: Freud's Papers on Technique, 1953–54*, 232.

63. See Berthold Hoeckner, *Programming the Absolute: Nineteenth-Century German Music and the Hermeneutics of the Moment* (Princeton, NJ: Princeton University Press, 2002). Hoeckner's memorable phrase "refer[s] to the interpretive practice of seizing on moments in music that seem ineffable, and nevertheless of putting their meaning in words" (10). While Hoeckner engages the long "Romantic century," his formulation collides fruitfully with my propositions about twentieth-century musical modernism. Specifically, modernism might be seen as a radicalization of such programming of the absolute: to the degree

that various modernisms have a direct hand in disenchanting the—often "romanticized"—absolute, traversing its fantasy and laying bare a Real antagonism now seemingly unprogrammable, still this does not lead to a renunciation of programs. Rather, it leads to their hypostasizing: a repression of a Real truth that takes the form of an explosion of discourse, and hence of meaning making, leading eventually to the most elaborate and formalized forms of programming in the era of "high modernisms."

64. The (non-)ending of *Moses und Aron* has long been a source of intense scholarly engagement. For two recent examples, see Matthias Schmidt, "'O Wort, du Wort, das mir fehlt': Die Gottesfrage in Arnold Schönbergs Oper *Moses und Aron*. Zur Theologie eines musikalischen Kunst-Werkes im 20. Jahrhundert," *Musik und Ästhetik* 10, no. 37 (2006): 111–15; and, less directly, Mark P. Risinger, "Schoenberg's Modern Psalm, op. 50c and the Unattainable Ending," in *Political and Religious Ideas in the Works of Arnold Schoenberg*, ed. Charlotte M. Cross and Russell A. Berman (New York: Garland, 2000), 289–306.

65. Harold Bloom, *The Anxiety of Influence: A Theory of Poetry*, 2nd ed. (Oxford: Oxford University Press, 1997), 96.

66. T. J. Clark, *Farewell to an Idea*, 13.

67. See Slavoj Žižek, *The Sublime Object of Ideology* (London: Verso, 1989), xxix–xxx.

68. Jacques Lacan, *Le séminaire de Jacques Lacan, livre VI: Le Désir et son interprétation, 1958–1959* (Paris, France: Éditions de la Martinière, Le Champ freudien, 2013), 353.

69. Sigmund Freud, *Beyond the Pleasure Principle* (1920), in *SE* 18:14–15.

70. Theodor W. Adorno, *Mahler: A Physiognomy*, 138.

71. Adorno, agreeing with Pfitzner, considered the first movement's call a kind of daemonization: "The invocation ["Veni Creator Spiritus"] is addressed, according to an objective sense of form, to the music itself. That the Spirit should come is a plea that the composition should be inspired" (ibid.).

72. Rick Noack, "WATCH: A Hungarian Camerawoman Trips Refugees Who Are Running from Police," *Washington Post*, September 8, 2015, https://www.washingtonpost.com/news/worldviews/wp/2015/09/08/watch-a-hungarian-camerawoman-trips-refugees-who-are-running-from-police/.

73. Anne Dunand, "The End of Analysis (II)," in *Reading Seminar XI: Lacan's Four Fundamental Concepts of Psychoanalysis*, ed. Richard Feldstein, Bruce Fink, and Maire Jaanus (Albany, NY: SUNY Press, 1994), 254.

CHAPTER ONE

1. In his autograph from August 18, 1837, Schumann's original expressive designation for "Des Abends" is simply "Einfach und innig" (simply and inwardly); only with the first publication the following year by Breitkopf and Härtel is the designation changed to "Sehr innig zu spielen" (to be played very inwardly).

2. See "David Performing Tonight at Berlin's Brandenburg Gate—Watch on ZDF!" at http://davidhasselhoffonline.com/2014/12/david-performing-tonight-at-berlins-brandenburg-gate-watch-on-zdf/ (it appears to be a Swedish re-airing of the original ZDF clip).

3. March 31–May 19; the single was also number one in Switzerland for a month and in Austria for a week. Interestingly, it was never released in the United States, where, according to the *Boston Globe*'s Brian Rogers, Hasselhoff was already "something of a parody of him-

self," edging into Eddie Murphy territory as far as actor-singer metamorphoses were concerned. See Brian Rogers, "How David Hasselhoff Brought Down the Berlin Wall," *Boston Globe*, April 8, 2008, http://bostonglobe.longjaunt.com/blog/2008/04/14/how-david-hasselhoff-brought-down-the-berlin-wall.

4. For a fuller autobiographical account, see David Hasselhoff, *Don't Hassel the Hoff: The Autobiography* (New York: Thomas Dunne Books, 2007), 92–93, 139.

5. Ibid., 139.

6. Ibid., 140.

7. "Point sur place Berlin," November 11, 1989. Available online at http://www.ina.fr/histoire-et-conflits/guerre-froide/video/CAB89047741/point-sur-place-berlin.fr.html. Antenne 2 (1975–92) is now known as France 2.

8. Christian Merlin, "À Berlin, Rostropovitch a joué pour l'histoire," November 9, 2011, *Le Figaro Online*, http://www.lefigaro.fr/international/2009/11/07/01003-20091107ARTFIG00224--berlin-rostropovitch-a-joue-pour-l-histoire-.php.

9. Hartmut Cramer, "Interview: Mstislav Rostropovich, Cellist and Conductor: 'We Carry Out a Divine Service with our Music,'" *Fidelio* 8, no. 1 (Spring 1999): 85.

10. Mark Robinson and Joel Schechter, "Revolution from 1789 to 1989: An Introduction" in *Theater* 21, nos. 1–2 (1990): 4–5.

11. See Joel Brouwer's collection *Exactly What Happened* (West Lafayette, IN: Purdue University Press, 1999), 29–30; see also notable obituaries, including Jeffrey Freymann-Weyr, "Master Cellist, Conductor Rostropovich Dies at 80," NPR, Friday, April 27, 2007, http://www.npr.org/templates/story/story.php?storyId=9870484; and "Russian Maestro Rostropovich Dies," BBC News, April 27, 2007, http://news.bbc.co.uk/2/hi/6598895.stm.

12. Richard Taruskin, "Six Times Six: A Bach Suite Selection," in *The Danger of Music and Other Anti-Utopian Essays* (Berkeley: University of California Press, 2008), 68.

13. Hartmut Cramer, "Interview: Mstislav Rostropovich, Cellist and Conductor," 85.

14. This performance has been elegantly glossed by numerous writers, including: David B. Dennis, *Beethoven in German Politics 1870–1989* (New Haven, CT: Yale University Press, 1996), 200–203; Esteban Buch, *Beethovens Neunte: Eine Biographie*, trans. Silke Hass (Berlin: Propyläen, 2000), 333–37; and Richard Taruskin, "A Beethoven Season? Like Last Season, the One Before . . . ," *New York Times*, September 10, 1995. See also Taruskin's addendum in his *The Danger of Music* (Berkeley: University of California Press, 2010).

15. See David B. Dennis, *Beethoven in German Politics, 1870–1989*, 200.

16. Alex Rehding, *Music and Monumentality* (Oxford: Oxford University Press, 2009). See also Uwe Martin, "Freude, Freiheit, Brüderlichkeit: Über Schillers Schwierigkeiten beim Schreiben von Freiheit," *Cahiers d'études germaniques* 8 (1990): 9–10.

17. Leonard Bernstein, "Aesthetic News Bulletin," notes to *Ode an die Freiheit: Bernstein in Berlin*, Deutsche Grammophon 429 861–2, compact disc.

18. David Dennis found only one "editorial attack" on Bernstein's move, from one Wolfgang Pötzsch of the East Berlin *National-Zeitung*, December 28, 1989. Pötzsch wrote that Bernstein "falsified Beethoven's humanistic intensions and degraded the otherwise excellent performance into a semi-newsworthy [*pseudoaktuellen*] propaganda vehicle for the American sponsors." David B. Dennis, *Beethoven in German Politics, 1870–1989*, 243n96.

19. Friedrich Nietzsche, *Beyond Good and Evil*, ed. Rolf-Peter Horstmann and Judith Norman, trans. Judith Norman (Cambridge, England: Cambridge University Press, 2002), 137.

CHAPTER TWO

1. Jacqueline Rose, *States of Fantasy* (London: Oxford University Press, 1995), 2.

2. In *The Romantic Generation* (Cambridge, MA: Harvard University Press, 1995), Charles Rosen gives a virtually bar-by-bar account of "Des Abends," savoring its intimacies at length. The crossing thumbs of the performer—as private a scene as one might stage on a piano—become the piece's central characters: "Until bar 12 the two thumbs are always a third or fourth apart, but in bar 11 the right-hand thumb rises out of the accompaniment and starts to follow the melody at the lower octave. This corrupts the integrity of the voice leading and creates the most telling of dissonances in bar 12, the minor second that inflects the climax of the melody: there is no more beautiful nuance in all of Schumann" (35).

3. See Luis de Milán, *El maestro* (Valencia, 1536), ed., trans., and transcribed by Charles Jacobs (University Park: Pennsylvania State University Press, 1971); Christopher Simpson, *The Principles of Practical Musick* (London, 1665), ed. P. J. Lord (Oxford: Oxford University Press, 1970), 141–42.

4. The first two quotes are from the composer and theorist Daniel Gottlob Türk, the third from the philosopher Christian Friedrich Michaelis, the fourth from Beethoven. See Annette Richards, *The Free Fantasia and the Musical Picturesque* (Cambridge, England: Cambridge University Press, 2001), 39 (Türk), 135 (Michaelis), and 198 (Beethoven).

5. E. T. A. Hoffmann, *E. T. A. Hoffmann's Musical Writings*, ed. David Charlton, trans. Martyn Clarke (Cambridge, England: Cambridge University Press, 2004), 52, emphases mine.

6. Annette Richards, *The Free Fantasia and the Musical Picturesque*, 226.

7. The earlier passage comes from an anonymous review in the *Allgemeine musikalische Zeitung* 7, no. 20 (February 13, 1805); the latter is from Amadeus Wendt, "Gedanken über die neuere Tonkunst, und van Beethovens Musik, namentlich dessen Fidelio," *AmZ* 17, no. 23 (June 7, 1815), cited in Annette Richards, *The Free Fantasia and the Musical Picturesque*, 207.

8. Ernst Ludwig Gerber, in a letter to C. H. Rinck, 1817, in Friedrich Noack, "Eine Briefsammlung aus der ersten Hälfte des 19. Jahrhunderts," *Archive für Musikwissenschaft* (1935), 326; cited in Annette Richards, *The Free Fantasia and the Musical Picturesque*, 199.

9. Annette Richards, *The Free Fantasia and the Musical Picturesque*, 198.

10. See Georg August Griesinger, *Biographische Notizen über Joseph Haydn* (Leipzig: Breitkopf and Härtel, 1810), 78; cited in Annette Richards, *The Free Fantasia and the Musical Picturesque*, 85. For more on this particular theme, see also Elaine Sisman, "After the Heroic Style," *Beethoven Forum* 6, no. 1 (1998), 75ff.

11. Richards quotes Heinrich Christoph Koch: *fantasieren* designates the process whereby "the composer arouses the activity of his genius." See Christoph Koch, *Musikalisches Lexikon* (Offenbach am Main: A. Hermann dem Jüngern, 1802); cited in Annette Richards, *The Free Fantasia and the Musical Picturesque*, 85. While *fantasieren* and *improvisieren* were often conflated in contemporary discourse, the peculiar specificity of the fantasy genre ought not itself be conflated with musical improvisation. Or rather, it was in musical fantasies that the more generic musical category of improvisation attained a new power and heightened meaning—namely, the theatricalization of genius and, more generally, individual self-determination.

12. Daniel K. L. Chua, "Beethoven Going Blank," in a special issue in honor of Richard Taruskin, *Journal of Musicology* 31, no. 3 (2014): 301n8.

13. Ibid., 301 (first quote), 316 (second quote).

14. Ibid., 316. Chua cites Beethoven's own well-known letter from March 1824 in which the composer explicitly acknowledged the Ninth as a reenactment of the *Choral Fantasy*'s dramaturgy "but on a far grander scale." See Emily Anderson, ed., *The Letters of Beethoven*, vol. 3 (New York: St. Martin's Press, 1961), 1114.

15. Ibid., 320.

16. Ibid., 324.

17. I borrow this formulation from Todd McGowan's account of the psychoanalytic "lost object," which he describes as "constitutively rather than empirically lost." Todd McGowan, *Enjoying What We Don't Have: The Psychoanalytic Project of Psychoanalysis* (Lincoln: University of Nebraska Press, 2013), 29.

18. Ryan Minor, *Choral Fantasies: Music, Festivity, and Nationhood in Nineteenth-Century Germany* (Cambridge, England: Cambridge University Press, 2012), 16.

19. Maria Torok, "Fantasy: An Attempt to Define Its Structure and Operation" (1959), in Nicolas Abraham and Maria Torok, *The Shell and the Kernel: Renewals of Psychoanalysis*, vol. 1, ed., trans., with an introduction by Nicholas T. Rand (Chicago: University of Chicago Press, 1994), 35; cited in Jacqueline Rose, *States of Fantasy*, 5.

20. Henri F. Ellenberger, *The Discovery of the Unconscious: The History and Evolution of Dynamic Psychiatry* (New York: Basic Books, 1970).

21. Matt ffytche, *The Foundation of the Unconscious: Schelling, Freud and the Birth of the Modern Psyche* (Cambridge, England: Cambridge University Press, 2012). ffytche identifies four particular obstacles to historicizing the Western unconscious of the nineteenth and twentieth centuries: "the diffuse application of the concept of an unconscious; the difficulty of historicizing concepts of mind; paradigmatic confusion over the terms of German idealism; and the resistance of psychoanalysis to its historicization" (14).

22. Ibid., 23. ffytche cites, among others, "psychiatry, medicine and psychology, but also philosophy, religion and metaphysics and theories of nature and history, as well as more popular psychological and cultural elaborations in novels, poems and moral essays" (9).

23. Maud Ellmann, review of Matt ffytche's *The Foundation of the Unconscious, Critical Inquiry* 42, no. 1 (2015): 220.

24. Matt ffytche, *The Foundation of the Unconscious*, 23, emphasis mine.

25. While ffytche offers a novel historicization of Schelling's conception of the unconscious and its eventual ramifications for Freudian and post-Freudian psychoanalysis, he is by no means the first to link Schelling to the latter. Slavoj Žižek's formidable engagement with Schelling in the mid- to late 1990s is considered only one—especially robust—"rediscovery." But following the philosopher's fall into disrepute throughout the later nineteenth century, the "Schelling renaissance" has been recurring continually; see for instance the introductions to *The New Schelling*, ed. Judith Norman and Alistair Welchman (London: Continuum Press, 2004), and *Interpreting Schelling: Critical Essays*, ed. Lara Oštarić (Cambridge, England: Cambridge University Press, 2014). For Žižek's two most important works specifically on Schelling, see Slavoj Žižek, *The Indivisible Remainder: Essays on Schelling and Related Matters* (London: Verso, 1996), and Slavoj Žižek / F. W. J. von Schelling, *The Abyss of Freedom / Ages of the World*, trans. Judith Norman (Ann Arbor: University of Michigan Press, 1997).

26. Matt ffytche, *The Foundation of the Unconscious*, 137. Historicity here is understood in dialectical tension with what cannot be recalled, and as such, resists historicization

absolutely: "For experience to be historical, argues Schelling, there must be aspects of the past that simply cannot be remembered. Seen from this point of view, the self now constructs its identity back towards an unknown historical ground, retracing 'the long path of developments from the present back into the deepest night of the past.'" ffytche here quotes from an early version of Schelling's unfinished *Weltalter* (Ages of the World) manuscript; see Slavoj Žižek / F. W. J. von Schelling, *The Abyss of Freedom / Ages of the World*, 114.

27. Friedrich Wilhelm Joseph von Schelling, *Philosophical Inquiries into the Essence of Human Freedom*, trans. with introduction by Jeff Love and Johannes Schmidt (Albany: State University of New York Press, 2006), 29.

28. Slavoj Žižek / F. W. J. von Schelling, *The Abyss of Freedom / Ages of the World*, 181.

29. Ibid., 181–82.

30. For a brief summary of the project's history—and a pellucid introduction to its contents—see Alistair Welchman and Judith Norman, "Creating the Past: Schelling's *Ages of the World*," *Journal of the Philosophy of History* 4 (2010): 23–43.

31. Ibid., 30.

32. Immanuel Kant, *Critique of Pure Reason*, trans. Werner S. Pluhar (Indianapolis: Hackett, 1996), 385.

33. Adrian Johnston, "Ghosts of Substance Past: Schelling, Lacan, and the Denaturalization of Nature," in *Lacan: The Silent Partners*, ed. Slavoj Žižek (London: Verso, 2006), 50–51.

34. Comparisons between Beethoven and Schelling have often been made, though little direct relationship or influence is documented; see for instance William Kinderman, *Beethoven*, 2nd ed. (Oxford: Oxford University Press, 2009), 7–8. Kinderman does cite an amusing passage from one Friedrich Wähner in Beethoven's conversation books of 1820: "Long live philosophy and music! You have to read Plato in the German translation by Schleiermacher. You must, I'll bring it to you. He and Schelling are the greatest!" (299).

35. Friedrich Wilhelm Joseph von Schelling, *Philosophical Investigations*, 70.

36. Slavoj Žižek, *Enjoy Your Symptom!: Jacques Lacan in Hollywood and Out* (New York: Routledge, 1992), 136, emphasis in the original.

37. Adrian Johnston, *Žižek's Ontology: A Transcendental Materialist Theory of Subjectivity* (Evanston, IL: Northwestern University Press, 2008), 43.

38. See Friedrich Wilhelm Joseph von Schelling, *The Ages of the World*, trans. with introduction by Jason M. Wirth (Albany: State University of New York Press, 2000), 140–41n52.

39. Pierre Hadot, *The Veil of Isis: An Essay on the History of the Idea of Nature*, trans. Michael Chase (Cambridge, MA: Belknap Press, 2006).

40. See Johann Wolfgang von Goethe, "Genius die Büste der Natur enthüllend," in *Goethes Werke (Weimarer Ausgabe)* (Weimar: H. Böhlau, 1887–1919), I, 4, 127; Friedrich Schlegel, *Ideas*, no. 1, in *Friedrich Schlegel's "Lucinde" and the Fragments*, ed. and trans. Peter Firchow (Minneapolis: University of Minnesota Press, 1971), 241; Friedrich Schiller, *The Works of Friedrich Schiller: Poems*, ed. Nathan Haskell Dole, trans. E. P. Arnold Forster (New York: Bigelow and Brown, 1902), 227–29; Novalis, *The Novices of Sais, with Illustrations by Paul Klee*, trans. Ralph Manheim (New York: Archipelago Books, 2005), 17. Such is the canonical status of the figure of the veiled Isis that these citations are often found grouped together in histories of German Romanticism. For a swift appraisal from the perspective of contemporary music, see Annette Richards, *The Free Fantasia and the Musical Picturesque*,

221–23; and Maynard Solomon, "Some Romantic Images," in *Late Beethoven: Music, Thought, Imagination* (Berkeley: University of California Press, 2003), esp. 67–70.

41. Maynard Solomon, *Late Beethoven*, 68–69.

42. Letter from September 19, 1815, in *The Letters of Beethoven*, vol. 2, 527–28n563.

43. Annette Richards, *The Free Fantasia and the Musical Picturesque*, 226.

44. Richards cites Leonard Ratner as one instance of linking fantasy and sonata as mutual others; see Leonard Ratner, *Classic Music: Expression, Form, and Style* (New York: Schirmer, 1980), 233.

45. Theodor Adorno, "Vers une musique informelle," in *Quasi una Fantasia*, trans. Rodney Livingstone (London: Verso, 1992), 272–73. Interestingly, Richards cites Adorno's essay in her introduction, but not as a participant within her historical narrative. See Annette Richards, *The Free Fantasia and the Musical Picturesque*, 17n23.

46. Theodor Adorno, "Vers une musique informelle," 322.

47. Adrian Johnston, *Žižek's Ontology*, xxiv.

48. Silvana Dalto, "The Origin of the Subject from the Perspective of Freud's Scientific Materialism," trans. Luke Thurston, in *The Pre-Psychoanalytic Writings of Sigmund Freud*, ed. Gertrudis Van de Vijver and Filip Geerardyn (London: Karnac, 2002), 223; cited in Adrian Johnston, *Žižek's Ontology*, 43.

49. Nicholas Mathew, *Political Beethoven* (Cambridge, England: Cambridge University Press, 2013), 196.

50. Ibid., 194. Mathew cites Schmitt's strong charge that, for the political Romantic, "even the greatest external event—a revolution or a world war—is intrinsically indifferent. The incident becomes significant only when it has become the occasion for a great experience, a genial apprehension, or some other Romantic creation." Carl Schmitt, *Political Romanticism*, trans. Guy Oakes (Cambridge, MA: MIT Press, 1986), 96–97; cited in Nicholas Mathew, *Political Beethoven*, 190.

51. Nicholas Mathew, *Political Beethoven*, 194.

52. Ibid., 193.

53. Ibid., 196.

54. Daniel K. L. Chua, "Beethoven Going Blank," 304–5.

55. Ibid., 302 (first citation); Nicholas Mathew, *Political Beethoven*, 193 (second citation).

56. Nicholas Mathew, *Political Beethoven*, 193.

57. I thank one of my anonymous readers for this wonderful formulation. In his recent history of absolute music as a Kantian "regulative concept," Mark Evan Bonds stresses its constitutively migratory nature. While repertoires and historical moments may come and go, "the idea of absolute music will nevertheless continue to shape our attempts to identify and comprehend the essence of music, even if only as a regulative concept." Mark Evan Bonds, *Absolute Music: The History of an Idea* (Oxford: Oxford University Press, 2014), 299.

58. Jacques Lacan, *The Seminar of Jacques Lacan, Book XI: The Four Fundamental Principles of Psychoanalysis, 1964*, ed. Jacques-Alain Miller, trans. Alan Sheridan (New York: Norton, 1998), 24.

59. See Sigmund Freud, "The Unconscious," in *SE* XIV (1914–16), *On the History of the Psycho-Analytic Movement, Papers on Metapsychology and Other Works*, 159–215; see especially the essay's section V, "The Special Characteristics of the System *Ucs*." In his *Seminar XI*, Lacan will theorize unconscious knowledge as "truth," in contradistinction to what goes

by the name "knowledge," understood here as a conscious discursive activity or epistemological situation.

60. Jacques Lacan, *The Seminar, Book XI*, 25. Translation modified; the original French is "achoppement, défaillance, fêlure."

61. I address Lacan's notion of cause in its relation to repetition in more detail in part 3, especially chapter 12.

62. See for instance Sigmund Freud, *New Introductory Lectures on Psychoanalysis* (1933), in *SE* 22, 161n1. In addition to their citation in multiple letters, the lines also appear in chapter 6/1 of *The Interpretation of Dreams* (1900a), in *SE* 5, 490.

63. Sigmund Freud, "Lines of Advance in Psycho-Analytic Therapy" (1919a [1918]), in *SE* 17, 161.

64. Jacques Lacan, *The Seminar of Jacques Lacan, Book I: Freud's Papers on Technique, 1953–54*, ed. Jacques-Alain Miller, trans. with notes by John Forrester (New York: W. W. Norton, 1991), 232.

65. Jacques Lacan, *The Seminar of Jacques Lacan, Book VII: The Ethics of Psychoanalysis, 1959–60*, ed. Jacques-Alain Miller, trans. with notes by Dennis Porter (New York: W. W. Norton, 1992), 303–4. Lacan is reading Freud to the letter here; see Sigmund Freud, "Inhibitions, Symptoms and Anxiety" (1925–26), in *SE* XX, 75–176.

66. Jacques Lacan, *The Seminar of Jacques Lacan, Book XI: The Four Fundamental Concepts of Psychoanalysis, 1964*, trans. Alan Sheridan (New York: W. W. Norton, 1998), 273.

67. Rudolf Bernet, "Imagination et fantasme," in *L'homme et ses destins*, ed. Antone Vergote (Louvain: Peeters, 1993), 193. Cited and translated in Ed Pluth, *Signifiers and Acts: Freedom in Lacan's Theory of the Subject* (Albany: State University of New York Press, 2007), 82. Bernet describes in Freud a "progressive differentiation between imagination understood as 'imaginativeness' [*fantaisie*] and imagination understood as 'fantasy' [*fantasme*]."

68. See the letter from September 21, 1897, in *The Complete Letters of Sigmund Freud to Wilhelm Fliess, 1887–1904*, trans. Jeffrey Moussaieff Masson (Cambridge, MA: Belknap Press, 1986), 264. See also Sigmund Freud, "Constructions in Analysis," (1937b), in *SE* 23, 358–71.

69. Sigmund Freud, "Constructions in Analysis." Many have suggested that the Oedipus complex is not only Freud's hypothesis of a mass unconscious fantasy, but indeed his *own* unconscious fantasy, a construction that provided a way forward at what would have otherwise been psychoanalysis's great impasse, its moment of failing. There would be others; see Kenneth Reinhard, "Lacan and Monotheism: Psychoanalysis and the Traversal of Cultural Fantasy" (1999), http://english.chass.ncsu.edu/jouvert/v3i12/reinha.htm.

70. Alexander Wheelock Thayer, *Ludwig van Beethovens Leben*, vol. 5 (Leipzig: Breitkopf and Härtel, 1908), 318–19.

71. Anonymous, "Einige Worte zu den vielen über Beethoven's letzte Werke," *AmZ* 31 (1829): 272, cited in K. M. Knittel, "Wagner, Deafness, and the Reception of Beethoven's Late Style," *Journal of the American Musicological Society* 51, no. 1 (1998): 55. Knittel translates *wüstes Gewirr* slightly differently, as "wild jumble"; in *Political Beethoven*, Nicholas Mathew opts for the more elaborate "desolate entanglement." Keeping in mind that the root *wüst-* connotes something wild and disarrayed, I have aimed somewhere in the middle.

72. Alexandre Oulibicheff, *Beethoven, ses critiques et ses glossateurs* (Leipzig and Paris: Brockhaus, 1857), 270; cited in K. M. Knittel, "Wagner, Deafness, and the Reception of Beethoven's Late Style," 51.

73. Joseph Kerman, *The Beethoven Quartets* (New York: Alfred A. Knopf, 1966), 349.

74. Ibid., 326.

75. See Stephen Rumph, *Beethoven after Napoleon: Political Romanticism in the Late Works* (Berkeley: University of California Press, 2004), especially chapter 9, "A Modernist Epilogue," 222–45; K. M. Knittel, "Wagner, Deafness, and the Reception of Beethoven's Late Style"; K. M. Knittel, "Imitation, Individuality, and Illness: Behind Beethoven's 'Three Styles,'" *Beethoven Forum* 4, ed. Christopher Reynolds (Lincoln: University of Nebraska Press, 1995), 17–36; K. M. Knittel, "From Chaos to History: The Reception of Beethoven's Late Quartets" (PhD diss., Princeton University, 1992).

76. Wagner of course performed an about-face on Beethoven's deafness when it no longer suited his designs; see K. M. Knittel, "Wagner, Deafness, and the Reception of Beethoven's Late Style," 75ff.

77. See Theodor Adorno, "Beethoven's Late Style" (1937), in *Night Music: Essays on Music 1928–1962*, ed. Rolf Tiedemann, trans. Wieland Hoban (London: Seagull Books, 2009), 11–18.

78. The cited passages in order are Walter Riezler, *Beethoven*, trans. G. D. H. Pidcock (New York: E. P. Dutton, 1938), 109, 237, cited in Stephen Rumph, *Beethoven after Napoleon*, 226, 227; Heinrich Schenker, *Beethoven: die letzten Sonaten. Sonata in A, Op. 101: Kritische Ausgabe mit Einführung und Erläuterung*, ed. Oswald Jonas (Vienna: Universal Edition, 1971), 9, in Stephen Rumph, *Beethoven after Napoleon*, 231; Charles Rosen, *The Classical Style: Haydn, Mozart, and Beethoven* (New York: W. W. Norton, 1972), 407, in Stephen Rumph, *Beethoven after Napoleon*, 237; Maynard Solomon, "Beethoven's Ninth Symphony: A Search for Order," in *Beethoven Essays* (Cambridge, MA: Harvard University Press, 1988), 26, in Stephen Rumph, *Beethoven after Napoleon*, 240.

79. Theodor Adorno, "Beethoven's Late Style," 18.

80. Stephen Rumph, *Beethoven after Napoleon*, 242.

81. Theodor Adorno, "Beethoven's Late Style," 18.

82. This is Chua's specific formulation in Daniel K. L. Chua, *The "Galitzin" Quartets of Beethoven* (Princeton, NJ: Princeton University Press, 1995), 246.

83. Theodor Adorno, *Beethoven: The Philosophy of Music*, ed. Rolf Tiedemann, trans. Edmund Jephcott (Oxford: Polity Press, 1998), 137.

84. Theodor Adorno, "Beethoven's Late Style," 17.

85. Nicholas Mathew, *Political Beethoven*, 189.

86. Daniel K. L. Chua, *The "Galitzin" Quartets of Beethoven*, 240. Though Chua's first monograph does not exactly go out of its way to critique Adorno's vision—rather, it seems to share or at least "inhabit" it, like a Method actor—Chua is nonetheless quite careful to present all such statements as Adorno's, and (quite) his own.

87. T. J. Clark, *Farewell to an Idea: Episodes in a History of Modernism* (New Haven, CT: Yale University Press, 2001), 15.

88. Ibid., 52.

89. Ibid.

90. See Sigmund Freud, "Project for a Scientific Psychology" (1895), in *SE* I, 356. For still one of the best excavations of the term's meanings and uses, see Jean Laplanche and J. B. Pontalis, "Deferred Action, Deferred," in *The Language of Psycho-Analysis*, trans. Donald Nicholson-Smith (New York: W. W. Norton, 1974), 111–14. For a brief but efficacious

introduction to Lacanian conceptualizations of time, see Dylan Evans, "time," in *An Introductory Dictionary of Lacanian Psychoanalysis* (London: Routledge, 1996), 208–9.

91. See for instance Ursula Günther, "Das Ende der Ars Nova," *Die Musikforschung* 16 (1963): 105–20; and Maria Rika Maniates, *Mannerism in Italian Music and Culture, 1530–1630* (Chapel Hill: University of North Carolina Press, 1979).

92. Susan McClary makes a compelling argument for the entire madrigal tradition as "always already Mannerist," which would certainly complicate my argument; suffice to say in the present context that the question of "proto-modernisms" is not at all closed, but I would argue that the capacity to articulate and engage them requires keeping the question of historical—that is, a paradoxical later, "original"—modernism at least conceptually open. See Susan McClary, *Modal Subjectivities: Self-Fashioning in the Italian Madrigal* (Berkeley: University of California Press, 2004).

CHAPTER THREE

1. Richard Taruskin, "Afterword: Nicht blutbefleckt?," *Journal of Musicology* 26, no. 2 (Spring 2009): 274–84. I am not of course suggesting that Bach's legacy is not "bloodstained," but rather that this scene's intention, however unconscious, is to place Bach in the context of such an imposing signifier of barbarism that it "adsorbs" anything problematic in Bach's legacy. The irony is that the problematic history of Bach's music is *normally* an invisible one; only in such a politicized context as Rostropovich's outdoor performance might one actually be provoked to wonder about it.

2. Reinhart Koselleck, "Historical Criteria of the Modern Concept of Revolution," in *Futures Past: On the Semantics of Historical Time*, trans. Keith Tribe (New York: Columbia University Press, 2004), 43–57.

3. See Michael D. Coogan et al., eds., *The New Oxford Annotated Bible, New Revised Standard Edition with the Apocrypha* (Oxford: Oxford University Press, 2010), 2063.

4. See Harold Bloom, *The Anxiety of Influence* (Oxford: Oxford University Press, 1973), 14–15. As Bloom, with characteristic iconoclasm, defines kenosis, "the later poet, apparently emptying himself of his own afflatus, his imaginative godhood, seems to humble himself as though he were ceasing to be a poet, but this ebbing is so performed in relation to a precursor's poem-of-ebbing that the precursor is emptied out also, and so the later poem of deflation is not as absolute as it seems." For a more recent treatment of kenosis from the point of view of language, see Elisabeth Loevlie, "Poetic Language and the Expression of Nothing," *Angelaki: Journal of the Theoretical Humanities* 17, no. 3 (2012): 85–96.

5. "Mark Seaberg: Looking for Freedom," Discogs, http://www.discogs.com/Marc-Seaberg-Looking-For-Freedom-Shorty/release/1281693.

6. The original subject of the song was more of an "Escape to Bavaria" than a simple road trip down south.

7. Slavoj Žižek, *The Plague of Fantasies* (London: Verso, 1997), 7. Though Žižek follows a doggedly Lacanian exposition of fantasy, this point is one of the historical constants of the concept, reaching back to Freud's "A child is being beaten," and back up through Jean Laplanche and Jean-Bertrand Pontalis's now-canonic "Fantasy and the Origins of Sexuality," *International Journal of Psycho-Analysis* 49 (1968): 22.

8. Edgar Allan Poe, "The Imp of the Perverse," in *Collected Works of Edgar Allan Poe: Tales and Sketches, 1843–1849*, vol. 3, ed. Thomas Ollive Mabbott (Cambridge, MA: Belknap Press, 1969).

9. On this point, see again Richard Taruskin, "Postscript, 2008" to "A Beethoven Season?," in *The Danger of Music and Other Anti-Utopian Essays* (Berkeley: University of California Press, 2008), 74–80.

10. In one of the many interviews conducted by David Dennis, an East German man at the November 12 concert at the Berliner Philharmonie was happy to hear Beethoven's Seventh, but would have preferred the Ninth since "we are now brothers again." See David B. Dennis, *Beethoven in German Politics 1870–1989* (New Haven, CT: Yale University Press, 1996), 242n86.

11. Klaus Geitel, "Exulting Freedom in Music" (1989), available at http://www.leonardbernstein.com/hc_berlin.htm.

12. Jacqueline Rose, *States of Fantasy* (London: Oxford University Press, 1995), 3.

13. Ibid.

CHAPTER FOUR

1. Jacques-Alain Miller, "Les six paradigmes de la jouissance," *La cause freudienne: Revue de psychanalyse* 43 (1999): 7–29.

2. See Bruce Fink, "Fantasies and the Fundamental Fantasy," in *Against Understanding, Vol. 2: Cases and Commentary in a Lacanian Key* (New York: Routledge, 2014), 41–42. Though I jest slightly here, Fink is indeed one of the most Talmudic readers of Lacan, which is to say he follows the letter with remarkable and tireless fidelity and lucidity—which entails, as any Lacanian would tell you, infidelities, creativities, leaps.

3. See Jacques Lacan, *Television: A Challenge to the Psychoanalytic Establishment*, ed. Joan Copcec, trans. Denis Hollier, Rosalind Krauss, and Annette Michelson (New York: W. W. Norton, 1990), 3; translated and amended to reflect more closely the original transcript.

4. Ernesto Laclau, preface to Slavoj Žižek, *The Sublime Object of Ideology* (London: Verso, 1989), xii.

5. Jacques Lacan, *The Seminar of Jacques Lacan, Book XX: Encore, 1972–73, On Feminine Sexuality, the Limits of Love and Knowledge*, ed. Jacques-Alain Miller, trans. with notes by Bruce Fink (New York: W. W. Norton, 1998), 26.

6. The accolade comes from Marcus Browne, "Slavoj Žižek: 'Trump Is Really a Centrist Liberal,'" *The Guardian*, April 28, 2016, http://www.theguardian.com/books/2016/apr/28/slavoj-zizek-donald-trump-is-really-a-centrist-liberal.

7. *Žižek!*, directed by Astra Taylor (2005; New York: Zeitgeist Films, 2006), DVD.

8. Slavoj Žižek, *The Sublime Object of Ideology*, 2nd ed. (London: Verso, 2008), xxx. Future citations of this book reference the second edition.

9. Ibid. See also Francis Fukuyama, "The End of History?," *National Interest* 16 (Summer 1989): 3–18.

10. See Daniel Bell, *The End of Ideology: On the Exhaustion of Political Ideas in the Fifties* (New York: Free Press, 1960).

11. Anna Kornbluh, "Reading the Real: Žižek's Literary Materialism," in *Everything You Always Wanted to Know about Literature but Were Afraid to Ask Žižek: SIC 10*, ed. Russell Sbriglia (Durham, NC: Duke University Press, forthcoming).

12. Adrian Johnston maintains that this is still one of Žižek's "most startling claims"; see Adrian Johnston, *Žižek's Ontology: A Transcendental Materialist Theory of Subjectivity* (Evanston, IL: Northwestern University Press, 2008), xxiii.

13. Bruno Latour, *We Have Never Been Modern*, trans. Catherine Porter (Cambridge, MA: Harvard University Press, 1993), 9.

14. Slavoj Žižek, *The Sublime Object of Ideology*, xxiv. Žižek cites in particular Louis Althusser, *For Marx* (Paris: François Maspero, 1965).

15. Slavoj Žižek, *The Sublime Object of Ideology*, 16.

16. Ibid., 47.

17. Ibid., 45.

18. The first citation comes from Jacques Lacan, *The Seminar of Jacques Lacan, Book I: Freud's Papers on Technique, 1953–1954*, ed. Jacques-Alain Miller, trans. with notes by John Forrester (New York: W. W. Norton, 1991), 66. The second comes from Jacques Lacan, *The Seminar of Jacques Lacan, Book II: The Ego in Freud's Theory and in the Technique of Psychoanalysis, 1954–55*, ed. Jacques-Alain Miller, trans. Sylvana Tomaselli (New York: W. W. Norton, 1988), 164.

19. Jacques Lacan, *The Seminar, Book II*, 97 (first citation), 313 (second citation).

20. In his "Seminar on 'The Purloined Letter'" (1956), Lacan emphasizes how the Real doesn't have a place *within* the symbolic, but is its other, and as such the other of the very concept of place. "For it can literally [*à la lettre*] be said that something is not in its place only of what can change places—that is, of the symbolic. For the real, whatever upheaval we subject it to, is always and in every case in its place; it carries its place stuck to the sole of its shoe, there being nothing that can exile it from it." Jacques Lacan, *Écrits: The First Complete Edition in English*, trans. Bruce Fink (New York: W. W. Norton, 2006), 17.

21. Jacques Lacan, *The Seminar of Jacques Lacan, Book XX: Encore, 1972–73, On Feminine Sexuality, the Limits of Love and Knowledge*, trans. with notes by Bruce Fink (New York: W. W. Norton, 1998), 94 (first citation); Jacques Lacan, *The Seminar of Jacques Lacan, Book XI: The Four Fundamental Principles of Psychoanalysis, 1964*, trans. Alan Sheridan (New York: W. W. Norton, 1998), 167 (second citation).

22. Slavoj Žižek, *The Sublime Object of Ideology*, 195; cited in Anna Kornbluh, "Reading the Real." Kornbluh is adamant that "on the whole, Žižek's Lacan is the Real Lacan, the Lacan of the Real, the Lacan with whom it is possible to advance that earlier tarrying with the Real which Žižek finds in Schelling and Hegel."

23. Slavoj Žižek, *The Sublime Object of Ideology*, 195; emphasis mine.

24. I explore this premise in more detail in relation to Schoenberg's *Erwartung* and the scene of early twentieth-century modernism in "Waiting, Still, or Is Psychoanalysis Tonal?," *Opera Quarterly* (forthcoming).

25. The first citation comes from Jacques Lacan, *Autres écrits* (Paris: Seuil, 2001), 254.

26. Jacques Lacan, *The Seminar, Book II*, 29 (first citation); Jacques Lacan, *Television*, 6 (second citation).

27. Jacques Lacan, *The Seminar of Jacques Lacan, Book XVII: The Other Side of Psychoanalysis, 1969–1970*, ed. Jacques-Alain Miller, trans. with notes by Russell Grigg (New York: W. W. Norton, 2007), 53.

28. Jacques Lacan, *The Seminar of Jacques Lacan, Book III: The Psychoses, 1955–1956*, ed. Jacques-Alain Miller, trans. with notes by Russell Grigg (New York: W. W. Norton, 1993), 267.

29. See Jacques Lacan, *The Seminar, Book XI*, 237–38, for a discussion of "the model for a whole series of cases" in which "there is no interval between S_1 and S_2, when the first dyad of signifiers become solidified, holophrased." He is speaking of certain kinds of psychosis.

30. Jacques Lacan, *The Seminar, Book XI*, 46.

31. Ernesto Laclau and Chantal Mouffe, *Hegemony and Socialist Strategy: Towards a Radical Democratic Politics* (London: Verso, 1985); see in particular chapter 3, "Beyond the Positivity of the Social: Antagonisms and Hegemony," 93–148.

32. Ibid., 113. "The practice of articulation," Laclau and Mouffe write, "consists in the construction of nodal points which partially fix meaning; and the partial character of this fixation proceeds from the openness of the social, a result, in its turn, of the constant overflowing of every discourse by the infinitude of the field of discursivity."

33. Ernesto Laclau, "Why Do Empty Signifiers Matter to Politics?," in *Emancipation(s)* (London: Verso, 1996), 44.

34. Ernesto Laclau and Chantal Mouffe, *Hegemony and Socialist Strategy*, 114.

35. Ibid., 122. In the preface to the second edition (2000) of *Hegemony and Socialist Strategy*, Laclau and Mouffe reaffirm that antagonism "is, perhaps, the most central argument of our book," adding, "our thesis is that antagonisms are not objective relations, but relations which reveal the limits of all objectivity. Society is constituted around these limits, and they are antagonistic limits" (xiv).

36. Jacques Lacan employs this formulation throughout his work; see for instance his "Position of the Unconscious," in *Écrits: The First Complete Edition in English*, 713. Contrast this with Lacan's definition of the sign, which "represents something to someone" (*The Seminar, Book XI*, 207). For a particularly vivid parable of this definition, see Žižek's account of the patient in his "old-style hospital bed" in "Lacan's Four Discourses: A Political Reading," in *Desire of the Analysts: Psychoanalysis and Cultural Criticism*, ed. Greg Forter and Paul Allen Miller (Albany: State University of New York Press, 2008), 83–84.

37. For an exploration of the history of psychoanalysis's politicization in light of contemporary Lacanian theory, see Todd McGowan, *Enjoying What We Don't Have: The Psychoanalytic Project of Psychoanalysis* (Lincoln: University of Nebraska Press, 2013).

38. See Jacques Lacan, *Le Séminaire de Jacques Lacan, livre V: Les formations de l'inconscient, 1957–1958*, ed. Jacques-Alain Miller (Paris: Seuil, 1998), 311. For Lacan's comments on the career-defining status of his concept of *objet a*, see Jacques Lacan, *Le Séminaire de Jacques Lacan, livre XXI: Les non-dupes errent, 1973–1974*, unpublished, in particular the meeting of April 9, 1974, cited in Bruce Fink, *The Lacanian Subject: Between Language and Jouissance* (Princeton, NJ: Princeton University Press, 1996), 83.

39. Lacan's most famous account of this order, indeed his most famous theory generally, is "The Mirror Stage as Formative of the *I* Function as Revealed in Psychoanalytic Experience," in *Écrits: The First Complete Edition in English*, 75–81.

40. The most extensive exploration to date of Lacan's debt to Lévi-Strauss is Markos Zafiropoulos, *Lacan and Lévi-Strauss or the Return to Freud (1951–1957)*, trans. John Holland (London: Karnac Press, 2010).

41. Jacques Lacan, *Le Séminaire de Jacques Lacan, livre V*, 409 (first citation), cited in Bruce Fink, "Fantasies and the Fundamental Fantasy," 40; Jacques Lacan, "The Direction of

the Treatment and the Principles of its Power," in *Écrits: The First Complete Edition in English*, 532.

42. Bruce Fink, *The Lacanian Subject*, 83.

43. Levi Bryant, "Some Scattered Observations on Fantasy," *Larval Subjects* blog, November 13, 2006, http://larval-subjects.blogspot.com/2006/11/some-scattered-observations-on-fantasy.html.

44. Jacques Lacan, *The Seminar, Book XI*, 185.

45. For a careful and nuanced discussion of this question, see Ed Pluth, *Signifiers and Acts: Freedom in Lacan's Theory of the Subject* (Albany: State University of New York Press, 2007), chapter 5, "The Fundamental Fantasy," 81–95.

46. Todd McGowan, *Enjoying What We Don't Have.*

47. See Christopher Simpson, *The Principles of Practical Musick* (London, 1665), ed. P. J. Lord (Oxford: Oxford University Press, 1970), 141–42.

48. Ernesto Laclau, "The Impossibility of Society," *Canadian Journal of Political and Social Science* 15, no. 3 (1991): 27; cited in Jason Glynos, "The Grip of Ideology: A Lacanian Approach to the Theory of Ideology," *Journal of Political Ideologies* 6, no. 2 (2001): 198.

49. Glynos's "The Grip of Ideology" still provides one of the most robust distillations of this thesis.

50. Jacques Lacan, *Le Séminaire de Jacques Lacan, livre VI, Le Désir et son interprétation, 1958–1959*, session on April 8, 1959, unpublished.

51. Ibid. Lorenzo Chiesa, one of Lacan's most dogged, careful, and philosophically acute exegetes in recent years, traces Lacan's evolution from a belief that "there is an Other of the Other" to his thesis that "there is no Other of the Other" in *Subjectivity and Otherness* (Cambridge, MA: MIT Press, 2007), 104–39.

52. Lacan's conception of discourse here is antithetical to the more popular "communication theories" of the day, with their aspirations to the maximization of signal over noise. But neither is Lacan's conception harmonious with Foucault's, a year after Lacan's seminar, in Foucault's inaugural Collège de France lecture. See Michel Foucault, "Orders of Discourse," *Social Science Information* 10, no. 2 (1971): 7–30. For a lucid rehearsal of the quite "heterogeneous and transdisciplinary" strains of discourse analysis in the last half century, and their relation to Lacan, see Ian Parker and David Pavón-Cuéllar's introduction to their ambitious edited volume *Lacan, Discourse, Event: New Psychoanalytic Approaches to Textual Indeterminacy* (New York: Routledge, 2014), 1–13.

53. In addition to Lacan's own exposition of the discourses in *Seminar XVII*, there are a great many glosses, critiques, and applications whose divergences reveal particularly well the openness (and precariousness) of Lacan's teachings. For the most efficacious exegesis, see Paul Verhaeghe, "From Impossibility to Inability: Lacan's Theory of the Four Discourses," in *Beyond Gender: From Subject to Drive* (New York: Other Press, 2001), 17–34. For other nuanced accounts, see also Mark Bracher, Marshall W. Alcorn, and Ronald J. Corthell, eds., *Lacanian Theory of Discourse: Subject, Structure, and Society* (New York: New York University Press, 1994); and Justin Clemens and Russell Grigg, eds., *Jacques Lacan and the Other Side of Psychoanalysis: Reflections on Seminar XVII, SIC 6* (Durham, NC: Duke University Press, 2006).

54. It ought not go without saying that Lacan's critics remain skeptical of his claim of psychoanalysis's un- or anti-mastery. The most vocal critic in this regard is Mikkel Borch-

Jacobsen, whose brilliant and (by Lacanians at least) under-read book *The Absolute Master* is a polemical attack on exactly this point; Borch-Jacobsen maintains that Lacan's mastery is absolute precisely *because* it deigns to stage for the analysand that, behind the analyst's stony silence, there is nothing to hide, nothing "there." See Mikkel Borch-Jacobsen, *Lacan: The Absolute Master*, trans. Douglas Brick (Stanford, CA: Stanford University Press, 1991).

55. Jacques Lacan, *The Seminar, Book XVII*, 99.

56. See Sigmund Freud, "A Difficulty in the Path of Psycho-Analysis" (1917a), in *SE* 17, 139–43; emphasis mine. See also Freud, "The Resistance to Psycho-Analysis" (1925e), in *SE* 19, 221.

57. Jacques Lacan, *The Seminar, Book XVII*, 207.

58. The master signifier can in this sense be understood as the booming voice of the Wizard of Oz, and its goal is to collect other signifiers around it the way that sound collects reverberations in a hall—the audience is, strictly speaking, optional. The subject, meanwhile—the man behind the curtain—is not itself master but servant, of its desire. Regarding Lacan's Hegelianism, Borch-Jacobsen makes a compelling case for how deeply Lacan misreads Hegel, or rather Alexandre Kojève, Lacan's own "master" in all things Hegel; see Mikkel Borch-Jacobsen, *Lacan: The Absolute Master*, 8ff. Žižek, meanwhile, also maintains that Lacan misreads Hegel—*when he reads him*: "We have to take it as an axiom that Lacan's own reading of Hegel is fundamentally misguided. Lacan gets Hegel wrong, perhaps even very wrong." But paradoxically, Lacan becomes for Žižek one of the great Hegelians once he talks about anything else but Hegel. For a brief account, see "'From Lacan to Hegel': Interview with Slavoj Žižek," in *Žižek and his Contemporaries: On the Emergence of the Slovenian Lacan*, ed. Jones Irwin and Helena Motoh (New York: Bloomsbury, 2014), 130ff.

59. For Lacan and Lacanians—arguably for Freudians, too—the ultimate expression of such an aspired unity is the notion of a "sexual relationship" (*un rapport sexuel*). Lacan's famous statement in 1970 that "il n'y a pas de rapport sexuel" (there is no such thing as a sexual relationship) is thus a claim on the impossibility of any such relationship between subject and other predicated on an absolute unity, harmony, perfection, or completion, but also on other such utopian premises, such as that of undistorted communication (in the case of Habermas). Jacques Lacan, *The Seminar, Book XVII*, 116.

60. Late in his career, Lacan will reformulate *jouissance* as *plus-de-jouir.*

61. Hence the ample (and excellent) entry devoted to the word in the truly epic, recently translated *Dictionary of Untranslatables*, ed. Barbara Cassin, trans. Steven Rendall, Christian Hubert, Jeffrey Mehlman, Nathanael Stein, and Michael Syrotinski, translation ed. Emily Apter, Jacques Lezra, Michael Wood (Princeton, NJ: Princeton University Press, 2014).

62. See Jacques Lacan, *The Seminar, Book XX*, 3.

63. As is often pointed out in connection with Lacanian *jouissance*, Freud originally thought of his principle as the *Unlustprinzip*, a principle guarding *against* a kind of difficult or unbearable pleasure. See Sigmund Freud, "The Interpretation of Dreams" (1900a), in *SE* V, 599ff.

64. Sigmund Freud, "Introductory Lectures on Psycho-Analysis" (1916–17), in *SE* 15/16, 365–66; cited in Bruce Fink, "Against Understanding: Why Understanding Should Not be Viewed as an Essential Aim of Psychoanalytic Treatment," in *Against Understanding, Vol. 1: Commentary and Critique in a Lacanian Key* (New York: Routledge, 2014), 26n7.

65. Fink describes *jouissance* as fundamentally beyond the subject's control, but crucially, as a by-product of our attempts to control. It is not something we seek out, but what simply "happens" to us, to our happy or miserable surprise, while we seek out other things. See again Bruce Fink, "Against Understanding," 278n7.

66. Despite the clarity of Verhaeghe's "From Impossibility to Inability," I differ with it on one major point: taking his cue from Lacan himself, he describes the relation between "agent" and "other" as one of impossibility, and that between "truth" and "product" as one of inability, but I find this distinction unhelpful and a bit sophistic, and would argue for their reversal: as I read Lacanian discourse theory, the relation between agent and other is marked by an inadequacy (to communicate *fully*, to achieve *complete* identification, consensus, understanding, et cetera). Meanwhile, the relation between truth and product does not, strictly speaking, exist; they are barred from one another, and this barring of any actual connection *constitutes* the relationship, rather like two lovers otherwise separated by an infinite glass pane.

67. Bruce Fink, "Fantasies and the Fundamental Fantasy," 47. For Lacan's own formulations on the relation between fundamental fantasy and axiom, see the concluding sections of *The Seminar of Jacques Lacan, Book XVI: From an Other to the Other, 1968–1969*, trans. Cormac Gallagher (London: Karnac Books, 2002).

68. This is what Žižek, after Kant, calls fantasy's "transcendental schematism": "it literally 'teaches us how to desire.'" Slavoj Žižek, *The Plague of Fantasies* (London: Verso, 1997), 7.

69. Anne Dunand, "The End of Analysis (II)," in *Reading Seminar XI: Lacan's Four Fundamental Concepts of Psychoanalysis*, ed. Richard Feldstein, Bruce Fink, and Maire Jaanus (Albany, NY: SUNY Press, 1994), 254.

70. "Slavoj Žižek: What Is Freedom Today?—Video," prod. Nicole Jackson, Ben Marshall, Bruno Rinvolucri, Anetta Jones, Robbie Kilgour, and Caterina Monzani, *The Guardian,* December 3, 2014, http://www.theguardian.com/commentisfree/video/2014/dec/03/slavoj-zizek-philosopher-what-is-freedom-today-video.

71. Žižek has at various points, but especially in the late 1990s, come close to styling his own project thusly.

72. Matt ffytche, *Foundation of the Unconscious: Schelling, Freud and the Birth of the Modern Psyche* (Cambridge, England: Cambridge University Press, 2012), 23.

73. Eric Dean Rasmussen, "Liberation Hurts: An Interview with Slavoj Žižek," *electronic book review*, July 1, 2004, http://www.electronicbookreview.com/thread/endconstruction/desublimation. Perspicacious early reviews of *The Sublime Object of Ideology* noted Žižek's priorities; see for instance Peter Dews, "Hegel in Analysis: Slavoj Žižek's Lacanian Dialectics," *Bulletin of the Hegel Society of Great Britain* 21–22 (1990): 1–18.

74. Adrian Johnston, *Žižek's Ontology*, xiv.

75. Slavoj Žižek, "Appendix II. Robert Schumann: The Romantic Anti-Humanist," in *The Plague of Fantasies*, 245. For an excellent critical discussion of Žižek's larger engagement with music, including his claims in the Schumann essay, see Holly Watkins, "Slavoj Žižek: Responding from the Void," *Contemporary Music Review* 31, nos. 5–6 (2012): 449–60.

76. Slavoj Žižek, *The Sublime Object of Ideology*, 126.

77. Ibid., xxx.

78. Slavoj Žižek, *The Plague of Fantasies*, 3–44.

79. Žižek borrows the phrase "material sincerity" from Henri Bergson, *Laughter: An Essay on the Meaning of the Comic*, trans. Cloudesley Brereton and Fred Rothwell (New York: Macmillan, 1914), 144.

80. Slavoj Žižek, "Appendix II. Robert Schumann," 245; emphasis in the original.

81. T. J. Clark, "Modernism, Postmodernism, and Steam," *October* 100 (2002): 165–66.

82. Mark Evan Bonds, *Absolute Music: The History of an Idea* (Oxford: Oxford University Press, 2014), 299.

CHAPTER FIVE

1. Jacques Lacan, *The Seminar of Jacques Lacan, Book XVII: The Other Side of Psychoanalysis, 1969–1970*, ed. Jacques-Alain Miller, trans. with notes Russell Grigg (New York: W. W. Norton, 2007), 207.

2. See, respectively, Oliver Fritz, "Did Pop Bring Down the Berlin Wall?," BBC Two *Newsnight Review*, November 16, 2009, http://news.bbc.co.uk/2/hi/programmes/newsnight/review/8362668.stm; "Did the Boss Help Bring Down the Berlin Wall?," *Wall Street Journal*, July 8, 2013, http://blogs.wsj.com/speakeasy/2013/07/08/did-the-boss-help-bring-down-the-berlin-wall/; "Chimes of Freedom: How Springsteen Helped Tear Down the Wall," *Spiegel Online*, http://www.spiegel.de/international/germany/book-says-springsteen-concert-helped-bring-down-berlin-wall-a-906236.html; "Did Bowie Bring Down the Berlin Wall?," *The Week*, http://www.theweek.co.uk/25027/did-bowie-bring-down-berlin-wall; "How Mr. Hasselhoff Tore Down This Wall," NPR, http://www.npr.org/2014/11/09/362595983/how-mr-hasselhoff-tore-down-this-wall. For an early scholarly address, see Jolanta Pekacz, "Did Rock Smash the Wall? The Role of Rock in Political Transition," *Popular Music* 13, no. 1 (1994): 41–49.

3. Freud's essay on fetishism (*SE* 21, 152–59) points out that the fetishist can be in thrall to his or her fantasy while simultaneously knowing that it is "but" a fantasy. This is a special kind of knowledge, in that it not only fails to diminish the grip of the fantasy itself, but arguably even strengthens it. The phrase "I know very well, but all the same . . ." forms the basis of a canonical sequel to Freud's essay by Octave Mannoni: "Je sais bien, mais quand-même . . . ," in *Clefs pour l'imaginaire ou l'autre scène* (Paris: Seuil, 1969), 9–33.

4. Oliver Fritz, "Did Pop Bring Down the Berlin Wall?"

5. Paul Berman, "Two Decades after the Fall: Optimism of the Intellect," *Dissent*, September 9, 2009, https://www.dissentmagazine.org/online_articles/two-decades-after-the-fall-optimism-of-the-intellect.

6. For a particularly dubious recent effort to support the Hasselhoff Thesis—technically the Boss Thesis—see Erik Kirschbaum's multi-colon *Rocking the Wall: Bruce Springsteen: The Untold Story of a Concert in East Berlin That Changed the World* (New York: Berlinica Publishing, 2013). For a decent appraisal, see also John A. Gans Jr.'s review, "Did Bruce Springsteen Win the Cold War?," *Survival* 55, no. 6 (2013): 169–78.

7. Richard Taruskin, "A Beethoven Season?," in *The Danger of Music and Other Anti-Utopian Essays* (Berkeley: University of California Press, 2008), 72. Originally published in the *New York Times*, September 10, 1995.

8. Claude Lefort, "The Permanence of the Theologico-Political?," in *Democracy and Political Theory*, trans. David Macey (Minneapolis: University of Minnesota Press, 1988), 225.

9. See Caryl Clark's careful and critical "Forging Identity: Beethoven's 'Ode' as European Anthem," *Critical Inquiry* 23 (1997): 789–807, for the most thorough background on the process of making the Ode into the anthem of the European Union.

10. Benedict Anderson, *Imagined Communities: Reflections on the Origin and Spread of Nationalism* (London: Verso, 1991), 145.

11. Both Žižek and Laclau take pains to point out that, in Žižek's words, "There is no reason to be dismissive of the discourse of the Master, to identify it too hastily with 'authoritarian repression': the Master's gesture is the founding gesture of every social link." Slavoj Žižek, "Lacan's Four Discourses," in *The Desire of the Analysts: Psychoanalysis and Cultural Criticism*, ed. Greg Forter and Paul Allen Miller (Albany: State University of New York Press, 2008), 87; and, for a similar point, Ernesto Laclau, "Why Do Empty Signifiers Matter to Politics?," in *Emancipation(s)* (London: Verso 1996), 44.

12. Joe Moran provides wonderful detail of the days surrounding the opening of the borders between East and West Berlin, particularly the aura of meaninglessness emanating from the interstices of the otherwise joyous moment. Joe Moran, "November in Berlin: The End of the Everyday," *History Workshop Journal* 57, no. 1 (2004): 216–34.

13. Friedrich Wilhelm Joseph von Schelling, "Clara," in *Sämtliche Werke IX* (Stuttgart: Cotta 1856–61), 39; cited in Slavoj Žižek, "Introduction: The Specter of Ideology," in *Mapping Ideology*, ed. Slavoj Žižek (London and New York: Verso, 2012), 27. See also Slavoj Žižek / F. W. J. von Schelling, *The Abyss of Freedom* / Ages of the World, trans. Judith Norman (Ann Arbor: University of Michigan Press, 1997). Žižek translates *scheuen sich vor* as "are terrified of," a—rather Žižekian—exaggeration. The German implies less a feeling of horror than of deep apprehension: "Die meisten Menschen scheuen sich vor der Freiheit, wie sie sich vor der Magie, vor allem Unerklärbaren, und besonders vor der Geisterwelt scheuen."

14. Dennis points out what has now become a generally acknowledged fact: that Bernstein's performance was not at all an endeavor in post-partisanship, even less a triumph over ideology, but rather a gloating (if politically unconscious) victory dance for late global capitalism. David B. Dennis, *Beethoven in German Politics 1870–1989* (New Haven, CT: Yale University Press, 1996), 260.

15. See Lydia Goehr's now-classic formulation of *Werktreue* in *The Imaginary Museum of Musical Works: An Essay in the Philosophy of Music* (New York: Oxford University Press, 2002): "A performance met the *Werktreue* ideal most satisfactorily, it was finally decided, when it achieved complete transparency. For transparency allowed the work to 'shine' through and be heard in and for itself" (232). See also Karen Leistra-Jones's fascinating recent article "Staging Authenticity: Joachim, Brahms, and the Politics of *Werktreue* Performance," *Journal of the American Musicological Society* 66, no. 2 (2013): 397–436.

16. Jacques Lacan, *The Seminar of Jacques Lacan, Book XI: The Four Fundamental Principles of Psychoanalysis, 1964*, ed. Jacques-Alain Miller, trans. Alan Sheridan (New York: W. W. Norton, 1998), 257.

17. Jacques Lacan, *The Seminar of Jacques Lacan, Book XX: Encore, 1972–73, On Feminine Sexuality, the Limits of Love and Knowledge*, ed. Jacques-Alain Miller, trans. with notes by Bruce Fink (New York: W. W. Norton, 1998), 26.

18. Claude Lefort, "The Logic of Totalitarianism," in *The Political Forms of Modern Society: Bureaucracy, Democracy, Totalitarianism*, trans. J. B. Thompson (Cambridge, MA: MIT Press, 1986), 280.

19. Eric Santner, *The Royal Remains: The People's Two Bodies and the Endgames of Sovereignty* (Chicago: University of Chicago Press, 2011), 4.

20. In *The Royal Remains*, Eric Santner articulates this as one of the central theses of much recent work in political theology; he also cites Lacan's discourse of the master as a specific means of conceptualizing how any biocratic "knowledge of the body," no matter how disenchantedly "modern" in its efforts at accumulation and deployment, nonetheless fails in the encounter with a "strange and physical presence," as Foucault called the body of the king. Lacan, among others, helps political theology to think of how "the real object of the new physics of power is not simply the body or life but rather the flesh that has become separated from the body of the king and has entered, like a strange alien presence, into that of the people (as we shall see, science fiction, horror, and political theory are not as far apart as one might think)" (11).

21. Bruce Fink, "Fantasies and the Fundamental Fantasy," in *Against Understanding, Vol. 2: Cases and Commentary in a Lacanian Key* (New York: Routledge, 2014), 47.

22. Slavoj Žižek, "Robert Schumann: The Romantic Anti-Humanist," in *The Plague of Fantasies* (London: Verso, 1997), 245.

23. Heinrich Besseler, discussed briefly in Carl Dahlhaus, *Foundations of Music History*, trans. J. B. Robinson (Cambridge, England: Cambridge University Press, 1993), 108.

24. Northrop Frye, *Anatomy of Criticism* (Princeton, NJ: Princeton University Press, 1953), 193, quoted in Fredric Jameson, *The Political Unconscious* (Ithaca, NY: Cornell University Press, 1982).

25. Walter Benjamin, "Theses on the Philosophy of History," in *Illuminations*, ed. Hannah Arendt, trans. Harry Zohn (New York: Schoken Books, 1969), 253.

26. Jacques Lacan, "Seminar on 'The Purloined Letter,'" in *Écrits: The First Complete Edition in English*, trans. Bruce Fink (New York: Norton, 2007), 30.

27. Joshua Clover, *1989: Bob Dylan Didn't Have This to Sing About* (Berkeley: University of California Press, 2010), 109.

28. Fredric Jameson, *The Political Unconscious*, 35: "History is not a text, not a narrative, master or otherwise, but . . . an absent cause[,] inaccessible to us except in textual form, and . . . our approach to it and to the Real itself necessarily passes through its prior textualization, its narrativization in the political unconscious."

29. Joshua Clover, *1989*, 108.

30. Quoted in Gopal Balakrishnan, *Antagonistics: Capitalism and Power in an Age of War* (London: Verso, 2008), vii, cited in Joshua Clover, *1989*, 126. I cite Balakrishnan less as an interlocutor than to stay within the frame of Clover's argument.

31. Ibid., viii.

32. Joshua Clover, *1989*, 12–13. Compare Clover here with Žižek's account of fantasy as "the narrative occlusion of antagonism . . . the primordial form of narrative, which serves to occult some original deadlock" (Slavoj Žižek, *The Plague of Fantasies*, 11). Clover is relentless in pursuing his thesis, with which I otherwise generally agree: "1989" as an idea represents for him "a closure of space, now rendered unipolar; it is a closure of time, no longer open to change and thus emptied; it is a closure of meaning around the single idea of the victory of the West. This is '1989' as instantaneous and total: the closure of historical thought" (135). Where I diverge is a matter of subtle but crucial distinction: I would argue that "1989" represents a falling into (ideological) fantasy of especially robust efficacy, such

that the first real threats to it in the West, after 9/11, trigger not a loosening of its grip, but a tightening, an exacerbation. This is what Eric Santner and Robert Esposito, among others, conceptualize as the "immunological dialectic." See Roberto Esposito, *Bios: Biopolitics and Philosophy*, trans. Timothy Campbell (Minneapolis: University of Minnesota Press, 2008).

33. Marius Carboni, *Marketing Strategies in the UK Classical Music Business: The Significance of 1989* (Saarbrücken, Germany: LAP Lambert Academic Publishing, 2011); I thank University of Chicago PhD candidate Woo Chan (Chaz) Lee for bringing this source to my attention. The book on this late twentieth-century transformation of the concept of "classical music" has yet to be written, though certainly the worn trope of its death in the last quarter century hits on something of the truth. But this transformation may in the end have significantly more to do with Derridean spectrality than with any more traditional conceptions of mortality and obsolescence. The basic operation, I would argue, involves a series of practices, beliefs, and texts being sealed off and sealed together—fantasized—in such a way that renders them absolutely self-consistent (a fantasmatic "enjoying substance") and also perpetually out of reach or impossible (a "Real object"). This would involve a simultaneous process of disembodiment *and* corporatization. The post-Wall transition of Deutsche Grammophon—the label that originally released Bernstein's 1989 performance of the Ninth—provides one allegorical starting point: for previous decades a subsidiary of Polygram, it was eventually sold to Seagram and Universal Music Group, a division of Vivendi and the largest American music corporation in the world. In a piquant irony for this book, it also holds the rights to the song "Looking for Freedom."

34. Roxette's "Listen to Your Heart," for instance, actually became the soundtrack in 1990 television spots for Civic Forum, Václav Havel's popular reform movement. More ominously, it was also employed by Hungary's nationalist party Fidesz, whose campaign slogan that year was *Listen to your heart—Vote Fidesz!* (which actually rhymes in Hungarian). As of the writing of this book, Fidesz had, as the ruling party in Hungary, turned the country into the only non-democracy in Europe. For an interesting journalistic exploration of state-(mis)hearings of song lyrics, see Parker Molloy, "Are Politicians Too Dumb to Understand the Lyrics to 'Born in the USA'?," http://www.thedailybeast.com/articles/2014/11/06/are-politicians-too-dumb-to-understand-the-lyrics-to-born-in-the-usa.html.

35. Francis Fukuyama, "The End of History?," *National Interest* 16 (Summer 1989): 3.

36. See Francis Fukuyama, "The Future of History," *Foreign Affairs* 91, no. 1 (2012): 53–61; and Francis Fukuyama with Jacques Attali, "The Beginning of a New History," *New Perspectives Quarterly* 31, no. 1 (2014): 20–24. For a representative neoliberal reassessment, see Cato Institute Senior Fellow John Mueller, "Did History End? Assessing the Fukuyama Thesis," *Political Science Quarterly* 129, no. 1 (2014): 35–54.

37. Francis Fukuyama, "The End of History?," 18. Fukuyama's lines are admittedly the enactment of a well-established trope in writing on the realization of grand wishes. As antithetical a thinker as Adorno articulates something strikingly similar in his 1964 discussion with Ernst Bloch on utopia, as he reminds the audience that "numerous so-called Utopian dreams . . . have been fulfilled . . . [but] all operate as though the best thing about them had been forgotten—one is not happy about them." See "Über die Möglichkeiten der Utopie Heute" (SWF 1964), https://archive.org/details/AdornoErnstBloch-MglichkeitenDerUtopieHeuteswf1964.

38. Russell Jacoby, *The End of Utopia* (New York: Basic Books, 1999), 9. On bangless whimpers, see T. S. Eliot, "The Hollow Men" (1925):

> This is the way the world ends
> This is the way the world ends
> This is the way the world ends
> Not with a bang but a whimper.

T. S. Eliot, *Collected Poems, 1909–1962*
(New York: Harcourt, Brace and World, 1963), 82.

CHAPTER SIX

1. The exact date of Szymański's premiere is not known, and publishers and biographers provide conflicting information.

2. Luciano Berio-Franz Schubert, *Rendering* (Vienna: Universal Edition, 1989), preface.

3. *Fifty Years Holland: A Dutch Miracle,* Globe/GLO 6900, 1997, compact disc.

4. Thomas Gartmann, "*. . . dass nichts sich von jemals vollendet ist . . .*": *Untersuchungen zum Instrumentalschaffen von Luciano Berio* (Bern: Verlag Paul Haupt, 1995), 127ff.

5. See the "Base de Documentation sur la Musique Contemporaine" (BRAHMS) maintained by IRCAM in Paris, at http://brahms.ircam.fr/. See also, among other similar sites, the Music Information Center Austria at http://www.musicaustria.at/en.

6. For a recent account of *détournement*, see McKenzie Wark's deft (and controversial) history of the Situationist International, *The Beach Beneath the Street: The Everyday Life and Glorious Times of the Situationist International* (New York: Verso, 2011).

7. Northrop Frye, *Anatomy of Criticism* (Princeton, NJ: Princeton University Press, 1953), 193.

CHAPTER SEVEN

1. Fredric Jameson, *A Singular Modernity: Essay on the Ontology of the Present* (London: Verso, 2002), 34.

2. Philip Bohlman, "Ontologies of Music," in *Rethinking Music*, ed. Nicholas Cook and Mark Everist (Oxford: Oxford University Press, 1999), 17.

3. Throughout this book I will follow Lydia Goehr's cue in capitalizing the phrase "New Music," and thereby treating it as a term of art. Goehr does so in connection with Adorno's use (in German) of the phrase. See Lydia Goehr, "Dissonant Works and Listening Publics," in *The Cambridge Companion to Adorno*, ed. Tom Huhn (Cambridge, England: Cambridge University Press, 2004), 245n2.

4. Jacques Rancière's recent *Aisthesis*, an immodest revision of Erich Auerbach's classic appraisal *Mimesis* (1953), is robust in its assertion of forms over "contents," beginning with the structuring power of the very signifiers "aesthetic" and "art." See Jacques Rancière, *Aisthesis: Scenes from the Aesthetic Regime of Art*, trans. Zakir Paul (London: Verso, 2013), x. For a deft exploration of the implications of Rancière's thought for music studies, see Jairo Moreno and Gavin Steingo, "Rancière's Equal Music," *Contemporary Music Review* 31, nos. 5–6 (2012): 487–505.

5. See Andreas Ballstaedt's excavation of the term "New Music" in *Wege zur Neue Musik* (Mainz: Schott, 2003).

6. Fredric Jameson coins the word "ideologeme" in *The Political Unconscious* (Ithaca, NY: Cornell University Press, 1981), 77: "Our object of study will prove to be the ideologeme, that is, the smallest intelligible unit of the essentially antagonistic collective discourses of social classes."

7. See in particular Hettie Malcomsen, "Composing Individuals: Ethnographic Reflections on Success and Prestige in the British New Music Network," *Twentieth-Century Music* 10, no. 1 (2013): 115–36; Yara El-Ghadban, "Facing the Music: Rituals of Belonging and Recognition in Contemporary Western Art Music," *American Ethnologist* 36, no. 1 (2009): 140–60; Charles Wilson, "György Ligeti and the Rhetoric of Autonomy," *Twentieth-Century Music* 1, no. 1 (2004): 5–28; Georgina Born, *Rationalizing Culture: IRCAM, Boulez, and the Institutionalization of the Musical Avant-Garde* (Berkeley: University of California Press, 1995); and Susan McClary, "Terminal Prestige: The Case of Avant-Garde Music Composition," *Cultural Critique* 12 (1989): 57–81.

8. See Howard Becker, *Art Worlds* (Berkeley: University of California Press, 1984); see also Pierre Bourdieu, *Outline of a Theory of Practice* (Cambridge, England: Cambridge University Press, 1977).

9. Ian Buchanan, "Schizoanalytic Modernism: The Case of Antonin Artaud," in *Understanding Deleuze, Understanding Modernism*, ed. Paul Ardoin, S. E. Gontarski, and Laci Mattison (New York: Bloomsbury Academic, 2014), 196. Buchanan is making use here of a definition of the concept in Gilles Deleuze and Félix Guattari, *What Is Philosophy?*, trans. Graham Burchell and Hugh Tomlinson (London: Verso, 1994), 22.

10. See Walter Frisch, *German Modernism: Music and the Arts* (Berkeley: University of California Press, 2007).

11. See the last chapter in Lydia Goehr's *The Imaginary Museum of Musical Works: An Essay in the Philosophy of Music* (New York: Oxford University Press, 2002), titled "*Werktreue*: Confirmation and Challenge in Contemporary Movements," 243–86, for an especially interesting take on New Music's complicated, sometimes contradictory relationship to the work-concept and the canon.

12. Peter Hallward, *Alain Badiou: Subject to Truth* (Minneapolis: University of Minnesota Press, 2003), 115.

13. Paul Bekker, "Neue Musik," in *Neue Musik: Dritter Band der gesammelten Schriften* (Stuttgart and Berlin: deutsche Verlags-anstalt, 1923), 85–118; Theodor W. Adorno, *Philosophie der neuen Musik* (Tübingen: Verlag J. C. B. Mohr, 1949).

14. Christoph von Blumröder, *Der Begriff "Neue Musik" im 20. Jahrhundert*, Freiburger Schriften zur Musikwissenschaft, Band XII (Munich and Salzburg: Musikverlag Emil Katzbichler, 1981); Andreas Ballstaedt, *Wege zur Neuen Musik: Über einige Grundlagen der Musikgeschichtsschreibung des 20. Jahrhunderts*, Neue Studien zur Musikwissenschaft, Band VIII (Mainz: Schott Verlag, 2003).

15. "Was beibt? 100 Jahre Neue Musik," http://www.mh-stuttgart.de/fileadmin/downloads/Musikwissenschaft/2008-09%20100JahreFlyer.PDF. See also Wolfgang Rathert's critical review, "Was bleibt? 100 Jahre Neue Musik," *Musik und Ästhetik* 18 (2014): 112–16.

16. The entire series ended with a performance of *Erwartung*, cited multiply throughout the brochure and its events, and providing something of an ouroborosian teleology: "expec-

tation" of a return to the beginning of the new. Strikingly, *Erwartung* was paired in concert—as it often is—with Béla Bartók's *Bluebeard's Castle*, but Bartók himself was presented within the series's frames only under the sign of "Alternative Histories" and as the unnamed surplus designated by the concert title itself: *Erwartung und mehr.*

17. See the opening page of Daniel Albright's introduction to his anthology *Modernism and Music* (Chicago: University of Chicago Press, 2003) for a swift history of the term "modern." Also see Raymond Williams's yet swifter but equally indispensable entry on "modern" in *Keywords: A Vocabulary of Culture and Society*, rev. ed. (Oxford: Oxford University Press, 1983), 208–9.

18. Björn Heile, ed., *The Modernist Legacy: Essays on New Music* (Farnham, England: Ashgate, 2009).

19. Susan McClary, "Terminal Prestige: The Case of Avant-Garde Music," in the special issue "Discursive Strategies and the Economy of Prestige," *Cultural Critique* 12 (1989): 72.

20. See Harry Levin, "What Was Modernism?," *Massachusetts Review* 1, no. 4 (1960): 609–30; Robert Martin Adams, "What Was Modernism?," *Hudson Review* 31, no. 1 (1978): 19–33; Raymond Williams, "When Was Modernism?," *New Left Review* 175, no. 1 (1989): 48–53.

21. See in particular Dai Griffiths, "Genre: Grammar Schoolboy Music," *Critical Musicology Newsletter* 3 (1995): n.p., reprinted in *Music, Culture and Society: A Reader*, ed. Derek B. Scott (Cambridge, England: Cambridge University Press, 2000), 143–45. Just as *From 1989* was going into production, McClary published a remarkable reassessment of musical modernism; see Susan McClary, "The Lure of the Sublime: Revisiting the Modernist Project," in *Transformations of Musical Modernism*, ed. Erling E. Guldbrandsen and Julian Johnson (Cambridge, England: Cambridge University Press, 2015), 21–35.

22. Ben Earle, "'The Real Thing—At Last?' Historicizing Humphrey Searle," in *British Music and Modernism, 1895–1960*, ed. Matthew Riley (Aldershot, England: Ashgate, 2010), 301; cited in Björn Heile, "Musical Modernism, Sanitized," *Modernism/Modernity* 18, no. 3 (2011): 631–37. Earle is likely referring to a trove of books that began appearing shortly after the turn of the millennium, many of them with either Oxford or Cambridge University Press, among them J. P. E. Harper-Scott, *Edward Elgar, Modernist* (Cambridge, England: Cambridge University Press, 2006), and Daniel M. Grimley, *Carl Nielsen and the Idea of Modernism* (Woodbridge, England: Boydell and Brewer, 2011). James Hepokoski's introduction to his *Sibelius: Symphony No. 5* (Cambridge, England: Cambridge University Press, 1993) constitutes a *locus classicus* in this increasingly catholic approach to a "canonical" musical modernism.

23. Daniel Albright, *Modernism and Music: An Anthology of Sources* (Chicago: University of Chicago Press, 2004), 11.

24. David Metzer, *Musical Modernism at the Turn of the Twenty-First Century* (Cambridge, England: Cambridge University Press, 2009), 7.

25. Arved Mark Ashby, ed., *The Pleasure of Modernist Music* (Rochester, NY: University of Rochester Press, 2004), 4.

26. Tamara Levitz, *Modernist Mysteries: Persèphone* (Oxford: Oxford University Press, 2012), 45.

27. Richard Taruskin, *The Oxford History of Western Music*, vol. 5 (Oxford: Oxford University Press, 2009), 2.

28. Alastair Williams, "Ageing of the New: The Museum of Musical Modernism," in *The Cambridge History of Twentieth-Century Music*, ed. Nicholas Cook and Anthony Pople (Cambridge, England: Cambridge University Press, 2004), 506.

29. Ibid., 536.

30. Peter Franklin, "Between the Wars: Traditions, Modernisms, and the 'Little People from the Suburbs,'" in *The Cambridge History of Twentieth-Century Music*, 186. Franklin references Robert Schumann, "Florestan's Shrove Tuesday Address Delivered after a Performance of Beethoven's Last Symphony," in *Strunk's Source Readings in Music History*, vol. 6, ed. Ruth Solie (New York: W. W. Norton, 1997), 104–6.

31. Gianmario Borio, "Musical Communication and the Process of Modernity," *Journal of the Royal Musical Association* 139, no. 1 (2014): 179.

32. See for instance Douglas Mao and Rebecca L. Walkowitz, "The New Modernist Studies," *PMLA* 123, no. 3 (2008): 737–48. Essential to this turn were the founding of two journals, *Modernism/Modernity* and *Modernist Cultures*—and, in 1999, the Modernist Studies Association.

33. Jacques Rancière, *Aisthesis*, 262. For the most sustained revisionist assessment of Clement Greenberg and his legacy, see Caroline A. Jones, *Eyesight Alone: Clement Greenberg's Modernism and the Bureaucratization of the Senses* (Chicago: University of Chicago Press, 2006).

34. See *The Oxford Handbook of Global Modernisms*, ed. Mark Wollaeger and Matt Eatough (Oxford: Oxford University Press, 2012) and *The Cambridge Companion to Modernist Culture*, ed. Celia Marshik (Cambridge, England: Cambridge University Press, 2014). For pioneering work integrating modernist studies and work in the digital humanities, see in particular Hoyt Long and Richard Jean So, "Network Analysis and the Sociology of Modernism," *boundary 2* 40, no. 2 (2013): 147–82; and Hoyt Long and Richard Jean So, "Literary Pattern Recognition: Modernism between Close Reading and Machine Learning," *Critical Inquiry* 42, no. 2 (2016): 235–67.

35. See in particular Raymond Williams, "The Metropolis and the Emergence of Modernism," in *Unreal City: Urban Experience in Modern European Literature and Art*, ed. Edward Timms and David Kelley (Manchester, England: Manchester University Press, 1985), 13–24.

36. Brigid Cohen, "Diasporic Dialogues in Mid-Century New York: Stefan Wolpe, George Russell, Hannah Arendt, and the Historiography of Displacement," *Journal of the Society for American Music* 6, no. 2 (2012): 145. See also Brigid Cohen, *Stefan Wolpe and the Avant-Garde Diaspora* (Cambridge, England: Cambridge University Press, 2012).

37. Brigid Cohen, "Diasporic Dialogues in Mid-Century New York," 146.

38. Ezra Pound, *Confucius* (New York: New Directions, 1951), 36; Harold Rosenberg, *The Tradition of the New* (New York: Horizon Press, 1959). Daniel Albright, in *Modernism and Music: An Anthology*, notes with irony that Pound "discovered [the phrase] in the Great Digest of Confucius, who noted that it was written in letters of gold on the Emperor T'ang's bathtub" (8).

39. Michael Levenson, *Modernism* (New Haven, CT: Yale University Press, 2011), 5.

40. Peter Osborne, *Anywhere or Not at All: Philosophy of Contemporary Art* (London: Verso, 2013), 73–74; italics mine. Osborne is obviously heavily indebted to Habermas's conception of the "time consciousness" of avant-garde art, but also to the work of the conceptual historian Reinhart Koselleck, whom he engages fulsomely in his book.

41. Matei Călinescu, *Five Faces of Modernity: Modernism, Avant-Garde, Decadence, Kitsch, Postmodernism* (Durham, NC: Duke University Press, 1977), 86.

42. See, among other sources, Fredric Jameson, *A Singular Modernity*; T. J. Clark, *Farewell to an Idea: Episodes in a History of Modernism* (New Haven, CT: Yale University Press, 2001); and Susan Stanford Friedman, "Definitional Excursions: The Meanings of Modern/Modernity/Modernism," *Modernism/Modernity* 8, no. 3 (2001): 493–513.

43. Susan Stanford Friedman, "Definitional Excursions," 510.

44. Fredric Jameson, *A Singular Modernity*, 4.

45. Ibid., 121.

46. Ibid., 4–5.

47. "A Tradition against Itself" is the first chapter of Octavio Paz, *Children of the Mire: Modern Poetry from Romanticism to the Avant-Garde* (Cambridge, MA: Harvard University Press, 1991), first published in 1971.

48. Gustave Flaubert, in a letter from January 16, 1852, to Louise Colet: "What I would like to write is a book about nothing, a book without exterior attachments, which would be held together by the inner force of its style, as the earth without support is held in the air—a book that would have almost no subject or at least in which the subject would be almost invisible." Gustave Flaubert, *Correspondance, vol. 2, Juillet 1851-Décembre 1858*, ed. Jean Bruneau (Paris: Gallimard, 1980), 31.

49. Hugo Friedrich, *Die Struktur der modernen Lyrik* (Hamburg: Rowohlt Verlag, 1956); published in English as *The Structure of Modern Poetry*, trans. Joachim Neugroschel (Evanston, IL: Northwestern University Press, 1974), 7. Friedrich goes on to give an excerpt of a theoretically endless catalogue of negativities: "Disorientation, disintegration of the familiar, loss of order, incoherence, fragmentism, reversibility, additive style, depoeticized poetry, bolts of annihilation, strident imagery, brutal abruptness, dislocation, astigmatism, alienation." In *A Singular Modernity*, Fredric Jameson offers a two-tiered analysis of Friedrich's argument, tracing simultaneously Paul de Man's own quietly eviscerating deconstruction of it.

50. Fredric Jameson, *A Singular Modernity*, 126–27, citing Theodor W. Adorno, *Ästhetische Theorie*, ed. Gretel Adorno and Rolf Tiedemann (Frankfurt: Suhrkamp, 1970), 36–48; in English as *Aesthetic Theory*, trans. Robert Hullot-Kentor (Minneapolis: Minnesota University Press, 1997), 20–27.

51. Charles Baudelaire, "The Salon of 1859," in *Baudelaire: Selected Writings on Art and Artists*, ed. and trans. P.E. Charve (Cambridge, England: Cambridge University Press, 1972), 299.

52. In this sense, the profusion of eulogies (to modernism) and litanies (about the inflation or deflation of the term) seem moments of perfect misrecognition: the loss of meaning is there at modernism's beginnings, its "origins." The loss is modernism's gain, its grip and footing on the cultures in which it proposed to intervene.

53. In *Less Than Nothing: Hegel and the Shadow of Dialectical Materialism* (London: Verso, 2012), Slavoj Žižek cites Mladen Dolar, *Oficirji, služkinje in dimnikarji* (Ljubljana, Slovenia: Analecta, 2010): "In literature, the corresponding couple is perhaps that of Sophocles versus Aeschylus: the tragic deadlock versus a new order, terror versus a new harmony" (963).

54. Jacques Lacan, *Le Séminaire de Jacques Lacan, Livre XVII: L'envers de la psychanalyse, 1969–1970*, ed. Jacques-Alain Miller (Paris: Seuil, 1991), 178.

55. See Christopher Prendergast's review of Jameson's *A Singular Modernity*, "Codeword Modernity," *New Left Review* 24 (2003): 104, http://newleftreview.org/II/24/christopher-prendergast-codeword-modernity.

56. Slavoj Žižek, *The Sublime Object of Ideology*, 2nd ed. (London: Verso, 2008), 140.

57. For an extended discussion of the doctor as the archetypal figure and "office" of modernity, see chapter 3, "Toward a Science of the Flesh," in Eric Santner, *The Royal Remains: The People's Two Bodies and the Endgames of Sovereignty* (Chicago: University of Chicago Press, 2011).

58. Marshall Berman, *All That Is Solid Melts into Air: The Experience of Modernity*, 2nd ed. (New York: Penguin Books, 1988), 15.

59. Charles Taylor, *Sources of the Self: The Making of Modern Identity* (Cambridge, MA: Harvard University Press, 1989).

60. Charles Taylor, "Two Theories of Modernity," *Hastings Center Report* 25, no. 2 (1995): 24. Later published in *Alternative Modernities*, ed. Dilip Parameshwar Gaonkar (Durham, NC: Duke University Press, 2001), 172–96.

61. Dilip Parameshwar Gaonkar, "On Alternative Modernities," in *Alternative Modernities*, 14.

62. Ibid., 16.

63. Jameson is rather brutally dismissive of theories of "alternate modernity," and is generally acknowledged as neither the most enlightened, progressive, nor informed reader of cultural difference (see the famous Ahmad-Jameson debates in *Social Text* in the autumn issues of 1986–87). Nonetheless, even a semi-charitable reading would understand this dismissal as part and parcel of Jameson's understanding of modernity *as* capitalism, and capitalism not as an essence, but as a site of antagonism, a radically interventionist force disrupting any and all global imaginaries. "Alternate modernity" becomes a way—often compromised and degraded—of living with a certain kind of nothing, a symptom; to celebrate one's "own" modernity is hence to celebrate one's symptom. See Jameson's pointed response to this critique in *A Singular Modernity*, 12. For an alternative critique of alternate modernities, see Volker H. Schmidt, "Multiple Modernities or Varieties of Modernity?," *Current Sociology* 54, no. 1 (2006): 77–97.

64. Karl Marx and Friedrich Engels, *The Communist Manifesto*, trans. Samuel Moore, introduction by Gareth Stedman Jones (New York: Penguin Classics, 2002), 223; partially cited and glossed in Marshall Berman, *All That Is Solid Melts into Air*, 88ff.

65. Peter Wagner, *Modernity: Understanding the Present* (Cambridge, England: Polity Press, 2012), 4. Wagner also appends the corollary of self-determination: "In a first step towards concreteness, this basic commitment translates into the principles of individual and collective self-determination and in the expectation of ever-increasing mastery of nature and ever more reasonable interaction between human beings" (4).

66. Fredric Jameson, *A Singular Modernity*, 31–32.

67. Fredric Jameson has always had much to say about this matter, and *A Singular Modernity* is no exception: "I am tempted to argue that the present cannot feel itself to be a historical period in its own right without this gaze from the future, which seals it off and expels it as powerfully from time to come as it was able to do with its own immediate precedents" (34).

68. Ibid., 34–35.

69. For Kant's own conceptualization of transcendental illusion, see Immanuel Kant, *Critique of Pure Reason*, trans. Werner S. Pluhar (Indianapolis: Hackett, 1996), "On Transcendental Illusion," 346ff. The premise is, unsurprisingly, an important one for post-Lacanians as well; see for instance Alenka Zupančič, "On Love as Comedy," *Lacanian Ink* 20 (2002): 69; and Adrian Johnston, *Žižek's Ontology: A Transcendental Materialist Theory of Subjectivity* (Evanston, IL: Northwestern University Press, 2008), 34.

70. Michel Foucault, "What Is Enlightenment?," in *The Foucault Reader*, ed. Paul Rabinow (New York: Pantheon Books, 1984), 312. See also Jürgen Habermas's "Modernity: An Incomplete Project?," trans. Seyla Benhabib, in *The Anti-Aesthetic: Essays on Postmodern Culture*, ed. Hal Foster (Port Townsend, WA: Bay Press, 1983), 3–15.

71. Fredric Jameson devotes a good deal of discussion to modernity-as-break, using Schelling in particular as a guide; see among other passages *A Singular Modernity*, 25.

72. Slavoj Žižek, *The Parallax View* (Cambridge, MA: MIT Press, 2006), 34–35; adapted from the slightly earlier *Organs without Bodies: On Deleuze and Consequences* (New York: Routledge, 2004), 166.

73. T. J. Clark, *Farewell to an Idea*, 8.

74. Jean Laplanche and Jean-Bertrand Pontalis, "Parapraxis," in *The Language of Psycho-Analysis*, trans. Donald Nicholson-Smith (New York: W. W. Norton, 1974), 300.

75. Jameson concludes *A Singular Modernity* with a discussion of Rimbaud's phrase, in which he maintains a similar thesis: "Ironic or not, Rimbaud's great cry has always been felt to be exciting: probably because it does not limit itself to assuring us that we are modern already, but gives us something to do."

76. Bruno Latour, *We Have Never Been Modern*, trans. Catherine Porter (Cambridge, MA: Harvard University Press, 1993).

77. T. J. Clark, *Farewell to an Idea*, 8 (first citation); Raymond Williams, *Politics of Modernism: Against the New Conformists* (London: Verso, 2007), 43 (second citation).

78. To take one among countless examples, here from music: for every Cage who presents silence itself (as both "silence" and "the impossibility of silence"), there is a Stockhausen who conceptualizes the *gefärbte Pause* (colored pause). "True silence" never ceases toggling between utopian endeavors to stage the cessation of all sound and the (equally utopian) endeavor to stage the auditory revelation of "the sound of silence."

79. T. J. Clark, "Origins of the Present Crisis," *New Left Review* 2 (2000): 95, at http://newleftreview.org/II/2/t-j-clark-origins-of-the-present-crisis.

80. See Alenka Zupančič, *Ethics of the Real: Kant, Lacan* (London: Verso, 2000), 200ff, for a brilliant discussion of Oedipus as institutional founder.

81. See Yuri Lotman, "On the Semiosphere" (1984), trans. Wilma Clark, *Sign Systems Studies* 33, no. 1 (2005): 205–26.

CHAPTER EIGHT

1. I am thinking of Claus-Steffen Mahnkopf's impressive but problematic intervention in New Music, in particular his theory, based on the work of Ulrich Beck, of a "second modernity," one that calls for a new fidelity of theory and practice in the aesthetic field. See among (many)

other titles *Facets of the Second Modernity: New Music and Aesthetics in the 21st Century*, vol. 6, ed. Claus-Steffen Mahnkopf, Frank Cox, and Wolfram Schurig (Hofheim: Wolke Verlag, 2006).

2. Jameson admits as much in the conclusion to *A Singular Modernity*, where he calls for "a wholesale displacement of the thematics of modernity by the desire called Utopia." Clark is unfailingly self-conscious of his own melancholy throughout *Farewell to an Idea*, but for an actual critical assessment of this melancholy's ramifications for his project, see Jay Bernstein, "Social Signs and Natural Bodies: On T. J. Clark's *Farewell to an Idea*," *Radical Philosophy* 104 (2000): 25–38.

3. Laura Doyle and Regenia Gagnier, "The Global Circulation Project's Forum on Global Modernisms," *Literature Compass* 9, no. 9 (2012): 590. This definition reflects a generally shared orientation in *The Oxford Handbook of Global Modernisms*, for which Doyle wrote the afterword, and this orientation, itself formulated in part from the work of Jameson on "singular modernity," has been the aim of some criticism and wariness; see Stephen Yao's response essay in the same collection.

4. See for instance Fredric Jameson, *Postmodernism, or the Logic of Late Capitalism* (Durham, NC: Duke University Press, 1991), 45–46.

5. Ibid., ix.

6. Alexander Kluge, *Der Angriff der Gegenwart auf die übrige Zeit* (Frankfurt: Syndikat Autoren und Verlagsgesellschaft, 1985). The book eventually inspired a film, known in the United States as *The Blind Director* and first screened at the New York Film Festival in October 1985. See also Alexander Kluge, "The Assault of the Present on the Rest of Time," trans. Tamara Evans and Stewart Liebman, *New German Critique* 49 (1990): 11–22.

7. "Tall tales" and "white lies" is how Jonathan Arac translates Lyotard's famous formulation of the *grand récits* of modernity (otherwise translated as "grand narratives") and *petit récits* (otherwise "language games") of postmodernity. See Jonathan Arac, *Postmodernism and Politics* (Minneapolis: University of Minnesota Press, 1989), xiii.

8. Steven Connor, "Introduction," in *The Cambridge Companion to Postmodernism*, ed. Steven Connor (Cambridge, England: Cambridge University Press, 2004), 10–11.

9. Fredric Jameson, *A Singular Modernity* (London: Verso, 2002), 94.

10. See Friedrich Wilhelm Joseph von Schelling, *The Ages of the World*, trans. with introduction by Jason M. Wirth (Albany: State University of New York Press, 2000), 42: "Most people know no past except for the one that in each moment, precisely because of the moment, expands itself, which is still becoming itself, but which is not itself. There is no past without a determinate and decisive present." Cited in Fredric Jameson, *A Singular Modernity*, 24; note that Jameson provides an alternate translation from an unspecified source.

11. Fredric Jameson, *A Singular Modernity*, 24.

12. Steven Connor, "Introduction," 10.

13. Joshua Clover, *1989: Bob Dylan Didn't Have This to Sing About* (Berkeley: University of California Press, 2010), 135: "Against Fukuyama pop we might pose Jameson pop. This mode is necessarily less celebratory, as Jameson's sense of history includes no fanfare for its accelerating collapse into a kind of pop itself. Jameson's method of reading is to a great extent a meditation on defeat. Nonetheless, it is able to unfold from that condition the possibility that within defeat, within historic closure, something remains: a knowledge in hiding, which cannot be seen directly."

14. Ibid., 135 (first citation), 137 (second citation).

15. Further developing an ongoing theme in his work, Rancière argues in *Aisthesis* that the aesthetic experience—a kind of radical *far niente*—is indeed inextricable from "the fullest expression of the fighting workers' collective . . . the general strike, an exemplary equivalence of strategic action and radical inaction." See Jacques Rancière, *Aisthesis: Scenes from the Aesthetic Regime of Art*, trans. Zakir Paul (London: Verso, 2013), xiv.

16. Michel Foucault, "Des espaces autres" (1967), in *Dits et écrits*, vol. 2 (Paris: Gallimard, 2001), 1571–81. Translated by Lieven de Cauter and Michiel Dehaene as "Of Other Spaces," in *Heterotopia and the City: Public Space in a Postcivil Society*, ed. Michiel Dehaene and Lieven de Cauter (London: Routledge, 2008), 13–29.

17. Sigmund Freud, "Lines of Advance in Psycho-Analytic Therapy" (1919a [1918]), in *SE* 17, 159ff.

18. See Bruce Fink, "Against Understanding: Why Understanding Should Not be Viewed as an Essential Aim of Psychoanalytic Treatment," in *Against Understanding, Vol. 1: Commentary and Critique in a Lacanian Key* (New York: Routledge, 2014). Linking "understanding" with "explanation," Fink cites an especially pertinent point of Freud's from *The Interpretation of Dreams*: "To explain a thing means to trace it back to something already known." Sigmund Freud (1900a), in *SE* V, 549.

19. "Slavoj Žižek: What Is Freedom Today?—Video," prod. Nicole Jackson, Ben Marshall, Bruno Rinvolucri, Anetta Jones, Robbie Kilgour, and Caterina Monzani, *The Guardian*, December 3, 2014, http://www.theguardian.com/commentisfree/video/2014/dec/03/slavoj-zizek-philosopher-what-is-freedom-today-video.

20. The quote comes from Sigmund Freud and Josef Breuer, *Studies in Hysteria* (1895), in *SE* 2, 305. For Freud's most substantial assessment of the therapeutic efficacy of psychoanalysis, see "Analysis Terminable and Interminable" (1937a), in *SE* 23, 211–53.

21. In *Picture Imperfect: Utopian Thought for an Anti-Utopian Age* (New York: Columbia University Press, 2005), Russell Jacoby provides a useful if ultimately problematic distinction between "two currents of utopian thought: the blueprint tradition and the iconoclastic tradition" (xiv–xvi). I will return to this distinction in chapter 15 via Adorno's work, but in general, I find the distinction offered by Žižek and Badiou a more fruitful one: that between utopia as a state—both as a political body and structure, and also an enduring situation or condition—and utopia as an event—a moment, a turn, an experience that fundamentally restructures the situation.

22. "Changing the coordinates of the possible" is how Žižek, following Badiou, defines the true utopian political act. See, among many other texts in which he uses this formulation, Slavoj Žižek, *Iraq: The Borrowed Kettle* (London: Verso, 2004).

CHAPTER NINE

1. Michel Foucault, "Of Other Spaces," in *Heterotopia and the City: Public Space in a Postcivil Society*, ed. Michiel Dehaene and Lieven de Cauter (London: Routledge, 2008), 13–29.

2. Ibid., 22.

3. Ibid., 16.

4. On the subject of music and heterotopia, see Yayoi Uno Everett, *The Music of Louis Andriessen* (Cambridge, England: Cambridge University Press, 2006), 163ff ("New music

community as a heterotopian site"); see also Nicholas Reyland's extremely rich article "The Spaces of Dream: Lutosławski's Modernist Heterotopias," *Twentieth-Century Music* 12, no. 1 (2015): 37–70. Reyland's is certainly the most ambitious and extensive theorization to date of the concept in relation to composition, modernity, and modernism, and a wonderful introduction to its use in post-Foucauldian scholarship. It also shows the slipperiness of the topic, and its constitutional openness to debate and application: heterotopia is a different concept than "zone." Reyland generally conceives the noumenal "other space" of the musical works themselves as the locus of heterotopia, something I am hesitant to do here. In contrast is the treatment of the concept provided by Philip Bohlman in "Jüdische Lebenswelten zwischen Utopie und Heterotopie, jüdische Musik zwischen Schtetl und Ghetto," *Lied und populäre Kultur* 47 (2002): 29–57. Here Bohlman is faithful to an anthropological and sociological conception, arguably closer to Foucault's initial conception, which identifies actual social and cultural spaces in which people work, live, and enjoy. While my application is limited here, I would hope to suggest that—precisely here, where the "real world" and the noumenal space of the aesthetic interweave inextricably—the middle ground is especially fertile. To put it simply, "the aesthetic" is not simply that set of activities, objects, texts, et cetera that can be allocated to heterotopian spaces like the museum and the concert hall. "The aesthetic" is what emerges as the name for precisely the slipping remainder or surplus of such allocations, that is, a way of naming the fact that, as a classic example, Beethoven's Fifth is in excess of its status as performance by being a work, but *also* in excess of its status as a work by being a performance. This is something that philosophers of the ontology of the work of art (Nelson Goodman, Lydia Goehr, Brian Kane, et al.) appear to take limited interest in; here the concept of heterotopia might open up (indeed!) new spaces.

5. See T. J. Clark's allusion to Weber in the introduction to his *Farewell to an Idea: Episodes in a History of Modernism* (New Haven, CT: Yale University Press, 2001). In a characteristically thoughtful review of Joseph Straus's book on dodecaphonic music in America, Martin Brody also develops some striking thoughts about New Music as a heterotopia; see Martin Brody, "Review: *Twelve-Tone Music in America* by Joseph N. Straus," *Journal of the American Musicological Society* 65, no. 1 (2012): 291–97.

6. Michel Foucault, *Les Mots et les choses: Une archéologie des sciences humaines* (Paris: Gallimard, 1966), 9; trans. Alan Sheridan as *The Order of Things: An Archaeology of the Human Sciences*, 4th ed. (London: Routledge, 2004), xix.

7. Despite the general assumption that Foucault and Lacan were geographically close but otherwise worlds apart, Yannis Stavrakakis and others have noted how the two were at least somewhat engaged with each other and each other's work, not least during the mid-1960s, when Lacan was formulating a more concrete conception of fantasy, traversal, and *objet a*, and Foucault was finishing *Les Mots et les choses*. Lacan asked his seminar attendees to read *Les Mots* on April 27, 1966 (its publication year), and Foucault attended the same seminar less than a month later. For a generous unfolding of the larger dispute, see Thomas Brockelman, "The Other Side of the Canvas: Lacan Flips Foucault over Velázquez," *Continental Philosophy Review* 46, no. 2 (2013): 271–90.

8. David Harvey, *Spaces of Hope* (Berkeley: University of California Press, 2000), 183–84. See also Kevin Hetherington, *The Badlands of Modernity: Heterotopia and Social Ordering* (London: Routledge, 1997). For an early, not explicitly acknowledged reception of Foucault's

concept, see Henri Lefebvre's classic *The Urban Revolution*, trans. Robert Bononno (Minneapolis: University of Minnesota Press, 2003), 38ff.

9. See Heiner Goebbels, "La Jalousie, Red Run, Herakles 2, Befreiung" (1993), http://www.heinergoebbels.com/en/archive/works/complete/view/218/details.

10. Rainald Goetz rose to fame rapidly in the early to mid-1980s as one of Germany's most brazen young Leftist writers. In this context, his audacious project *1989: Material*, 3 vols. (Frankfurt: Suhrkamp, 2004) provides a fascinating context on the events of the *Wende*. As Ulrich Plass describes it, the "material" comprises a "monumental attempt to transcribe the history of the years 1989 and 1990 as seen and heard on television (the first published entry is dated February 10, 1989, the last one October 3, 1990, the day of German reunification). These three volumes, containing more than 1,500 pages, recorded like a paradoxically impersonal diary, bear the simple title *1989: Material 1–3*." Ulrich Plass, "Journalism, Television, Poetry: Rainald Goetz's *1989*," *Germanic Review: Literature, Culture, Theory* 81, no. 3 (2006): 202–20.

11. Heiner Goebbels, "La Jalousie, Red Run, Herakles 2, Befreiung" (1993).

12. See in particular Slavoj Žižek, "The Seven Veils of Fantasy," in *The Plague of Fantasies* (London: Verso, 1997), specifically the section "The Inherent Transgression," 24–36.

13. One of Žižek's favored examples of the voice in cinema is the famous scene in Fritz Lang's *Das Testament des Dr. Mabuse* (1933): two characters, thinking they have discovered the source of a voice gloating over their impending demise, pull back a proscenium curtain only to discover a desk, microphone, loudspeaker, and silhouette. This scene also becomes one of Michel Chion's favored examples of an *acousmêtre*, "the strange cinematic figure of an audible voice without a clearly visible body." See Michel Chion, *The Voice in Cinema*, ed. and trans. Claudia Gorbman (New York: Columbia University Press, 1999), 23; and see also Brian Kane, *Sound Unseen: Acousmatic Sound in Theory and Practice* (Oxford: Oxford University Press, 2014), 39.

14. Jonathan Kalb, in *The Theater of Heiner Müller* (Oxford: Oxford University Press, 1998), provides a lurid and, indeed, Müllerian account of the playwright's "typical practices," which he divides into two: "1) to adopt the manner of the source author entirely, style, tone and all, occupying the corpus like a vampire or virus in order to explode it from within, or 2) to set up a source author or composite of several authors as a broad paradigm, a nexus of ideas drawn from fable and fact, and then embarrass it with similar occupation—these exploding or embarrassing processes coming to full fruition only in the public arena of production. . . . History being a perennial bloodbath, all previous creators were, to him, guilty shadows with whom the living had a bloody obligation to grapple" (15–16).

15. See Michael Bloom's review of Jonathan Kalb's *The Theater of Heiner Müller*, *American Theatre* 16, no. 2 (1999): 70.

16. Jonathan Kalb, *The Theater of Heiner Müller*, 50.

17. Ibid., 19.

18. Ibid., 16.

19. Philip Bohlman and Brian Currid, "Suturing History, Healing Europe: German National Temporality in *Wolokolamsk Highway*," *Musical Quarterly* 85, no. 4 (2001): 681–717. Bohlman and Currid's argument is rich and sophisticated, and certainly the most extensive and sensitive treatment of the work; nonetheless, I differ in my conclusions about it.

20. See Max Nyffeler, "Wer spricht? Isabel Mundry und Heiner Goebbels über Konstellationen des Ich. Erstes Gespräch mit Max Nyffeler," Beckmesser.de, March 2003, http://www.beckmesser.de/komponisten/goebbels/goebbels-mundry-1.html.

21. Cassiber, *A Face We All Know*, ReR Megacorp/RERCCD 3/91 4DA1X, compact disc. Goetz was a textual source for the album, and Frank Zappa—with whom Ensemble Modern had already enjoyed a long working relationship—is also undoubtedly an influence.

22. Eisler would continue to be one of Goebbels's most enduring preoccupations, reaching something of an apotheosis with his ambivalent hour-long tribute to the composer, *Eislermaterial* (1998). In founding the *Sogenannte Linksradikale Blasorchester*, Goebbels was expressly interested in Eislerian precepts: the creation of a music "that is enmeshed in social action, that displays a strong communicative dimension, but that doesn't 'dumb itself down.'" See Kersten Glandien, "En Route—Eine monographische Studie zum Œuvre von Heiner Goebbels," http://www.heinergoebbels.com/download.php?itemID=2.

23. This particular constellation of influences—Stravinskian neoclassicism, jazz, and *Neue Sachlichkeit*, fused together with a strong political charge—brings to mind the music of Louis Andriessen, particularly Andriessen's works of the 1970s and early 1980s (*De Volharding* and *De Staat* are two exemplary works, though passages from myriad other works, *Hoketus* and *De Stijl* for instance, belong in this network, too).

24. Rainald Goetz, *Krieg*; translation mine.

25. See Max Nyffeler, "Cross-Country: On the Compositional Work of Heiner Goebbels" (1995), http://www.heinergoebbels.com/en/archive/texts/articles/read/173.

26. Max Nyffeler, "Der dialektische Sampler: Zur kompositorischen Arbeit von Heiner Goebbels," in *Heiner Goebbels: Komposition als Inszenierung*, ed. Wolfgang Sandner (Berlin: Henschel, 2002), 173–80.

27. Heiner Goebbels, "Prince and the Revolution: Über das Neue," in *Heiner Goebbels: Komposition als Inszenierung*, 207; translation mine.

28. Goebbels's note to *Wolokolamsker Chausee* is especially illuminating here; see http://www.hoerdat.in-berlin.de/select.php?S=0&col1=ti&a=Wolokolamsker+Chaussee+1–5.

29. See Heiner Müller, "The Hamletmachine," in *Hamletmachine and Other Texts for the Stage*, ed. and trans. Carl Weber (Ann Arbor, MI: Performing Arts Journal Publications, 1984), 56–57. Müller's 1979 play exerted a considerable influence on European writers and artists in the 1980s, including Goetz and Goebbels, the latter working closely with Müller on a number of collaborations throughout the decade.

30. Paweł Szymański, liner notes to *A Kaleidoscope for M. C. E.*, in Szymon Krzeszowiec, *Kaleidoscope*, DUX 0688, compact disc.

31. Ibid.

32. Adrian Thomas, *Polish Music since Szymanowski* (Cambridge, England: Cambridge University Press, 2005), 300. Ligeti, as has been well documented, was listening closely to the works of Steve Reich, Philip Glass, Terry Riley, and La Monte Young beginning in the mid- to late 1960s, and their music appears to serve as source of parody in Ligeti's *Continuum* from 1968.

33. Paweł Szymański, "From Idea to Sound: A Few Remarks on My Way of Composing," in *From Idea to Sound*, ed. Miloš Velimirovič (Krakow: FZE, 1993), 134. See also Jan Stęszewski, "Kreative Impulse: Polnische Zeitgenössische Komponisten und ihr Schaffen," *Österreichische Musikzeitschrift* 57, nos. 8–9 (2002): 10–19.

34. Paweł Szymański, "From Idea to Sound," 136. In a 1993 interview with Anders Beyer, Szymański clarifies what he understands as "a new trend . . . a musical freedom [that] relies on the notion that each composer can write music as he himself thinks fit and each is free to collect historical elements and insert them into the music. Now, late in the 20th century, we can hear music from the last ten centuries, both live and recorded. It is an amazing situation because it is part of our consciousness. . . . This basic attitude has something to do with pluralism, some call it 'postmodernism.'" Anders Beyer, ed., *The Voice of Music: Conversations with Composers of Our Time*, trans. Jean Christensen (Aldershot, England: Ashgate, 2001), 262.

35. Ibid., 262.

36. Paweł Szymański, "From Idea to Sound," 136.

37. While Szymański maintains that the score can be realized in 7'45", the dedicatee Ivan Monighetti's live recording is around 11 minutes. The fastest performance on record is 8'23", and was only realized nearly twenty years after the score was premiered. See Mikołaj Pałosz, *Cellovator*, DUX 0628, compact disc.

38. In *Polish Music since Szymanowski*, Adrian Thomas outlines, in his chapter on "Young Poland," 289–316, the degree of neoclassical tendencies. As just one example, Thomas mentions Krzysztof Baculewski's *Antitheton I*, also from 1989, which is considerably less subtle than *Kaleidoscope* in its baroque employments.

39. It's interesting to note that *Kaleidoscope*'s fashioning of a puppet and/or machine doesn't restrict itself to Bach alone; the performer becomes one as well, submitted as she is to a series of increasingly unfeasible—or downright impossible—demands as the score unfolds. One kind of servant—Rostropovich's music-priest—is switched out for a very different kind: the twittering machine.

40. See Alan Megill on R.G. Collingwood in *Historical Knowledge, Historical Error: A Contemporary Guide to Practice* (Chicago: University of Chicago Press, 2007), 54–58.

41. The lyrics to "Looking for Freedom" are, from a certain point of view, a shameless plug for the work and life ethic of late liberal capitalism.

42. Ernesto Laclau, "The Impossibility of Society," *Canadian Journal of Political and Social Science* 15, no. 3 (1991): 24.

43. Frederic Jameson, *Postmodernism: or, the Cultural Logic of Late Capitalism* (London: Verso, 1991), 17. Jameson's assessment of postmodernism's "blank parody," or parody without any claims, is often compared with Linda Hutcheon's more critical conception, formulated in 1989 in *The Politics of Postmodernism* (New York: Routledge, 1989).

44. Heiner Goebbels, "La Jalousie, Red Run, Herakles 2, Befreiung" (1993).

45. In Szymański's case, the status of the signifier "Bach" far exceeds Rostropovich; "Bach" is a ubiquitous and endlessly contested signifier in Polish new music, and a thorough exploration of such contestations would look well beyond 1989. Adrian Thomas, for instance, notes in *Polish Music since Szymanowski* (see p. 54ff) how, earlier in the postwar period, Bach served as a master signifier for one the more reactionary socialist realist programs in contemporary music, the socialist cantata.

46. The sketches were originally but incorrectly catalogued by Otto Erich Deutsch in 1951 as part of a group of nine distinct and incomplete movements. Only in 1978, as the sketches were revisited in preparation for various anniversary celebrations, did it become clear that three of the nine were written significantly later than the other six. Eventually

these sketches were dated to 1828, the last year of Schubert's life, and presumed to be those for a "Letzte Symphonie" mentioned by Schubert's friend Eduard von Bauernfeld in 1829. For more on the history of the sketches, see Brian Newbould, "Schubert's Last Symphony," *Musical Times* 126, no. 1707 (1985): 272.

47. See Luciano Berio-Franz Schubert, *Rendering* (Vienna: Universal Edition, 1989), preface; the line "complete the Symphony as Schubert himself might have done" comes directly from Brian Newbould.

48. Hartmut Lück, "Die symphonischen Fragmente Franz Schuberts zwischen wissenschaftlichenm Eifer und Kommzerzialisierung," *Österreichische Musikzeitung* 40 (1985): 432, cited in Thomas Gartmann, "*. . . dass nichts sich von jemals vollendet ist . . .*": *Untersuchungen zum Instrumentalschaffen von Luciano Berio* (Bern: Verlag Paul Haupt, 1995), 127. This particular issue of the *Österreichische Musikzeitung* was heavily devoted to the subject of Schubert's unfinished works, and could be said to represent the peak of European public and scholarly activity around the issue. See also, in the following issue, Paul-Gilbert Langevin, "Franz Schuberts symphonische Fragmente im Werden. Plädoyer für eine schöpferische Musikologie," *Österreichische Musikzeitung* 41 (1986): 506–9.

49. In a review of *Rendering*'s UK premiere, Paul Griffiths describes how "Berio's tremulous, sensuous score sometimes effects a Mahlerian separation of layers, as when muted trumpets call through a haze of flutes and strings, and Schubert pre-figures Mahler in the third and final movement, a triple-time funeral march. But the Mahler most precisely recalled is the Mahler of Berio's own *Sinfonia*. The weave of foreign material (including foreign Schubertian material among the new echoings) is now subtler and defter, but again Berio shows himself the master of musical time travel." Paul Griffiths, "Concertgebouw/ Harnoncourt; Concerts," *The Times*, June 20, 1989.

50. Axel Fuhrmann, "Geschichte, Geschichten. Luciano Berio über das Verhältnis von Musik und Text," *Neue Zeitschrift für Musik* 152, no. 5 (1991): 28–32. See also David Osmond-Smith, "Berio and the Art of Commentary," *Musical Times* 116, no. 1592 (1975): 871–72; in this short essay, written more than a decade before *Rendering*, Osmond-Smith largely discusses Berio's use of his own solo *Sequenze* in his concertante-like *Chemins* works. But his assertions reflect quite strikingly on the latter score's methods.

51. Luciano Berio-Franz Schubert, *Rendering*, preface.

52. Gartmann's examination of *Rendering*'s sketch materials (located at the Paul Sacher Stiftung in Basel, Switzerland) reveals that Berio possessed both Gülke's and Newbould's published scores, and had corresponded with Moser. It is worth pointing out that, however dismissive Berio was of the previous treatments, they were indispensable to his own orchestration, and in many places provided a clear model. See Thomas Gartmann, "*. . . dass nichts sich von jemals vollendet ist . . .* ," 135–36.

53. David Osmond-Smith (among others) writes of the subtleties of Berio's orchestrations of the both the Mahler songs and Brahms's Sonata. In both cases, Berio remains generally loyal to the sound of the respective composers' orchestrational styles, but simultaneously Osmond-Smith identifies moments in each score where the composer's music looks forward or back, to past and future influences, and allows these pockets of history or potentiality to "speak for themselves"—with Berio's "help." David Osmond-Smith, "La mesure de la distance: *Rendering* de Berio," *InHarmoniques* 7 (1991): 147–52.

54. Luciano Berio-Franz Schubert, *Rendering*, preface.

55. Nicholas Kenyon, "Bright Stars in the Suffolk Sky," *The Observer*, June 25, 1989; David Osmond-Smith, "La mesure de la distance," 150.

56. Paul Driver, "How to Add New Facets to Schubert's Gems," *Sunday Times*, June 25, 1989 (first quote); Wilfried Gruhn, "Schubert Spielen: Berios Sinfonische Ergänzungen Zu Schuberts Sinfonie-Fragment D.936a," *Musica* (Germany) 44, no. 5 (1990): 290–96 (second quote); David Metzer, "Musical Decay: Luciano Berio's *Rendering* and John Cage's *Europera 5*," *Journal of the Royal Musical Association* 125, no. 1 (2000): 93–114 (third quote). Many thanks to Tamara Levitz for suggesting an especially eloquent translation of Gruhn's hard-working sentence.

57. Thomas Gartmann, " . . . *dass nichts sich von jemals vollendet ist* . . . ," 153, from a conversation between the author and Berio on September 27, 1993, in Freiburg.

58. Though a powerfully disenchanting film in its own right, Fritz Lehner's 1986 Schubert biopic *Notturno/Love Has Lied* does not shy away from depicting precisely such a scene—multiple times, no less.

59. Thomas Gartmann, " . . . *dass nichts sich von jemals vollendet ist* . . . ," 154.

60. An extensive multi-installment conversation ensued in the early 1960s over the correct rendering of this small rhythmic detail; see Desmond Shawe-Taylor et al., "Schubert as Written and as Performed," *Musical Times* 104, no. 1447 (1963): 626–28.

61. I owe the spotting of this quotation to Gartmann.

62. Italo Calvino, *If on a Winter's Night a Traveler*, trans. William Weaver (Orlando, FL: Harcourt, 1981), 176.

63. In his 1915 essay on the unconscious, Freud outlined four distinct characteristics of the "system Ucs.": "exemption from mutual contradiction, primary process (mobility of cathexes), timelessness, and replacement of external by psychical reality" (*SE* 14, 187). Of all the commentators on *Rendering*, Gartmann comes closest to articulating this quality: "The quotations, mostly hidden in subsidiary voices or in the bass and also through their combination barely discernible, unleash a nightmarish irritation [*lösen eine beklemmende Irritation aus*]. In their appeal to an unconscious memory, they function like a kind of dream world, or like a Romantic 'realm of the imagination' carried over into the present day." Thomas Gartmann, " . . . *dass nichts sich von jemals vollendet ist* . . . ," 133, translation mine.

64. See Jacques Lacan, *The Seminar of Jacques Lacan, Book XI: The Four Fundamental Concepts of Psychoanalysis, 1964*, ed. Jacques-Alain Miller, trans. Alan Sheridan (New York: Norton, 1998), 184: "What I have metaphorically called a headless subjectification, a subjectification without a subject, a bone."

65. It is perhaps no coincidence that the appearance of the very first connective episode in Berio—Schubert's first movement recalls clearly the entrance of proliferating birdsong in the prelude to Richard Strauss's *Der Rosenkavalier.*

66. See Christopher H. Gibbs, "'Poor Schubert': Images and Legends of the Composer," in *The Cambridge Companion to Schubert*, ed. Christopher H. Gibbs (Cambridge, England: Cambridge University Press, 1997), 36–55. "There is an intriguing psychological phenomenon whereby every listener constructs his or her own image of the composer. (In the language of psychoanalysis one might even refer to this process as something like 'transference' with the composer.) The affectionate expression 'our Schubert,' commonly used by Schubert's own family and friends, captures a possessiveness often directed toward beloved figures, although in Schubert's case the propriety was especially pronounced. The writer

Heinrich Hoffmann von Fallersleben, for example, described meeting Schubert for the first time and registered disappointment at the composer's ordinariness: Schubert 'is absolutely not different from any other Viennese; he speaks Viennese, like every other Viennese he has fine linen, a clean coat, a shiny hat and in his face, in his whole being, nothing that resembles my Schubert'" (37, citing Otto Erich Deutsch, ed., *Schubert: Memoirs by His Friends*, trans. Rosamond Ley and John Nowell (London: Adam and Charles Black, 1958).

67. Heinrich Kreissle von Hellborn, *Franz Schubert* (Vienna, 1865), 580; translation modified in Arthur Duke Coleridge, *The Life of Franz Schubert*, vol. 2 (London: Longmans, Green and Co., 1869), 255.

68. Christopher H. Gibbs, introduction to *The Cambridge Companion to Schubert*, 2: "That the public, for example, had to wait more than forty years for the premiere of the 'Unfinished' Symphony (D759) meant that a defining work, so revealing of Schubert's artistic maturity and compositional style, remained both 'outside' history and buried within it, the kernel of its eventual revision."

69. Christopher H. Gibbs, "'Poor Schubert,'" in *The Cambridge Companion to Schubert*, 52.

70. Adalbert Stifter, quoted in Leon Botstein, "Realism Transformed: Franz Schubert and Vienna," in *The Cambridge Companion to Schubert*, 26.

71. Luciano Berio-Franz Schubert, *Rendering*, preface.

72. See Leonard Bernstein, "Lecture Five: The Twentieth Century Crisis," in *The Unanswered Question: Six Talks at Harvard* (Cambridge, MA: Harvard University Press, 1976), 321. Bernstein was much admired by Berio, who had dedicated his *Sinfonia* to him; in particular Berio respected Bernstein's advocacy of Mahler. "Using Mahler was also a tribute to Leonard Bernstein who has done so much for his music," Berio said in a famous interview with Rossana Dalmonte; see Luciano Berio, Rossana Dalmonte, and Bálint András Varga, *Two Interviews*, ed. and trans. David Osmond-Smith (New York: Marion Boyars, 1985), 108.

73. See again David Osmond-Smith, "La mesure de la distance," and also for instance Christine Masts's program annotations for the work's performance by the Berliner Philharmoniker under Seymon Bychkov: "a poetic meditation on the fascination exerted by an ultimately insurmountable distance," https://www.digitalconcerthall.com/en/concert/2451.

CHAPTER TEN

1. Ligeti's "Galamb borong" received its considerably hyped world premiere on September 23, 1989, at the Berliner Festwochen by pianist Volker Banfield, who commissioned it along with "Fém"; the pair became the first two in a second book of études.

2. Stefano Gervasoni, notes to *An. Serenata con la complicità di Schubert*, available online at CEMAT (Centri musicali attrezzati), http://www.cematitalia.it/index.php?id=5.1&lg=it&pag=opera&wh=254, translation mine.

3. Dieter Schnebel, liner notes, *Schubert-Phantasie, für Orchester / Diapason / In Motu Proprio*, Sinfonieorchester des SWF, dir. Zoltan Peško et al., Wergo, WER 60108, 1985, LP.

4. Ibid.

5. "Programmheft der Wittener Tage für neue Musik 1991," cited in Vera Lumpe, liner notes, *Adriana Hölszky: Hängebrücken*, Nomos Quartett, Pellegrini Quartett, et al., cpo 999112–2, 2013, compact disc.

6. Jörn Peter Hiekel, "Brücken zur eigenen Zeit schlagen; Triokompositionen von Georg Kröll," *Musiktexte: Zeitschrift für neue Musik* 114 (2007–8): 13, translation mine.

7. Theodor Adorno, "Schubert" (1928), in *Night Music: Essays on Music 1928–1962*, ed. Rolf Tiedemann, trans. Wieland Hoban (London: Seagull Books, 2009), 32. In *Analyzing Schubert* (Cambridge, England: Cambridge University Press, 2011), Suzannah Clark points out how Carl Dahlhaus preserves the trope, purging it of its morbidities and rendering a more passably neutral analytical observation (167).

8. Rolf Riehm in a letter to Jörn Peter Hiekel from January 19, 1997, cited in Jörn Peter Hiekel, "Schubert und das eigene Selbstverständnis: Beispiele für die Rezeption in der Musik nach 1950," in *Dialekt ohne Erde . . . : Franz Schubert und das 20. Jahrhundert* (Graz: Universal Edition, 1998), 286.

9. Theodor Adorno, "Schubert" (1928), 45. While Hoban translates *zitiert* as the more neutral "refers," I wanted to preserve word's textual connotation.

10. In discussing Helmut Lachenmann's early *Schubertvariationen*, Rainer Nonnenmann paraphrases Adorno's line: "But nowhere is Lachenmann further from musical tradition than where he cites it." Rainer Nonnenmann, "Melancholie in Franz Schuberts Walzer in cis-Moll D 643 und Helmut Lachenmanns *Schubertvariationen* (1956)," *Archiv für Musikwissenschaft* 54, no. 4 (1997): 268.

11. Christoph von Blumröder, *Der Begriff "Neue Musik" im 20. Jahrhundert*, Freiburger Schriften zur Musikwissenschaft, Band XII (Munich and Salzburg: Musikverlag Emil Katzbichler, 1981), 146.

12. Ulrich Leyendecker, liner notes to *Streichquartett Nr. 3, Ricercar zur Kunst der Fuge, Musik in Deutschland, 1950–2000. Instrumentale Kammermusik, CD 2: Traditionelle Ensembles 1970–1990*, Auryn-Quartett et al., Sony BMG/Deutsche Musikrat, 74321 73590 2, 2007, compact disc.

13. See Poul Ruders's interview with Sven Erik Werner, "Den Indre Scene," in *Skrålys: Musik, Politik, Musik. Udvalgte Artikler af Sven Erik Werner* (Copenhagen: Edition Samfundet, 2007), 62–67.

14. Poul Ruders, program note to *Symfoni nr. 1 (1989)*, available at http://www.musicsalesclassical.com/composer/work/1342/19164.

15. Yayoi Uno Everett, *The Music of Louis Andriessen* (Cambridge, England: Cambridge University Press, 2006), 100.

16. Louis Andriessen and Maja Trochimczyk, "Dialogue 1: Learning," in *The Music of Louis Andriessen*, ed. Maja Trochimczyk (New York: Routledge, 2002), 10.

17. Yayoi Uno Everett, *The Music of Louis Andriessen*, 138.

18. The first two quotes come from Nadia Boulanger's review of the premiere of Stravinsky's *Octuor*; see "Concerts Koussevitsky," *Le Monde musical*, November 1923, cited in Scott Messing, *Neoclassicism in Music: From the Genesis of the Concept through the Schoenberg /Stravinsky Polemic* (Ann Arbor, MI: UMI Research Press, 1988), 133. The third quote comes from a letter from Bartók's wife to his mother, cited in Richard Taruskin, "Bartók and Stravinsky," in *The Danger of Music* (Berkeley: University of California Press, 2009), 135.

19. There is a history still to be written of Andriessen's co-reception of both Stravinsky *and* the Dutch early music movement.

20. Jürgen Habermas, "The New Obscurity: The Crisis of the Welfare State and the Exhaustion of Utopian Energies," trans. Phillip Jacobs, *Philosophy and Social Criticism* 11,

no. 2 (1986): 2. Originally published as "Die Neue Unübersichtlichkeit. Die Krise des Wohlfahrtsstaates und die Erschöpfung utopischer Energien," *Merkur* 39 (1985): 1–14.

21. Jürgen Habermas, "The New Obscurity," 2.

22. Perry Anderson, "Modernity and Revolution," *New Left Review* 144 (1984): 109.

23. Phillip Jacobs, the first English translator of Habermas's article, renders the phrase as "the future is occupied with the merely negative." Shierry Weber Nicholsen, who translated the essay as part of the 1989 English volume *The New Conservatism: Cultural Criticism and the Historians' Debate* (Cambridge, MA: MIT Press, 1989), provides to my mind the better translation, "the future is negatively cathected."

24. Theodor Adorno, *Aesthetic Theory*, trans. Robert Hullot-Kentor (Minneapolis: Minnesota University Press, 1997), 136.

25. The complete list of supporters includes official commissioners Instituts Français of Bremen and Bonn and the Fondation Louis Vuitton pour l'Opéra et la Musique; coproducer (along with the Festival d'Avignon and eventually the Opera Montpellier) Programme Musical France Culture; and with the assistance of the Association Française d'Action Artistique and the Mission du Bicentenaire de la Révolution Française et de la Déclaration des Droits de l'Homme.

26. Pascal Dusapin, "La Femme qui pleure," in *Une Musique en train de se faire* (Paris: Éditions du Seuil, 2009), 140–41. See also Michelle Biget, "Roméo et Juliette, ou La Révolution en Chantant," *Les Cahiers du CIREM* 12–13 (1989): 73–95, and, in the same volume, Michelle Biget, "Un Vrai Faux Livret D'opéra," 131–42.

27. Antoine Gindt, "Synopsis," in "Texte" for Pascal Dusapin, *Roméo et Juliette*, Groupe Vocal de France, Orchestre Symphonique de Mulhouse et al., dir. Luca Pfaff, Accord 201162, 1990, compact disc; my translation slightly modifies the one given in the booklet.

28. Ibid., 5.

29. Helmut Lachenmann, *Musik als existentielle Erfahrung*, ed. Josef Häusler (Wiesbaden: Breitkopf and Härtel, 1996), 399.

30. See David Fanning's rather damning review, with which I am inclined to agree, of a recent recording of the work in *Gramophone*, http://www.gramophone.co.uk/review/penderecki-symphony-no-4-adagio.

31. Given my reading, it ought not be surprising that I strongly disagree with Ewa Siemdaj's almost inscrutable assessment of the work in her article "Types of Climaxes in Krzysztof Penderecki's Symphonic Works," in *Krzysztof Penderecki: Musik im Kontext—Konferenzbericht Leipzig 2003* (Leipzig: Schröder, 2006), 182–201. More on point, interestingly enough, are the odd reviews and program notes of the work, which all stumble over its formal torpor while legitimizing both the work's and the composer's prestige. Ivan Hewitt, classical music critic for the *London Telegraph*, loses some credibility when he refers to "the little-known Polish composer Krzysztof Penderecki," but is otherwise on the mark: "The problem is that the music's strange mixture of styles undercut its bid for profundity. It's hard to take an agonised string fugue seriously, when it's suddenly cut off by a burst of 1960s avant-gardism such as a deafening brass cluster or a thundering roulade on tuned drums." See Ivan Hewett, "Penderecki's 4th Symphony, Bournemouth S.O., Lighthouse, Poole, Review: 'Fascinating but Frustrating,'" http://www.telegraph.co.uk/culture/music/classicalconcertreviews/11435521/Pendereckis-4th-Symphony-Bournemouth-S.O.-Lighthouse-Poole-review-fascinating-but-frustrating.html.

32. Another point of interest in the comparison is the love both composers share for the symphonies of Bruckner, and the difference in its "expression." Lachenmann allegedly expresses this love in private, as Richard Toop recalls in an anecdote about the composer playing piano arrangements of the Eighth Symphony in his composing *Häuschen*; see Richard Toop, liner notes, *Helmut Lachenmann 1: Tanzsuite mit Deutschlandlied; Reigen seliger Geister*, Arditti Quartet, Deutsches Symphonie-Orchester Berlin, dir. Olaf Henzold, Auvidis Montaigne MO 782019, 1994, compact disc. Penderecki, on the other hand, could be said to "play" Bruckner very much in public, on the symphonic stage itself, as virtually every program annotator and concert reviewer of his symphonies cannot refrain from pointing out. But these antithetical venues for the expression of beloved tradition shouldn't mask a crucial commonality: in the music of both composers, "Bruckner" *doesn't work*, the beloved tradition is broken, and broken with. The Brucknerian tension-arc *leading to* a transfigurative apotheosis is a prohibited topic. Either the arc or the apotheosis must be denied or undone; one may happen, but only at the cost of the other's failure.

33. One of the more remarkable aspects of the opera is how seriously it maintains an almost mimetic fidelity to the associations conjured by its numbers' titles. The music for "morning" is foggy and caffeinated at once, quick, incipient, comic, and breakable; the following number "before" carries more weight and consolidated forward motion, with longer extended passages building in ever-increasing waves; and so on.

34. Hans-Peter Jahn, "Anlaß und Absicht: Einige Bemerkungen Zu Mauricio Kagels Fragende Ode für Doppelchor, Bläser und Schlagzeug," in *Kagel . . . /1991* (Cologne: DuMont, 1991), 200.

35. Björn Heile, *The Music of Mauricio Kagel* (Aldershot, England: Ashgate, 2006), 158.

36. Jahn articulates especially well—and in perhaps a more charitable way than I would—the awkward but intimate ethical bond between *Fragende Ode* and Beethoven's Ninth, namely the way both scores' "impetus towards humanity" pushes them "from spiritual into the embarrassing. It is the emptiness of all great leaps." See Hans-Peter Jahn, "Anlaß und Absicht," 202.

37. Perry Anderson, *The Origins of Postmodernity* (London: Verso, 1998), 81, cited in T. J. Clark, "Origins of the Present Crisis," *New Left Review* 2 (2000): 86.

38. T. J. Clark, "Origins of the Present Crisis," 87–88.

39. Perry Anderson, *The Origins of Postmodernity*, 89.

40. Ibid., 92.

41. Ovid, *Metamorphoses: A New Verse Translation*, trans. David Raeburn (New York: Penguin Books, 2004), 110.

42. T. J. Clark, "Origins of the Present Crisis," 90. The goal of Clark's review was adamantly not to demonstrate something that by 2000 had long become a cliché: namely, the pointing out of the fact that "descriptions of postmodernism almost invariably thrive on a kind of blindness to the presence within *modernism* of the very features that are supposed to make postmodernism what it is" (ibid.). Clark cites Anderson as an example: "Virtually every aesthetic device or feature attributed to postmodernism—*bricolage* of tradition, play with the popular, reflexivity, hybridity, pastiche, figurality, decentering of the subject—could be found" (Perry Anderson, *Origins of Postmodernity*, 80).

43. T. J. Clark, "Origins of the Present Crisis," 91.

44. Ibid., 93.

45. For a good discussion on the dynamics of this and surrounding passages, see Karol Berger's fascinating book—surely one of the more exhaustive and sensitive treatments of musical modernity in the last few decades—*Bach's Cycle, Mozart's Arrow: An Essay on the Origins of Musical Modernity* (Berkeley: University of California Press, 2007), 251ff.

46. Slavoj Žižek, *The Parallax View* (Cambridge, MA: MIT Press, 2006), 35. Žižek is here talking not about music at all, but about "the Universal," and more specifically about Jameson's notion of a "singular modernity," but his words apply well to "Bach" as an object-cause of desire, reconfigured by the New Musical work into "modern" experience—that is, one of antagonism.

47. Ibid., 34.

48. Todd McGowan, in *Enjoying What We Don't Have: The Psychoanalytic Project of Psychoanalysis* (Lincoln: University of Nebraska Press, 2013), makes an especially strong recent case for the "political project of psychoanalysis" as a process of embracing impossibility—an anti-transcendental moment of resignation, of sinking into what one always already was, as prior to precisely a process of revolutionary change: "The cure is more a recognition of who one is rather than a transformation of one's subjectivity. Though psychoanalysis does view this recognition as the most radical kind of revolution, the revolution changes how the subject relates to its activity, not the activity itself" (4).

49. Georg Katzer, notes to a concert performance of *HEX*, 18, Zepernick Randspiele, Sankt-Annen-Kirche, http://lists.mur.at/pipermail/sumpfhahn/2010-July/000216.html.

50. Anaximander, as translated by Nietzsche in his *Die Philosophie im tragischen Zeitalter der Griechen* (1873); I adapt my translation from Dale Wilkinson, *Nietzsche and the Greeks* (New York: Bloomsbury, 2006), 111.

51. See Martha Sprigge, "Abilities to Mourn: Musical Commemoration in the German Democratic Republic (1945–1989)" (PhD diss., University of Chicago, 2013), 321–29. Sprigge also looks in considerably more depth at Katzer's *Aide-mémoire* for tape from 1983, a veritable nightmare of a piece and a prototype for both *Mon 1789* and its follow-up the next year, *Mein 1989*. For more commentary on the latter works, see Elaine Kelly, "Reflective Nostalgia and Diasporic Memory: Composing East Germany after 1989," in *Remembering and Rethinking the GDR: Multiple Perspectives and Plural Authenticities*, Palgrave Macmillan Memory Studies, ed. Anna Saunders and Debbie Pinfold (New York: Palgrave Macmillan, 2013), 122ff.

52. Martha Sprigge, "Abilities to Mourn," 328–29.

53. Ibid., 329.

54. Email correspondence with Armando Maggi, professor of Italian literature at the University of Chicago, August 25, 2015.

55. Salvatore Sciarrino, "A Statement on *La lontananza nostalgica utopica futura*," liner notes, *Luigi Nono: La lontananza nostalgica utopica futura*, Melise Mellinger and Salvatore Sciarrino, Kairos 0012102KAI, 2000, compact disc, 13. Stefan Drees offers a thicker exegesis in the notes to the same recording.

56. Interestingly, Nono's original title for the 1988 version of the piece, *La lontananza nostalgica-futura; utopica*, was added only after Nono "revised the composition completely and changed the entire score radically." Stefan Drees, liner notes, *Luigi Nono: La lontananza nostalgica utopica futura*, 17.

57. Gidon Kremer, "Luigi Nono: The Highways and Byways of a Friendship," liner notes, *Luigi Nono: La lontananza nostalgica utopica futura/"Hay Que Caminar" Soñando*,

Gidon Kremer, Tatjana Gridenko, et al., Deutsche Grammophon 474 326–2, 1992, compact disc, 4.

58. Salvatore Sciarrino, "A Statement on *La lontananza nostalgica utopica futura*," 13.

59. Stefan Drees, liner notes, *Luigi Nono: La lontananza nostalgica utopica futura*, 16.

60. Gidon Kremer, "Luigi Nono," 4.

61. Stefan Drees, "*La lontananza nostalgica utopica futura*," 16. For a much more substantial examination of *La lontananza*, see Stefan Drees, *Architektur und Fragment: Studien zu späten Kompositionen Luigi Nonos* (Saarbrücken, Germany: Pfau-Verlag, 1998).

62. Trent Leipert, "Feeling in the Cracks: Subjective Binds in European New Music" (PhD diss., University of Chicago, 2014), chapter 3, "Late Nono and the Uncertain Interval of the Subject," 61–113.

63. Luigi Nono, *La lontananza nostalgica utopica futura*, Versione KOE 232 (Milan: Ricordi, 1990), performance directions.

64. Christopher Burns, email to the author, August 22, 2015. Burns was a tremendous source of help in navigating the complexities of *La lontananza* and Nono's late work in general.

65. Luigi Nono, *La lontananza nostalgica utopica futura*, performance directions.

66. Luigi Pestalozza, liner notes, *Luigi Nono: La lontananza nostalgica utopica futura / "Hay Que Caminar" Soñando*," Deutsche Grammophon 474 326–2, 0.

67. Gidon Kremer, "Luigi Nono," 3.

68. Miranda Cuckson, "Nono's 'La Lontananza,'" http://www.mirandacuckson.com/2011/09/08/nonos-la-lontananza/. Cuckson and her collaborator Christopher Burns are dedicated performers of the work, and she has done considerable interpretive and analytical work on the score, including providing the first realization of Nono's directions to sing at various points. Some of her more salient observations on the work and her collaboration with Burns can be found on her website.

69. See Reinhart Koselleck, "The Temporalization of Utopia," in *The Practice of Conceptual History: Timing History, Spacing Concepts*, trans. Todd Presner (Stanford, CA: Stanford University Press, 2002), 84–99.

70. Derrida coins the term "hauntology" (a punning of "ontology," especially effective with a French haccent) in his *Specters of Marx: The State of the Debt, the Work of Mourning and the New International*, trans. Peggy Kamuf (New York: Routledge, 1994), 10ff. For an inspired and nuanced exegesis of the term in relation to music, see Tamara Levitz, "Hauntology: An Excursus on a Hermeneutics of Loss," in *Modernist Mysteries: Perséphone* (Oxford: Oxford University Press, 2012), 475–84.

71. Tom Rutherford-Johnson, "The Ghost of the Avant-Garde," *Guardian Online*, April 23, 2012, http://www.theguardian.com/music/musicblog/2012/apr/23/luigi-nono-future-creative-utopia.

72. This "collapsing" was the basis of a controversy Katzer courted with *Aide-mémoire*, which some East German critics found a confounding and potentially inaccurate representation of history. See Martha Sprigge, "Abilities to Mourn," 313–14.

73. Fredric Jameson, *Postmodernism, or the Logic of Late Capitalism* (Durham, NC: Duke University Press, 1991), 18.

74. See Simonetta Sargenti, "Tempo, Spazio, Suono in *La lontananza nostalgica utopica futura*, per violino e nastro, di Luigi Nono," *De Musica: Annuario in Divenire* 12 (2008): 17.

75. Sprigge and others have pointed out that *after* the neutralization of the GDR, something like longing does become significantly more prominent in the work of Katzer and his compatriots, though both Sprigge and Kelly take pains to emphasize that this longing is put in dialectical tension with a persisting analytical acuity.

76. Though it raises a line of argument that falls outside the aims of this book, one could certainly find in 1989 works that seem to have in common their own distance from those I discuss above. One thinks of, for instance, the works of Michael Nyman, quite a few of which were premiered that year.

77. On the intimate agon between Debussy and Wagner, see Robin Holloway's *locus classicus Debussy and Wagner* (London: Eulenberg, 1979); and Carolyn Abbate, "'Tristan' in the Composition of 'Pelléas,'" *Nineteenth-Century Music* (1981): 117–41. For a recent reappraisal see Gianmario Borio, "' . . . après Wagner et non pas d'après Wagner . . .': Réflexions sur les rapports entre le texte, la musique et l'image dans *Pelléas et Mélisande*," in *Regards sur Debussy*, ed. Myriam Chimènes and Alexandra Laederich (Paris: Fayard, 2013), 121–36.

78. David Metzer, *Musical Modernism at the Turn of the Twenty-First Century* (Cambridge, England: Cambridge University Press, 2009), 6ff.

79. "Katzer's works are, in essence, sites of confusion that can elicit an array of emotional reactions, particularly for those who witness their pasts for purchase in a manner that is equal parts distressing and nostalgic." Martha Sprigge, "Abilities to Mourn," 355.

80. Jean Laplanche and Jean-Bertrand Pontalis, "Fantasy and the Origins of Sexuality," in *Formations of Fantasy*, ed. Victor Burgin, James Donald, and Cora Kaplan (New York: Methuen, 1986), 5–34. Strikingly, Laplanche and Pontalis go back to an example from Freud—his first mention of the concept of a "primal fantasy"—that focuses on the modality of hearing; see 18ff.

81. Georges Bataille, *Inner Experience*, trans. Leslie Anne Boldt (Albany: State University of New York Press, 1988), 69; cited in Adrian Johnston, *Žižek's Ontology: A Transcendental Materialist Theory of Subjectivity* (Evanston, IL: Northwestern University Press, 2008).

82. Slavoj Žižek, *For They Know Not What They Do: Enjoyment as a Political Factor* (London: Verso, 2002), 197.

83. Penderecki's Symphony No. 2, "Christmas," an unrelieved dark half hour complete with morose quotations of *Stille Nacht*, was begun on Christmas Eve 1979 and premiered at the Warsaw Autumn festival in 1981. While Penderecki worked on his Third Symphony throughout the 1980s, he did not complete it until the mid-1990s.

84. See Rainer Nonnenmann, *Beethoven und Helmut Lachenmanns "Staub für Orchester" (1985/87). Analytische Betrachtung eines Werkes* (Saarbrücken: Pfau, 2000); Helmut Lachenmann, "Nicht mit Beethoven und nicht vor Späth," in Helmut Lachenmann, *Musik als existentielle Erfahrung*, ed. Josef Häusler (Wiesbaden: Breitkopf and Härtel, 1996), 186–90; Alastair Williams, *Music in Germany since 1968* (Cambridge, England: Cambridge University Press, 2013), 105–6.

CHAPTER ELEVEN

1. Louis Althusser, "Ideology and Ideological State Apparatuses," in *Lenin and Philosophy, and Other Essays*, trans. Ben Brewster (London: New Left Books, 1971), 132–33.

2. See in particular the chapters by Richard Adlington and Gianmario Borio in *Music and Protest since 1968*, ed. Beate Kutschke and Barley Norton (Cambridge, England: Cambridge University Press, 2013). My scandalously brief list ought not imply there were not a great many works that could be grouped under the signifier "revolution" from the mid-1960s through at least the early 1970s. And these works stretched their network to the representative extremes of what could be thought as New Music at the time; I might suggest as such poles Bernd Alois Zimmermann's *Requiem für einen jungen Dichter* (1967–69) on the one hand, and Cornelius Cardew's 1969 cofounding of the Scratch Orchestra and his *The Great Learning* (1968–71) on the other. There is, happily, much excellent recent work on the topic of composition and political activism in the late 1960s; see among other works Eric Drott, *Music and the Elusive Revolution: Cultural Politics and Political Culture in France, 1968–1981* (Berkeley: University of California Press, 2011); Robert Adlington, *Composing Dissent: Avant-Garde Music in 1960s Amsterdam* (Oxford: Oxford University Press, 2013); Beate Kutschke, *Neue Linke / Neue Musik: Kulturtheorien und künstlerische Avantgarde in den 1960er und 70er Jahren* (Cologne: Böhlau, 2007); and Robert Adlington, ed., *Sound Commitments: Avant-Garde Music and the Sixties* (Oxford: Oxford University Press, 2009).

3. Søren Kierkegaard, *Repetition and Philosophical Crumbs*, trans. M.G. Piety, with introduction and notes by Edward F. Mooney (Oxford: Oxford University Press, 2009), 38.

4. Luigi Nono, "The Historical Reality of Music Today," first published in English in *The Score* 27 (1960): 41. The authorship of the text has long been a source of confusion. It seems it was actually not written by Nono himself, but by Lachenmann, who was at that time Nono's student in Venice: "I was the ghostwriter of this piece. . . . They were entirely Nono's critical thoughts but entirely my words, and I put my whole heart into it. Today I can see it was wrong-footed, but then it was helpful for the debate." See Philip Clark, "The Human Torch," *The Wire* 228 (2003): 26. See also Massimo Mila and Luigi Nono, *Nulla di oscuro tra noi. Lettere 1952–1988*, ed. Angela Ida De Benedictis and Venieri Rizzardi (Milan: il Saggiatore S.P.A., 2010), 23.

5. There is here a vast bibliography, but two particular texts stick out in relation to Bach and New Music: Rudolf Stefan's canonical "Johann Sebastian Bach und die Anfänge der Neuen Musik," *Melos/Neue Zeitschrift für Musik* 2, no. 1 (1976): 3–7; and the proceedings from the ambitious 1984 Kassel conference *Bach im 20. Jahrhundert*, ed. Kurt Fischer (Kassel: Kasseler Musiktage, 1985).

6. "'Mortify the past.' The past as a wish that creates the probability pattern of the future? Did John of the Cross mean that, and the fear of changing the past which is fear of the present? I mortify my past every time I sit at the piano to compose." Igor Stravinsky and Robert Craft, *Dialogues and a Diary* (New York: Doubleday, 1968), 128.

7. Daniel K.L. Chua, *The "Galitzin" Quartets of Beethoven* (Princeton, NJ: Princeton University Press, 1995), 7.

8. Debussy, letter to Chausson, October 2, 1893, in *Debussy Letters*, ed. François Lesure and Roger Nichols, trans. Roger Nichols (London: Faber, 1987), 56.

9. This last register arguably reinstalls Berio into the chain, given that his palpable influence on Dusapin involves the stylistic refashioning of "negative algorithms," ways of fashioning melodies *without* melody, tonality *without* tonic, scenario *without* scene.

10. Joseph Kerman, *Opera as Drama*, rev. ed. (Berkeley: University of California Press, 1988), 141; Pierre Boulez, "Reflections on *Pelléas et Melisande*," in Pierre Boulez,

Orientations, ed. J. J. Nattiez and trans. Martin Cooper (Cambridge, MA: Harvard University Press, 1986), 317.

11. Kerman's complaint comes after a marvelous reading of the opera, unambivalent in its celebration of Debussy's achievement. But it seems to me that Kerman has performed an exemplary good-object/bad-object split, and all the more surprisingly, given how he asserts near the chapter's beginning that Debussy's labors cannot be extricated from the whole of Maeterlinck's system. See Joseph Kerman, *Opera as Drama*, 155.

12. Critics have long struggled to read the strange silences of *Pelléas*, and my rushed reading does not speak to them all, but to a strain originally formulated (so far as I can tell) in Kerman's book, and enjoying something of a renaissance beginning in the aughts; see Jann Pasler, "Mélisande's Charm and the Truth of Her Music," in *Rethinking Debussy*, ed. Elliott Antokoletz and Marianne Wheeldon (Oxford: Oxford University Press, 2011); and especially Peter Dayan, "Nature, Music, and Meaning in Debussy's Writings," *19th-Century Music* 28, no. 3 (2005): 214–29; as well as Peter Dayan's remarkable book from the following year, *Music Writing Literature, from Sand via Debussy to Derrida* (Aldershot, England: Ashgate, 2006), 55–75. For a swift assessment of Beckett's well-known "debt" to Maeterlinck, see Ashley Taggart, "Maeterlinck and Beckett: Paying Lip-Service to Silence," in *Samuel Beckett: Debts and Legacies*, ed. Erik Tonning, Matthew Feldman, Matthijs Engelberts, and Dirk Van Hulle, no. 22 (2010) in the journal series *Samuel Beckett Today/Aujourd'hui* (Amsterdam: Rodopi), 93–106.

13. Tom Eyers, in his *Lacan and the Concept of the "Real"* (New York: Palgrave Macmillan, 2012), offers the most careful and inspired analysis I know of Lacan's conception of the image of the other, and traces its development from the early work on the "mirror stage" through the early and "mature" formulations of the *objet a*. See in particular "From 'ideal-ego' i(a) to *objet petit a*" in chapter 2, "The Imaginary and the Real," 31–35.

CHAPTER TWELVE

1. My argument in this section relies heavily on Mladen Dolar's two recent accounts, cogent and clarifying, of *tyche* and *automaton* in both Aristotle and Lacan; see Mladen Dolar, "Tyche, clinamen, den," *Continental Philosophy Review* 46 (2013): 223–39; and "Which Repetition?" (October 2013), an unpublished manuscript existing in PDF form that partially overlaps with "Tyche, clinamen, den." Readers will find a number of the manuscript's arguments, and some of its prose, rehearsed in an earlier essay: Mladen Dolar, "Comedy and Its Double," in *Schluß mit der Komödie!: zur schleichenden Vorherrschaft des Tragischen in unserer Kultur*, ed. Robert Pfaller (Vienna: Sonderzahl, 2005), 181–209. Slavoj Žižek, *Less Than Nothing: Hegel and the Shadow of Dialectical Materialism* (London: Verso, 2012), addresses many of the same issues, but I find Dolar's argument considerably more concise and practicable.

2. Alan Sheridan's translation of Lacan's *Seminar XI* preserves the French *tuché*. I will follow Mladen Dolar's lead, however, and refer to it by its "original" spelling, *tyche*.

3. Aristotle, *The Basic Writings of Aristotle*, ed. Richard McKeon (New York: Modern Library, 2001), 777 (*automaton*), 246–47 (*tyche*). For a classic (non-Lacanian) account of *tyche* and *automaton*, see Jonathan Lear, *Aristotle: The Desire to Understand* (Cambridge, England: Cambridge University Press, 1988), 36ff. For an inspired discussion of the concepts

in relation to (early) modernity, see Michael Witmore, *Culture of Accidents: Unexpected Knowledges in Early Modern England* (Stanford, CA: Stanford University Press, 2001), 33–34.

4. See Slavoj Žižek, "Introduction: Lacan with (x)," in *Lacan: The Silent Partners*, ed. Slavoj Žižek (London: Verso, 2006), 1–3.

5. Jacques Lacan, *The Seminar of Jacques Lacan, Book XI: The Four Fundamental Concepts of Psychoanalysis, 1964*, ed. Jacques-Alain Miller, trans. Alan Sheridan (New York: W. W. Norton, 1998), 53–54.

6. There is a rich field of investigation into the influence of information theory and early cybernetics on Lacan's work, and especially his conception of the unconscious. For a concise elaboration of the Lacanian unconscious as a site of *automaton*-like assemblage, see Bruce Fink, *The Lacanian Subject: Between Language and Jouissance* (Princeton, NJ: Princeton University Press, 1996), 20–24. For a more substantial and historically oriented discussion, see Lydia H. Lui, *The Freudian Robot: Digital Media and the Future of the Unconscious* (Chicago: University of Chicago, 2011), chapter 4, "The Cybernetic Unconscious."

7. Sigmund Freud, "Recent and Indifferent Material," in *The Interpretation of Dreams*, *SE* 4/1, 165.

8. Jacques Lacan, *The Seminar, Book XI*, 67.

9. See Mladen Dolar, "Tyche, clinamen, den," 227.

10. Dolar cites the effect of comic repetition as a classic example, whereby the simple reiteration of an utterly unfunny line can balloon into volatile hilarity. See Jude Stewart's account—itself quite funny—of "the mystery of *Dinner for One*," an early-1960s British television sketch that has attained enormous popularity in Germany (to the point of becoming a New Year's Eve ritual), and is anchored by the constant refrain "Same procedure as *every* year, James." http://www.slate.com/articles/arts/culturebox/2005/12/the_mystery_of_dinner_for_one.html.

11. Mladen Dolar, "Tyche, clinamen, den," 227.

12. Ibid., 228.

13. Alain Badiou and Barbara Cassin, *Il n'y pas de rapport sexuel: Deux leçons sur "L'Étourdit" de Lacan* (Paris: Editions Fayard, 2010), 83–84, cited in Mladen Dolar, "Tyche, clinamen, den" 237. Badiou and Cassin are not discussing *tyche* in this passage, but rather a related concept—related through Lacan's insistence—from Democritus: *den*, a word that the philosopher coins from *to meden*, meaning "not-being" or "what-is-not"; *den* is simultaneously also not being, or "what-is," *to den*; rather, it remains a surplus to the void, and subtraction from the one. In "Tyche, clinamen, den" Dolar considers it, along with *tyche* and *clinamen* (after Lucretius), as one of three ways of conceptualizing "the birth of the object out of the spirit of ancient philosophy" ("object" here relating to the Lacanian "Real object").

14. Jacques Lacan, "Seminar on 'The Purloined Letter,'" in *Écrits: The First Complete Edition in English*, trans. Bruce Fink (New York: W. W. Norton, 2006), 17.

15. Sigi Jöttkandt makes a case for Badiou's inclusion in the pair Lacan-Kierkegaard, maintaining that "in every name we give to the Event there is something that cannot be accounted for—nonsense, an excess escapes every attempt to count to One." Jöttkandt also makes the compelling claim for Badiou as "a profoundly *comic* thinker," for reasons that would suggest Lacan's inclusion. See Sigi Jöttkandt, "No Three without Two: Badiou with

Lacan with Kierkegaard," in *Kierkegaard and Political Theory: Religion, Aesthetics, Politics and the Intervention of the Single Individual*, ed. Armen Avanessian and Sophie Wennerscheid (Copenhagen: Museum Tusculanum Press, 2014), 236.

16. Jacques Lacan, *On the Names-of-the-Father*, trans. Bruce Fink (Cambridge, England: Polity Press, 2013), 61.

17. Ibid., 57: "When anxious, the subject is affected, as I told you, by the Other's desire, *d(A)* here on the board. The subject is affected by that desire in an immediate manner, which cannot be dialectized. It is in this respect that anxiety is, among the subject's affects, the one that does not mislead [*ne trompe pas*]." See also Tom Eyers, *Lacan and the Concept of the "Real"* (New York: Palgrave Macmillan, 2012), 31ff, for a discussion of this and proximate passages.

18. As I cited in chapter 2, Žižek in particular is adamant that "Lacan gets Hegel wrong, perhaps even very wrong," but it could be argued that Žižek's strongly revisionist Hegel in many ways comes to resemble Lacan's Kierkegaard. The matter is in any case a complex one. See "'From Lacan to Hegel': Interview with Slavoj Žižek," in *Žižek and His Contemporaries: On the Emergence of the Slovenian Lacan*, ed. Jones Irwin and Helena Motoh (New York: Bloomsbury, 2014), 130ff.

19. I am here adapting the original French transcript of Lacan's *Seminar XI*, April 15, 1964, since the corresponding Sheridan translation (128) is somewhat misleading.

20. Lacanians would doubtless qualify all these points. To take one instance, in many cases symptoms cannot be clarified without first being constructed in the process of analysis. But in general, Lacan reenacts and intensifies Freud's famous moment of rhetorical *litotes*, or "diminution" regarding the promise of happiness ("much will be gained if we succeed in transforming your hysterical misery into common unhappiness"), many times, among them in *Seminar VII*. See Jacques Lacan, *The Seminar of Jacques Lacan, Book VII: The Ethics of Psychoanalysis, 1959–60*, ed. Jacques-Alain Miller, trans. with notes by Dennis Porter (New York: W. W. Norton, 1992), 392–93.

21. To paraphrase Philip Larkin, who pretty much had it right, your mum and dad, they lack you up, they fill you with the lacks they had, and add some extra, just for you.

22. These latter paraphrases are closer to what Lacan meant by the phrase, and to its original reference, which Bruce Fink traces to Jacques Cazotte's fantastic novel *Le diable amoureux* (1772), specifically the annotated French edition by Annalisa Bottacin (Milan: Cisalpino-La Goliardica, 1983), 56–57.

23. See for instance Jacques Lacan, "The Subversion of the Subject and the Dialectic of Desire," in *Écrits*, 690.

24. Sigmund Freud, "On Beginning the Treatment" (1913), in *SE* 12, 130.

25. Sigmund Freud, "Analysis Terminable and Interminable" (1937a), in *SE* 23, 209–54.

26. As far as institutional matters go, the variable-length session was arguably Lacan's most controversial invention.

27. See Heinz Hartmann, Ernst Kris, and Rudolph M. Loewenstein, "Notes on the Theory of Aggression," *Psychoanalytic Study of the Child* 3, no. 4 (1949): 14. For the clearest exposition of Lacan's critique of analytic orientations based on identification and ego-fortification, see Bruce Fink, "Lacan's Critique of the Ego Psychology Troika: Hartman, Kris, and Loewenstein," in *Lacan to the Letter: Reading "Écrits" Closely* (Minneapolis: University of Minnesota Press, 2004), 38–62.

28. Jacques Lacan, *The Seminar, Book XI*, 274, 276.

29. Jacques Lacan, "The Function and Field of Speech and Language in Psychoanalysis" (1953), in *Écrits*, 213, 217.

30. In *Subjectivity and Otherness* (Cambridge, MA: MIT Press, 2007), Lorenzo Chiesa points out that desire—at least, when it remains veiled by fantasy—cannot but lead to repetition: "The desire of the Other cannot be *desired* directly, and so one *repeats* one's desire for it" (150).

31. Mladen Dolar, "Which Repetition?"

32. Tom Eyers (*Lacan and the Concept of the "Real"*) and Lorenzo Chiesa (*Subjectivity and Otherness*) provide excellent recent demonstrations of Lacan's "super-periodic" consistencies.

33. Jacques Lacan, "The Function and Field of Speech and Language in Psychoanalysis," 249: "Analysis can have as its goal only the advent of true speech and the subject's realization of his history in its relation to a future."

34. Jacques Lacan, *The Seminar of Jacques Lacan, Book I: Freud's Papers on Technique, 1953–54*, ed. Jacques-Alain Miller, trans. with notes by John Forrester (New York: W. W. Norton, 1991), 232.

35. Jacques Lacan, *The Seminar of Jacques Lacan, Book VII*, 303–4. See also Sigmund Freud, "Inhibitions, Symptoms and Anxiety" (1925–26), in *SE* XX (1925–26), 75–176.

36. Bruce Fink, *The Lacanian Subject*, 79.

37. Jacques Lacan, "Proposition of 9 October 1967 on the Psychoanalyst of the School," trans. Russell Grigg, *Analysis* 6 (1995): 1–13. First published by Lacan himself in 1967, the "Proposition" still generates controversy among Lacanians, and Lacan himself expressed ambivalence and regret about it late in life. In it, he laid out his conception of "the pass," an "institutional framework" through which analysands testify to their completion of the analytic process, putting into words what—in the spirit of analysis itself—shouldn't after all remain a mystical or ineffable experience. See Dylan Evans, "pass," in *An Introductory Dictionary of Lacanian Psychoanalysis* (London: Routledge, 1996), 138–39, for a brief summary. For a more substantial discussion see Anne Dunand, "The End of Analysis (II)," in *Reading Seminar XI: Lacan's Four Fundamental Concepts of Psychoanalysis*, ed. Richard Feldstein, Bruce Fink, and Maire Jaanus (Albany, NY: SUNY Press, 1994), 251–56.

38. Dylan Evans, "end of analysis," in *An Introductory Dictionary of Lacanian Psychoanalysis* (London: Routledge, 1996), 55.

39. Colette Soler, "The Aim of the Analytic Act," *Umbr(a): Incurable* 1 (2006): 61.

40. Ian Parker, a practicing Lacanian with great interest and enterprise in the critical implementation and practicability of Lacan's teachings, expresses due skepticism of the "high Lacanese" formulation of the end of analysis. Ian Parker, *Lacanian Psychoanalysis: Revolutions in Psychoanalysis* (New York: Routledge, 2011), 13.

41. Jacques Lacan, *The Seminar, Book XI*, 274. Accepting different nuances, this is a widespread precept across the many psychoanalytic orientations. Jonathan Lear, a philosopher and practicing analyst (trained in Freudian technique and that of Hans Loewald), writes eloquently, and in a distinctly Kierkegaardian vein, of how "the process [of analysis] is unending," and that "being a psychoanalyst is in part a never-ending task of bringing oneself back to the activity of being a psychoanalyst." Jonathan Lear, *Therapeutic Action: An Earnest Plea for Irony* (London: Karnac Books, 2003), 32. Lear expands significantly on the

connections between psychoanalysis and what Kierkegaard conceives as a "calling" in *A Case for Irony* (Cambridge, MA: Harvard University Press, 2011).

42. To call a protester a "hysteric" is, of course, a classic master-discourse move, and often a sexist one, too: the master, refusing to budge, tells the protesters their demands are ridiculously unrealistic, they are out of their heads, et cetera. Lacan does not apply the term pejoratively, however, but understands it structurally: the hysterical structure, as Mark Bracher puts it, "is in force wherever a discourse is dominated by the speaker's symptom . . . as the failure of the subject, $, to coincide with or be satisfied by the master signifiers offered by society and embraced as the subject's ideals." The hysteric's discourse is, for Lacan, an extremely productive one, a "motor force," as Fink puts it. See Bruce Fink, *The Lacanian Subject*, 133–35; and Mark Bracher, "On the Psychological and Social Functions of Language," in *Lacanian Theory of Discourse: Subject, Structure, and Society*, ed. Mark Bracher, Marshall W. Alcorn, and Ronald J. Corthell (New York: New York University Press, 1994), 122.

43. Eric Santner, *The Royal Remains: The People's Two Bodies and the Endgames of Sovereignty* (Chicago: University of Chicago Press, 2011), 6–7. Santner is not writing of "discourses" but "cultures" in this passage, but I think the dynamic—and the collective experience of this dynamic—are the same. Santner adds a crucial detail, the assumption by the subject of the very qualities being defended against: "In numerous spheres of activity, strategies of self-preservation can, in short, become a form of mortification; in each case, out of a fear of breakdown or dying, of exposing oneself to what is perceived to be mortal risk, one preemptively deadens oneself" (7).

44. Paul Verhaeghe, *Beyond Gender: From Subject to Drive* (New York: Other Press, 2001), 31.

45. Mladen Dolar, "Hegel as the Other Side of Psychoanalysis," in *Jacques Lacan and the Other Side of Psychoanalysis: Reflections on Seminar XVII, SIC 6* (Durham, NC: Duke University Press, 2006), 152. Lacan speaks of the analyst trying "to represent, in some way, the discourse's reject-producing effect [*effet de rejet*]." See Jacques Lacan, *The Seminar of Jacques Lacan, Book XVII: The Other Side of Psychoanalysis, 1969–1970*, ed. Jacques-Alain Miller, trans. with notes by Russell Grigg (New York: W. W. Norton, 2007), 44.

46. Mark Bracher, "On the Psychological and Social Functions of Language," 125: "Mythic knowledge [as S_2] . . . is a disjoint knowledge, a form that is completely alien to the discourse of science."

47. Verhaeghe, following Freud's gradual realization that it was either useless or disadvantageous to tell his analysands what was "wrong with them," suggests that the knowledge in the analyst's discourse is not so much repressed by the analyst as prohibited, somewhat like real but inadmissible evidence in a court of law.

48. The *Poordjeli* signifier, famous in Lacanian circles, was unearthed in an analysis conducted by Serge Leclaire. For a recounting of the analysis, see Serge Leclaire, *A Child Is Being Killed: On Primary Narcissism and the Death Drive*, trans. Marie-Claude Hays (Stanford, CA: Stanford University Press, 1998), 36ff.

49. Eyers is here referring to the *trait unaire* (unary trait) derived from Freud's *einziger Zug*. The unary trait is often identified with the master signifier, and here I follow Bruce Fink's formulation in *The Lacanian Subject*; but as Eyers points out, the former concept is a shadowy one, bridging the divide between imaginary and symbolic in ways that generate inevitable ambiguity. See Tom Eyers, *Lacan and the Concept of the "Real,"* 55ff.

50. Jacques Lacan, *The Seminar of Jacques Lacan, Book XX: Encore, 1972–73, On Feminine Sexuality, the Limits of Love and Knowledge*, ed. Jacques-Alain Miller, trans. with notes by Bruce Fink (New York: W. W. Norton, 1998), 11ff. Lacan's discussion of the master signifier as *la bêtise* alludes to Freud's proxy case on "Little Hans," who called his horse phobia *Dummheit*, translated by Strachey as "nonsense."

51. The master signifier seems perpetually to oscillate between the sublime and the simpleton, between the Hebrew God's all-knowing reply to Moses, *Ehyeh asher ehyeh* (I am that I am, or I will be what I will be) and Popeye's infinitely unself-conscious "I yam what I yam." Regarding angelic smiles, see Jacques Lacan, *The Seminar, Book XX*, 20–21.

52. Some readers of Lacan focus less on the psycho-archaeological aspect of spoken master signifiers, and more on the logic of liberation implied in the act of speaking "new" master signifiers that are one's "own"; the ambiguity is there in Lacan's *Seminar XVII*. See for instance Mark Bracher, "On the Psychological and Social Functions of Language," who qualifies this liberation by reminding that production of master signifiers "does not constitute a radical break with tyranny and an accession to freedom [since] the subject remains in thrall to a master signifier." But unlike in the master's discourse, here "master signifiers are produced by the subject rather than imposed upon the subject from the outside . . . a little less oppressive . . . less absolute, exclusive, and rigid in its establishment of the subject's identity, and more open, fluid, processual—constituted, in a word, by relativity and textuality" (123–24).

53. Bruce Fink, *The Lacanian Subject*, 135.

54. Mladen Dolar, "Which Repetition?" Dolar is here alluding to Hegel's famous formulation, in the *Grundlinien der Philosophie des Rechts* (1820), that "What is reasonable is actual; and what is actual, is reasonable" (*Was vernünftig ist, das ist Wirklich; und was wirklich ist, das ist vernünftig*).

55. Mladen Dolar, "Which Repetition?"

CHAPTER THIRTEEN

1. Fredric Jameson, *A Singular Modernity* (London: Verso, 2002), 135.

2. In the as-yet-unwritten book about Lacan, Freud, and the anxiety of influence, Aaron Copland's famous point about Mahler and Beethoven might provide some insight, not least into Lacan's actual style(s) of performance, his "revisionary ratios": "The difference between listening to Beethoven and listening to Mahler is the difference between watching a great man walk down the street and watching a great actor act the part of a great man walking down the street." Howard Pollack, *Aaron Copland: The Life and Work of an Uncommon Man* (New York: H. Holt, 1999), 63.

3. Hugo Friedrich, *The Structure of Modern Poetry*, trans. Joachim Neugroschel (Evanston, IL: Northwestern University Press, 1974), 7.

4. Hugo Friedrich, *The Structure of the Modern Lyric*, trans. Joachim Neugroschel (New York: Columbia University Press, 1974), 8.

5. Jacques Lacan, *Le Séminaire de Jacques Lacan, livre VI, Le Désir et son interprétation, 1958–1959*, session on April 8, 1959, unpublished.

6. Lacan founded the EFP with, among other things, a "Founding Act." Dedicated to "[restoring] the cutting edge of [Freud's] discovery" and "[denouncing] the deviations and

compromises that blunt its progress while degrading its use," the document reads as both a document of its "high modernist" moment and also a continuation of the great modernist manifestos in the first two decades of the century. Jacques Lacan, "Founding Act," trans. Jeffrey Mehlman, *October* 40 (1987): 96.

7. T. J. Clark, "Clement Greenberg's Theory of Art," *Critical Inquiry* 9, no. 1 (1982): 153–54. Clark, unsurprisingly for a social historian of art, is emphatic that this negativity has a social basis. It is a form of mirroring, or even mimesis, of what it sees around it: its "dance of negation" is a complex re-creation of "the decline of ruling-class elites, the absence of a 'social base' for artistic production, the paradox involved in making bourgeois art in the absence of a bourgeoisie" (154). Clark's thesis is important to Ben Earle as well, and becomes a crucial part of his argument in *Luigi Dallapiccola and Musical Modernism in Fascist Italy* (Cambridge, England: Cambridge University Press, 2012).

8. Perry Anderson, *In the Tracks of Historical Materialism* (London: Verso, 1983), 37, cited in Paul Sheehan, "Postmodernism and Philosophy," in *The Cambridge Companion to Postmodernism*, ed. Steven Connor (Cambridge, England: Cambridge University Press, 2004), 25. Sheehan makes precisely this move.

9. "Every real signifier is, as such, a signifier that signifies nothing. The more the signifier signifies nothing, the more indestructible it is." Jacques Lacan, *The Seminar, Book III: The Psychoses, 1955–56*, trans. Russell Grigg (London: Routledge, 1993), 185. See also Raymond Williams's comments on Freud and Lacan in "Marxism and Literature," in *Politics and Letters: Interviews with New Left Review*, introduction by Geoff Dyer (London: Verso, 2015). Williams is keen on assessing Lacan as a writer—as opposed to a scientist—while I think it is precisely Lacan's clinical teachings that make the strongest case for thinking of his relationship to aesthetic modernism.

10. I say "migrates (back)" in reference to Freudian psychoanalysis, which was unquestionably bound up in uncountable ways with the currents of early twentieth-century aesthetic modernism, and which Lacan considered his entire teachings and practice a "return to." The thesis of psychoanalysis's propinquity to modernism, their breathing of the same timely spirit, has been rehearsed constantly in the historical literature on psychoanalysis (Peter Gay and Carl Schorske being two classic examples), but to my knowledge, there is here too a limited attempt to think more analytically about the structural parallels between, say, psychoanalytic and aesthetic techniques. For an interesting recent historical appraisal of psychoanalysis *as* a modernism, see Eli Zaretsky, *Secrets of the Soul: A Social and Cultural History of Psychoanalysis* (New York: Vintage Books, 2005).

11. In his more than fifty books, Žižek mentions living composers only—actually, less than—a handful of times. Lacan was notoriously stingy in addressing music, even more than Freud. There is some evidence he was holding back; see "Lacan, Music: Judith Miller Talks with Diego Masson," trans. Asunción Alvarez, *Lacanian Ink* 39 (2012): 52–65.

12. I thank Brian Kane for lightly dousing the "resonance" trope with some needed terminological acid.

13. Shoshana Felman, "To Open the Question," *Yale French Studies* 55–56 (1977): 5–10.

14. At the least, I might suggest that any future "opening of the question" in a Lacanian direction would do well to head off at the pass as quickly as possible—or deconstruct as patiently as possible—the notion of music as the other of language, the Real or imaginary to its symbolic.

15. Shoshana Felman, "To Open the Question," 8.

16. Or "deconstructionist." It could be said that Felman's (non-pejoratively) negative approach to "authority" here, seeking to undo and re-implicate both literature and psychoanalysis in at least a *potentially* more collaborative relationship, relies on a (non-vanishing, but still spectral) mediator—Derrida—who allows a temporary sublimation of the opposition *interpret(read)/analyze* into the term *deconstruct.*

17. Jacques Lacan, *The Seminar of Jacques Lacan, Book III: The Psychoses, 1955–1956*, ed. Jacques-Alain Miller, trans. with notes by Russell Grigg (New York: W. W. Norton, 1993), 185.

18. Fredric Jameson, *A Singular Modernity*, 136.

19. Ibid., 137.

20. Ibid.

21. Rainer Maria Rilke, "Der Engel," in *Neue Gedichte* (Frankfurt: Insel, 1974), 37; for an English translation, see Rainer Maria Rilke, *New Poems*, trans. Edward Snow (Boston: North Point Press, 1984), 83, cited in Fredric Jameson, *A Singular Modernity*, 135.

22. Fredric Jameson, *A Singular Modernity*, 136.

23. Perry Anderson, "Modernity and Revolution," *New Left Review* 144 (1984): 104–5.

24. Fredric Jameson, *A Singular Modernity*, 136.

25. Bruce Fink, "Fantasies and the Fundamental Fantasy," in *Against Understanding, Vol. 2: Cases and Commentary in a Lacanian Key* (New York: Routledge, 2014), 47.

26. Mark Bracher, "On the Psychological and Social Functions of Language," in *Lacanian Theory of Discourse: Subject, Structure, and Society*, ed. Mark Bracher, Marshall W. Alcorn, and Ronald J. Corthell (New York: New York University Press, 1994), 126. In his own text, Bracher is not explicit about this redaction, and it is not clear why it fails to appear in the official version prepared by Miller.

27. Jacques Lacan, *The Seminar of Jacques Lacan, Book XVII: The Other Side of Psychoanalysis, 1969–1970*, ed. Jacques-Alain Miller, trans. with notes by Russell Grigg (New York: W. W. Norton, 2007), 207.

28. Jacques Lacan, "Appendix A: Analyticon," in ibid., 208.

29. Ibid., 99.

30. Slavoj Žižek / F. W. J. von Schelling, *The Abyss of Freedom / Ages of the World*, trans. Judith Norman (Ann Arbor: University of Michigan Press, 1997), 181.

31. Mladen Dolar, "Tyche, clinamen, den," *Continental Philosophy Review* 46 (2013): 228.

32. See Sigmund Freud's famous evocation of the psyche as an archaeological site in *Civilization and Its Discontents.* See also Carl E. Schorske, "Freud: The Psychoarcheology of Civilizations," in *The Cambridge Companion to Freud* (Cambridge, England: Cambridge University Press, 1991), 8–24. Whitney Davis, perhaps the most astute writer on the relation between psychoanalysis and archaeology, conceives of psychoanalysis as "a version of impossible archaeology, a not-archaeology." Whitney Davis, *Replications: Archaeology, Art History, Psychoanalysis* (University Park, PA: Penn State University Press, 1996), 30.

CHAPTER FOURTEEN

1. Rainer Maria Rilke, *The Notebooks of Malte Laurids Brigge*, trans. Stephen Mitchell (New York: Vintage, 1990), 22–23. I thank Eric Santner for drawing my attention to this passage in his remarkable reading of the novel in *The Royal Remains: The People's Two Bodies*

and the Endgames of Sovereignty (Chicago: University of Chicago Press, 2011), 188–244. Citing Zupančič on the Lacanian *objet a*, Santner assesses the novel as "among the more compelling literary efforts we possess that try to show us what this labor might look like [of taking] on not simply one's finitude but the 'hole in finitude'"—*without* trying to fill it in" (210).

2. Eric Santner, *The Royal Remains*, 211.

3. Among other explorations of Kierkegaard's influence on Rilke, see Leonardo Lisi, "Rainer Maria Rilke: Unsatisfied Love and the Poetry of Living," in *Kierkegaard's Influence on Literature, Criticism and Art. Tome I: The Germanophone World*, Kierkegaard Research: Sources, Reception and Resources 10, ed. Jon Stewart (Aldershot, England: Ashgate, 2013), 213–35.

4. Mladen Dolar, "Which Repetition?" (October 2013), unpublished manuscript existing in PDF form.

5. Hugo von Hofmannsthal, *The Lord Chandos Letter: And Other Writings*, trans. Joel Rotenberg, introduction by John Banville (New York: New York Review of Books, 2005), 121.

6. While a great deal has been made of the biographical connections between Hofmannsthal and Chandos, Erwin Kobel's point still holds: Hofmannsthal achieves in his "letter" a kind of absolute difference from his "role." See Erwin Kobel, *Hugo Von Hofmannsthal* (Berlin: De Gruyter, 1970).

7. In a number of writings, Keathley provides one of the most compelling readings—which is also to say, a reading that presents some problems—of *Erwartung* as a proto-feminist work. She rightly disrupts the long-standing and often absolute prioritization of Schoenberg over Pappenheim, emphasizing their collaboration. Taking Pappenheim's own activist feminism into consideration, Keathley makes a case for the monodrama as a precedent (if not prototype) for future feminist emancipatory fictions, rather than just the eminently gawkable post-Charcotian amphitheater of female hysteria it has long been taken as. I nonetheless share Julie Brown's recent reservations about Keathley's dismissal of the "hysteria thesis"; while there is little evidence that Schoenberg himself was especially embroiled in Freud's ideas, Alexander Carpenter has done peerless detective work to uncover the many connections between Pappenheim and the Freudian scene, including finally verifying the blood relation between Marie Pappenheim and Bertha Pappenheim, known in psychoanalytic history as "Anna O," the "patient zero" of psychoanalysis. See Elizabeth L. Keathley, "'Die *Frauenfrage*' in *Erwartung*: Schoenberg's Collaboration with Marie Pappenheim," in *Opera after 1900*, ed. Margaret Notley (Aldershot, England: Ashgate, 2010), 11–50; Elizabeth L. Keathley, "Interpreting *Erwartung*: Collaborative Process and Early Reception," in *The Cambridge Companion to Schoenberg*, ed. Jennifer Shaw and Joseph Auner (Cambridge, England: Cambridge University Press, 2010), 81–93; and Elizabeth L. Keathley, "Revisioning Musical Modernism: Arnold Schoenberg, Marie Pappenheim, and *Erwartung*'s New Woman" (PhD diss., State University of New York at Stony Brook, 1999). See also Julie Brown, *Schoenberg and Redemption* (Cambridge, England: Cambridge University Press, 2014), 152; and Alexander Carpenter, "Schoenberg's Vienna, Freud's Vienna: Re-Examining the Connections between the Monodrama *Erwartung* and the Early History of Psychoanalysis," *Musical Quarterly* 93, no. 1 (2010): 144–81.

8. Slavoj Žižek, "Appendix II. Robert Schumann: The Romantic Anti-Humanist," in *The Plague of Fantasies* (London: Verso, 1997), 245.

9. Keathley, in "Interpreting *Erwartung*," comes to similar conclusions, though obviously without relying on a psychoanalytic framework: despite the lack of a "definitive conclusion," the Woman "finally achieves awareness of herself as utterly alone in a world without meaning except what she imparts to it. This flicker of insight opens up the possibility for an independent and meaningful existence" (93).

10. Carl Dahlhaus, "Expressive Principle and Orchestral Polyphony in Schoenberg's *Erwartung*," in *Schoenberg and the New Music: Essays by Carl Dahlhaus*, trans. Derrick Puffett and Alfred Clayton (Cambridge, England: Cambridge University Press, 1989), 149–55.

11. Mladen Dolar, "Tyche, clinamen, den," *Continental Philosophy Review* 46 (2013): 228.

12. Ethan Haimo, "The Rise and Fall of Radical Athematicism," in *The Cambridge Companion to Arnold Schoenberg*, ed. Jennifer Shaw and Joseph Auner (Cambridge, England: Cambridge University Press), 94–107.

13. See Berthold Hoeckner, "Elsa Screams, or The Birth of Music Drama," *Cambridge Opera Journal* 9, no. 2 (1997): 97–132; and Philip Friedheim, "Wagner and the Aesthetics of the Scream," *19th-Century Music* 7, no. 1 (1983): 63–70.

14. Theodor Adorno, *Negative Dialectics*, trans. E.B. Ashton (New York: Continuum, 1973), 5.

15. The *Grundgestalt* is a central topic in Schoenberg's work, and one of his most crucial means of maintaining a link with the canonical tradition from which he was constantly in the process of breaking. "Whatever happens in a piece of music is the endless reshaping of the basic shape. . . . There is nothing in a piece of music but what comes from the theme, springs from it and can be traced back to it; to put it still more severely, nothing but the theme itself." Arnold Schoenberg, "Linear Counterpoint," in *Style and Idea*, ed. Leonard Stein, trans. Leo Black (New York: Faber and Faber, 1975), 289–95. The first analyst to begin to trace methodically the presence of the [014] *Grundgestalt* throughout *Erwartung* was Herbert H. Buchanan, in "A Key to Schoenberg's *Erwartung* (Op. 17)," *Journal of the American Musicological Society* 20, no. 3 (1967): 434–49.

16. Paul Verhaeghe, "From Impossibility to Inability: Lacan's Theory of the Four Discourses," in *Beyond Gender: From Subject to Drive* (New York: Other Press, 2001), 32.

17. See Elizabeth L. Keathley, "Revisioning Musical Modernism," 347–61, for the most fulsome (non-analytic) treatment of the song, and of speculation into Pappenheim's own connections to it.

18. Taruskin, in his treatment of the song's role in *Erwartung*, returns to the "unanswerable question [of] whether [Schoenberg] consciously mined a tonal piece for a motif to abstract and as it were 'denature,' or whether memories of 'Am Wegrand' were stirred when Schoenberg found himself playing so extensively with the tones (or, more precisely, with the intervallic relationships) of one of its characteristic motifs." See Richard Taruskin, chapter 6, "Inner Occurrences (Transcendentalism, III)," in *The Oxford History of Western Music*, vol. 5 (Oxford: Oxford University Press, 2009), 337 (the culmination of a larger discussion of the work on pp. 326–37).

19. In the margins of his copy of Paul Bekker's essay on *Erwartung* (in which Bekker calls it "a music of liberation, transformation, and redemption") Schoenberg scribbled gruffly, "Not at all. . . . What does *Erwartung* have to do with redemption? The woman may have been wrong in her fearful states of mind, or not (this is not clear, but, all the same, there are only fearful imaginings and these become manifest). She is not at all redeemed by

them." Paul Bekker, "*Erwartung*," in "Arnold Schönberg zum fünfzigsten Geburtstage," special issue of *Musikblätter des Anbruch* 6, nos. 7–8 (1924): 277. Copy with Schoenberg's marginal annotation in Arnold Schönberg Center (ASC) archive, Vienna; cited in Elizabeth L. Keathley, "Interpreting *Erwartung*," 82–83.

20. Hugo von Hofmannsthal, *The Lord Chandos Letter*, 127–28.

21. Andreas Huyssen, for instance, calls the letter a "founding text of literary high modernism," and more recently, Patrick Greaney suggests it as a remarkably prescient call for a "literary knowledge" that bears uncanny resemblances to Lacan's discursive account of the unconscious. See Andreas Huyssen, "The Disturbance of Vision in Vienna Modernism," *MODERNISM/Modernity* 5, no. 3 (1998), 36; and Patrick Greaney, "On the Chaos in Chandos: Hofmannsthal on Modernity's Threshold," *MLN* 129 (2014), 563–64.

22. Jacques Lacan, *The Seminar of Jacques Lacan, Book XI: The Four Fundamental Concepts of Psychoanalysis, 1964*, ed. Jacques-Alain Miller, trans. Alan Sheridan (New York: W. W. Norton, 1998), 273.

23. The first quote comes from a letter from Schoenberg to Busoni in the days before the composition of *Erwartung*; see Ferruccio Busoni, *Selected Letters*, ed. and trans. Antony Beaumont (London: Faber and Faber, 1987), 389. The second quote has a complicated history; my citation comes from Josef Rufer, *The Works of Arnold Schoenberg: A Catalogue of His Compositions, Writings, and Paintings*, trans. Dika Newlin (London: Faber and Faber, 1962), 45. But Fusako Hamao details some dispute over the authenticity of this statement, which relies on Rufer's own recollections, particularly regarding its nationalistic insinuation. Most interestingly, she cites Schoenberg's grandson, E. Randol Schoenberg, who cites a letter from his grandfather to Alma Mahler from July 26, 1921, paraphrasing his remark to Rufer in a considerably more sarcastic light. See E. Randol Schoenberg, "The Most Famous Thing He Never Said," *Jewish Music Institute International Centre for Suppressed Music Newsletter* 4 (November 2002). See also Fusako Hamao, "Redating Schoenberg's Announcement of the Twelve-Tone Method: A Study of Recollections," in "A Music-Theoretical Matrix: Essays in Honor of Allen Forte (Part III)," ed. David Carson Berry, a special issue of *Gamut* 4, no. 1 (2011): 231–97, particularly 244–45 and 277–78.

24. Herbert H. Buchanan, "A Key to Schoenberg's *Erwartung* (Op. 17: 442)".

25. Charles Rosen, *Arnold Schoenberg* (New York: Viking Books, 1975), 57–58.

CHAPTER FIFTEEN

1. Theodor Adorno, *Mahler: A Musical Physiognomy*, trans. Edmund Jephcott (Chicago: University of Chicago Press, 1992), 154.

2. For a transcript of all three panels, see "'Die Nähe zu Mahler war wie eine Mauer.' Drei Podiumsdiskussionen über das Verhältnis neuer Musik zu Gustav Mahler," ed. Klaus Hinrich Stahmer, in *Das Gustav-Mahler-Fest Hamburg 1989: Bericht über den Internationalen Gustav-Mahler-Kongress*, ed. Matthias Theodor Vogt (Kassel: Bärenreiter, 1991), 415–29; the title comes from a comment by Michael Denhoff in the second panel (422). For more on the Gustav Mahler Vereinigung e.V., Hamburg, and on their activities in their founding year, see http://www.gustav-mahler-vereinigung.de/1989.htm.

3. See Björn Heile, "'Transcending Quotation': Cross-Cultural Musical Representation in Mauricio Kagel's *Die Stücke der Windrose* für Salonorchester" (PhD diss., University of South-

ampton, 2001), 52: "It is evident that what we hear is neither 'genuine' klezmer or salon music, nor is it Kagel's music in a direct way, but klezmer or salon music represented by Kagel."

4. See Helmut Lachenmann, "*Tableau.* Stück für Orchester (1988/89)," in Helmut Lachenmann, *Musik als existentielle Erfahrung*, ed. Josef Häusler (Wiesbaden: Breitkopf and Härtel, 2004), 400. For a rich condensation of Lachenmann's thoughts on Mahler, see his essay "Mahler—eine Herausforderung. Antworten auf fünf Fragen" in that same volume, 263–69.

5. Georges Bataille, *Inner Experience*, trans. Leslie Anne Boldt (Albany: State University of New York Press, 1988), 69.

6. The complete list of commissioned composers includes Michael Denhoff, Detlev Glanert, Hans-Joachim Hespos, Thomas Jahn, Babette Koblenz, Walter Zimmermann, Manfred Trojahn, and Klaus K. Hübler. Many of the works are reengaged a few years later in Klaus Hinrich Stahmer, "Zwischen Nostalgie und Utopie. Musik über und zu Gustav Mahler von Peter Ruzicka, Helmut Lachenmann, Wilhelm Killmayer, Vittorio Fellegara, Detlev Glanert, Michael Denhoff, Walter Zimmermann, Babette Koblenz und Thomas Jahn," in *Franz Schubert und Gustav Mahler in der Musik der Gegenwart*, ed. Klaus Hinrich Stahmer (Mainz: Schott, 1997), 93–105.

7. See Michael Denhoff, "NACHTBILD op. 57 (1989) (Mahler-Momente) für Kammer-ensemble," available at http://www.denhoff.de/werkkommentare.htm#op57; translation mine. Denhoff's last line is a series of plays on the German root *-bild*: "Trugbild, Zerrbild, Vexierbild, Abbild und Negativbild."

8. Klaus Angermann, liner notes to *Mahler/Skizze*, trans. J. Bradford Robinson, in *Detlev Glanert—Sinfonie Nr. 1/Vier Fantasien/Mahler/Skizze/Drei Gesänge aus Carmen*, Wergo, WER 6522-2, 1994, compact disc.

9. See Klaus Hinrich Stahmer, "Zwischen Nostalgie und Utopie," 103–5, for a more detailed account of this passage in context of the score as a whole.

10. Thomas Jahn, "Background," available at http://www.thomasjahn.com/english/t-back.htm (English) and http://www.thomasjahn.com/german/t-back.htm (original German); translation modified from German. I thank Thomas Jahn for graciously providing me with an unreleased recording of *Background*.

11. Many authors have speculated about the effect Mahler's famous 1910 meeting with Freud had on the (non)completion of the composer's Tenth Symphony; the day after their meeting, Mahler wrote his wife Alma the following poem—"Then flowed together into a single chord / My hesitant thinking and raging feelings"—and some commentators cannot resist hypothesizing this as the "scream" chord in the Tenth. See for instance Constantin Floros, *Gustav Mahler* (Munich: C. H. Beck oHG, 2010), 43–44.

12. "'Die Nähe zu Mahler war wie eine Mauer,'" 418–19; translation mine.

13. Ibid., 417.

14. Ibid., 427.

15. Slavoj Žižek, *The Sublime Object of Ideology*, 2nd ed. (London: Verso, 2008), 195.

16. Sigmund Freud, "Mourning and Melancholia" (1917), in *SE* 16, 247.

17. "'Die Nähe zu Mahler war wie eine Mauer,'" 420–21.

18. Ibid., 421; translation mine. I have tried to preserve Hespos's neologisms and (seemingly) deliberate awkwardness of phrasing, punctuation, mixing of metaphors, et cetera.

19. Fredric Jameson, *A Singular Modernity* (London: Verso, 2002), 135.

20. T. J.Clark, "Clement Greenberg's Theory of Art," *Critical Inquiry* 9, no. 1 (1982): 154.

21. The example is one of Žižek's better known and oft-rehearsed, initially formulated in the early 1990s and first published in Slavoj Žižek, *Looking Awry: An Introduction to Jacques Lacan through Popular Culture* (Cambridge, MA: MIT Press, 1992), 171–72n6.

22. Alain Badiou and Barbara Cassin, *Il n'y pas de rapport sexuel: Deux leçons sur "L'Étourdit" de Lacan* (Paris: Editions Fayard, 2010), 83–84.

23. Mladen Dolar, "Which Repetition?" (October 2013), unpublished manuscript existing in PDF form.

24. Alexander Wheelock Thayer, *Ludwig van Beethovens Leben*, vol. 5 (Leipzig: Breitkopf and Härtel, 1908), 318–19.

25. Theodor Adorno, "Beethoven's Late Style" (1937), in *Night Music: Essays on Music 1928–1962*, ed. Rolf Tiedemann, trans. Wieland Hoban (London: Seagull Books, 2009), 17.

26. "Programmheft der Wittener Tage für neue Musik 1991," cited in Vera Lumpe, liner notes, *Adriana Hölszky: Hängebrücken*, Nomos Quartett, Pellegrini Quartett, et al., cpo 999112–2, 2013, compact disc.

27. Harry Vogt, "Musikmensch der neuesten Zeit?: Zum Schubert-Rezeption in 20. Jahrhundert," in *Programmheft des Rheinischen Musikfestes 1989* (Cologne: WDR, 1989), 39–40. Many thanks to Rita Friedrich, music librarian of Stadtbibliothek Aachen, for her invaluable assistance in helping me access materials related to the Musikfest '89.

28. Jacques Lacan, "The Direction of the Treatment," in *Écrits: The First Complete Edition in English*, trans. Bruce Fink (New York: W. W. Norton, 2006), 532. I have slightly modified Fink's translation—he gives the subject the pronoun "he"—by making the pronoun consistent with my own gender-neutral treatment of the word in this book.

29. See T. J. Clark's discussion of Jackson Pollock in chapter 6, "The Unhappy Consciousness," of *Farewell to an Idea: Episodes in a History of Modernism* (New Haven, CT: Yale University Press, 2001), 298–369; for Clark's specific discussion of modernism's "bad dream," see 306ff.

30. Charles Baudelaire, "The Salon of 1859," in *Baudelaire: Selected Writings on Art and Artists*, ed. and trans. P. E. Charve (Cambridge, England: Cambridge University Press, 1972), 299.

31. Leonard Bernstein, "Lecture Five: The Twentieth Century Crisis," in *The Unanswered Question: Six Talks at Harvard* (Cambridge, MA: Harvard University Press, 1976), 321.

32. Leonard Bernstein, "Mahler: His Time Has Come," *High Fidelity/Musical America* 17 (1967): 54. For an excellent exploration of Bernstein's moderate Mahlerian modernism, see Matthew Mugmon, "Beyond the Composer-Conductor Dichotomy: Bernstein's Copland-Inspired Mahler Advocacy," *Music and Letters* 94, no. 4 (2014): 606–27. Among other things, Mugmon points out how, paradoxically, Mahler's "good-by" became a means of sanctioning Bernstein's continued use of tonality and more "traditional" idioms.

33. Paul Bekker, *Gustav Mahlers Sinfonien* (Berlin: Schuster und Loeffler, 1921), 340.

34. See the eponymous essay in Lewis Thomas, *Late Night Thoughts on Listening to Mahler's Ninth Symphony* (New York: Penguin Books, 1980), 166.

35. Ibid., 168.

36. Hugo von Hofmannsthal, *The Lord Chandos Letter: And Other Writings*, trans. Joel Rotenberg, introduction by John Banville (New York: New York Review of Books, 2005), 128.

37. As Mahler biographer Jens Malte Fischer points out in *Gustav Mahler*, trans. Stewart Spencer (New Haven, CT: Yale University Press, 2011), despite the seeming appropriateness of relating Mahler's Ninth to Hofmannsthal's "Chandos Letter," there is not much biograph-

ical evidence that Mahler shared the "questionable delights" of his younger, more "modern" Viennese contemporaries (132). This doesn't, however, keep Fischer from making exactly such a link: "The 'speechless' Ninth Symphony," he writes, "is the answer to Lord Chandos's questions, and it provides this answer in a more immediate, more fluent and white-hot way than language itself could ever do" (614).

38. Peter Oswald, "Subkutane Seismographen: Zeit und Geschichte im ersten Satz von Mahlers IX. Symphonie," in *Musik-Konzepte, Sonderband: Gustav Mahler*, ed. Heinz-Klaus Metzger and Rainer Riehn (Munich: edition text + kritik, 1989), 276. Oswald would take up directorship of Klangforum Wien in 1993, found the influential New Music label Kairos Music in 1999, and direct the esteemed "steirischer herbst" festival from 2000 to 2005.

39. Fredric Jameson, *A Singular Modernity* (London: Verso, 2002), 34.

40. Erwin Schrödinger, "The Present Situation in Quantum Mechanics," trans. John D. Trimmer, *Proceedings of the American Philosophical Society* 124 (1980): 323–28.

41. In this sense, I agree with Schrödinger's oft-misconstrued assessment of his own thought experiment: he considered his "Copenhagen School" account of the simultaneously living-and-dead cat "absurd," a "blurred model," a "shaky or out-of-focus photograph," when what was preferred was "a snapshot of clouds and fog banks." See Erwin Schrödinger, "The Present Situation in Quantum Mechanics," 328.

42. Theodor Adorno, *Negative Dialectics*, trans. E. B. Ashton (New York: Continuum, 1973), 5.

43. Theodor Adorno, *Mahler: A Musical Physiognomy*, 155 (first and second citations), 166 (third citation).

44. Adorno in a letter to Hans G. Helms, September 12, 1960, in the Theodor W. Adorno Archive, Frankfurt am Main (Br 588/64); cited in Stefan Müller-Doohm, *Adorno: A Biography*, trans. Rodney Livingstone (Cambridge, England: Polity Press, 2005), 395.

45. Theodor Adorno, "Vers une musique informelle" (1960), in *Gesammelte Schriften*, vol. 16, ed. Rolf Tiedemann (Frankfurt am Main: Surhkamp Verlag, 1978), 540; translation mine. The original line is "Die Gestalt aller künstlerischen Utopie heute ist: Dinge machen, von denen wir nicht wissen, was sie sind."

46. Theodor Adorno, *Mahler: A Musical Physiognomy*, 156 (first citation), 29 (second citation), 154 (third citation).

47. Ibid., 166.

48. Ibid., 157.

49. Ibid., 161–62.

50. Ibid., 162–64.

51. Theodor Adorno, "Mahler" (1960), in *Quasi una Fantasia*, trans. Rodney Livingstone (London: Verso, 1992), 92.

52. Theodor Adorno, *Mahler: A Musical Physiognomy*, 166 (first two citations); the third citation is from Hugo von Hofmannsthal, *The Lord Chandos Letter*, 127–28.

53. Theodor Adorno, "Mahler," 85.

54. Ibid., 96.

55. Ibid., 93.

56. Ibid.

57. Ibid.

58. Ibid., 97 (first citation), 92 (second citation).

59. Ibid., 97.

60. Theodor Adorno, *Mahler: A Musical Physiognomy*, 147. Elsewhere in the monograph, Adorno writes similarly of the originality of the third movement in Mahler's First Symphony: "Its striking originality is produced by the unity of the disorganized and the significant" (124).

61. Theodor Adorno, "Music and New Music" (1960), in *Quasi una Fantasia*, 249–68.

62. Ibid., 256.

63. Ibid., 264 (first three citations), 257 (fourth citation).

64. Ibid., 264.

65. Ibid., 257.

66. Ibid., 258.

67. Ibid., 260.

68. Ibid., 261.

69. Ibid., 262.

70. Ibid., 263.

71. Ibid., 265.

72. Ibid., 256. Adorno is referring to New Music's "tone of menace," but I think the phrase well describes Adorno's own account.

73. Theodor Adorno, "Beethoven's Late Style," 17 (first citation), 18 (second citation), 16 (third citation).

74. Ibid., 15.

75. Ibid., 17.

76. Ibid., 18.

77. Theodor Adorno, "Mahler," 86.

78. Ibid., 99. The line comes from "Zu meinem träumen floh ich vor dem wolke," the second of George's "Überschriften und Widmungen," in Stefan George, *Gesamtausgabe: Endgültige Fassung in 18 Bänden von Georg Bondi in einem Buch*, ed. Georg Bondi (Berlin: Hofenberg, 2014), 124.

79. Arguably it is Adorno's 1928 essay on Schubert that first formulates the trope of "objective" landscape and "subjective" glow. Its epigraph from Louis Aragon—"The whole useless body was consumed by transparency. / Little by little the body turned into light, its blood into rays . . ."—sets a tone that returns, its purpura now mostly healed, in the Beethoven essay. See "Schubert," in Theodor Adorno, *Night Music*, 19–46. See also Stephen Decatur Smith's excellent work, equally genealogical and critical, on the dual figures of light and decay in Adorno et al. in "'Even Money Decays': Transience and Hope in Adorno, Benjamin, and *Wozzeck*," *Opera Quarterly* 29, nos. 3–4 (2013): 212–43. Of invaluable help to my own thinking is also Stephen Decatur Smith, "The Light of Decay: Hope and Natural History in Adorno's Late Style," paper presented at the American Comparative Literature Association, New York University, March 2014.

80. Freud's well-known epigraph to *The Interpretation of Dreams* is taken from Virgil's *Aeneid*: "Flectere si nequeo superos, Acheronta movebo," translated roughly as "If I cannot bend the upper gods, then I will the lower ones."

81. Robert Hass, "Meditation at Lagunitas," in *Praise* (New York: Ecco Press, 1979), 4.

82. David Riesman, *The Lonely Crowd, Revised Edition: A Study of the Changing American Character* (New Haven, CT: Yale University Press, 2001).

83. Jean-Luc Nancy, *The Inoperative Community*, ed. Peter Connor, trans. Peter Connor, Lisa Garbus, Michael Holland, and Simona Sawhney (Minneapolis: University of Minnesota Press, 1991), 9.

84. See for instance Tobias Bleek's painstaking and exhaustive exploration of an eleven-minute quartet by György Kurtág, *Musikalische Intertextualität als Schaffensprinzip: eine Studie zu György Kurtágs Streichquartett "Officium breve," op. 28* (Saarbrücken: Pfau, 2010).

85. The Invisible Committee, *To Our Friends* (Cambridge, MA: MIT Press, 2015), 17.

86. See http://hgnm.org/composer/marek-poliks/.

87. Post on Marek Poliks's Facebook page, October 16, 2014 (6:47 p.m.), https://www.facebook.com/mpoliks.

88. The reception of Nono's score has been remarkably consistent vis-à-vis its "secrecies" and "inwardness"; see for instance the shared framing and concerns in Heinz-Klaus Metzger, "Wendepunkt Quartett?," in *Musik-Konzepte 20: Luigi Nono*, ed. Heinz-Klaus Metzger and Rainer Riehn (Munich: Edition text + kritik, 1981), 93–112, and, almost two decades later, in Dietrich Eberhard Sattler, "'Geheimere Welt': Zu Luigi Nonos Streichquartett *Fragmente-Stille, an Diotima*," *Musik und Ästhetik* 14 (2010): 74–86.

89. For by far the most expert and inspired analysis of Nono's quartet in English, see Carola Nielinger-Vakil, "*Fragmente-Stille, an Diotima*: World of Greater Compositional Secrets," *Acta Musicologica* 82, no. 1 (2010). She discusses Nono's sketches and compositional method throughout, and examines his notion of *campi* and *onde* on 119ff.

90. Paul-Heinz Dittrich, *"Nie vollendbare poetische Anstrengung": Texte zur Musik 1957–1999*, ed. Stefan Fricke and Alexandra Raetzer (Saarbrücken: Pfau, 2003), 354.

91. Richard Toop, liner notes to *Henri Dutilleux/Pascal Dusapin—Ainsi La Nuit/Time Zones, Quatuor III*, Arditti Quartet, Audivis Montaigne, MO 782016, compact disc. Toop is citing Theodor Adorno, *Alban Berg: Master of the Smallest Link*, trans., introduced, and annotated by Juliane Brand and Christopher Hailey (Cambridge, England: Cambridge University Press, 1991), 104ff.

92. Wolfgang Rihm, *ausgesprochen: Schriften und Gespräche*, vol. 2, ed. Ulrich Mosch (Mainz: Schott, 1997), 371; translation mine.

93. See Douglass M. Green, "Berg's *De Profundis*: The Finale of the Lyric Suite," *International Alban Berg Society Newsletter* 5 (June 1977): 13–23. Green's work was first introduced to German-speaking audiences in George Perle, "Das geheime Programm der *Lyrischen Suite*. I and II," *Österreichische Musikzeitschrift* 33, no. 2 (1978): 64–79 (part 1), and *Österreichische Musikzeitschrift* 33, no. 3 (1978): 113–119 (part 2). For an exemplar of how the *Lyrische Suite* was already considered an encrypted score, see for instance Constantin Floros, "Das esoterische Programm der *Lyrischen Suite* von Alban Berg. Eine semantische Analyse," *Hamburger Jahrbuch für Musikwissenschaft* 1 (1975): 101–45. By the time of Adorno's 1968 book on Berg (in which the score is coined a "latent opera"), Adorno had known for decades about the secret program; see his confessional letter from April 16, 1936, to Berg's widow, Helene, in *Theodor W. Adorno and Alban Berg: Correspondence 1925–1935*, ed. Henri Lonitz, trans. Wieland Hoban (Cambridge, MA: Polity Press, 2005), 232–36.

94. Silvestrov's comment about "the end of music" comes from Valentin Sil'vestrov and Tat'yana Frumkis, "Sokhranyat' dostoinstvo . . .," *Sovetskaya muzïka* 4 (1990): 13. Translation by Peter Schmelz.

95. Peter Schmelz, "Valentin Silvestrov and the Echoes of Music History," *Journal of Musicology* 31, no. 2 (2014): 270. Schmelz is not discussing Silvestrov's Second Quartet, but his general "postlude" style.

96. Theodor Adorno, *Alban Berg: Master of the Smallest Link*, 112. In this context, Ulrich Leyendecker's Third Quartet, discussed in chapter 10, reveals another intertext: its theatrical incapacity to "complete" Bach's unfinished Contrapunctus from *Die Kunst der Fuge* actually *sounds* less like Bach or Beethoven—whose *Grosse Fuge* it ostensibly channels as it progresses—than it does like the "Allegro misterioso" from Berg's *Lyrische Suite*, itself a dramatic "undoing" ritual.

97. Marco Stroppa, liner notes to *Traiettoria/Spirali*, Pierre-Laurent Aimard, Arditti Quartet, Stradivarius, STR 57008, compact disc.

98. Pascal Dusapin, *Quatuor II, "Time Zones," 24 pièces pour quatuor à cordes* (Paris: Éditions Salabert, 1990), preface; translation mine.

99. Anonymous, "Einige Worte zu den vielen über Beethoven's letzte Werke," *Allgemeine musikalische Zeitung* 31 (1829): 272 (first quote); Alexandre Oulibicheff, *Beethoven, ses critiques et ses glossateurs* (Leipzig and Paris: Brockhaus, 1857), 270 (second quote).

100. For an excellent recent exploration of the concept, see Ilya Kliger, "On 'Genre Memory' in Bakhtin," in *Persistent Forms: Explorations in Historical Poetics*, ed. Ilya Kliger and Boris Maslov, foreword by Eric Hayot (New York: Fordham University Press, 2015), 227–51.

101. Ibid., 244.

102. Mikhail Bakhtin, "Rable i Gogol," in *Voprosy literatury i estetiki* (Moscow: Khudozhestvennaia literature, 1975), 492; Ilya Kliger, "On 'Genre Memory' in Bakhtin," 245.

103. See Helmut Lachenmann, *Musik als existentielle Erfahrung*, 237; for an English translation, see Lachenmann, "On My Second String Quartet," trans. Evan Johnson, *Contemporary Music Review* 23, no. 3 (2004): 67.

104. See again Carola Nielinger-Vakil, "*Fragmente-Stille, an Diotima*: World of Greater Compositional Secrets"; see also Luigi Nono, "Wie Hölderlin komponierte," in Kay-Uwe Kirchert, *Wahrnehmung und Fragmentierung: Luigi Nonos Kompositionen zwischen "Al gran sole carico d'amore" und "Prometeo"* (Saarbrücken: Pfau, 2006), 207–8. I am using the Hölderin translation found in Friedrich Hölderlin, *Odes and Elegies*, trans. and ed. Nick Hoff (Middletown, CT: Wesleyan University Press, 2008), 96–97.

105. See Rainer Nonnenmann, *Der Gang durch die Klippen: Helmut Lachenmanns Begegnungen mit Luigi Nono anhand ihres Briefwechsels und anderer Quellen 1957–1990* (Wiesbaden: Breitkopf and Härtel, 2013).

106. On the subject of the fifth-movement "cavatina" from Beethoven's Quartet, Op. 130, see Daniel K. L. Chua, "Beethoven's Other Humanism," *Journal of the American Musicological Society* 62, no. 3 (2009): 571–645. For a prolonged exploration of the voice in late musical modernism, see Marcelle Pierson, "The Voice under Erasure: Singing, Melody, and Expression in Late Modernist Music" (PhD diss., University of Chicago, 2015).

107. Samuel Beckett, *Krapp's Last Tape and Other Dramatic Pieces* (New York: Grove Press, 2009), 10.

108. Ned Beauman, "Fail Worse," *New Inquiry*, February 9, 2012, http://thenewinquiry.com/essays/fail-worse/.

INDEX

The italicized abbreviation "fig." following a page number indicates that an illustration appears on that page.

www.ingramcontent.com/pod-product-compliance
Ingram Content Group UK Ltd.
Pitfield, Milton Keynes, MK11 3LW, UK
UKHW041854031026
15587UKWH00006B/1231/J

9 780520 279360